The
400
Best
Garden
Plants

The 400 Best Garden Plants

A practical encyclopedia of
annuals, perennials, bulbs,
trees, and shrubs

ELVIN McDONALD

Quantum
Books

A QUANTUM BOOK

This book is produced by
Quantum Publishing Ltd.
6 Blundell Street
London
N7 9BH

Text and photography by Elvin McDonald
Designed by Yasuo Kubota, Kubota & Bender

ISBN 0 681 28919 8

QUMBGP

Colour separations by Hong Kong Scanner Arts Int'l Ltd.

Printed in Singapore by Star Standard Industries (Pte) Ltd.

Acknowledgments

Dedicated to Marta Hallet

Thanks to the home team, pals and friends, particularly:

Kristen Schilo, editor; Mary Forsell, copyeditor; Yasuo Kubota, designer; Tatiana Ginsberg, production manager; Catherine San Filippo, proofreader; Lillien Waller, helping hand; Carla Glasser, agent; Douglas Askew, research; Tom Osborn, driver/gardener; Rosalind Creasy, focalizer; James R. Bailey, neighbor; Janis Blackschleger, telekineticist; Diane Ofner, gardening student; JoAnn Trial, scientist, and Don Trial, teacher; R. Michael Lee, architect; Charles Gulick, gardener; Michael Berryhill, poet; Linda Starr, head coach; Hila Paldi, body coach; Mark Inabnit, Publisher and Editor-in-Chief, *Houston Life*; David Walker, Editorial Director, *Houston Life*; Catherine Beason, angel unaware; Maria Moss, Executive Editor, *Houston Life*; David Warren, artist/gardenmaker; Audrey Scachnow, tweak expressionist; Christy Barthelme, envisionary; Tino and Richard, Stark Cleaning Services; Tony Williams, yard man; Dan Twyman, pruner; and Leslie Williams, cheering.

Elvin McDonald
Houston, TX
March 31, 1995

Introduction/8

Part One:
Annuals

CHAPTER ONE
The Annual Garden/14

CHAPTER TWO
The 100 Best Annuals for Your Garden/24

CHAPTER THREE
Troubleshooting Guide for Annuals/108

CHAPTER FOUR
Bringing Annuals into Your Home/110

Part Two:
Perennials

CHAPTER FIVE
The Perennial Garden/114

CHAPTER SIX
The 100 Best Perennials for Your Garden/124

CHAPTER SEVEN
Troubleshooting Guide for Perennials/208

CHAPTER EIGHT
Bringing Perennials into Your Home/210

Part Three:
Bulbs

CHAPTER NINE
The Bulb Garden/214

CHAPTER TEN
The 100 Best Bulbs for Your Garden/222

CHAPTER ELEVEN
Troubleshooting Guide for Bulbs/308

CHAPTER TWELVE
Bringing Bulbs into Your Home/310

Part Four:
Trees and Shrubs

CHAPTER THIRTEEN
The Woody Plant Garden/314

CHAPTER FOURTEEN
The 100 Best Trees, Shrubs, and Ground Covers/324

CHAPTER FIFTEEN
Troubleshooting Guide for Woody Plants/408

CHAPTER SIXTEEN
Bringing Woody Plants into Your Home/410

BIBLIOGRAPHY/413

RESOURCES/415

CREDITS/418

INDEX/422

U.S.D.A. PLANT HARDINESS ZONE MAP/431

Introduction

The four hundred plants that appear in these colorful pages represent my pick of the crop as a lifelong gardener and horticultural journalist. They are far from being the only "best" plants. Some vast families and categories—for instance, orchids and aquatic plants—certainly deserve more attention. Most assuredly, I am already growing the plants and assembling the photography for a sequel. One of the most wonderful aspects of gardening is that we can never know all of the plants. For this reason, dedicated gardeners will always experience the thrill of the hunt, the excitement upon discovering a flower or plant more beguiling than could have been imagined.

How to Read an Entry

Within each of the four parts of the book, plants appear in alphabetical order by botanical genus name. If you know only the plant's common name, look for it in the Index. The botanical name and suggested pronunciation are followed by common name or names, many of which are interchangeable, and then by the plant's family name, appearing first in botanical Latin followed by the name in English. For example, plants of the bulb genus *Chionodoxa* (botanical name) are commonly referred to as glory-of-the-snow (common name). They are members of the Liliaceae (botanical family name), or lily family (common family name).

Within the entries, species names sometimes appear, where applicable. For instance, in the *Lychnis*, or campion, entry in the perennials section, the species names *L. coronaria* and *L. flos-jovis* both appear. Both are broadly referred to as campion. Oftentimes, species do not have common names and, as a result, are known in the plant trade only by their botanical names.

Particularly with shrubs and trees, I have listed some of the best prospects from sometimes vast possibilities. In all, four hundred different plants are pictured in this volume, yet many more are actually named, a resource unto itself for tracking down worthwhile species and cultivars.

Within each entry, there is also a guide for cultivation:

Height/habit: Despite the inexactness of horticulture and botanical differences, I sum up here as much as can be said about a genus in as few words as possible.

Leaves: Many plants are appreciated for their foliage as much as—or even more so—than their flowers. Here I provide a succinct description of leaf shapes and characteristics.

Flowers: Dimensions, arrangement and color and fragrance characteristics are noted.

Season: The plant's high season appears here.

When to plant: I have used the phrase, "Set out transplants when available" for nearly all plants in the book. In other words, if a gardener shops regularly for plants, both through mail order and locally (nurseries, garden centers, and plant auctions held by public gardens), they will be delivered or sold at approximately the correct planting time for

that person's hardiness zone. Containerization, lightweight growing mediums, remarkably efficient distribution, and computer brain power have revolutionized the plant business. Yes, there are still plants shipped at the wrong time and local retailers who sell inappropriate choices, but on the whole, the system works.

I have also provided each plant's tolerance for cold and heat according to zone, as appears on the United States Department of Agriculture's Plant Hardiness Zone Map (see page 431). (This information can also appear under "Season," if applicable.) However, please note that the U.S.D.A. map has traditionally been based on cold tolerance, not heat. Now the billion-dollar industry of gardening is working to generate maps and zone awareness for heat as well as cold, also taking into account the relative dryness or wetness of a particular climate. To establish heat tolerance zones for this book, I have used a variety of references, including the catalogs of Louisiana Nursery, Wayside Gardens, and Yucca Do Nursery (see Resources). As well, I consulted the books listed in the Bibliography, especially *A Garden Book for Houston* and *Hortica*. When in doubt, ask a neighbor who gardens for details about your hardiness zone. There are lots of variables and a host of gardeners who like nothing better than trying to succeed with a plant that is not rated for their zone.

Light: To prosper, most plants need strong light or some sun, in a site that affords air movement. Here, I provide specific light or shade requirements.

Soil: Most plants need well-drained soil that is kept evenly moist to on the dry side. There are rainy seasons when gardens are wet for long periods of time. If water stands longer than a few hours in your yard, this does not bode well for gardening—unless you are undertaking a water or bog garden. There are also dry seasons and gardeners today generally subscribe

to the concept of Xeriscaping: Not to set in motion any garden that will require undue irrigation during normal times of drought.

Fertilizer: Generally speaking, 5-10-5 and 15-30-15 are good for flowering-fruiting plants. Timed-release 14-14-14 is an all-purpose, long-serving (up to a whole season from one application) fertilizer for a wide variety of plants. For acid-loving plants, choose 30-10-10 or chelated iron. Careful, consistent application of these or entirely organic fertilizers will result in vigorous growth.

Pruning: This has been included for the woody plants, and instructions are as specific as possible. Pruning is best learned by observing someone who is knowledgeable and then by practicing. If you select the right tool, never squeeze the handles until all your fingers are accounted for, and never do it when you're angry. Pruning is not only therapeutic for plants, it also benefits the gardener, as a way of generating discipline and instilling a sense of order in outdoor chores.

Propagation: Lots of gardeners favor propagation over just about everything else done in the course of a gardening season. It is fun to see little seeds sprout and roots take hold from brown-looking cuttings. It is also practical if you have elaborate plantings in mind. Annuals are not discussed under propagation as they are not increased from existing plants.

Uses: Under this heading, each plant's strong points are discussed, though you the gardener may find your own unique usages.

As much as I can provide detailed information about the art of gardening, you will be your own best teacher, a philosophy stated most eloquently in this old garden verse:

> *If you seek answers,*
> *leave your questions*
> *outside the garden gate.*

Elvin McDonald
Houston, Texas   June 29, 1994

Part One:
Annuals

Chapter One:
The Annual Garden

Annuals can truly make the garden. They are the scented, flowering plants that enter the picture at the beginning of one growing season and exit by its end, having grown up from seeds into a new generation of blooms. Once they have returned to seed, they die back to the ground.

This wonderful rainbow of plants offers instant gratification, especially when purchased already blooming in packs of transplants. When a yard looks bleak, a patio pot bereft of hopeful signs, they are the ticket, a convenient way to color in the garden and focus on the bright side.

Annuals are the answer to an intrepid beginner's prayer. They encourage us to let go, to get on with the planting and not be paralyzed by questions about the unknown. They permit the gardener to try various planting and design ideas without the expense, hard work, or long-range commitment required by perennials and woody specimens.

Like many plants, annuals are extraordinarily adaptable. Usually they will only not do well if the site poses extremes: whether too sunny or shady, too wet or dry, too hot or cold. Even if the plant does not fare well, it could still have a second life: Though annuals complete their lives in one garden cycle, they have the potential to quickly regenerate from seeds, keeping your garden budget intact.

Planning and Designing the Annual Garden

You can make a garden entirely with annuals or feature them in special roles, whether star players or mere extras in the company of all other classes of plants: bulbs and shrubs, trees and ground covers, perennials and vines, vegetables, fruits, and herbs.

Annuals and various tender or quick-to-bloom perennials treated as annuals run the gamut from edgers, creepers, and ground covers to hedgers, quick screeners, and viners and bloom variously from spring until fall. In zone 9 and warmer, an exciting array blooms through winter and into spring, then goes to seed and dies rapidly

at the onset of torrid summer weather. To plan your garden, look through Chapter Two to find the most appealing choices in color combinations and to decide which annuals best correspond to your own personal uses, whether in bouquets, to cover a trellis, or to act as ground covers.

"Mass for effect" is the number one rule for getting the most from annuals. Their impact is diminished by lining in a single row or by spotting here and there randomly or regularly, polka-dot style. Whether different colors and different shapes or textures are mixed or matched is largely a matter of personal taste. Whatever gives you pleasure is probably correct for your garden.

One of the easiest ways to feel success with a garden is to organize according to color. The all-white garden is one of the most romantic, but it also has a simplicity and gives a sense of order. By direct contrast, there are gardeners who wouldn't be happy without a fiesta mix of every flower color imaginable. The wise gardener Gertrude Jekyll noted that "...the blue garden needn't be all blue, merely beautiful."

Soil Preparation

Above all, annuals need well-drained soil. Don't plant them in ground where water stands several hours or overnight following rain. If you grow them in containers, be sure they have drain holes. So long as the soil is well drained, any site can be made hospitable.

To prepare the garden, dig ground beds the depth of a garden spade. Remove any weeds, clumps or runners of lawn grass, sticks, stones, and other debris. Top-dress with fertilizer,

Buying and Planting Annuals

Gardeners at all stages from rank beginner to seasoned veteran will always grow certain plants from seeds. However, this takes extra planning. For quicker results, you might want to rely mostly on transplants started by professional growers and offered for sale at retail when blooms are in evidence.

One advantage of starting with plants coming into flower is that you can mix and match colors on the spot. Transplants are

preferably an organic product. Add 2 to 6 inches (5 to 15 centimeters) of well-rotted compost. Fork, turn, rake, or till all of this together. Ideally this needs to stand a week or two to cure, but if you are in a hurry, soil preparation and planting can be done the same day.

If you are planting annuals in containers, the rule of thumb is the bigger the pot, the better the plant. Small pots outdoors don't fare well since they are prone to overheating and underwatering. Use fresh potting soil each season, or at least top-dress with well-rotted compost every year.

offered for as long a season as feasible in each region. This means you don't necessarily have to do all of your planting at once. Buying in installments can help you be a better, more satisfied gardener.

By the time transplants reach retail, the containers in which they are growing are already packed with roots. This can mean thorough watering daily or they may be permanently stunted. Therefore, it might be better not to bring home plants until you are actually ready and able to set them in permanent places.

After soil preparation, the next step to success with annual transplants is promptly to set each in place, teasing out the roots from the original soil mass so that they are able to make contact with the endemic soil. Set at the same level in the ground as they were growing previously in the container. Water well. In the event you are transplanting a seedling and the soil falls away, exposing the roots to air and light, set it quickly and gently into moist soil, then water well and provide shade from direct sun until the roots have time—a few days—to reestablish.

If you wish to start annuals from seed, keep in mind that seed packets are somewhat less reliable as indicators of proper planting time since they can be purchased year-round through catalogs and from local racks. Seeds for annuals that bloom in the spring are usually sown the previous fall or winter in mild regions and greenhouses. Seeds for summer through fall annuals can often be sown where they are to grow and bloom in the garden or containers as soon as the ground is warm and the weather settled in spring.

The easiest way to start annuals from seeds is to sow them on the site where they will grow and bloom. Prepare the soil, then sow in a natural drift or in short rows according to the space and your plan. In a mixed garden it is often possible to start seeds in a place protected a bit by the next-door perennial or shrub. This improvised nursery plot may be outlined with sand or a dribble of vermiculite, just to remind you or your helper to take special care.

The annuals that self-sow, or "volunteer," are among every gardener's favorites. They are often planted first in one place, but in succeeding seasons their charm is one of serendipity, popping up where we'd least expect to see them. Moreover, self-sown seedlings have a way of taking root and growing marvelously in nooks and crevices where setting a proper transplant would be impossible.

Caring for Annuals Throughout the Seasons

Be sure to give your annuals well-drained soil and the proper amounts of sun or shade, as indicated in Chapter Two. Additionally, provide adequate water from rain and irrigation, as well as fertilizer. With all of these elements in balance, the only routine cares for annuals are to remove the spent flowers before seeds form and to stake up any that have gotten too tall to stand on their own. Insects and diseases are hardly a consideration, with a few exceptions (see Chapter Three).

Essential Tools

Growing, showing, and in general enjoying annual flowers requires hardly any tools. Transplants in particular are perfect for townhouse gardeners or anyone whose space is limited. It is nice to have a trowel and some hand pruners of the by-pass variety (with blades arranged more-or-less as scissors). Bamboo stakes or twiggy brush saved from general yard cleanup come in handy for holding or guiding growth, along with green twist-ties, jute garden twine, or raffia for securing branches to supports.

Year-round Gardening Calendar

Note planting reminders in a datebook or on a wall calendar. Become familiar with the United States Department of Agriculture Plant Hardiness Zone Map, which will help you learn the effects of cold on plants. Gardeners in zone 8 and colder to zone 3 in parts of the United States and Canada enjoy some annuals along with the spring bulbs, shrubs, and flowering trees. The greatest show usually takes place throughout summer with a final flourish before frost by 'Sensation' cosmos and annual types of chrysanthemum.

Gardeners in zone 9 and warmer, from subtropical to tropical, depend on a different group of annuals for each season, with major plantings occurring in fall or early winter for blooms through spring, and again in late spring with plants that thrive in torrid conditions. The particular needs of each annual are noted with the individual descriptions in Chapter Two.

Here is a calendar of seasonal reminders:

SPRING:

Till and prepare soil in garden beds and top-dress with fertilizer.

Sow seeds of annuals or transplant seedlings after danger of frost has passed.

Bring transplants to the garden.

Mulch with organic matter.

Start a gardening watering schedule, soaking soil thoroughly yet infrequently as a conservation measure. To check if soil needs to be watered, see if it feels dry 3 to 4 inches (7.5 to 10 centimeters) down.

Bring spring annual bouquets indoors.

Deadhead spent blooms.

SUMMER:

Continue weeding, watering, and deadheading.

Sow seeds of late-blooming annuals.

Bring summer annual bouquets indoors.

FALL:

Continue watering, weeding, and deadheading.

Bring late summer/early fall annual bouquets indoors.

In warm climates, sow annual seeds for spring blooms.

WINTER:

Begin designing your annual garden on paper.

Order everything you'll need: tools, seeds, flats, starting mixes.

Start annual seeds indoors.

Chapter Two:
The 100 Best Annuals for Your Garden

ABELMOSCHUS	26	*Flowering Okra*
ABUTILON	27	*Flowering Maple*
AGERATUM	28	*Flossflower*
AMARANTHUS	28	*Joseph's Coat; Tampala;* *Love-lies-bleeding*
ANTIRRHINUM	29	*Snapdragon*
ARCTOTIS	30	*African Daisy*
BEGONIA	31	*Wax Begonia*
BELAMCANDA	32	*Blackberry Lily;* *Leopard Flower*
BORAGO	33	*Borage*
BRACHYCOME	33	*Swan River Daisy*
BRASSICA	34	*Ornamental or Flowering* *Cabbage; Kale*
BROWALLIA	35	*Bush Violet*
CALENDULA	36	*Pot Marigold*
CALLISTEPHUS	37	*China Aster; Annual Aster*
CAPSICUM	37	*Ornamental Pepper*
CATHARANTHUS	38	*Madagascar Periwinkle;* *Annual Vinca*
CELOSIA	38	*Cockscomb*
CENTAUREA	39	*Bachelor's Button;* *Cornflower; Dusty Miller*
CHRYSANTHEMUM	40	*Annual Chrysanthemum*
CLARKIA	41	*Farewell-to-spring;* *Satin Flower; Godetia*
CLEOME	42	*Spider Flower*
CLITORIA	42	*Butterfly Pea*
COLEUS	43	*Painted Nettle*
CONSOLIDA	44	*Larkspur;* *Annual Delphinium*
CONVOLVULUS	45	*Dwarf Morning Glory*
COREOPSIS	46	*Pot of Gold*
CORIANDRUM	46	*Coriander; Cilantro* *(Chinese Parsley)*
COSMOS	47	*Cosmos*
CUCURBITA	48	*Gourd*
DAHLIA	49	*Annual Dahlia*
DATURA	49	*Angel's Trumpet*
DIANTHUS	50	*Pink; Carnation;* *Sweet William*

DOLICHOS	51	Purple Hyacinth Bean
DOROTHEANTHUS	52	Ice Plant; Livingstone Daisy
DYSSODIA	53	Dahlberg Daisy
EMILIA	53	Tassel Flower; Flora's Paintbrush
ESCHSCHOLZIA	54	California Poppy
EUPHORBIA	55	Summer Poinsettia; Snow-on-the-mountain
FELICIA	56	Blue Daisy
GAILLARDIA	57	Blanketflower
GAZANIA	58	Treasure Flower
GERBERA	59	Transvaal Daisy
GILIA	60	Globe Gilia
GOMPHRENA	60	Globe Amaranth; Everlasting Bachelor's Button
HELIANTHUS	61	Annual Sunflower
HELICHRYSUM	62	Everlasting; Strawflower
HELIOTROPIUM	62	Heliotrope; Cherry Pie
HELIPTERUM	63	Everlasting; Strawflower; Rhodanthe
HUNNEMANNIA	64	Mexican Tulip Poppy; Golden Cup
IBERIS	65	Annual Candytuft
IMPATIENS	66	Busy Lizzie; Patience; Sultana
IPOMOEA	67	Morning Glory; Moonflower; Cardinal Climber
LATHYRUS	68	Sweet Pea
LAVATERA	69	Tree Mallow
LIMONIUM	69	Statice
LINUM	70	Annual Flax
LISIANTHUS	71	Eustoma; Texas Bluebell
LOBELIA	72	Edging Lobelia
LOBULARIA	73	Sweet Alyssum
MATTHIOLA	74	Stock
MELAMPODIUM	74	'Medallion' Daisy
MENTZELIA	75	Blazing Star; Bartonia
MIMULUS	76	Monkey Flower
MIRABILIS	76	Four-o'clock
MONARDA	77	Lemon Mint
MYOSOTIS	78	Forget-me-not
NEMESIA	79	Cape Jewels
NICOTIANA	80	Flowering Tobacco
NIEREMBERGIA	81	Cup Flower
NIGELLA	82	Love-in-a-mist
NOLANA	83	Chilean Bellflower
OCIMUM	84	Basil
PAPAVER	84	Iceland, Opium and Shirley Poppies
PELARGONIUM	85	Bedding Geranium
PENSTEMON	86	Beardtongue
PERILLA	87	Shiso
PETROSELINUM	88	Parsley
PETUNIA	88	Garden Petunia
PHLOX	89	Annual Phlox
PORTULACA	90	Rose Moss; Purslane
RATABIDA	91	Mexican Hat; Prairie Coneflower
RESEDA	92	Mignonette
RICINUS	93	Castor Bean
RUDBECKIA	94	Black-eyed Susan; Gloriosa Daisy
SALPIGLOSSIS	95	Painted Tongue
SALVIA	96	Annual Sage
SANVITALIA	97	Creeping Zinnia
SCABIOSA	98	Pincushion Flower; Mourning Bride
SCHIZANTHUS	99	Butterfly Flower; Poor-man's-Orchid
SENECIO	99	Cineraria; Dusty Miller
TAGETES	100	Marigold
THUNBERGIA	101	Black-eyed-Susan Vine
TITHONIA	102	Mexican Sunflower
TORENIA	103	Wishbone Flower
TRACHYMENE	103	Blue Lace Flower; Didiscus
TROPAEOLUM	104	Nasturtium
VERBENA	104	Garden Verbena; Vervain
VIOLA	105	Pansy; Viola
XERANTHEMUM	106	Everlasting; Immortelle
ZINNIA	107	Common Zinnia; Youth-and-old-age

ABELMOSCHUS
(able-MOS-kus)

Flowering Okra

MALVACEAE; mallow family

Height/habit: Spreading bushes, 1–6 ft. (30–180 cm.).
Leaves: Palmate, 3–12 in. (7.5–30 cm.) across.
Flowers: Round, 3–5 in. (7.5–12.5 cm.) across; pink, red, rose, or yellow; open fresh daily.

Season: Summer.
When to plant: Sow seeds indoors at 75–80°F (24–26°C) 12–16 weeks before frost-free weather. Set out transplants when available. Often reseeds zone 7 and warmer.
Light: Sun half day or more.
Soil: Well drained, moist.
Fertilizer: 5-10-5.
Uses: Beds, borders, pots.

ABUTILON
(ab-YEW-till-on)

Flowering Maple

MALVACEAE; mallow family

Height/habit: Upright varieties, 3–4 ft. (1–1.2 m.) on lightly woody stems; lax-stemmed varieties spread and cascade 2–3 ft. (61–90 cm.).

Leaves: Maple-shaped, 2–3 in. (5–7.5 cm.) across.

Flowers: Bell-shaped, hanging, 1–3 in. (2.5–7.5 cm.) across; most colors except blue.

Season: Summer in cold climates; all year zone 9 and warmer. Flowers on new growth when nights are at least 10°F (about 3–5°C) cooler than days.

When to plant: Sow seeds indoors at 70–75°F (21–24°C) 12–16 weeks before frost-free weather. Root tip cuttings winter through spring in a warm, sunny place. Set out transplants when available.

Light: Sun half day or more.

Soil: Well drained, moist.

Fertilizer: Alternate 30-10-10 with 15-30-15.

Uses: Beds, borders, pots, bouquets.

AGERATUM
(adj-er-RAY-tum)

Flossflower

COMPOSITAE; daisy family

Height/habit: Bedding varieties, 8-12 in. (20–30 cm.); cut-flower varieties 2 ft. (61 cm.).
Leaves: Lightly quilted, 2 in. (5 cm.) long.
Flowers: Fuzzy, flattened clusters, 2–4 in. (5–10 cm.) across; exceptional blues, also pink and white.
Season: Summer in cold climates; winter until spring zone 9 and warmer.
When to plant: Sow seeds indoors at 70–75°F (21–24°C) 8–12 weeks before planting-out weather; sow outdoors where they are to grow and bloom when soil is warm. Seeds need light to sprout; do not cover. Set out transplants when available.
Light: Sun half day or more.
Soil: Well drained, moist.
Fertilizer: 5-10-5.
Uses: Beds, borders, pots, bouquets.

AMARANTHUS
(am-uh-RANTH-us)

Joseph's Coat; Tampala; Love-lies-bleeding

AMARANTHACEAE; amaranth family

Height/habit: Upright, 2–8 ft. (61–240 cm.).
Leaves: Long or oval, 2–4 in. (5–10 cm.) long, beginning green or dark red, turning at the tops to bright yellow, orange, or phosphorescent pink.
Flowers: Tiny, dry, of little consequence in varieties having colorful leaves, such as Joseph's coat (*A. tricolor* 'Splendens') and tampala (*A. tricolor*); hanging panicles in curiously showy, wine red, or chartreuse on love-lies-bleeding (*A. caudatus*).
Season: Summer until fall frost; all zones.
When to plant: Sow seeds indoors at 70–75°F (21–24°C) 6–8 weeks before frost-free weather; outdoors as soon as soil is warm and there is no danger of frost. Set out transplants when available.
Light: Sun half day or more.
Soil: Well drained, moist.
Fertilizer: None required. Overly rich soil could result in less colorful leaves.
Uses: Beds, borders, pots, bouquets.

ANTIRRHINUM
(an-tir-EYE-num)

Snapdragon

SCROPHULARIACEAE; figwort
family

Height/habit: Dwarf varieties
in mounds, 8–12 in. (20–30
cm.); standard ('Maximum')
types, 2–5 ft. (61–150 cm.).
Leaves: Lanceolate or oblong
to 3 in. (7.5 cm.); pale green to
reddish.
Flowers: Pouched to 2 in.
(5 cm.) long in terminal
racemes; most colors except
blue. Deadheading increases
bloom.
Season: Summer until hard
frost in cold climates; winter
until spring zone 9 and
warmer.
When to plant: In the North,
sow seeds indoors 70°F (21°C)
12–16 weeks before planting-
out weather in the spring; in
the South, sow seeds late
summer through early fall.
Prechill seeds in refrigerator
1 week before sowing. Seeds
need light to sprout; do not
cover. After sprouting, grow
in cool temperature, about
45–50°F (7–10°C) to produce
strong seedlings. Set out
transplants when available.
Light: Sun half day or more.
Soil: Well drained, moist.
Fertilizer: 5-10-5.
Uses: Beds, borders, pots,
bouquets.

ARCTOTIS
(ark-TOH-tiss)

African Daisy

COMPOSITAE; daisy family

Height/habit: Spreading, 6–18 in. (15–45 cm.) high/wide.
Leaves: Rosettes, pinnately lobed, to 6 in. (15 cm.) long.
Flowers: Single, to 2 in. (5 cm.) across; most colors except blue, from pastel to bright tones.
Season: Summer until frost in cold climates; fall until spring zone 9 and warmer.

When to plant: Sow seeds indoors at 60–70˚F (15–21˚C) 6–8 weeks before planting-out weather; sow outdoors where they are to grow and bloom when soil is warm.
Light: Sun half day or more.
Soil: Well drained, moist to dry; tolerates drought.
Fertilizer: 5-10-5.
Uses: Beds, borders, ground cover, rock gardens, pots.

BEGONIA
(be-GO-nee-ah)

Wax Begonia

BEGONIACEAE; begonia family

Height/habit: *B. semperflorens* in tidy, upright mounds, 6–18 in. (15–45 cm.).

Leaves: Oval, 1–3 in. (2.5–7.5 cm.) across; cupped, waxy; bright green, olive, or reddish bronze.

Flowers: Small clusters from the leaf axils, 1–2 in. (2.5–5 cm.) across; single if from seeds, double in certain cultivars propagated vegetatively; pink, red, rose, or white.

Season: Summer until frost in cold climates; year-round zone 9 and warmer.

When to plant: Sow seeds indoors at 70°F (21°C) 16 weeks before first blooms. Though tiny, seeds sprout readily when sown in moist medium. Seeds need light to sprout; do not cover. Set out transplants when available.

Light: Full sun to part shade.

Soil: Well drained, moist to slightly dry.

Fertilizer: 5-10-5.

Uses: Beds, borders, pots.

BELAMCANDA
(bell-am-KAN-dah)

Blackberry Lily; Leopard Flower

IRIDACEAE; iris family

Height/habit: Upright, 2–4 ft. (61–120 cm.).

Leaves: Resemble German iris; grow in flattened fans 1–1.5 ft. (30–45 cm.) long/wide.

Flowers: Single, 6 petals, to 2 in. (5 cm.) across; orange with red spots. Candy lily (*Pardancanda*) closely related, with same habit, but flowers in many pastel shades, often bicolored.

Season: Late summer until early fall, followed by seed clusters resembling large blackberries. Thrives in zone 5.

When to plant: Sow seeds indoors at 70°F (21°C) 8–12 weeks before planting-out weather; sow outdoors when soil is warm. Set transplants when available. Technically a rhizomatous bulb/perennial, but blooms reliably the first year from seeds.

Light: Sun half day or more.

Soil: Well drained, moist.

Fertilizer: 5-10-5.

Uses: Beds, borders, pots, seed heads for arrangements.

BORAGO
(boh-RAY-go)

Borage

BORAGINACEAE; borage family

Height/habit: Upright, sprawling, 1–2 ft. (30–61 cm.) high/wide.

Leaves: Hairy, pebbled, oblong, to 6 in. (15 cm.).

Flowers: Starry, 5-pointed, to 1 in. (2.5 cm.) across; blue.

Season: Summer until frost in cold climates; variously through the year zone 8 and warmer. Reseeds.

When to plant: Prechill seeds in refrigerator 1 week before planting. Sow seeds outdoors where they are to grow and bloom when soil is workable but cool.

Light: Sun half day or more.

Soil: Well drained; moist to on the dry side; tolerates drought.

Fertilizer: 5-10-5.

Uses: Beds, borders, herb gardens, bee plant, pots.

BRACHYCOME
(BRACKY-comb)

Swan River Daisy

COMPOSITAE; daisy family

Height/habit: Mounds, 6–10 in. (15–25 cm.).

Leaves: Finely dissected, fernlike, to 2 in. (5 cm.) long, growing mostly from the base.

Flowers: Nickel-sized daisies; various shades of blue, occasionally white; centers can be yellow or nearly black.

Season: Summer until frost in cold climates; winter until spring zone 9 and warmer.

When to plant: Sow seeds indoors at 70°F (21°C) 6–8 weeks before planting-out weather in spring; sow outdoors where they are to grow and bloom as soon as soil is warm and there is no danger of frost. Set out transplants when available.

Light: Sun half day or more.

Soil: Well drained, moist.

Fertilizer: 5-10-5.

Uses: Edging, rock gardens, pots.

BRASSICA
(BRASS-ick-ah)

Ornamental or Flowering Cabbage; Kale

CRUCIFERAE; mustard family

Height/habit: Symmetrical rosettes, 1–1.5 ft. (30–45 cm.) high/wide.

Leaves: Rounded (cabbage) or lacy (kale); blue-green at first, changing from the centers outward to white, cream, chartreuse, pink, or lavender.

Flowers: Yellow, 4-petaled, dime-sized, ascending gracefully above the leaves in spring until early summer.

Season: Best leaf coloration occurs in cool weather: fall in the North, fall until early spring zone 7 and warmer.

When to plant: Sow seeds 60–70°F (15–21°C) late spring until early summer in the North, late summer in mild climates. Seeds need light to sprout; a scant covering of horticultural vermiculite helps maintain desired moisture during germination. Set transplants when available.

Light: Sun half day or more.

Soil: Well drained, moist.

Fertilizer: 5-10-5. Too much nitrogen delays coloration.

Uses: Beds, borders, pots, arrangements.

BROWALLIA
(broh-WALL-ee-ah)
Bush Violet
SOLANACEAE; nightshade family

Height/habit: Mounds, 10–16 in. (25–40 cm.).
Leaves: Oval, 2–3 in. (5–7.5 cm.) long.
Flowers: 5-lobed stylized stars, 1–2 in. (2.5–5 cm.) across; blue or white.
Season: Spring until fall; through winter in sunny climes with temperatures of 55–70°F (13–21°C), zone 9–10.
When to plant: Sow seeds indoors at 70–72°F (21–22°C) 10–12 weeks before frost-free weather. Seeds need light to sprout; do not cover. After sprouting, grow at 55°F (13°C) and keep on dry side in early stages. Set out transplants when available.
Light: Mostly sun in cool weather, more shade in heat.
Soil: Well drained, moist.
Fertilizer: 5-10-5.
Uses: Beds, borders, pots, hanging baskets.

CALENDULA
(kal-END-yew-lah)

Pot Marigold
COMPOSITAE; daisy family

Height/habit: Dwarfs in mounds, 8–12 in. (20–30 cm.); cutting varieties, 14–30 in. (35–75 cm.).

Leaves: Oblong, 3–6 in. (7.5–15 cm.) long.

Flowers: 2–4 in. (5–10 cm.) across, atop straight stems; cream, orange, or yellow. Deadheading increases bloom.

Season: Late spring to frost in the North; fall until spring zone 9 and warmer. Cool nights, with temperatures of 45–55°F (7–13°C), favor quality.

When to plant: In the North, sow seeds indoors at 70°F (21°C) 6–8 weeks before planting-out weather in spring; provide continual darkness until seeds sprout; sow outdoors where they are to grow and bloom as soon as soil can be worked. In mild climates, sow seeds late summer until early fall. Set transplants when available.

Light: Sun half day or more.

Soil: Well drained, moist.

Fertilizer: 5-10-5.

Uses: Beds, borders, pots, bouquets.

CALLISTEPHUS
(kal-is-STEE-fuss)

China Aster;
Annual Aster

COMPOSITAE; daisy family

Height/habit: Dwarf bedding varieties in mounds, 8–16 in. (20–40 cm.); cutting varieties, 16–30 in. (40–75 cm.).
Leaves: Broad or triangular ovals, 3–4 in. (7.5–10 cm.) long, mostly in basal rosettes.
Flowers: Single or double, 2–4 in. (5–10 cm.) across; blue, lavender, pink, red, rose, or white.
Season: Summer in cold climates; late spring until early summer zone 8 and warmer.
When to plant: Sow seeds indoors at 70°F (21°C) 6–8 weeks before planting-out weather in spring; sow outdoors where they are to grow and bloom as soon as soil is warm. Set transplants when available.
Light: Sun half day or more.
Soil: Well drained, moist. Avoid extremes of wet and dry. Do not grow China asters on the same site every year.
Fertilizer: 5-10-5.
Uses: Dwarfs for bedding and pots. Tall varieties for beds, borders, and bouquets.

CAPSICUM
(KAP-sick-um)

Ornamental
Pepper

SOLANACEAE; nightshade family

Height/habit: Tidy, bushy, many branches, 10–18 in. (25–45 cm.) high/wide.
Leaves: Ovate or lanceolate, 1–2 in. (2.5–5 cm.) long.
Flowers: Starry, to .5 in. (1.2 cm.) across; white, followed by conical, fingerlike, or round peppers; green, chartreuse, cream, orange, red, or purple.
Season: Late summer until frost; fall until winter in frost-free zones (9-10).
When to plant: Sow seeds indoors at 70°F (21°C) 6–8 weeks before planting-out weather; sow outdoors where they are to grow and bloom when soil is warm. Set transplants when available.
Light: Sun half day or more.
Soil: Well drained, moist.
Fertilizer: 5-10-5.
Uses: Beds, borders, pots.

CATHARANTHUS
(kath-uh-RANTH-us)

Madagascar Periwinkle; Annual Vinca

APOCYNACEAE; dogbane family

Height/habit: Mounds, 6–18 in. (15–45 cm.).

Leaves: Oblong, lanceolate, 1–2 in. (2.5–5 cm.) long.

Flowers: 1–2 in. (2.5–5 cm.) across, 5 petals resembling a pinwheel; white, pink, rose, or cherry red, often with contrasting eye.

Season: Summer until fall frost; all zones.

When to plant: Sow seeds indoors at 70–75°F (21–24°C) 8–10 weeks before planting-out weather in spring. Keep in continual darkness until they sprout. Outdoors, sow where they are to grow and bloom when soil is warm. Set out transplants when available.

Light: Sunny to partly sunny. Hardly any flower can match the performance of this one in dry summer heat.

Soil: Well drained, moist to on dry side. Caution: Avoid cold—below 60°F (15°C)— and wet conditions.

Fertilizer: 5-10-5.

Uses: Beds, borders, pots.

CELOSIA
(sel-LOW-shah)

Cockscomb

AMARANTHACEAE; amaranth family

Height/habit: Upright; dwarf, 8 in. (20 cm.); medium, 14–16 in. (35–40 cm.); tall, 3 ft. (1 m.).

Leaves: Lanceolate, to 3–4 in. (7.5–10 cm.) long.

Flowers: Crested (cockscomb) to 12 in. (30 cm.) across or plumed to 12 in. (30 cm.) tall; creamy white, yellow, pink, rose, to darkest red.

Season: Summer until fall frost.

When to plant: Sow seeds indoors at 70–75°F (21–24°C) 6–8 weeks before planting-out weather; sow outdoors where they are to grow and bloom when soil is warm. Set out transplants when available. Sowing too early as well as cold temperatures—below 65°F (18°C)—result in premature flowering; all zones.

Light: Sun half day or more.

Soil: Well drained, moist.

Fertilizer: 5-10-5.

Uses: Beds, borders, pots, bouquets, drying.

CENTAUREA
(sen-TAW-ree-ah)

Bachelor's Button; Cornflower; Dusty Miller

COMPOSITAE; daisy family

Height/habit: Dwarf bachelor's button *(C. cyanus)* and dusty miller *(C. cineraria)*, 8–10 in. (20–25 cm.) high/wide; standard bachelor's button (cornflower), 1.5–2 ft. (45–61 cm.).

Leaves: Gray-green in bachelor's button, .5 in. (1.2 cm.) wide; 2–3 in. (5–7.5 cm.) long. Silver-gray in dusty miller, deeply cut, lacy; 1–2 in. (2.5–5 cm.) wide, 4–5 in. (10–12.5 cm.) long.

Flowers: 2 in. (5 cm.) across in bachelor's button; blue, mauve, maroon, pink, rose, or white. Dusty miller grown for its silver leaves—the .5-in. (1.2 cm.) yellow flowers are incidental.

Season: Bachelor's button late spring until summer in cold climates; winter until spring zone 8 and warmer. Dusty miller late spring until killing frost.

When to plant: Sow bachelor's button seeds outdoors where they are to grow and bloom in earliest spring or fall zone 8 and warmer. Set transplants when available. Sow dusty miller seeds indoors at 65°F (18°C) 8–12 weeks before planting-out weather. Set out transplants when available.

Light: Sun half day or more.

Soil: Well drained, moist to on dry side.

Fertilizer: 5-10-5.

Uses: Beds, borders, pots, bouquets.

CHRYSANTHEMUM
(kriss-ANTH-ee-mum)

Annual Chrysanthemum

COMPOSITAE; daisy family

Height/habit: Erect bushes, many branches, 1–3 ft. (30–90 cm.) high/wide.

Leaves: Deeply cut or finely divided, 4–6 in. (10–15 cm.) long.

Flowers: Single daisies, 1–3 in. (2.5–7.5 cm.) across; white, yellow, pink, or rose, often bicolored in annual chrysanthemum (*C. carinatum*). Other choice species are *C. multicaule* and *C. paludosum.*

Season: Summer or until frost; all zones.

When to plant: Sow seeds indoors at 65–70°F (18–21°C) 6–8 weeks before planting-out weather; sow outdoors where they are to grow and bloom when soil is warm. Set transplants when available.

Light: Sun half day or more.

Soil: Well drained, moist.

Fertilizer: 5-10-5.

Uses: Beds, borders, pots, bouquets.

CLARKIA
(KLARK-ee-ah)

Farewell-to-spring; Satin Flower; Godetia

ONAGRACEAE; evening prim-rose family

Height/habit: Bushy, upright to sprawling, 1.5–3 ft. (45–90 cm.) high/wide.
Leaves: Lanceolate, to 2 in. (5 cm.) long.
Flowers: Single or double, 2–4 in. (5–10 cm.) across, in loose spikes; white, pink, rose, red, or salmon.
Season: Spring until summer, best in cool weather; all zones.
When to plant: Sow seeds where they are to grow and bloom, fall in mild-winter regions, early spring elsewhere. Set transplants when available.
Light: Sun half day or more.
Soil: Well drained, moist to on the dry side.
Fertilizer: 5-10-5.
Uses: Beds, borders, pots, bouquets.

CLEOME
(klee-OH-me)
Spider Flower
CAPARACEAE; caper family

Height/habit: 2–6 ft. (61 to 180 cm.) high/wide.

Leaves: Compound with 5–7 leaflets, to 5 in. (12.5 cm.) across, on rigid stems with spines.

Flowers: Racemes to 5–6 in. (12.5–15 cm.) across; spidery, ephemeral; white, pink, or cherry rose.

Season: Summer or until killing frost; all zones.

When to plant: Prechill seeds 1 week in refrigerator. Sow seeds indoors at 70–75°F (21–24°C) 8–10 weeks before planting-out weather; sow outdoors where they are to grow and bloom when soil is warm. Set out transplants when available. Often reseeds.

Light: Sun half day or more.

Soil: Well drained, moist to on the dry side.

Fertilizer: 5-10-5.

Uses: Beds, borders, backgrounds, large pots.

CLITORIA
(klih-TOH-ree-ah)
Butterfly Pea
LEGUMINOSAE; pea family

Height/habit: Slender twining vine, 10–20 ft. (3–6 m.).

Leaves: 5–7 leaflets to 4 in. (10 cm.) long.

Flowers: To 2 in. (5 cm.); sea blue or white.

Season: Summer or until killing frost; all zones.

When to plant: Soak seeds 24–48 hours in room-temperature water, then sow indoors at 70–75°F (21–24°C) 12 weeks before warm, frost-free weather arrives. Set out transplants when available.

Light: Sun half day or more.

Soil: Well drained, moist.

Fertilizer: 5-10-5.

Uses: Quick cover for lattice, trellis, arbor, chain-link fence.

COLEUS
(KOH-lee-us)

Painted Nettle

LABIATAE; mint family

Height/habit: 8–20 in.
(20–50 cm.) high/wide.
Leaves: Crenate-serrate, some
with extra cuts and ruffles;
2–4 in. (5–10 cm.) long; many
colors and combinations.
Flowers: Thin blue spikes to
4 in. (10 cm.) long; late summer through fall. Grown
primarily for colorful leaves.
Season: Late spring until fall;
all zones.

When to plant: Sow seeds
indoors at 70°F (21°C) 8–12
weeks before frost-free
weather. Seeds need light to
sprout; do not cover. Set
transplants when available.
Cuttings from favorite plants
carried over the winter in
warmth root easily in spring.
Light: Sunbelt varieties need
a half day or more; others
thrive in part shade.
Soil: Well drained, moist.
Fertilizer: 5-10-5.
Uses: Beds, borders, pots.

CONSOLIDA
(kohn-SOL-id-ah)
Larkspur; Annual Delphinium
RANUNCULACEAE; buttercup family

Height/habit: 2–4 ft. (61–120 cm.).
Leaves: Mostly basal, finely cut.
Flowers: Each about 1 in. (2.5 cm.) across in vertical racemes or panicles; shades of blue, mauve, pink, or white.
Season: Late spring until summer in the North; late winter until spring zone 8 and warmer.
When to plant: Sow seeds in late fall or winter (or earliest spring in the North) where plants are to grow and bloom. Set out transplants when available. Often reseeds.
Light: Sun half day or more.
Soil: Well drained, moist.
Fertilizer: 5-10-5.
Uses: Beds, borders, bouquets.

CONVOLVULUS
(kohn-VOLV-yew-lus)

Dwarf Morning Glory

CONVOLVULACEAE; morning-glory family

Height/habit: Bushy, spreading, 1 ft. (30 cm.) high, 2 ft. (61 cm.) wide.
Leaves: Linear, oblong, to 3 in. (7.5 cm.).
Flowers: Funnelform trumpets, 2–3 in. (5–7.5 cm.) across; blue, white, yellow ('Royal Ensign'), or dark red ('Crimson Monarch').
Season: Summer; flowers open only in sun.
When to plant: First nick seed with file, then plant in warm soil where it is to grow and bloom. Set transplants when available.
Light: Sun half day or more.
Soil: Well drained, moist to on the dry side; tolerates drought.
Fertilizer: 5-10-5.
Uses: Beds, borders, rock gardens, pots.

COREOPSIS
(koh-ree-OP-siss)

Pot of Gold
COMPOSITAE; daisy family

Height/habit: Bushes, 1–1.5 ft. (30–45 cm.).
Leaves: Entire or pinnately lobed, mostly in basal rosettes.
Flowers: Single or double, 2 in. (5 cm.) across; intense yellow. Deadheading increases bloom.
Season: Summer until frost in cold climates; spring until early summer zone 8 and warmer. Cultivars 'Early Sunrise' and 'Sunray' behave as hardy perennials zones 4 and warmer.
When to plant: Sow seeds indoors at 70°F (21°C) 4–6 weeks before frost-free weather; sow outdoors where they are to grow and bloom when soil is warm. Set transplants when available.
Light: Sun half day or more.
Soil: Well drained, moist to on the dry side.
Fertilizer: 5-10-5.
Uses: Beds, borders, pots, bouquets.

CORIANDRUM
(koh-ree-AND-rum)

Coriander; Cilantro (Chinese Parsley)
UMBELLIFERAE; carrot family

Height/habit: Tidy rosettes or clumps, 6–12 in. (15–30 cm.) high/wide.
Leaves: Resemble Italian parsley, to 6 in. (15 cm.) long/wide.
Flowers: Umbels to 1 ft. (30 cm.) above the leaves, lacy; white; followed by seed heads that are the herbalist's coriander.
Season: Leaves in cool weather; flowers beginning of summer; all zones.
When to plant: Sow seeds where they are to grow and bloom in early spring; fall in climates with mild winters. Set transplants when available. Reseeds.
Light: Sun half day or more; tolerates more shade than most herbs.
Soil: Well drained, moist.
Fertilizer: 5-10-5.
Uses: Beds, borders, edging, pots; cilantro leaves for the kitchen.

COSMOS
(KOZ-mose)
Cosmos
COMPOSITAE; daisy family

Height/habit: Bushy, 1-6 ft.
(30–180 cm.)
Leaves: Pinnately cut, 3–5 in.
(7.5–12.5 cm.) long.
Flowers: Single or double,
2–3 in. (5–7.5 cm.) across
in 'Klondyke' types
(*C. sulphureus*, which are
yellow, orange, or mahogany
red); 4-6 in. (10-15 cm.)
across in 'Sensation' types
(*C. bipinnatus*, which are lilac
pink, rose, crimson, or white).
Deadheading increases bloom.
Season: Summer until frost
in cold climates; at almost any
time zone 9 and warmer.
When to plant: Sow seeds
indoors at 70°F (21°C) 4–6
weeks before frost-free
weather; sow outdoors
where they are to grow and
bloom when soil is warm.
Set transplants when available.
Light: Sun half day or more.
Soil: Well drained, moist.
Fertilizer: 5-10-5.
Uses: Beds, borders, pots,
bouquets.

CUCURBITA
(kew-KURB-it-ah)

Gourd

CUCURBITACEAE; gourd family

Height/habit: Tendril-climbing vine, 10–20 ft. (3–6 m.).
Leaves: Coarse, triangular to ovate, lobed, 1–1.5 ft. (30–45 cm.) long/wide.
Flowers: Male and female on same plant, 5-lobed, to 5 in. (12.5 cm.) across; yellow; followed by the fruit in various shapes, sizes, and colors.

Season: Summer until frost.
When to plant: Sow seeds where they are to grow and bloom when soil is thoroughly warm.
Light: Sun half day or more.
Soil: Well drained, moist to on the dry side; tolerates drought.
Fertilizer: 5-10-5.
Uses: Quick cover for fence, trellis, unsightly brush; decorative gourds for household ornament.

DATURA
(dah-TOO-rah)
Angel's Trumpet
SOLANACEAE; nightshade family

Height/habit: Bushy,
spreading, 3–6 ft. (1–1.8 m.).
Leaves: Ovate, entire to den-
tate, 8–10 in. (20–25 cm.) long;
green, grayish, or purplish.
Flowers: Outward-facing
trumpets to 8 in. (20 cm.) long
by 2–3 in. (5–7.5 cm.) across;
white, cream, yellow, purple,
often bicolored and doubled
hose-in-hose style; fragrant.
Season: Summer until frost;
perennial zone 9 and warmer.
When to plant: Sow seeds
indoors at 70–75°F (21–24°C)
8–10 weeks before frost-free
weather. Set transplants
when available.
Light: Sun half day or more.
Soil: Well drained, moist to
on the dry side.
Fertilizer: 5-10-5.
Uses: Beds, borders, pots.

DAHLIA
(DAL-ee-ah)
Annual Dahlia
COMPOSITAE; daisy family

Height/habit: Bushy, 10–18 in.
(25–45 cm.).
Leaves: Pinnate, to 6 in.
(15 cm.) long.
Flowers: Single or double,
2–4 in. (5–10 cm.) across;
most colors except blue.
Season: Summer until frost.
When to plant: Sow seeds
indoors at 70°F (21°C) 12–16
weeks before frost-free
weather; grow seedlings at cool
temperature, 50°F (10°C). Set
transplants when available.
Light: Sun half day or more.
Soil: Well drained, moist.
Fertilizer: 5-10-5.
Uses: Beds, borders, pots,
bouquets.

DIANTHUS
(die-ANTH-us)

Pink; Carnation; Sweet William

CARYOPHYLLACEAE; pink family

Height/habit: Rainbow pink (*D. chinensis*) varieties grown as annuals form 6–8-in. (15–20-cm.) mounds. *D. caryophyllus* as annual garden carnations grow 1–1.5 ft. (30–45 cm.). *D. barbatus* in annual varieties of sweet William grow 6–12 in. (15–30 cm.).

Leaves: Lanceolate, to 2 in. (5 cm.) long; mostly basal, green, or blue-green.

Flowers: Solitary, panicled, or in heads; individuals 1–2 in. (2.5–5 cm.) across; white, pink, rose, red, often bicolored; some clove-scented. Garden carnations are also orange or yellow. Deadheading increases bloom.

Season: Late spring until fall frost in the North; fall until early summer zone 9 and warmer.

When to plant: Sow seeds indoors at 70°F (21°C) 8–10 weeks before planting-out weather; sow outdoors where they are to grow and bloom, as soon as soil is warm. Set transplants when available.

Light: Sun half day or more.

Soil: Well drained, moist to on the dry side.

Fertilizer: 5-10-5. Caution: Do not use ammonia-based fertilizer.

Uses: Beds, borders, edgings, rock gardens, pots, nosegays, bouquets.

DOLICHOS
(DOLE-ick-os)
Purple Hyacinth Bean
LEGUMINOSAE; pea family

Height/habit: Twining, purple-stemmed vine, 10–30 ft. (3–9 m.).

Leaves: 3 leaflets, 3–6 in. (7.5–15 cm.) long.

Flowers: Resemble small butterflies, to 1 in. (2.5 cm.) across, in loose racemes to 1 ft. (30 cm.) long; lavender purple and fragrant; followed by bright purple pods.

Season: Summer or until frost; all zones.

When to plant: Sow seeds where they are to grow and bloom when soil is warm. Set transplants when available.

Light: Sun half day or more.

Soil: Well drained, moist.

Fertilizer: 5-10-5.

Uses: Quick cover for fence, trellis, arbor, tepee.

DOROTHEANTHUS
(doh-roth-ee-ANTH-us)

Ice Plant; Livingstone Daisy

AIZOACEAE; carpetweed family

Height/habit: Spreading, trailing, 4–6 in. (10–15 cm.) high x 1–1.5 ft. (30–45 cm.) wide.
Leaves: Succulent, thin, tapered, to 3 in. (7.5 cm.) long, green to bluish.
Flowers: Daisylike, to 2 in. (5 cm.) across; pink, white, rose, yellow, often bicolored.

Season: Summer until frost in cold climates; spring until summer zone 9 and warmer.
When to plant: Sow seeds indoors at 65°F (18°C) 8–10 weeks before frost-free weather; provide continual darkness until seeds sprout. Set transplants when available.
Light: Full sun, the more the better.
Soil: Well drained, on the dry side.
Fertilizer: 5-10-5.
Uses: Beds, dry banks/slopes, rock gardens, pots.

DYSSODIA
(diss-OH-dee-ah)
Dahlberg Daisy
COMPOSITAE; daisy family

Height/habit: 8-in. (20-cm.) mounds.

Leaves: Finely dissected, to 2 in. (5 cm.) long.

Flowers: 1 in. (2.5 cm.) across; bright yellow.

Season: Summer until frost in cold climates; winter until spring zone 9 and warmer.

When to plant: Sow seeds indoors at 70°F (21°C) 6–8 weeks before frost-free weather. Seeds need light to sprout; do not cover. Sow fall through early winter in mild climates. Set transplants when available. Often reseeds.

Light: Sun half day or more.

Soil: Well drained, moist to on dry side.

Fertilizer: 5-10-5.

Uses: Beds, border edging, rock gardens, pots, hanging baskets.

EMILIA
(ee-MEE-lee-ah)
Tassel Flower; Flora's Paintbrush
COMPOSITAE; daisy family

Height/habit: Flowering stems thin, wiry, 1.5–2 ft. (45–61 cm.).

Leaves: Mostly in basal rosettes to 6 in. (15 cm.) long, reminiscent of dandelion.

Flowers: Brushlike, rounded, to 1 in. (2.5 cm) across; orange, red, or yellow. Deadheading increases bloom.

Season: Summer or until fall frost; all zones.

When to plant: Sow seeds indoors at 70°F (21°C) 6–8 weeks before frost-free weather; sow outdoors where they are to grow and bloom as soon as soil is warm. Provide continual darkness until seeds sprout. Set transplants when available.

Light: Sun half day or more.

Soil: Well drained, moist to on the dry side.

Fertilizer: 5-10-5.

Uses: Beds, borders, pots, bouquets.

ESCHSCHOLZIA
(esh-SCHOLTZ-ee-ah)

California Poppy

PAPAVERACEAE; poppy family

Height/habit: Mounded,
10–18 in. (25–45 cm.).
Leaves: Dissected finely into
segments, blue-green.
Flowers: Single or double,
1–2 in. (2.5–5 cm.) across,
borne singly above the foliage;
creamy yellow, vivid orange,
or salmon pink.
Season: Spring zone 8 and
warmer; summer in colder
climates.

When to plant: Sow seeds
outdoors in late fall or earliest
spring where they are to grow
and bloom. Transplanting is
difficult, but seeds sown
directly in 4-in. (10-cm.) pots
are often available as transplants; take care not to disturb
rootball when setting into
garden.
Light: Sun half day or more.
Soil: Sandy, well drained,
moist to on the dry side.
Fertilizer: 5-10-5.
Uses: Beds, edging, rock
gardens, pots.

EUPHORBIA
(yew-FOR-bee-uh)

Summer Poinsettia; Snow-on-the-mountain

EUPHORBIACEAE; spurge family

Height/habit: Erect bush, 2–4 ft. (61–122 cm.).
Leaves: Resemble those of poinsettia in *E. cyathophora* (*E. heterophylla* of trade, also called summer poinsettia), turning orange-red at the plant tops; white-margined, blue-green in *E. marginata* (snow-on-the-mountain).

Flowers: Inconspicuous.
Season: Summer or until fall frost; all zones.
When to plant: Prechill seeds 1 week in refrigerator, then sow indoors 70°F (21°C) 6–8 weeks before frost-free weather; sow outdoors where they are to grow and bloom as soon as soil is warm. Set transplants when available. Often reseeds.
Light: Sun half day or more.
Soil: Well drained, moist to on the dry side.
Fertilizer: 5-10-5.
Uses: Beds, borders, pots.

FELICIA
(fel-EE-shah)
Blue Daisy
COMPOSITAE; daisy family

Height/habit: Bushy mounds, to 1 ft. (30 cm.) tall/wide.
Leaves: Finely cut, fernlike, 1–2 in. (2.5–5 cm.) long.
Flowers: Single, to 1 in. (2.5 cm.) across; blue with yellow centers.
Season: Winter until spring in mild climates; summer zone 7 and colder.
When to plant: Sow seeds indoors at 68–86°F (20–30°C) 8–10 weeks before planting-out weather; sow outdoors where they are to grow and bloom when soil is warm. Set transplants when available. Reseeds.
Light: Sun half day or more.
Soil: Well drained, moist.
Fertilizer: 5-10-5.
Uses: Beds, borders, edging, rock gardens, pots, hanging baskets.

GAILLARDIA
(gay-LARD-ee-ah)

Blanketflower

COMPOSITAE; daisy family

Height/habit: Bushy mounds, 8–18 in. (20–45 cm.).
Leaves: Mostly basal, linear to lanceolate, often pinnately lobed, 3–4 in. (7.5–10 cm.).
Flowers: Solitary on wiry stems, single or double, 2–3 in. (5–7.5 cm.) across; yellow, orange, red, or mahogany. Deadheading increases bloom.
Season: Summer until frost in cold climates; spring until summer zone 8 and warmer.

When to plant: Sow seeds indoors at 70°F (21°C) 6–8 weeks before frost-free weather; sow outdoors where they are to grow and bloom when soil is warm. Set transplants when available. Often reseeds.
Light: Sun half day or more.
Soil: Well drained, moist to on the dry side.
Fertilizer: 5-10-5.
Uses: Beds, borders, rock gardens, pots, bouquets.

GAZANIA
(gah-ZAY-nee-ah).
Treasure Flower
COMPOSITAE; daisy family

Height/habit: Low mounds, 6–10 in. (15–25 cm.).

Leaves: Form a basal rosette reminiscent of dandelion but waxy; green above, silvery white below, 3–5 in. (7.5–12.5 cm.) long.

Flowers: Solitary on peduncle 6–8 in. (15–20 cm.) long; single daisies to 3 in. (7.5 cm.) across, closing at night and in cloudy weather; white, yellow, orange, pink, or mahogany, often bicolored. Deadheading increases bloom.

Season: Summer until frost in cold climates; spring until fall zone 8 and warmer (where the plants can persist as perennials).

When to plant: Sow seeds indoors at 60°F (15°C) 14–16 weeks before frost-free weather; grow seedlings at 55–60°F (13–15°C). Set transplants when available.

Light: Sun half day or more.

Soil: Well drained, moist to quite dry.

Fertilizer: 5-10-5.

Uses: Beds, edging, rock gardens, ground cover, pots.

GERBERA
(GURB-er-ah)
Transvaal Daisy
COMPOSITAE; daisy family

Height/habit: Mounds 6–12 in. (15–30 cm.) tall/wide.

Leaves: Form basal rosette, reminiscent of dandelion, 4–6 in. (10–15 cm.) long.

Flowers: Single or double, 3–5 in. (7.5–12.5 cm.) across, solitary atop graceful stems, 6–18 in. (15–45 cm.) tall; most colors except blue. Deadheading increases bloom.

Season: Late summer until fall frost in cold climates, late winter until spring zone 9 and warmer (where the plants persist as perennials). Short days initiate flower buds.

When to plant: Sow seeds indoors at 70°F (21°C) 12–16 weeks before frost-free weather. Plant fresh seeds with the pointed end down, other end exposed; they need light to sprout. Grow at 60°F (15°C) nights, 70–75°F (21–24°C) days. Set transplants when available (but do not subject to freezing).

Light: Sun half day or more in cooler climates, shade midday in high temperatures (above 80°F [26°C]).

Soil: Well drained, moist.

Fertilizer: 5-10-5.

Uses: Beds, borders, pots, bouquets.

GILIA
(JILL-ee-ah)

Globe Gilia

POLEMONIACEAE; phlox family

Height/habit: Erect to sprawling, 2–3 ft. (61–90 cm.) high/wide.

Leaves: Finely cut, mostly toward the plant base.

Flowers: Dense in globes, to 1 in. (2.5 cm.) across; long, wiry stems; sky blue.

Season: Summer or until frost; all zones.

When to plant: Sow seeds indoors at 70°F (21°C) 6–8 weeks before planting-out weather; do not cover as light aids germination. Sow outdoors where they are to grow and bloom when soil is warm. Set transplants when available.

Light: Sun half day or more.

Soil: Well drained, moist.

Fertilizer: 5-10-5.

Uses: Beds, borders, pots, bouquets.

GOMPHRENA
(gom-FREE-nah)

Globe Amaranth; Everlasting Bachelor's Button

AMARANTHACEAE; amaranth family

Height/habit: Mounded or bushy, 6–24 in. (15–61 cm.) high/wide.

Leaves: Oblong to elliptic, to 4 in. (10 cm.) long.

Flowers: Dry, globular heads, to 1 in. (2.5 cm.) across; lavender, orange, pink, red, rose, purple, or white.

Season: Summer until fall frost; all zones.

When to plant: Sow seeds indoors at 70°F (21°C) 8–10 weeks before frost-free weather; sow outdoors where they are to grow and bloom after the soil is warm. Set transplants when available.

Light: Sun half day or more.

Soil: Well drained, moist to on the dry side.

Fertilizer: 5-10-5.

Uses: Beds, borders, edging, pots, bouquets, drying.

HELIANTHUS
(hee-lee-ANTH-us)

Annual Sunflower

COMPOSITAE; daisy family

Height/habit: Strongly upright, 2–12 ft. (61–360 cm. [3.6 m.])
Leaves: Ovate, to 1 ft. (30 cm.) long, rough to the touch.
Flowers: Single or double, 3–12 in. (7.5–30 cm.) across; orange, yellow, white, or mahogany.
Season: Summer until frost in cold climates; midspring until early summer zone 8 and warmer.

When to plant: Sow seeds indoors at 70–75°F (21–24°C) 4–6 weeks before frost-free weather, preferably in individual small pots so as not to disturb the roots when planting in the garden; or sow seeds where they are to grow and bloom in the garden as soon as soil is warm. Set transplants when available.
Light: Sun half day or more.
Soil: Well drained, moist.
Fertilizer: 5-10-5.
Uses: Beds, borders, backgrounds, dwarfs in pots, bouquets, edible seeds.

HELICHRYSUM
(hell-ee-CHRISS-um)

Everlasting; Strawflower

COMPOSITAE; daisy family

Height/habit: Tidy clumps
1.5–3 ft. (45–90 cm.).
Leaves: Oblong or lanceolate
to 5 in. (12.5 cm.) long.
Flowers: Composed of dry,
glossy, petal-like bracts, 2–3 in.
(5–7.5 cm.) across; most colors
except blue. Harvest for drying
just before they open fully.
Season: Late spring until early
summer zone 8 and warmer,
summer in cold climates.

When to plant: Sow seeds
indoors at 70°F (21°C)
8–10 weeks before frost-free
weather; sow outdoors where
they are to grow and bloom as
soon as soil is warm. Sow
seeds on surface; they need
light to sprout. Set transplants
when available.
Light: Sun half day or more.
Soil: Well drained, moist.
Fertilizer: 5-10-5.
Uses: Beds, borders, pots,
bouquets; best for drying.

HELIOTROPIUM
(hee-lee-oh-TROPE-ee-um)

Heliotrope; Cherry Pie

BORAGINACEAE; borage family

Height/habit: Bushy to
shrublike, 1–4 ft. (30–122 cm.)
high/wide.
Leaves: Elliptic or oblong to
lanceolate, to 3 in. (7.5 cm.)
long.
Flowers: Coiled cymes,
displaying clusters to 8 in.
(20 cm.) across; deep blue-
violet to purple, lavender,
near-white; legendary
fragrance.
Season: Midsummer to fall
frost in cold climates, late
winter until spring zone 9
and warmer.
When to plant: Sow seeds
indoors at 70°F (21°C) 8–12
weeks before frost-free
weather. Set transplants
when available.
Light: Sun half day or more.
Soil: Well drained, moist.
Fertilizer: 5-10-5.
Uses: Beds, borders, pots,
bouquets.

HELIPTERUM
(hee-LIP-ter-um)

Everlasting; Strawflower; Rhodanthe

COMPOSITAE; daisy family

Height/habit: Erect, 1.5–2 ft.
(45–61 cm.) high/wide.
Leaves: Linear to lanceolate,
to 3 in. (7.5 cm.) long, bluish
green.
Flowers: Papery dry, petal-like
bracts; round blooms, 2–3 in.
(5–7.5 cm.) across; pink, rose,
or white.

Season: Summer; all zones.
When to plant: Sow seeds
indoors at 65–75°F (18–24°C)
8–10 weeks before frost-free
weather; sow outdoors where
they are to grow and bloom
as soon as soil is warm.
Set transplants when available.
Light: Sun half day or more.
Soil: Well drained, moist to
on the dry side.
Fertilizer: 5-10-5.
Uses: Beds, borders, pots,
bouquets, drying (harvest buds
for drying just as they are
about to open).

HUNNEMANNIA
(hun-nee-MAN-nee-ah)
Mexican Tulip Poppy; Golden Cup
PAPAVERACEAE; poppy family

Height/habit: Tidy mounds, 1.5–2 ft. (45–61 cm.) high/wide.
Leaves: Blue-green, finely dissected.
Flowers: Single poppies 2–3 in. (5–7.5 cm.) across; glowing yellow.
Season: Summer.
When to plant: Sow seeds indoors at 70–75°F (21–24°C) 8–12 weeks before frost-free weather; sow outdoors where they are to grow and bloom as soon as soil is warm. Sow seeds on surface; they need light to sprout. Set transplants when available.
Light: Sun half day or more.
Soil: Well drained, moist to on the dry side.
Fertilizer: 5-10-5.
Uses: Beds, borders, pots. Irresistible in the company of blue flowers, such as delphinium, larkspur, forget-me-not, and sage.

IBERIS
(eye-BEER-iss)

Annual Candytuft

CRUCIFERAE; mustard family

Height/habit: Mounded, bushy, 10–18 in. (25–45 cm.) high/wide.

Leaves: Lanceolate, 3–4 in. (7.5–10 cm.) long.

Flowers: Dense umbels 2–3 in. (5–7.5 cm.) across; white, pink, rose, or lavender; sometimes fragrant. Deadheading increases bloom.

Season: Summer in cold climates, late spring until early summer zone 8 and warmer. Best performance with warm days (70°F [21°C]), cool nights (50–60°F [10–15°C]).

When to plant: Sow seeds indoors at 70°F (21°C) for germination (then grow cool, at 50–65°F [10–18°C]), 8–10 weeks before frost-free weather; sow outdoors where they are to grow and bloom as soon as soil is warm. Set transplants when available.

Light: Sun half day or more.

Soil: Well drained, moist.

Fertilizer: 5-10-5.

Uses: Beds, borders, pots, nosegays, bouquets.

IMPATIENS
(im-PAY-shenz)

Busy Lizzie; Patience; Sultana

BALSAMINACEAE; balsam family

Height/habit: Bushy mounds, 8–18 in. (20–45 cm.) high/wide.

Leaves: Lanceolate-ovate to elliptic-oblong, 1–4 in. (2.5–10 cm.) long; green or reddish; New Guinea hybrids often variegated white, cream, pink, or red.

Flowers: Rounded, flattened, 1–3 in. (2.5–7.5 cm.) across, often with prominent, nectar-filled spur; nearly every color except true blue. Annual *I. balsamina* (balsam) flowers appear doubled.

Season: Summer until frost in cold climates; nearly all year zone 9 and warmer.

When to plant: Sow seeds indoors at 70°F (21°C) 8–12 weeks before frost-free weather. Do not cover; seeds need light to sprout. Seeds of annual *I. balsamina* require no special treatment and can be sown where they are to grow and bloom as soon as soil is warm. New Guinea impatiens are often propagated from cuttings. Set transplants when available.

Light: Common impatiens is the top-ranked flower for color in the shade. Annual and New Guinea impatiens require more sun. On average, the cooler the climate, the more direct sun is needed by impatiens. Failure to bloom indicates a need for more sun and blossom-booster fertilizer.

Soil: Well drained, moist.

Fertilizer: 5-10-5.

Uses: Beds, borders, edging, pots.

Morning Glory; Moonflower; Cardinal Climber

CONVOLVULACEAE; morning-glory family

Height/habit: Twining climber, 10–30 ft. (3–9 m.). Dwarf bush morning glory forms a mound to 3–4 ft. (1–1.2 m.) high/wide.

Leaves: Variously heart-shaped or shallowly 3-lobed, to 6 in. (15 cm.) across; plain green, sometimes variegated silvery white; finely cut in cardinal climber.

Flowers: 5-lobed funnels, to 4–5 in. (10–12.5 cm.) across; blue, white, red, pink, or rose; often bicolored by edging, stripes, or flecks; sometimes fragrant. Moonflower (*I. alba*) blooms at night; the others are best from dawn until midday heat.

Season: Summer or until fall frost; all zones.

When to plant: Sow seeds where they are to grow, first soaking 24–48 hours in room-temperature water, as soon as soil is warm.

Light: Sun half day or more.

Soil: Well drained, moist to on the dry side.

Fertilizer: 5-10-5.

Uses: Decorative cover for fence, arbor, trellis, tepee.

LATHYRUS
(LATH-er-us)

Sweet Pea

LEGUMINOSAE; pea family

Height/habit: Tendril-climbing vine to 6 ft. (1.8 m.); dwarf bush types 1–2 ft. (30–61 cm.).

Leaves: Blue-green paired leaflets, to 2 in. (5 cm.).

Flowers: To 2 in. (5 cm.) across, 1–4 per peduncle; white, pink, blue, rose, red, maroon, yellow, some bicolored; fragrant. Cutting for bouquets increases bloom.

Season: Late spring until summer in coolest climates; late spring until early summer elsewhere, with the exception of winter to midspring zone 8 and warmer.

When to plant: Soak seeds 24 hours in room-temperature water before planting. Sow outdoors where they are to grow and bloom as soon as soil is warm. Zone 8 and warmer, plant in fall. Set transplants, often available in 4-in.-(10-cm.-) diameter plastic pots, when available; take care not to disturb the roots.

Light: Sun half day or more.

Soil: Well drained, moist.

Fertilizer: 5-10-5.

Uses: Dwarf bush types for beds, borders, pots. Climbers for fence, trellis, arbor, tepees, perhaps paired with such deciduous shrubs as hamelia and beautyberry in zone 8 and warmer.

LAVATERA
(lav-uh-TEER-ah)

Tree Mallow

MALVACEAE; mallow family

Height/habit: Upright, shrublike, 1.5–2 ft. (45–61 cm.) high/wide.
Leaves: Rounded hearts, 2–3 in. (5–7.5 cm.) across; medium green.
Flowers: 5-petaled, glistening, to 3 in. (7.5 cm.) across; rose, pink, or white, often with contrasting veins.
Season: Summer or until frost; all zones.
When to plant: Sow seeds indoors at 70°F (21°C) 8–10 weeks before frost-free weather; sow outdoors where they are to grow and bloom when soil is warm.
Light: Sun half day or more.
Soil: Well drained, moist.
Fertilizer: 5-10-5.
Uses: Beds, borders, pots, quick hedging.

LIMONIUM
(lih-MOH-nee-um)

Statice

PLUMBAGINACEAE; leadwort or plumbago family

Height/habit: Upright clumps, 1–3 ft. (30–90 cm.).
Leaves: Mostly basal, 4–6 in. (10–15 cm.) long, resembling those of dandelion; coarse to the touch.
Flowers: Winged spikelets, dry, papery; blue, lavender, white, yellow, orange, apricot, peach, or rose red, often bicolored. Cut for drying just before they open fully.
Season: Summer; all zones.
When to plant: Sow seeds indoors at 70°F (21°C) 6–10 weeks before frost-free weather; sow outdoors where they are to grow and bloom as soon as soil is warm. Set transplants when available.
Light: Sun half day or more.
Soil: Well drained, moist to on the dry side.
Fertilizer: 5-10-5.
Uses: Beds, borders, pots, bouquets, principally for drying.

LINUM
(LEYE-num)

Annual Flax

LINACEAE; flax family

Height/habit: *L. grandiflorum*
erect, compact, to 2 ft.
(61 cm.).
Leaves: Linear to lanceolate,
1–2 in. (2.5–5 cm.)
long; bluish green.
Flowers: Loose panicles, 1–2 in.
(2.5–5 cm.) across; shades of
red, violet-blue, white with
carmine eye, or rose pink.
Season: Summer in the North;
spring until early summer
zone 8 and warmer.
When to plant: Sow seeds
indoors at 70°F (21°C)
8–10 weeks before frost-free
weather; sow outdoors where
they are to grow and bloom
as soon as soil is warm.
Set transplants when available.
Light: Sun half day or more.
Soil: Well drained, moist to
on the dry side.
Fertilizer: 5-10-5.
Uses: Beds, borders, rock
gardens.

LISIANTHUS
(liss-ee-ANTH-us)

Eustoma;
Texas Bluebell

GENTIANACEAE; gentian family

Height/habit: Erect, small clumps, 1–2.5 ft. (30–75 cm.).
Leaves: Waxy, blue-green, ovate or oblong, to 3 in. (7.5 cm.) long, occurring mostly toward the base.
Flowers: Single or double, resembling Canterbury bells, tulips, rosebuds; 2–3 in. (5–7.5 cm.) across; blue, white, pink, lavender, or rose, often bicolored.

Season: Summer; all zones.
When to plant: Sow seeds indoors at 68–77°F (20–25°C) 10–12 weeks before frost-free weather. Do not cover; seeds need light to sprout. Set transplants when available. (This plant is not easy to grow from seed.)
Light: Sun half day or more.
Soil: Well drained, moist to on the dry side.
Fertilizer: 5-10-5.
Uses: Beds, borders, pots, cutting.

LOBELIA
(loh-BEE-lee-ah)
Edging Lobelia
LOBELIACEAE; lobelia family

Height/habit: *L. erinus*
mounded to trailing, 4–12 in.
(10–30 cm.).

Leaves: Ovate to elliptic,
mostly at the base, narrower at
top; to 1 in. (2.5 cm.) long.

Flowers: 2 upper and 3 lower
lobes, to 1 in. (2.5 cm.) across;
exceptional blues, also lilac,
rose, crimson, or white.

Season: Summer to frost in
cold climates; spring until early
summer zone 8 and warmer.

When to plant: Sow seeds
indoors at 70–75°F (21–24°C)
8–12 weeks before frost-free
weather; sow in fall zone 8 and
warmer. Sow on surface, and
do not cover; seeds need light
to sprout. Grow at cool temperatures: 45–50°F (7–10°C).
Set transplants when available.

Light: Sun half day or more.

Soil: Well drained, moist.

Fertilizer: 5-10-5.

Uses: Beds, borders, edging,
rock gardens, pots, hanging
baskets.

LOBULARIA
(lob-yew-LAY-ree-ah)

Sweet Alyssum

CRUCIFERAE; mustard family

Height/habit: Mounded to trailing, 4–12 in. (10–30 cm.).
Leaves: Linear to lanceolate, gray-green, to 1 in. (2.5 cm.) long.
Flowers: Small, .25–.5 in. (.63–1.25 cm.) on slender pedicels, becoming so numerous as to hide the leaves; white, rose, violet, or purple. Deadheading by periodic light shearing increases bloom.

Season: Summer until frost in the North; late winter to early summer zone 8 and warmer.
When to plant: Sow seeds indoors at 70°F (21°C) 6–8 weeks before frost-free weather; sow outdoors where they are to grow and bloom when soil is warm. Sow fall until winter zone 8 and warmer. Set transplants when available.
Light: Sun half day or more.
Soil: Well drained, moist to on the dry side.
Fertilizer: 5-10-5.
Uses: Beds, borders, edging, pots, hanging baskets.

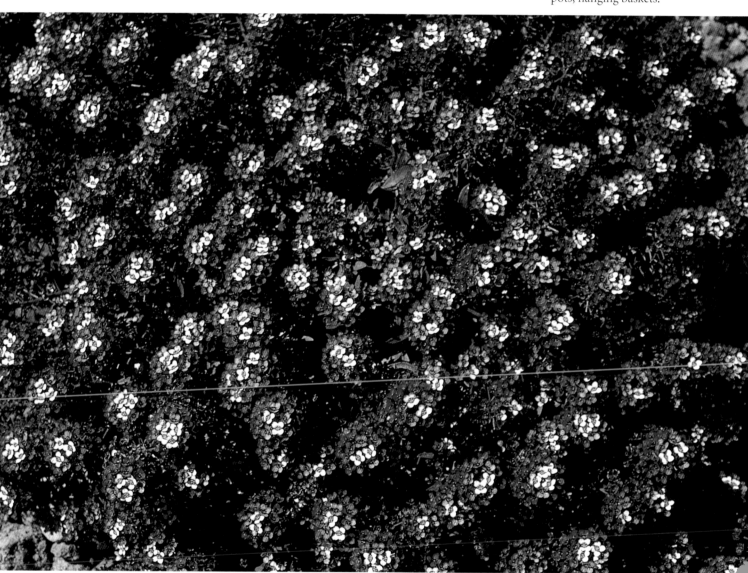

MELAMPODIUM
(mel-am-PODE-ee-um)

'Medallion' Daisy

COMPOSITAE; daisy family

Height/habit: Self-branching mounds, 2–4 ft. (61–122 cm.) high/wide.
Leaves: Heart-shaped, to 2 in. (5 cm.) long.
Flowers: Single, to 1.5 in. (3.7 cm.) across; vivid yellow, bronze-eyed. Self-cleaning (deadheading not required).
Season: Late spring to summer until frost (an outstanding, self-reliant performer over a long season); all zones.
When to plant: Sow seeds indoors at 70°F (21°C) 8–10 weeks before warm weather; darkness needed until seedlings appear, then grow on in high light. Set transplants when available.
Light: Sun half day or more.
Soil: Well drained, moist; when established, tolerates some drought.
Fertilizer: 5-10-5.
Uses: Beds, borders, large pots.

MATTHIOLA
(mat-ee-OH-lah)

Stock

CRUCIFERAE; mustard family

Height/habit: Upright in tidy clumps; dwarfs 8–12 in. (20–30 cm.), standards 2–2.5 ft. (61–75 cm.).
Leaves: Oblong to oblanceo-late, gray-green, to 4 in. (10 cm.) long.
Flowers: Single or double, to 1 in. (2.5 cm.) across, in terminal racemes; pink, purple, red, or white; fragrant. Deadheading increases bloom.
Season: Summer until frost in the North; winter until spring zone 8 and warmer.
When to plant: Sow seeds indoors at 70°F (21°C) 6–8 weeks before frost-free weather; sow outdoors where they are to grow and bloom when soil is warm. Sow late spring until summer or fall zone 8 and warmer. Set trans-plants when available.
Light: Sun half day or more.
Soil: Well drained, moist.
Fertilizer: 5-10-5.
Uses: Beds, borders, pots, bouquets.

MENTZELIA
(ment-ZEE-lee-ah)

Blazing Star; Bartonia

LOASACEAE; loasa family

Height/habit: Upright, vase-shaped, to 2 ft. (61 cm.) high/wide.

Leaves: Waxy, cut or toothed, 2–3 in. (5–7.5 cm.) long.

Flowers: Showy, to 5 in. (12.5 cm.) across; can resemble those of daisy, cactus, or passiflora; creamy white to greenish yellow; some open at night; fragrant.

Season: Summer; all zones.

When to plant: Refrigerate seeds 1 week before sowing. Sow seeds indoors at 70°F (21°C), then grow cool, at 50–65°F (10–18°C), or where they are to grow and bloom when soil is warm. Set transplants when available. Reseeds.

Light: Sun all day.

Soil: Well drained, moist to on the dry side; tolerates drought.

Fertilizer: 5-10-5.

Uses: Beds, borders, wild gardens.

MIMULUS
(MIM-yew-lus)
Monkey Flower
SCROPHULARIACEAE; figwort family

Height/habit: Self-branching clumps, 8–10 in. (20–25 cm.).
Leaves: Heart-shaped to oblong-lanceolate, 3–6 in. (7.5–15 cm.) long.
Flowers: Pouched, 1–2 in. (2.5–5 cm.) across; cream, red, rose, yellow, or wine, often marked with a contrasting color.
Season: Late spring until hot weather; late winter until early spring zone 8 and warmer.

When to plant: Sow seeds indoors at 65–70°F (18–21°C) 8–12 weeks before planting-out weather; grow at cool temperatures, 50–65°F (10–18°C). Zone 8 and warmer, sow fall until winter. Set transplants when available.
Light: Sun early or late in the day, mostly shade; needs more sun in cool temperatures, about 40–60°F (4–15°C).
Soil: Well drained, moist.
Fertilizer: 5-10-5.
Uses: Beds, borders, pots.

MIRABILIS
(mihr-AB-il-iss)
Four-o'clock
NYCTAGINACEAE; four-o'clock family

Height/habit: Upright, branching, to 4 ft. (1.2 m.) high/wide.
Leaves: Heart-shaped to ovate-lanceolate, to 3 in. (7.5 cm.) long.
Flowers: 5-lobed, whorled, growing from a tube, 1–2 in. (2.5–5 cm.) across; white, yellow, red, rose, pink, or salmon, often splashed with a second color. Fragrant blossoms open late afternoon. Self-cleaning (deadheading not required).

Season: Summer or until frost; all zones.
When to plant: Prechill seeds in refrigerator 1 week before planting. Sow indoors at 70–75°F (21–24°C) 6–8 weeks before frost-free weather; sow outdoors where they are to grow and bloom when the soil is warm. Set transplants when available.
Light: Sun half day or more.
Soil: Well drained, moist to on the dry side. Tolerates drought when established.
Fertilizer: 5-10-5.
Uses: Beds, borders, large pots. An outstanding performer in difficult situations.

MONARDA
(mon-ARD-ah)
Lemon Mint
LABIATAE; mint family

Height/habit: Tidy upright clumps of *M. citriodora* grow to 2 ft. (61 cm.).

Leaves: Lemon-scented, narrow lanceolate to oblong, 2 in. (5 cm.) long.

Flowers: Whorled, to 2 in. (5 cm.) across; white to pink and purplish.

Season: Late spring until early summer zone 8 and warmer; summer in cooler regions.

When to plant: Prechill seeds 1 week in refrigerator before planting. Sow indoors at 70°F (21°C) 8–10 weeks before planting-out weather; sow outdoors where they are to grow and bloom when soil is warm. Set transplants when available. Behaves variously as annual or biennial. Reseeds.

Light: Sun half day or more.

Soil: Well drained, moist to on the dry side; tolerates drought.

Fertilizer: 5-10-5.

Uses: Beds, borders, wild gardens, fresh or dried bouquets.

MYOSOTIS
(my-oh-SOH-tiss)

Forget-me-not

BORAGINACEAE; borage family

Height/habit: Thin flowering stems rise above mostly basal foliage, 8–24 in. (20–61 cm.).
Leaves: Oblong to linear or oblong to lanceolate, 2–3 in. (5–7.5 cm.) long/wide.
Flowers: Small, .25 in. (.63 cm.) across, but profuse; blue with white eye, also pink to white. Deadheading increases bloom.
Season: Winter until spring zone 8 and warmer; spring until early summer in colder climates.

When to plant: Sow seeds indoors at 65–70°F (18–21°C) and maintain in continual darkness until they sprout, 6–8 weeks before planting-out weather. In zone 8 and warmer sow seeds in fall. Set transplants when available.
Light: Sun half day or more in cool temperatures (below 60°F [15°C]); provide shade in heat.
Soil: Well drained, moist.
Fertilizer: 5-10-5.
Uses: Beds, borders, pots, bouquets. Recommended for interplanting with spring bulbs (tulip, daffodil).

NEMESIA
(nuh-MEE-zee-ah)

Cape Jewels

SCROPHULARIACEAE; figwort
family

Height/habit: Self-branching
bushlets to 1–2 ft. (30–61 cm.)
tall/wide.
Leaves: Lanceolate to linear,
to 4 in. (10 cm.) long.
Flowers: 4-in. (10-cm.)
panicles, 1 in. (2.5 cm.) across,
pouched; white, yellow,
orange, rose pink, scarlet, or
crimson, often marked on the
outside with darker color.
Season: Early summer until
hot weather; late winter until
spring zone 8 and warmer.
When to plant: Sow seeds
indoors at 65°F (18°C);
maintain continual darkness
until sprouts appear; grow
at cool temperatures, 50–65°F
(10–18°C), 8–10 weeks before
planting out. Start fall until
early winter zone 8 and
warmer. Set transplants when
available.
Light: Sun half day or more
in cool weather; more shade in
higher temperatures prolongs
season.
Soil: Well drained, moist.
Fertilizer: 5-10-5.
Uses: Beds, borders, pots; ideal
for cool greenhouse or frost-
free sun-heated pit in fall
through winter.

NICOTIANA
(nick-oh-she-YAY-nah)

Flowering Tobacco

SOLANACEAE; nightshade family

Height/habit: Dwarfs in tidy clumps, 1–2 ft. (30–61 cm.). *N. alata, N. rustica, N. sylvestris* are taller, to 3–5 ft. (1–1.5 m.), more graceful.

Leaves: Oval to heart-shaped to elliptic, more growing toward the base, 5–12 in. (12.5–30 cm.) long/wide.

Flowers: 5-lobed, tubular bell-like, to 2 in. (5 cm.) wide x 4 in. (10 cm.) long; white, chartreuse, pink, old rose, wine, or red. Species notably fragrant. Occasional deadheading improves appearance, increases bloom.

Season: Summer or until frost; all zones.

When to plant: Sow seeds indoors at 70°F (21°C) 8–10 weeks before warm weather. Do not cover; seeds need light to sprout. In zone 8 and warmer they can be started in fall; protect in the event of frost. Set transplants when available. Often reseeds.

Light: Sun half day or more in cool season; more shade as temperatures rise.

Soil: Well drained, moist.

Fertilizer: 5-10-5.

Uses: Beds, borders, pots.

NIEREMBERGIA
(neer-em-BERJ-ee-ah)

Cup Flower

SOLANACEAE; nightshade family

Height/habit: Tidy mounds,
to 12 in. (30 cm.) high/wide.
Leaves: Linear, to 1 in. (2.5
cm.) long.
Flowers: Shallow cups, 1–2 in.
(2.5–5 cm.) across; blue or
white.
Season: Summer or until frost
in the North; spring until early
summer in hottest climates,
zones 8–9.

When to plant: Sow seeds
indoors at 70–75°F (21–24°C)
8–12 weeks before planting-out
weather. Set transplants when
available.
Light: Sun half day or more;
more shade beneficial in hot
weather.
Soil: Well drained, moist.
Fertilizer: 5-10-5.
Uses: Beds, borders, pots,
hanging baskets.

NIGELLA
(nigh-JELL-ah)

Love-in-a-mist

RANUNCULACEAE; buttercup family

Height/habit: Bushy, self-branching, upright to sprawling, 1.5–2 ft. (45–61 cm.) high/wide.

Leaves: Finely segmented, similar to dill and fennel, to 3 in. (7.5 cm.) long.

Flowers: Finely laced, spidery, to 2 in. (5 cm.) across; white or pale to dark blue. Deadheading increases bloom but prevents seed capsules prized for drying.

Season: Summer in cold climates; spring until early summer zone 8 and warmer.

When to plant: Prechill seeds in refrigerator 1 week before planting. Sow outdoors where they are to grow and bloom as soon as soil can be worked. Set transplants when available; take care not to disturb roots.

Light: Sun half day or more.

Soil: Well drained, moist to on the dry side.

Fertilizer: 5-10-5.

Uses: Beds, borders, pots, bouquets, drying.

NOLANA
(no-LAY-nah)

Chilean Bellflower

NOLANACEAE; nolana family

Height/habit: Low, spreading mounds, 6–12 in. (15–30 cm.) high/wide.

Leaves: Ovate, obtuse, to 2 in. (5 cm.) long.

Flowers: 5-lobed, to 2 in. (5 cm.) wide; blue with white throat.

Season: Late spring until summer; all zones.

When to plant: Sow seeds indoors at 72°F (22°C) 6–8 weeks before frost-free weather; provide continuous light until seedlings emerge; sow outdoors where they are to grow and bloom when soil is warm. Set transplants when available.

Light: Sun half day or more.

Soil: Well drained, moist to on the dry side.

Fertilizer: 5-10-5.

Uses: Beds, borders, rock gardens, pots, hanging baskets.

OCIMUM
(OH-sim-um)
Basil
LABIATAE; mint family

Height/habit: Bushy, self-branching, 1–6 ft. (30–180 cm.) high/wide.

Leaves: Ovate to ovate-elliptic, .5–5 in. (1.25–12.5 cm.) long; green or red-purple (either color might be streaked or splashed with the other); edible; scents and tastes include sweet basil, lemon, anise, cinnamon, and clove. Thai basil hints of chocolate in both taste and color and makes a beautiful garden plant.

Flowers: Small, borne in spikes above the leaves; white to lavender pink or purplish (usually pinched to keep from forming).

Season: Summer or until frost; all zones. African blue basil often persists through mild winters, zones 9–10.

When to plant: Sow seeds indoors at 70–75˚F (21–24˚C) 6–8 weeks before warm, frost-free weather; sow outdoors where they are to grow and bloom when soil is warm. Set transplants when available.

Light: Sun half day or more.

Soil: Well drained, moist.

Fertilizer: 10-10-10.

Uses: Beds, borders, edging/hedging, pots; leaves for cookery.

PAPAVER
(pap-PAY-ver)
Iceland, Opium, and Shirley Poppies
PAPAVERACEAE; poppy family

Height/habit: Tendency toward basal foliage, above which the flowers rise on slender stems, 1–4 ft. (30–122 cm.).

Leaves: Cut or coarsely toothed, to 6 in. (15 cm.) long, blue-green in *P. somniferum* (opium poppy).

Flowers: Single to double with shimmery petals, 2–6 in. (5–15 cm.) across; all colors except blue (the fabled blue poppy is *Meconopsis*, a perennial). Iceland poppy (*P. nudicaule*) especially beautiful in yellow, coral, and pink. Shirley poppy (*P. rhoeas*) comes in shades of scarlet, pink, salmon, and white. Opium poppy can be white, delicate pink, red, or purple. Deadheading increases bloom but prevents formation of seed heads for drying.

Season: Late spring until summer in colder climates; spring until early summer zone 8 and warmer.

When to plant: Prechill seeds in refrigerator 1 week before planting. Sow where they are to grow and bloom as soon as soil can be worked in spring; zone 8 and warmer sow in fall. Set transplants when available.
Light: Sun half day or more.
Soil: Well drained, moist.
Fertilizer: 5-10-5.
Uses: Beds, borders, cutting, seedpods for drying (if decorative).

PELARGONIUM
(pel-ar-GO-nee-um)
Bedding Geranium
GERANIACEAE; geranium family

Height/habit: Upright-spreading bushlets, 1–2 ft. (30–61 cm.) high/wide.
Leaves: Rounded, crenate, often encircled by a darker color; primarily green in seed-grown varieties, variously variegated white, cream yellow, orange, mahogany in fancy-leaved cultivars propagated from cuttings.
Flowers: Single or double, in umbels of few or many; most colors except blue and yellow, strong in red, pink, salmon, orange, lavender, and white.

Season: Summer or until frost; all zones. They might go out of bloom in extremely hot, humid weather.
When to plant: Sow seeds indoors at 70°F (21°C) 8–12 weeks before warm weather. Hybrid geraniums come true from seed and start blooming in 3–4 months. Set transplants when available.
Light: Sun half day or more. Midday shade beneficial in torrid regions.
Soil: Well drained, moist to on the dry side.
Fertilizer: 5-10-5.
Uses: Beds, borders, pots, cut for nosegays.

PENSTEMON
(PEN-stem-on)

Beardtongue

SCROPHULARIACEAE; figwort
family

Height/habit: Stems upright,
in small clumps, 2–3 ft.
(61–90 cm.).

Leaves: Mostly basal, 2–3 in.
(5–7.5 cm.) long.

Flowers: Loose spikes resembling snapdragon, pouched,
to 2 in. (5 cm.) across; most
colors except blue and yellow,
often with contrasting throat
and veins. Deadheading
increases bloom and likelihood
of perennial behavior.

Season: Summer until frost in
cold climates; spring until early
summer zone 8 and warmer,
where the plants might behave
as perennials.

When to plant: Prechill seeds
1 week in refrigerator before
planting. Sow seeds indoors at
70°F (21°C) 12–16 weeks before
planting-out weather and grow
at cool temperatures, 50–65°F
(10–18°C). Set transplants
when available.

Light: Sun half day or more.

Soil: Well drained, moist to
on the dry side.

Fertilizer: 5-10-5.

Uses: Beds, borders, pots,
cutting.

PERILLA
(puh-RILL-ah)
Shiso
LABIATAE; mint family

Height/habit: Bushy, self-branching, 3–6 ft. (1–1.8 m.) high/wide.

Leaves: Resemble closely related sweet basil (the herb) but might also be ruffled, to 3 in. (7.5 cm.) long; purple or green.

Flowers: Typical of mint family but not showy. This plant is cultivated primarily for foliage effect.

Season: Summer or until frost; all zones; frequently self-sows in warmer parts of country.

When to plant: Prechill seeds in refrigerator 1 week before planting. Sow indoors at 65–70°F (18–21°C) 6–8 weeks before warm weather; sow outdoors where they are to grow and bloom when soil is warm. Do not cover; seeds need light to sprout.

Light: Sun half day or more.

Soil: Well drained, moist.

Fertilizer: 5-10-5.

Uses: Beds, borders, pots, in Asian cuisine.

PETROSELINUM
(pet-roh-SELL-ih-num)

Parsley

UMBELLIFERAE; carrot family

Height/habit: Tidy clumps or rosettes, to 1 ft. (30 cm.) high/wide first season; bolting to 6 ft. (1.8 m.) spring of second season.

Leaves: Divided, flat, celerylike in Italian, much cut and curled in 'Crispum' varieties, to 1 ft. (30 cm.) long/wide.

Flowers: Flattened umbels, to 6 in. (15 cm.) across, at beginning of second season; greenish yellow.

Season: Low, leafy growth through first summer, living over winter zones 6–7 and warmer; flowers second season, then dies. Reseeds.

When to plant: Soak seeds overnight in room-temperature water, then sow at 70°F (21°C) 6–8 weeks before planting-out weather; sow outdoors where they are to grow and bloom when soil is warm. Set transplants when available.

Light: Sun half day or more; tolerates some shade.

Soil: Well drained, moist.

Fertilizer: 10-10-10 or 5-10-5.

Uses: Beds, borders, edging, pots, leaves for culinary purposes.

PETUNIA
(puh-TOO-nee-ah)

Garden Petunia

SOLANACEAE; nightshade family

Height/habit: Self-branching mounds, bushy to cascading, 1–2 ft. (30–61 cm.).

Leaves: Ovate or ovate-lanceolate, 4–5 in. (10–12.5 cm.) long.

Flowers: Trumpet-shaped, single or double, 2–5 in. (5–12.5 cm.) across; all colors, often edged, striped, or starred with a contrasting color. Some are fragrant.

Season: Summer until fall frost in cold climates; spring until summer zone 8 and warmer.

When to plant: Sow seeds indoors at 70°F (21°C) 8–12 weeks before planting-out weather; sow in fall where winters are mild. Do not cover; seeds need light to sprout. Set transplants when available.

Light: Sun half day or more.

Soil: Well drained, moist.

Fertilizer: 5-10-5.

Uses: Beds, borders, pots, hanging baskets.

Annual Phlox

POLEMONIACEAE; phlox family

Height/habit: *P. drummondii* bushy to trailing, self-branching, 8–24 in. (20–61 cm.).
Leaves: Ovate to lanceolate, to 3 in. (7.5 cm.) long.
Flowers: Cluster to 1 in. (2.5 cm.) across; most colors, often with contrasting eye. Deadheading increases bloom.
Season: Summer in cold climates; spring until early summer zone 8 and warmer.
When to plant: Prechill seeds in refrigerator 1 week before planting. Sow indoors at 65°F (18°C) 8–10 weeks before planting-out weather; sow outdoors where they are to grow and bloom when soil is warm. Set transplants when available. Reseeds.
Light: Sun half day or more.
Soil: Well drained, sandy, moist to on the dry side.
Fertilizer: 5-10-5.
Uses: Beds, borders, ground cover, rock gardens, pots.

PORTULACA
(port-yew-LACK-ah)
Rose Moss;
Purslane

PORTULACACEAE; purslane
family

Height/habit: Mat-forming,
prostrate stems, to 12 in.
(30 cm.).
Leaves: Cylindrical to obovate,
to 1 in. (2.5 cm.) long.
Flowers: Single or double,
shimmery, cupped, 1–2 in.
(2.5–5 cm.) across; most colors
except blue.
Season: Summer or until frost;
all zones.
When to plant: Prechill seeds
in refrigerator 1 week before
planting. Sow indoors at 70°F
(21°C) 6–8 weeks before
planting-out weather; sow
outdoors where they are to
grow and bloom when soil is
warm. Seeds sprout best in
continual darkness. Set transplants when available. Reseeds.
Light: Sun half day or more.
Soil: Well drained, sandy,
moist to quite dry; tolerates
drought.
Fertilizer: 5-10-5.
Uses: Beds, borders, ground
cover, rock gardens, pots.

RATABIDA
(rah-tah-BID-ah)

Mexican Hat; Prairie Coneflower

COMPOSITAE; daisy family

Height/habit: Bushy, self-branching, 1–2 ft. (30–61 cm.) high/wide.

Leaves: Pinnate, 3–4 in. (7.5–10 cm.) long, growing mostly around the plant base.

Flowers: Distinctive disks surrounded by drooping petals, to 2 in. (5 cm.) across; yellow or brownish red.

Season: Summer; spring zone 8 and warmer.

When to plant: Prechill seeds 1 week in refrigerator before planting. Sow seeds indoors at 70°F (21°C) 8–12 weeks before planting-out weather; sow outdoors where they are to grow and bloom when soil is warm. Set transplants when available. Reseeds. Performs variously as annual/biennial/perennial.

Light: Sun half day or more.

Soil: Well drained, moist to on the dry side; tolerates drought.

Fertilizer: 5-10-5.

Uses: Beds, borders, pots, bouquets.

RESEDA
(REZ-uh-dah)
Mignonette
RESEDACEAE; mignonette family

Height/habit: Sprawling,
1–1.5 ft. (30–45 cm.).
Leaves: Elliptic to spatulate,
2–3 in. (5–7.5 cm.) long.
Flowers: Dense racemes,
to 2 in. (5 cm.) across; greenish
white with yellow or orange
highlights. Grown for
fragrance.
Season: Late spring until
summer or until hot weather;
all zones.
When to plant: Prechill seeds
1 week in refrigerator before
planting. Sow indoors at
70°F (21°C) 6–8 weeks before
planting-out weather; sow
outdoors where they are to
grow and bloom when soil is
warm. Set transplants when
available but do not disturb
roots.
Light: Sun half day or more in
cool temperatures, more shade
with increasing heat.
Soil: Well drained, moist.
Fertilizer: 5-10-5.
Uses: Beds, borders, pots,
bouquets.

(rih-SEE-nuss)

Castor Bean

EUPHORBIACEAE; spurge family

Height/habit: Strongly upright, 5–15 ft. (1.5–4.5 m.).
Leaves: Lobed, to 3 ft. (1 m.) across; green, bronze, or red. Caution: Contact can cause severe skin allergy.
Flowers: Many stamens, no petals, to 1 in. (2.5 cm.) across; orange-scarlet.
Season: Summer until frost; perennial zone 10 and warmer, becoming small tree to 40 ft. (12.1 m.).
When to plant: Sow seeds where they are to grow and bloom when soil is warm and there is no danger of frost. Caution: Seeds poisonous.
Light: Sun half day or more.
Soil: Well drained, moist.
Fertilizer: 5-10-5.
Uses: Border background, garden accent.

RUDBECKIA
(rood-BECK-ee-ah)

Black-eyed Susan; Gloriosa Daisy

COMPOSITAE; daisy family

Height/habit: Tidy clumps, 1–3 ft. (30–90 cm.) high/wide.

Leaves: Mostly basal, ovate to elliptic, 3–6 in. (7.5–15 cm.) long.

Flowers: Single or double, 2–6 in. (5–15 cm.) across; yellow, sometimes vividly bicolored red-brown. Deadheading increases bloom.

Season: Summer until frost; spring until summer zone 8 and warmer. Behaves variously as annual/biennial or short-lived perennial.

When to plant: Sow seeds indoors at 70–75°F (21–24°C) 8–10 weeks before planting-out weather; sow outdoors where they are to grow and bloom as soon as soil is warm. Set transplants when available.

Light: Sun half day or more.

Soil: Well drained, moist to on the dry side; tolerates drought.

Fertilizer: 5-10-5.

Uses: Beds, borders, pots, bouquets.

SALPIGLOSSIS
(sal-pee-GLOSS-iss)

Painted Tongue

SOLANACEAE; nightshade family

Height/habit: Tidy clumps
1–2 ft. (30–61 cm.) tall/wide.
Leaves: Mostly basal; elliptic,
narrow, or oblong, to 4 in.
(10 cm.).
Flowers: Resemble single
petunia, 2–3 in. (5–7.5 cm.)
across; velvety orange, red,
yellow, rose, purple, to near-
blue, netted/veined in contrasting color.

Season: Summer in cool
climates; late spring until
early summer zones 9–10.
When to plant: Sow seeds
indoors at 70–75°F (21–24°C)
12–16 weeks before planting-
out weather. Set transplants
when available.
Light: Sun half day or more.
Soil: Well drained, moist.
Fertilizer: 5-10-5.
Uses: Beds, borders, pots,
bouquets.

SALVIA
(SAL-vee-ah)

Annual Sage

LABIATAE; mint family

Height/habit: Well-branched clumps, 1–3 ft. (30–90 cm.) high/wide.

Leaves: Ovate or lanceolate, 2–4 in. (5–10 cm.) long.

Flowers: Spikes above the leaves, to 2 in. (5 cm.) wide x 6 in. (15 cm.) long; white to blue, all shades of red, purple, pink, rose, or violet. Hybrids of scarlet sage (*S. splendens*), mealycup sage (*S. farinacea*), and Texas sage (*S. coccinea*) are grown primarily as annuals, although they can be perennial in milder regions.

Season: Summer or until frost; all zones.

When to plant: Sow seeds indoors at 70°F (21°C), in continual darkness until they sprout, 8–10 weeks before planting-out weather; sow outdoors where they are to grow and bloom when soil is warm. Set transplants when available.

Light: Sun half day or more.

Soil: Well drained, moist.

Fertilizer: 5-10-5.

Uses: Beds, borders, pots, bouquets.

SANVITALIA
(san-vih-TAY-lee-ah)

Creeping Zinnia

COMPOSITAE; daisy family

Height/habit: Trailing, to 6 in.
(15 cm.), spreading 2–3 ft.
(61–90 cm.).
Leaves: Ovate to broadly
lanceolate, 2–3 in. (5–7.5 cm.)
long.
Flowers: Single or semidouble
daisies, 1 in. (2.5 cm.) across;
yellow.
Season: Summer or until frost;
all zones.
When to plant: Sow seeds
indoors at 70°F (21°C) 6–8
weeks before planting-out
weather; sow outdoors where
they are to grow and bloom
when soil is warm. Do not
cover; seeds need light to
sprout. Set transplants when
available.
Light: Sun half day or more.
Soil: Well drained, moist to
on the dry side.
Fertilizer: 5-10-5.
Uses: Ground cover, rock
gardens, hanging baskets.

SCABIOSA
(skab-ee-OH-sah)

Pincushion Flower; Mourning Bride

DIPSACACEAE; teasel family

Height/habit: Erect, 2–3 ft. (61–90 cm.) high/wide.
Leaves: Lanceolate, coarsely toothed, mostly at plant base, to 4 in. (10 cm.) long.
Flowers: Domed clusters with stamens protruding like pins from a pincushion, 2–3 in. (5–7.5 cm.) across; fragrant; reddish purple, pink, salmon, rose, violet-blue. Deadheading increases bloom.

Season: Summer until frost in cooler climates; late spring until early summer zone 8 and warmer.
When to plant: Sow seeds indoors at 70–75°F (21–24°C) 8–10 weeks before planting-out weather; sow outdoors where they are to grow and bloom when soil is warm. Set transplants when available.
Light: Sun half day or more.
Soil: Well drained, moist.
Fertilizer: 5-10-5.
Uses: Beds, borders, bouquets.

SCHIZANTHUS
(sky-ZANTH-us)

Butterfly Flower; Poor-man's Orchid

SOLANACEAE; nightshade family

Height/habit: Tidy, upright clumps, 15–30 in. (38–76 cm.) tall/wide.
Leaves: Pinnately cut and divided, to 6 in. (15 cm.), mostly toward the plant base.
Flowers: Complex, shallow cups to 2 in. (5 cm.) across; pink, lilac, violet, white, or purplish, often bicolored.
Season: Late winter until spring in milder climates; late spring until early summer in warm, temperate climes; summer in cool places.

When to plant: Sow seeds indoors at 70–75°F (21–24°C) 12–16 weeks before frost-free weather; zone 8 and warmer sow in fall. Maintain continual darkness until seeds sprout. Set transplants when available.
Light: Sun half day or more if cool; more shade in warmer weather.
Soil: Well drained, moist.
Fertilizer: 5-10-5.
Uses: Beds, borders, pots.

SENECIO
(suh-NEE-see-oh)

Cineraria; Dusty Miller

COMPOSITAE; daisy family

Height/habit: Cineraria grows 6–18 in. (15–45 cm.) high/wide; dusty miller forms tidy bush, 6–24 in. (15–61 cm.) high/wide.
Leaves: Cineraria (*Senecio* x *hybridus*) has basal foliage that is bright green, broad, oval, to 4 in. (10 cm.) long. The lacy leaves of dusty miller (*S. cineraria*) are gray-silver, to 4–8 in. (10–20 cm.) long/wide.
Flowers: Daisies 1–3 in. (2.5–7.5 cm.) across in dense trusses over plant top in cineraria, sweetly scented; smaller, yellow in dusty miller.
Season: Cineraria in late winter until spring in mild climates; late spring until early summer in the North. Dusty miller summer to frost in North; almost all year zone 8 and warmer.

When to plant: Sow cineraria seeds at beginning of cool but frost-free season; fall until early winter in mild climate; summer elsewhere (overwinter in cool greenhouse). Sow dusty miller seeds 8–12 weeks before planting-out weather. Sow on surface, and do not cover; seeds need light to sprout. Maintain 75°F (24°C) until seedlings appear, then grow in cool temperatures (40–60°F [4–15°C]). Set transplants when available.
Light: Sun half day or more. Shade for blooming cineraria prolongs flowers.
Soil: Well drained, moist.
Fertilizer: 5-10-5.
Uses: Beds, borders, dusty miller especially for edging/hedging, pots.

TAGETES
(tah-JEE-teez)

Marigold

COMPOSITAE; daisy family

Height/habit: Self-branching, bushy, upright, 1–4 ft. (30–122 cm.) high/wide.

Leaves: Fernlike, 2–4 in. (5–10 cm.) long/wide, often strong-scented. Those of Mexican mint marigold (*T. lucida*) grow in zone 9 and warmer.

Flowers: Single or double, 1–4 in. (2.5–10 cm.) across; creamy white to yellow, gold, orange, red, or mahogany. Deadheading increases bloom.

Season: Summer until frost in the North; late winter until summer zone 8 and warmer.

When to plant: Sow seeds indoors at 70°F (21°C) 6–12 weeks before frost-free weather, or sow where they are to grow and bloom when soil is warm. Set transplants when available.

Light: Sun half day or more.

Soil: Well drained, moist.

Fertilizer: 5-10-5.

Uses: Beds, borders, edging/hedging, pots, bouquets. Mexican mint marigold leaves are substitute for French tarragon.

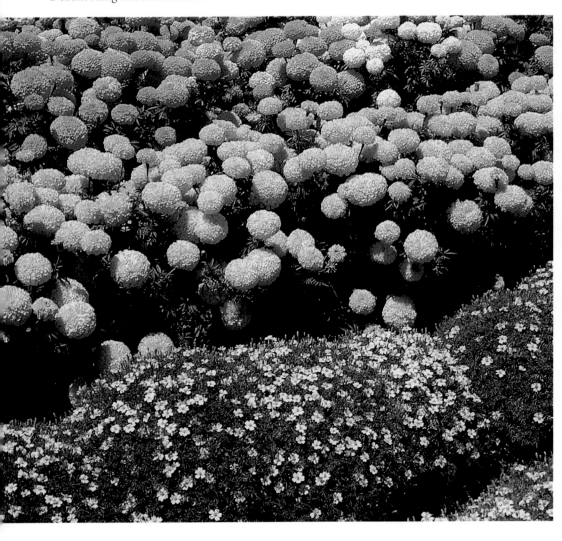

THUNBERGIA
(thun-BERJ-ee-ah)

Black-eyed-Susan Vine

ACANTHACEAE; acanthus family

Height/habit: Twining or trailing vine, 3–15 ft. (1–4.5 m.).
Leaves: Ovate to triangular, to 4 in. (10 cm.) long.
Flowers: Flaring tubes, 1–2 in. (2.5–5 cm.) across; orange, yellow, white, with or without brown-purple eye.
Season: Midsummer until frost in cold climates; winter until spring in mild, frost-free gardens (zone 10).

When to plant: Sow seeds indoors at 70–75°F (21–24°C) 6–8 weeks before planting-out weather; sow outdoors where they are to grow and bloom when soil is warm. Set transplants when available.
Light: Sun half day or more.
Soil: Well drained, moist.
Fertilizer: 5-10-5.
Uses: Cover for fence, lattice, arbor, tepee; also attractive spilling from hanging basket.

TITHONIA
(tith-OH-nee-ah)

Mexican Sunflower

COMPOSITAE; daisy family

Height/habit: Bushy, 3–6 ft. (1–1.8 m.) high/wide.
Leaves: Ovate to triangular, 6–12 in. (15–30 cm.) long/wide.
Flowers: Resemble single dahlia, 2–3 in. (5–7.5 cm.) across; orange-scarlet with yellow center.
Season: Summer or until frost; all zones.

When to plant: Sow seeds indoors at 70°F (21°C) 6–8 weeks before planting-out weather; sow outdoors where they are to grow and bloom when soil is warm. Set transplants when available.
Light: Sun half day or more.
Soil: Well drained, moist to on the dry side; tolerates drought.
Fertilizer: 5-10-5.
Uses: Back of border, hedge, large pots, bouquets.

TORENIA
(tor-EE-nee-ah)

Wishbone Flower

SCROPHULARIACEAE; figwort family

Height/habit: Much-branching bushlets, 1 ft. (30 cm.) high/wide.
Leaves: Ovate, serrate, to 2 in. (5 cm.) long.
Flowers: Pouched, to 1 in. (2.5 cm.) across; blue, pink, purple, lilac, or white, with yellow accent.
Season: Late spring or summer until frost; all zones.
When to plant: Sow seeds indoors at 70°F (21°C) 8–12 weeks before frost-free weather. Set transplants when available.
Light: Sun half day or more if cool; more shade if warm or hot.
Soil: Well drained, moist.
Fertilizer: 5-10-5.
Uses: Beds, borders, edging, pots, hanging baskets.

TRACHYMENE
(TRACKY-meen)

Blue Lace Flower; Didiscus

UMBELLIFERAE; carrot family

Height/habit: Erect to sprawling, 1–2 ft. (30–61 cm.)
Leaves: Lobed, cut, fernlike, 2–4 in. (5–10 cm.).
Flowers: Many in an umbel, to 3 in. (7.5 cm.) across; medium to pale blue. Deadheading increases bloom.

Season: Summer until frost; spring until early summer in torrid zones (9–10).
When to plant: Sow seeds indoors at 65°F (18°C) 8–10 weeks before planting-out weather; sow outdoors where they are to grow and bloom when soil is warm. Set transplants when available.
Light: Sun half day or more.
Soil: Well drained, moist.
Fertilizer: 5-10-5.
Uses: Beds, borders, pots, bouquets.

TROPAEOLUM
(trope-ee-OH-lum)

Nasturtium

TROPAEOLACEAE; nasturtium family

Height/habit: Bushy, self-branching, 1–1.5 ft. (30–45 cm.), to climbing/trailing, 4–6 ft. (1.2–1.8 m.).

Leaves: Rounded, peltate, to 2 in. (5 cm.) across, waxy green, white-splashed in some varieties.

Flowers: Irregular, 2–3 in. (5–7.5 cm.) across, with nectar-bearing spur; orange, rose pink, red, or yellow; fragrant; edible if pesticide-free. Cutting for bouquets or culinary purposes, as well as deadheading, increases bloom.

Season: Summer until frost in the North; spring zone 8 and warmer (but not hardy below 32°F [0°C]).

When to plant: Sow in individual pots indoors at 65°F (18°C) 6–8 weeks before frost-free weather; sow outdoors where they are to grow and bloom when soil is warm. Set transplants when available.

Light: Sun half day or more.

Soil: Well drained, sandy, moist.

Fertilizer: 5-10-5.

Uses: Beds, borders, pots, hanging baskets, bouquets.

VERBENA
(ver-BEE-nah)

Garden Verbena; Vervain

VERBENACEAE; verbena family

Height/habit: Bushy to creeping-trailing, 1–3 ft. (30–90 cm.).

Leaves: Toothed or cut, 1–3 in. (2.5–7.5 cm.) long.

Flowers: Flattened spikes, 2–3 in. (5–7.5 cm.) across; pink, peach, red, rose, purple, lavender, or blue, often with white eye. Lilac vervain (*V. bonariensis*), to 4 ft. (1.2 m.) tall/wide. Deadheading increases bloom.

Season: Late spring to fall frost; winter until early summer zone 8 and warmer, where verbena is often perennial.

When to plant: Sow seeds indoors at 65°F (18°C) 8–10 weeks before planting-out weather; sow outdoors where they are to grow and bloom when soil is warm. Set transplants when available.

Light: Sun half day or more.

Soil: Well drained, moist to on the dry side; tolerates drought.

Fertilizer: 5-10-5.

Uses: Beds, edging, pots, hanging baskets, bouquets. Lilac vervain often used in borders, where it laces pleasingly among bolder forms.

VIOLA
(veye-O-lah)

Pansy; Viola

VIOLACEAE; violet family

Height/habit: Bushy, much-branched mounds, 6–12 in. (15–30 cm.) high/wide.
Leaves: Ovate to cordate, 1–2 in. (2.5–5 cm.) long.
Flowers: Rounded, 1–4 in. (2.5–10 cm.) across; most colors, often bicolored; fragrant. Deadheading increases bloom.
Season: Spring until summer in the North; fall until spring zone 8 and warmer.

When to plant: Sow seeds indoors at 70°F (21°C) 12–16 weeks before planting-out weather; provide continual darkness until seeds sprout, then grow cool, 50–65°F (10–18°C), and in full sun. Or sow late summer to early fall where they are to grow and bloom. Set transplants when available.
Light: Sun half day or more.
Soil: Well drained, moist.
Fertilizer: 5-10-5.
Uses: Beds, borders, edging, pots, hanging baskets, bouquets; edible if pesticide-free.

XERANTHEMUM
(zuh-RANTH-ee-mum)

Everlasting; Immortelle

COMPOSITAE; daisy family

Height/habit: Much-branched, 1–2 ft. (30–61 cm.) high/wide.

Leaves: Oblong to lanceolate, to 2 in. (5 cm.) long; silvery.

Flowers: Papery, glossy, single, or semidouble, in heads to 2 in. (5 cm.) across; rose, pink, or white.

Season: Summer or until frost; all zones. Harvest for drying when buds begin opening. Left to dry on the plant, the flowers turn tan or light brown.

When to plant: Sow seeds outdoors where they are to grow and bloom when soil is warm. Set transplants when available.

Light: Sun half day or more.

Soil: Well drained, moist to on the dry side; tolerates drought.

Fertilizer: 5-10-5.

Uses: Beds, borders, rock gardens, pots, bouquets, drying.

ZINNIA
(ZIN-nee-ah)

Common Zinnia; Youth-and-old-age

COMPOSITAE; daisy family

Height/habit: Bushy, upright, self-branching, 1–4 ft. (30–122 cm.) high/wide; bushy trailing, 8–24 in. (20–61 cm.) in *Z. angustifolia* (*Z. linearis* of trade).

Leaves: Oval, clasping stems, 2–3 in. (5–7.5 cm.) long; narrow in *Z. angustifolia*.

Flowers: Single or double, ray petals flat or quilled, 1–8 in. (2.5–20 cm.) across; all colors except blue. Deadheading increases bloom.

Season: Summer until frost in cold climates; spring until summer zone 8 and warmer.

When to plant: Sow seeds indoors at 70–75°F (21–24°C) 6–8 weeks before planting-out weather; sow outdoors where they are to grow and bloom when soil is warm. Set transplants when available.

Light: Sun half day or more.

Soil: Well drained, moist to on the dry side.

Fertilizer: 5-10-5.

Uses: Beds, borders, edging/hedging, pots, bouquets.

Chapter Three:
Troubleshooting Guide for Annuals

Though annuals are relatively easy to care for, occasionally problems will beset the gardener. The following are the most common dilemmas with easy solutions provided.

Seedling or transplant wilts, collapses, or falls over at the soil line.

This indicates some kind of rot caused by too much water. When the growing medium stays soggy for too long, the roots die for lack of air.

Occasionally this kind of growth response can be traced to overfertilizing. There is always the possibility that what appears at first to be literally a dead wilt is only an indicator that the plant is badly in need of a thorough soaking. Conversely, plants that appear wilted despite their being in wet soil may recover as they begin to dry out.

Green or variously colored small insects clustered on growing tips.

This indicates the presence of aphids, also called plant lice. They can be rubbed off between the fingers or knocked off with strong sprays of water. The condition is generally not considered a long-term threat.

Few or no flowers despite lots of leafy, apparently healthy growth.

This indicates the need for more sunlight or applications of fertilizer labeled specifically for flowering plants, 15-30-15 for example.

Plant leaves flecked yellowish to grayish, overall lackluster appearance.

An indication of red spider mites, tiny insects that cluster on the leaf undersides and eventually cover every surface with tiny webs. Discourage by spraying the plant undersides with strong streams of water. Spider mites mostly attack plants under stress from lack of water when conditions are hot and dry.

Holes eaten from leaves, flowers gnawed or eaten through, sometimes trails of slime over surfaces.

These are indications of caterpillars, worms, or, in case of slime, slugs and snails. Solutions include hand-picking, lightly salting slugs on sight, setting out beer traps for slugs (low bowls of beer mixed with water), or spraying with safe products labeled for the control of caterpillars or slugs/snails.

Chapter Four:
Bringing Annuals Into Your Home

There are myriad tempting flowers that give joy in the garden and offer plenty of material for cutting. In fact, it is the mark of an annual that the more flowers are cut for bouquets, the more the plant will bloom. Cutting fresh flowers regularly and promptly removing the spent blooms—"deadheading"—keeps annuals productive over the longest season possible.

Annual flowers offer three distinct opportunities for enjoying their beauty indoors. If you purchase transplants in six-packs, 4-inch (10-centimeter), or quart- (liter-) size pots, with lots of buds and flowers, enjoy them immediately as table and floor decorations. Their utility pots can be hidden by setting them in baskets, slightly larger clay pots, window boxes, or a glazed ceramic cachepot. Just be sure there is a saucer to catch spills and that each plant is moistened well before it is placed in a temporary indoor garden spot.

A reason for growing of annual flowers is having a bounteous supply of material to cut for bouquets. Some gardeners are casual about this, others pursue flower arranging as an art form. Indeed, no part of the floral kingdom is richer in materials than the annuals.

The final harvest from annuals can consist of dried blossoms, scented herbs, wispy grasses, and elegant seed heads, all laid by during the active growing season for indoor decorations that add to the fall and winter pleasures of burrowing indoors, to celebrate the holidays, and anticipate the arrival of the seed and nursery catalogs that signal a new (and better-than-ever) gardening season.

To create effective arrangements, remember to blend a good balance of flower types.

For example:

❧ Rounded flowers include china aster, chrysanthemum, calendula, cosmos, dahlia, and bachelor's button

❧ Spiky flowers include snapdragon, sage, stock, and larkspur

❧ Flowers with graceful lines include salpiglossis, amaranthus, verbena, and abutilon

❧ Fragrant annual bouquets consist of candytuft, heliotrope, mignonette, flowering tobacco, petunia, pinks, stock, scabiosa, and sweet pea.

For everlastings arrangements and potpourri, the following air-dried flowers and seed heads are recommended:

❧ Blackberry lily dried seed heads with strawflowers or lemon mint

❧ Globe amaranth seed heads with gladiolus leaves or statice

❧ Sunflowers for displaying whole in still-life container arrangement

❧ Nigella seed heads with celosia

❧ Blue everlastings to brighten potpourri

❧ Calendula to brighten potpourri with shades of orange

❧ Whole pansy blossoms to add an elegant fillip to potpourri

❧ Pinks blossoms for adding a clove scent to potpourri

Part Two:
Perennials

Chapter Five:
The Perennial Garden

*M*any of the world's most breathtaking cultivated plants are classified as perennials, the mainstays of the garden. Technically speaking, a perennial is a plant that lives for more than two years; the term encompasses a great range of plants, including bulbs and trees. In this section, however, perennial flowers (often simply called perennials) and vines are the focus.

Locally adapted perennials and vines are all that you need to create an inviting outdoor "room." Vines can form the framework, covering fences and latticework (the "walls") as well as twining over arbors and pergolas (the "ceilings"). Perennials themselves are the "furnishings" and "accessories," perhaps intermingled with actual outdoor garden furniture.

The beauty of the perennial garden is that it lives on and on, returning every year without too much effort on the gardener's part. And there's always the ongoing quest for just the right perennial flowers and vines. Some gardeners like to grow only the newest introductions; others take pleasure in hunting down old garden flowers that are no longer common in commercial horticulture. Bringing a perennial garden to perfection can take years, but the pursuit is half the fun.

Planning and Designing the Perennial Garden

The most satisfactory perennial gardens are those planned according to the site and existing conditions. If the space is shaded, concentrate on perennials that do well in these conditions rather than languish. Daylilies, for example, will grow in shade but bloom little if at all. Primroses typically welcome lots of sun in cool spring weather, then prefer summer shade, making them ideal companions for deciduous trees and shrubs that do not leaf out until late in spring.

It helps to sketch ideas on graph paper, allowing each square to equal 1 foot (30 centimeters), or using any workable scale. Consider planting repetitive flower groupings, which lends a cohesive look to large spaces. A good gardener's rule of thumb is to set three plants or more together, in a triangle or circle, so that an established clump can form as rapidly as possible.

No matter what the dimensions of your outdoor space, there is always a workable design scheme. A narrow border, say 3 feet (1 meter) wide by 40 feet (12 meters) long, might be organized around four 8-foot (2.4-meter) tepees, which both train vines and provide vertical accent. They can be placed equidistantly, beginning 5 feet (1.5 meters) in from each end, with about 7.5 feet (2.2 meters) between them. (Specific instructions on how to construct a tepee appear later in this chapter.) Growing in the border could be a diverse selection of perennials that bloom throughout the seasons.

Some gardeners design according to color scheme. They enjoy devising a different palette for every season or maintaining the same color of choice year-round. Once you've chosen a color, you needn't be bound to a particular hue.

For instance, a garden of blue flowers looks beautiful interplanted with perennials having silvery leaves. Other accents can come from flowers in any other color of the rainbow (complementary colors for blue include soft yellows and oranges and also white) yet as long as blue and silver are used most abundantly, these serenely beautiful shades will dominate. Aside from color, there are many other design considerations in creating a perennial garden. Perennials and sociable vines are perfectly suited to mixing and matching with all other kinds of plants, from towering trees to alpine ground covers, and also respond well to being grown in containers. Here are some classic and contemporary design schemes:

Herbaceous Border

This style is associated with English gardens and involves planting densely. As one plant is fading, another is always just coming into bloom. Taller plants like peony, delphinium, and bleeding heart form the background, while medium-size plants like daylily, campion, and beardtongue bloom in the foreground. Planted so as to be clearly visible are the smaller perennials, such as lamb's ears and sedum.

Cottage Garden

Also associated with English gardens, the cottage style was originally a utilitarian garden of vegetables and herbs, with flowering and fragrant plants cultivated as well. Today, the cottage garden looks right at home in any geographical location. There are no rules for which types of plants look best, but classics include columbine, foxglove, lupine, primrose, evening primrose, and violet.

New American Garden

The idea for this style took root in a demonstration garden designed by Oehme van Sweden & Associates at the National Arboretum in Washington, D.C., under the directorship of Henry M. Cathey. By planting only locally adapted perennials, including

ornamental grasses, they achieved a natural yet bold effect that highlights the seasonal glory of the garden. The key is to mass the plantings and not to use too many different species.

Xeriscape

This type of garden involves using only plants that will require very little irrigation during dry weather. Though pioneered by the Denver

(Colorado) Water Department in the early 1980s, Xeriscaping is applicable everywhere, and plant selection varies to suit the particular locale.

Container Garden

For those whose gardening space is limited to a courtyard or deck, containers are the answer. They also appeal to gardeners who like to rearrange their plots frequently, adding pots here and there as they like—perhaps to punctuate the corners of an herbal knot garden or quickly brighten a corner of the yard where in-ground flowers have faded. Containers vary from clay and stone to wood, fiberglass, or even plastic (these retain moisture more efficiently than clay pots; if you want to hide the plastic, just slip them inside other, more attractive containers). Good perennial choices for containers are noted throughout Chapter Six, but a quick list includes bleeding heart, monkshood, chrysanthemum, coralbells, bee balm, gayfeather, and coneflower.

Tepees

To train vines and discipline unwieldy perennials, tepees are useful and decorative. Insert three or four bamboo stakes 6 to 8 feet (1.8 to 2.4 meters) long about 6 inches (15 centimeters) deep in the ground, 1.5 feet (45 centimeters) apart. Tie the tops together. The result will be a tripod or quadripod. Smaller or larger tepees are also possible. Sometimes it helps to fill the bottom interior of the structure with pea-vine brush, which allows tendril-climbing or twining vines to take hold.

Soil Preparation

Some perennials thrive in boggy conditions—perhaps by a body of water or along the banks of a stream—and they are noted throughout Chapter Six. Most, however, require soil that is well drained and that contains sufficient humus to give roots air and a reserve of moisture. If the endemic soil has a high clay or sand content, add 5 to 6 inches (12.5 to 15 centimeters) of well-rotted compost and mix thoroughly into the top 5 to 6 inches (12.5 to 15 centimeters) of soil.

If drainage is poor or your region experiences seasons of high heat and high humidity, such as along the Gulf Coast of the United States, raised planting beds are essential. These can be built of wood, landscape timbers, railroad ties, concrete blocks, or whatever material seems appropriate. The beds should be at least 6 to 8 inches (15 to 20 centimeters) deep and can then be filled with a mixture of endemic soil, well-rotted compost, and possibly sphagnum peat moss or leaf mold. Adding sand to the soil also helps drainage.

Theoretically, a perennial garden bed that is once or twice annually top-dressed with well-rotted compost will not need any additional fertilizer. However, in practice, gardeners often like to side-dress with 5-10-5 granules in the spring and again at midsummer. It is also common practice to mix in 14-14-14 or similar timed-release pellets at planting time.

Buying and Planting Perennials

Gardeners have several options in purchasing perennials. They can choose from container-grown perennials at their local nursery—a very convenient method as it allows for planting whenever you wish, from spring through fall in the North and year-round in zones 8 through 9. It is also a great help to purchase plants in bloom, so you'll know exactly what you're getting.

To plant a potted perennial, first water the ground thoroughly. Dig a hole a bit larger than the pot. Add compost to the hole to spur new plant growth. Turn over the pot and tap it lightly. The rootball should give easily, but if it does not, loosen the edges with a knife. Set the whole rootball in the hole with its top just beneath the surface of the soil. Water again, and add a little fertilizer if you wish.

The second option is to order special varieties

and cultivars from growers. They will ship at the proper time in spring for planting, usually sending the semidormant roots of herbaceous perennials. Plant these according to the enclosed directions. For a list of such growers, refer to the Resources section in the appendix of this book.

Another possibility is to plant from seed, which can be obtained both at the nursery and through the mail-order catalogs. You can also collect seeds from your own garden (though many perennials do not grow "true" from seed, and the plant you grow might not resemble the parent). Seeds from catalogs are usually planted in spring; seeds from your own plants go into the ground toward the end of summer, when they would naturally plant themselves. Some gardeners opt for raising perennial seeds in a cold frame, to protect them from the elements; after they are well developed after several months, they transplant them to a garden bed.

Caring for Perennials Throughout the Seasons

Catalog writers and garden book publishers may refer to them as "carefree," but in fact hardly any living plant is truly carefree. Throughout their long growing season, perennials respond to a bit of care nearly every day. Besides general training, tidying, and deadheading, there is also watering in time of drought, especially early in the season when roots are getting established; fertilizing if the soil is impoverished; and occasionally taking action against invasive weeds or insects. Except for the longest-lived perennials, such as herbaceous peony and baptisia, most perennials benefit from being dug and divided at least once every four or five years. Otherwise they are inclined to crowd themselves out in the centers.

You'll know it's time when you see new, stronger roots wrapping around the crown of the plant. Division rejuvenates the plant and is done before or after flowering. Most gardeners divide spring or summer bloomers in late summer to early fall and late bloomers the following spring. To divide, push two spading forks into the plant's crown and then pull the handles away from each other to detach the roots. Then pull the clump apart and replant young rootstocks.

Stems of tip cuttings are an expedient means of propagating perennials in spring and summer. A new plant grown this way will be exactly like the one from which it came. Use healthy, vital growth, usually at some medium age between the newest (at the tips) and the oldest (toward the base of the plant) and take cuttings 4 to 5 inches (10 to 12.5 centimeters) long.

Remove at least one or two sets of leaves from the base; roots develop at the nodes where leaves grew before. If leaves remaining at the top of the cutting are large and inclined to floppiness or wilting, cut them back by one-half to two-thirds. This reduces stress on the cutting and helps it concentrate energy on developing new roots. Set each cutting 1 to 2 inches (2.5 to 5 centimeters) deep in moist rooting medium. Bright light, moderate temperatures (55 to 75°F [13 to 24°C]), even moisture, and good circulation of moist air help cuttings take hold.

Perennials having fleshy roots often can be propagated by setting lengths 2 to 4 inches (5 to 10 centimeters) long in prepared soil in fall or early spring, about 1 inch (2.5 centimeters) deep. Some perennials that can be propagated from root cuttings include anemone, Oriental poppy, trollius, phlox, echinops, and verbascum.

Essential Tools

Aside from the usual trowel, Cape Cod weeder, and three-pronged cultivator, the perennial gardener seldom has a better friend than the border spade or woman's perennial spade. This works perfectly for digging holes to accommodate plants from gallon-size plastic pots, as well as for quick division and transplanting chores. For staking and tying, it also helps to have twigs and brush cut from the property, bamboo canes, and various means of tying, such as raffia, jute, and plastic-and-wire twist-ties.

Year-round Gardening Calendar
Here is a calendar of seasonal reminders:

SPRING:
Cut back and clean up dead growth as the weather warms and there is little danger of further killing frost.

Set brush stakes ("pea-vine sticks") over and around clumps of perennials that grow tall later—peonies, summer phlox, heliopsis.

Side-dress with 5-10-5 fertilizer.

Till and prepare soil in garden beds and top-dress with fertilizer.

Sow seeds of perennials or transplant seedlings after danger of frost has passed.

Bring transplants to the garden.

Mulch with organic matter.

Divide late-flowering perennials.

Start a garden watering schedule, watering soil thoroughly yet infrequently as a conservation measure. To check if soil needs to be watered, see if it feels dry 3 to 4 inches (7.5 to 10 centimeters) down.

Bring spring perennial bouquets indoors.

Deadhead spent blooms.

SUMMER:
Continue weeding and deadheading.

Water deeply in times of drought or, alternatively, rely on locally adapted perennials and mulching to conserve resources.

Plant seeds of perennials collected from your own garden.

Bring summer perennial bouquets indoors.

FALL:
Continue watering, weeding, and deadheading.

In late fall, side-dress with several inches of well-rotted compost or rotted manure. Left to cure over winter, this treatment enhances microlife in the soil and results in perennial plantings that are stronger and inherently more resistant to predatory insects and diseases.

Divide spring-flowering plants about a month before ground freezes.

Do not cut perennial stems and grasses to the ground—throughout the winter, they will provide cover for animals and add interest to the landscape.

Bring late summer/early fall perennial bouquets indoors.

WINTER:
Begin designing your perennial garden on paper.

Order everything you'll need: tools, seeds, flats, starting mixes.

Start perennial seeds indoors.

In the North, press back into the earth any crowns of perennials that may have been heaved up by alternate freezing and thawing.

Chapter Six:
The 100 Best Perennials for Your Garden

ACHILLEA	126	Yarrow
ACONITUM	127	Monkshood; Aconite
AJUGA	127	Bugleweed; Carpet Bugle
ALCHEMILLA	128	Lady's Mantle
ANEMONE	129	Windflower; European Pasqueflower; Japanese Anemone
AQUILEGIA	130	Columbine
ARABIS	130	Rock Cress
ARTEMISIA	131	Wormwood; Silver-king; Tarragon
ARUNCUS	132	Goat's Beard
ASARUM	133	Wild Ginger
ASCLEPIAS	134	Milkweed; Butterfly Weed; Bloodflower
ASTER	135	Michaelmas Daisy; New England and New York Asters
ASTILBE	136	False Goat's Beard
AURINIA	136	Basket-of-gold Alyssum
BAPTISIA	137	False Indigo
BERGENIA	138	Megasea
BOUGAINVILLEA	139	Paper Flower
CAMPANULA	140	Bellflower
CAREX	140	Sedge
CENTRANTHUS	141	Valerian; Jupiter's Beard
CHRYSANTHEMUM	142	Mum; Marguerite; Shasta, Painted, Oxeye, and Montauk Daisies
CIMICIFUGA	143	Bugbane
CLEMATIS	144	Clematis
CLERODENDRUM	145	Glory-bower
COREOPSIS	145	Tickseed
DELPHINIUM	146	Perennial Larkspur
DIANTHUS	147	Pink
DICENTRA	148	Bleeding Heart; Turkey Corn; Dutchman's breeches
DICTAMNUS	148	Gas Plant
DIGITALIS	149	Foxglove

ECHINACEA	150	Purple Coneflower
ECHINOPS	151	Globe-thistle; Hedgehog Flower
EPIMEDIUM	152	Barrenwort
ERYNGIUM	152	Sea Holly
EUPATORIUM	153	Boneset; Mist Flower; Hardy Ageratum; Joe-pye Weed; White Snakeroot
EUPHORBIA	154	Cypress Spurge
GAURA	155	Wild Honeysuckle
GERANIUM	156	Cranesbill
HELIOPSIS	157	Oxeye
HELLEBORUS	157	Christmas Rose; Lenten Rose; Stinking Hellebore
HEMEROCALLIS	158	Daylily
HEUCHERA	159	Coralbells; Alumroot
HOSTA	160	Plaintain Lily
HOUTTUYNIA	161	Houttuynia
INULA	161	Elecampane
IPOMOPSIS	162	Standing Cypress
IRIS	163	Flag; Fleur-de-lis
JASMINUM	164	Jasmine
JUSTICIA	164	Shrimp Plant; King's Crown
LAMIUM	165	Dead Nettle
LAVANDULA	166	Lavender
LIATRIS	167	Gay-feather
LIGULARIA	168	Leopard Plant; Silver Farfugium
LOBELIA	169	Cardinal Flower; Great Blue Lobelia
LONICERA	169	Honeysuckle
LUPINUS	170	Lupine; Texas Bluebonnet
LYCHNIS	171	Campion
LYSIMACHIA	172	Loosestrife; Creeping Jennie
MACLEAYA	173	Plume Poppy
MALVA	173	Mallow
MANDEVILLA	174	Mandeville; Chilean Jasmine
MISCANTHUS	175	Eulalia; Japanese Silver Grass
MONARDA	176	Bee Balm; Oswego Tea
NEPETA	177	Catmint
NEPHROLEPIS	177	Sword Fern; Boston Fern
OENOTHERA	178	Evening Primrose; Sun Drops
PAEONIA	179	Peony
PAPAVER	180	Perennial Poppy
PASSIFLORA	181	Passionflower
PENSTEMON	180	Beardtongue; Gulf Coast Penstemon
PEROVSKIA	182	Russian Sage
PHLOX	183	Phlox; Moss Pink
PHYSOSTEGIA	184	Obedient Plant
PLATYCODON	185	Balloon Flower
POLEMONIUM	186	Jacob's Ladder; Greek Valerian
POLYGONATUM	187	Solomon's Seal
POLYGONUM	187	Knotweed; Fleece Flower; Silver Lace Vine; Mexican Bamboo; Showy Bistort
POTENTILLA	188	Cinquefoil
PRIMULA	189	Primrose
PULMONARIA	190	Lungwort
RUDBECKIA	191	Coneflower; Black-eyed Susan
RUELLIA	192	Wild Petunia; Mexican Petunia
SALVIA	193	Sage
SEDUM	193	Stonecrop
SEMPERVIVUM	194	Houseleek; Live-forever
STACHYS	195	Lamb's Ears
STIGMAPHYLLON	195	Butterfly Vine
SYMPHYTUM	196	Comfrey
THALICTRUM	197	Meadow Rue
THUNBERGIA	198	Blue Trumpet Vine
TIARELLA	199	False Mitrewort
TRACHELOSPERMUM	200	Star Jasmine; Confederate Jasmine
TRADESCANTIA	200	Spiderwort
TRILLIUM	201	Wake-robin
TROLLIUS	202	Globeflower
VERBASCUM	203	Mullein
VERONICA	204	Speedwell
VIOLA	205	Violet
VITEX	206	Chaste Tree
YUCCA	207	Spanish Dagger

ACHILLEA
(ack-il-LEE-ah)

Yarrow

COMPOSITAE; daisy family

Height/habit: Lacy, often finely cut leaves in a basal rosette from which the flowering stems arise, 1–4 ft. (30–122 cm.) high/wide.

Leaves: Pinnately dissected, each 2–10 in. (5–25 cm.) long by one-third as wide, growing alternately or in a basal rosette, green to gray-green.

Flowers: Corymb-forming, 1–6 in. (2 .5–15 cm.) across, 1–4 ft. (30–122 cm.) high, rising above the foliage; white, yellow, red, orange, or pink. Hybrids of *A. millefolium* and *A. taygetea* have expanded the color range for this type into pastels. Prompt deadheading encourages a second blooming.

Season: Summer.

When to plant: Start seeds indoors 8–12 weeks ahead of planting-out weather for blooms in the same season; set transplants when available. If yarrow grows wild on your property, transplant some of the choicest clumps to your cultivated garden. If watered and shaded at first they can be transplanted while in bloom. Cold-hardy zones 2–3, heat-tolerant through zones 9–10.

Light: Sunny to half-sunny. Plants in light soil receiving full sun will grow barely one-third the size of those in rich soil receiving a half day of sun.

Soil: Well drained, moist to slightly on the dry side.

Fertilizer: 5-10-5.

Propagation: Sow seeds or divide plants having several crowns in spring or fall. Achilleas are at their best in the second and third seasons; rejuvenate by digging, dividing, and replanting only the strongest of the newer growths every 2–3 years.

Uses: Beds, borders, pots, cutting fresh or dried.

ACONITUM
(ack-oh-NEYE-tum)

Monkshood; Aconite

RANUNCULACEAE; buttercup family

Height/habit: Leafy shoots from the ground become flowering plants 3–6 ft. (1–1.8 m.) high/wide that often benefit from staking. Caution: Members of the Aconitum genus are poisonous.

Leaves: Finely cut, basal, similar to those of delphinium; 6–8 in. (15–20 cm.) across.

Flowers: Tubular to hood-shaped, 1–2 in. (2 .5–5 cm.) long/wide, growing in spikes showing well above the leaves; white through all shades of blue to purple; *A. anthora* is yellow and blooms before the blue types; *A. compactum* is pale pink.

Season: Midsummer through fall. Cold-hardy to zones 4–5 but diminished by heat zones 8–9 and warmer.

When to plant: Set transplants when available and do not disturb unless divisions are wanted.

Light: Sunny to half-sunny.

Soil: Humusy, well drained, moist to wet. Monkshood often colonizes moist banks.

Fertilizer: 5-10-5.

Propagation: Sow seeds outdoors in the fall for germination the following spring; seedlings bloom the third season. Established clumps can be divided when the soil is workable in spring.

Uses: Beds, borders, pots, cut flowers.

AJUGA
(ah-JEW-gah)

Bugleweed; Carpet Bugle

LABIATAE; mint family

Height/habit: Ground-hugging plants that form a dense mat, spreading via runners.

Leaves: Spatula-shaped, 1–4 in. (2.5–10 cm.) long by one-third as wide, mostly in basal rosettes; depending on the cultivar they may be green, burgundy, or silver.

Flowers: Compact spikes rising above the leaves, 3–6 in. (7.5-15 cm.) long; blue or white.

Season: Flowers in spring; foliage attractive most of the year. Cold–hardy zone 3; heat-tolerant through zone 9.

When to plant: Set transplants when available.

Light: Full sun (in cooler climates) to nearly full shade.

Soil: Humusy, well drained, moist.

Fertilizer: 5-10-5.

Propagation: Divide in spring or early fall or remove runners that have started to root.

Uses: Border edging, ground cover, outdoor pots.

ALCHEMILLA
(al-kem-MILL-ah)

Lady's Mantle

ROSACEAE; rose family

Height/habit: Low-mounding or carpeting herbs rarely exceeding 1 ft. (30 cm.) even in bloom, spreading 2–3 ft. (61–90 cm.) wide.

Leaves: Velvety, rounded, lobed, cut at the edges, 1–5 in. (2.5–12.5 cm.) wide; dewlike droplets from normal guttation (exudation of water from leaves) appear mornings on these beautiful leaves.

Flowers: Loose, feathery panicles 15 in. (38 cm.) high; yellow-green.

Season: Leaves from spring until fall frost; flowers midsummer. Cold-hardy zone 3, sometimes heat-tolerant through zone 8.

When to plant: Set transplants when available.

Light: Sun (cooler climates) to part shade.

Soil: Humusy, well drained, moist.

Fertilizer: 5-10-5.

Propagation: Sow seeds or divide in spring.

Uses: Edging, ground cover, outdoor pots.

ANEMONE
(ah-NEM-oh-nee)

Windflower; European Pasqueflower; Japanese Anemone

RANUNCULACEAE; buttercup family

Height/habit: Bushy, upright, 1–4 ft. (30–122 cm.) high/wide.

Leaves: Deeply cut, mostly from the base, plain green except notably silver-haired in European pasqueflower (*A. pulsatilla*), 1–2 ft. (30–61 cm.) high/wide.

Flowers: Single to double, often with showy stamens, 1–3 in. (2.5–7.5 cm.) across, on slender, graceful stems, 1–4 ft. (30–122 cm.) high; white, pink, mauve, blue, purple, or rosy carmine.

Season: Spring for the windflower (*A. canadensis* and *A. pulsatilla*); late summer through fall for the Japanese anemone (*A. hupehensis japonica*). Cold-hardy zones 3 (with protection) through 6, heat tolerance questionable zones 8 and warmer.

When to plant: Set transplants when available, ideally spring for those that bloom in the fall and fall for those that bloom in the spring.

Light: Full sun to part shade.

Soil: Humusy, well drained, moist.

Fertilizer: 5-10-5.

Propagation: Sow seeds or divide in spring or fall.

Uses: Beds, borders, outdoor pots, cut flowers.

AQUILEGIA
(ack-kwill-EE-jee-ah)
Columbine
RANUNCULACEAE; buttercup
family

Height/habit: Tidy clumps of
graceful, fernlike, blue-green
leaves, 1–2 ft. (30-61 cm.)
high/wide, surmounted by
elegant, wiry stems that bear
the showy flowers.
Leaves: Cut, mostly growing
from the base of the plant,
6–18 in. (15–45 cm.) long/wide,
from pale, bright green to quite
a glaucous blue-green. Leaf
miners often disfigure the leaves
but this seldom hurts the plants.
Flowers: Often have noticeable
spurs that give them a light,
airborne quality, 2–4 in.
(5–10 cm.) across; most colors,
typically bicolored.

Season: Spring. Cold-hardy
through zone 5; 'Hinckley's
Yellow' is the most reliable
columbine for humid, hot
gardens zone 8 and warmer.
When to plant: Set transplants
when available, ideally in early
spring or fall.
Light: Sun to half shade.
Soil: Humusy, well drained,
moist.
Fertilizer: 5-10-5.
Propagation: Sow seeds in
spring or fall, or transplant self-
sown seedlings (note: named
hybrid cultivars do not grow
true from seeds).
Uses: Beds, borders, rock gardens, pots, cut flowers. Also for
wild gardens and naturalizing:
A natural stand of blue-and-
white *A. caerulea* is particularly
memorable. Another favorite
for naturalizing is the delicate
red-and-yellow Canadian
columbine (*A. canadensis*).

 ## ARABIS
(AIR-abb-iss)
Rock Cress
CRUCIFERAE; mustard family

Height/habit: Mounding
or mat-forming, 6–12 in.
(15–30 cm.) high by several
times as wide.
Leaves: Small, gray-green,
mostly toward the base; 2–3 in.
(5–7.5 cm.) long.
Flowers: 4-petaled (occasionally doubled in choice cultivars),
each to .5 in. (1.25 cm.) across,
but appearing in such profusion that the foliage is nearly
obscured; white, pink, or rose.

Season: Early spring flowers.
When to plant: Set transplants
when available, best in early
spring or early fall. Cold-hardy
through zones 5–6 but intolerant of hot/humid summer conditions zones 8 and warmer.
Light: Full sun half day or
more.
Soil: Well drained, moist in
spring; keep on the dry side in
summer.
Fertilizer: 5-10-5.
Propagation: Sow seed, divide,
or take stem tip cuttings in
spring or fall.
Uses: Edging, spilling from a
rock wall, borders, outdoor
pots with bulbs in spring.

Wormwood; Silver-king; Tarragon

COMPOSITAE; daisy family

Height/habit: Clump-forming to colonizing, mostly upright, gray-leaved plants, 1–4 ft. (30–122 cm.) high/wide.
Leaves: Finely cut in many species, including wormwood (*A. absinthium*), entire in *A. albula* (silver-king) and *A. dracunculus* (tarragon). The leaves typically have a pungent odor when brushed against; those of 'Powis Castle' smell particularly sweet.
Flowers: Inconspicuous and tiny if present at all.

Season: Foliage color from spring until frost and even beyond.
When to plant: Set transplants when available, ideally in spring. Generally cold-hardy through zone 4. Silver-king and 'Powis Castle' adapt to humid, hot weather through zone 9.
Light: Sun half day or more.
Soil: Well drained, moist to on the dry side.
Propagation: Divide in spring or take stem tip cuttings.
Uses: Beds, borders, pots, cutting fresh or dried. These sturdy plants are chosen mostly for their silvery effect that, when repeated throughout a garden, helps pull together many different flower colors and forms.

ARUNCUS
(ah-RUNK-us)

Goat's Beard

ROSACEAE; rose family

Height/habit: Large clumps of compound leaves crowned by tiny flowers in spikes, 5–6 ft. (1.5–1.8 m.) high/wide.

Leaves: Compound, graceful, even feathery, 12–15 in. (30–38 cm.) long/wide, medium to dark green.

Flowers: Spikes 1–1.5 ft. (30–45 cm.) long rising above the foliage; flowers tiny but abundant; creamy white.

Season: Flowers early to mid-summer.

When to plant: Set transplants when available, ideally fall or early spring. Cold-hardy through zone 5; sometimes grows in hot, humid conditions in zone 9 and warmer.

Light: Half-sunny to half-shady.

Soil: Humusy, well drained, moist.

Fertilizer: 5-10-5.

Propagation: Divide in spring or transplant self-sown seedlings.

Uses: Borders, accents, large outdoor pots, streamside.

ASARUM
(ah-SAY-rum)

Wild Ginger

ARISTOLOCHIACEAE; birthwort
family

Height/habit: Low, ground-
covering, 6–10 in. (15–25 cm.)
high/wide.
Leaves: Heart-shaped, shiny,
dark green, to 5 in. (12.5 cm.)
across.
Flowers: Inconspicuous, purplish brown, borne under the
leaves.
Season: *A. canadense* is deciduous; the other species cultivated
are evergreen.

When to plant: Set transplants
when available. *A. canadense* is
cold-hardy through zone 3, the
evergreen species variously
zones 4–6. Questionably heat-
tolerant zone 8 and warmer.
Light: Half to full shade.
Soil: Humusy, well drained,
moist.
Fertilizer: 5-10-5.
Propagation: Divide roots in
spring or summer.
Uses: Edging or ground cover
in wild, woodland, or rock
gardens.

ASCLEPIAS
(az-KLEEP-ee-az)

Milkweed; Butterfly Weed; Bloodflower

ASCLEPIADACEAE; milkweed family

Height/habit: Upright, bushy, 2–5 ft. (61–150 cm.) high/wide.

Leaves: Narrow, 2–6 in. (5–15 cm.) long.

Flowers: Umbels 2–3 in. (5–7.5 cm.) across at the stem tips above the leaves; yellow, orange, red, pink, white, often bicolored.

Season: Summer.

When to plant: Set transplants when available; take care planting so as to disturb the roots as little as possible. Butterfly weed (*A. tuberosa*) cold-hardy through zone 3, also heat-tolerant through zone 10. Bloodflower (*A. curassavica*) tropical: Grow in ground zones 9–10, elsewhere in pots that can winter indoors in a warm place.

Light: Sun half day or more.

Soil: Well drained, moist. *A. tuberosa* often grows wild in sandy soil.

Fertilizer: 5-10-5.

Propagation: Sow seeds or take root cuttings in spring.

Uses: Beds, borders, outdoor pots, butterfly gardens.

ASTER
(AST-er)

Michaelmas Daisy; New England and New York Asters

COMPOSITAE; daisy family

Height/habit: Bushy mounds
1–6 ft. (30–180 cm.) high/wide.
Leaves: Simple, alternate, narrow, 2–6 in. (5–15 cm.) long,
dark green.
Flowers: Daisylike, each from
.25–4 in. (.63–10 cm.) across, in
loose heads, often hiding the
leaves; red, rose, pink, white,
blue, purple, or mauve.
Season: Summer for *A.* x
frikartii; late summer until
fall frost for most cultivars
of New England aster
(*A. novae-angliae*) and New
York aster (*A. novi-belgii*).

When to plant: Set transplants
when available, ideally in spring
as soon as the soil can be
worked. Cold-hardy through
zones 5–6 and surprisingly
tolerant of hot, humid summers
through zones 8–9.
Light: Full sun to light shade.
Soil: Humusy, well drained,
moist.
Fertilizer: 5-10-5.
Propagation: Divide or take
cuttings in spring or early
summer. Divide and replant
every third or fourth year to
keep the plants vigorous. Seeds
planted in spring bloom first
the following year but produce
unpredictable sizes and colors.
Uses: Beds, borders, outdoor
pots, cut flowers.

ASTILBE
(az-TILL-be)
False Goat's Beard
SAXIFRAGACEAE; saxifrage family

Height/habit: Tidy clumps 18–40 in. (45–100 cm.) high/wide.
Leaves: Compound and divided, 6–12 in. (15–30 cm.) long/wide; some deeply cut and feathery, bronzy to dark green.
Flowers: Showy panicles 2–4 in. (5–10 cm.) long or more consisting of tiny flowers rising above the leaves; white, pink, rose, red, lavender, or purple.
Season: Flowers about 4–6 weeks at the beginning of summer; foliage attractive spring through fall.

When to plant: Set transplants when available, ideally in spring or early fall. Cold-hardy through zone 5 but intolerant of hot, humid summers zone 9 and warmer.
Light: Half sun to half shade.
Soil: Humusy, well drained, moist.
Fertilizer: 5-10-5. Yellowish leaves with green veins could indicate a need for lower pH; treat by fertilizing with 30-10-10 or applying chelated iron according to product label instructions.
Propagation: Divide in spring.
Uses: Beds, borders, outdoor pots, cut flowers.

AURINIA
(aw-RINN-ee-ah)
Basket-of-gold Alyssum
CRUCIFERAE; mustard family

Height/habit: Sprawling, trailing, or cascading, 6–12 in. (15–30 cm.) high and several times as wide.
Leaves: Narrow, spatula-shaped, to 5 in. (12.5 cm.) long, gray-green.
Flowers: About .25 in. (.63 cm.) across in heads that completely cover the plants; pale to vivid yellow.
Season: Early to midspring. Cut or shear off the flower heads after bloom.

When to plant: Set transplants when available. Cold-hardy through zone 4, heat-tolerant through zone 8.
Light: Sun half day or more.
Soil: Well drained, moist to on the dry side.
Fertilizer: 5-10-5.
Propagation: Take stem cuttings in spring or summer or sow seeds in spring.
Uses: Edging at front of border, spilling over or from a rock wall, outdoor pots.

BAPTISIA
(bap-TIZ-ee-ah)
False Indigo
LEGUMINOSAE; pea family

Height/habit: Upright, shrub-like, to 3 ft. (90 cm.) high x 2 ft. (61 cm.) wide.

Leaves: Compound leaflets arranged in groups of 3; blue-green.

Flowers: Lupinelike in sprays at the top of the plant; dark blue in *B. australis*, yellow in *B. tinctoria* (both known as false indigo).

Season: Late spring through early summer for *B. australis*, all summer for *B. tinctoria*.

When to plant: Set transplants when available, ideally spring or fall. Cold-hardy zone 4, heat-tolerant zone 9.

Light: Sun half day or more.

Soil: Humusy, well drained, moist; tolerates drought but not alkaline pH.

Fertilizer: 5-10-5.

Propagation: Sow seeds in fall or divide in spring. Established plants can be left undisturbed indefinitely.

Uses: Beds, borders, wild gardens, dried seedpods for winter arrangements.

BERGENIA
(ber-JEE-nee-ah)

Megasea

SAXIFRAGACEAE; saxifrage family

Height/habit: Low clumps of bold foliage 1–1.5 ft. (30–45 cm.) high/wide.

Leaves: Evergreen, rounded, wavy at the edges, to 10 in. (25 cm.) long/wide; bright green to glowing burgundy, depending on the variety and the time of year.

Flowers: Loose panicles, 1–1.5 ft. (30–45 cm.) high, standing above the leaves; purplish red, bright pink, or white.

Season: Flowers early to mid-spring, leaves attractive at most times.

When to plant: Set transplants when available. Cold-hardy zones 2–3, heat-tolerant zone 9 (*B. crassifolia*, favored in California, is rated zones 3–10).

Light: More sun in cooler climates, more shade in hot places.

Soil: Sandy, well drained, moist.

Fertilizer: 5-10-5.

Propagation: Divide or sow seeds in spring.

Uses: Beds, borders, rock gardens, ground cover, pathway edging, leaves for flower arrangements.

BOUGAINVILLEA
(boog-in-VILL-ee-ah)

Paper Flower

NYCTAGINACEAE; four-o'clock
family

Height/habit: Potentially large
(to 60 ft. [18 m.] in some areas)
evergreen woody vines with
sharp spines along the stems.
Leaves: Smooth, alternate,
tapering at the base, to 4 in.
(10 cm.) long.
Flowers: Very small 5-lobed
trumpets, each barely .25 in.
(.63 cm.) wide; pale yellow to
white, several arising from the
center of each showy, papery,
long-lasting bract that can be
greenish white, yellow, orange,
peach, or brilliant magenta,
often profuse.
Season: Virtually everblooming
zone 10 and warmer; zone 9
and colder blooms appear
throughout most of summer
or, conversely, may soak up
energy outdoors all through
warm weather, then give it back
in the form of winter flowers
in a sunny garden room.

When to plant: Set transplants
when available, outdoors when
temperatures are above 50°F
(10°C). Take care not to over-
water in cool temperatures or
when the roots have been disturbed. Reliably winter-hardy
outdoors zone 10; elsewhere
move to a frost-free location as
necessary, with plenty of sun
and air circulation.
Light: Sun half day or more.
Soil: Well drained, moist to
quite dry.
Fertilizer: Potassium- (potash-)
rich blend, such as 12-12-17.
Propagation: Take stem
cuttings in spring. Training
and pruning techniques are
similar to those of wisteria:
First establish the permanent
framework, then cut back to
spurlike growths in the fall or
after a heavy flowering.
Uses: Zone 10 and warmer, use
as a screen or fence and arbor
cover; zone 9 and colder, keep
pots outdoors in frost-free
weather.

CAMPANULA
(kam-PAN-yew-lah)

Bellflower

CAMPANULACEAE; bellflower family

Height/habit: Variously upright or trailing, 1–4 ft. (30–122 cm.) high/wide.

Leaves: Often clustered in a basal rosette, oblong to lanceolate, to 8 in. (20 cm.) long.

Flowers: Bell-shaped, in racemes, also solitary or in heads, spikes, or panicles, 1–3 in. (2.5–7.5 cm.) across; blue, white, and occasionally pink or rose. Garden favorites include Carpathian bellflower (*C. carpatica*), Adriatic bellflower (*C. elatines*, an outstanding rock and wall plant), clustered bellflower (*C. glomerata*), peach-leaf bellflower (*C. persicifolia*), chimney bellflower (*C. pyramidalis*), and bluebells-of-Scotland (*C. rotundifolia*). Deadheading encourages a second blooming.

Season: Summer.

When to plant: Start seeds indoors 8–12 weeks ahead of planting-out weather for blooms in the second season; set transplants when available. Cold-hardy zone 3, heat-tolerant through zones 7–8.

Light: Sunny to half-sunny.

Soil: Well drained, evenly moist.

Fertilizer: 5-10-5.

Propagation: Sow seeds in spring or summer or divide plants having several crowns in spring or fall. Campanulas are at their best in the second and third seasons; rejuvenate by digging, dividing, and replanting only the strongest of the newer growths every 3–4 years.

Uses: Beds, borders, rock gardens, outdoor pots, cut flowers.

CAREX
(KAIR-ex)

Sedge

CYPERACEAE; sedge family

Height/habit: Upright to cascading grassy clumps, to 1 ft. (30 cm.) high/wide.

Leaves: Grasslike, to 1 ft. (30 cm.) long; extremely narrow in some varieties; green, gold, white, brown, buff to apricot.

Flowers: Brownish spikelets at the tips of leaflike stems. Grown mostly for foliage color and texture.

Season: Cultivated sorts are attractive for foliage effect from spring through fall, occasionally all winter.

When to plant: Set transplants when available. Cold-hardiness varies, zones 5–7; heat-tolerance for most through zone 9.

Light: Sunny to half-sunny.

Soil: Moist to boggy.

Fertilizer: 5-10-5.

Propagation: Divide established clumps in spring.

Uses: Beds, borders, pots. Ideal for pond banks and stream edges.

CENTRANTHUS
(sen-TRANTH-us)

Valerian;
Jupiter's Beard

VALERIANACEAE; valerian family

Height/habit: Bushy, upright, 2–3 ft. (61–90 cm.) high/wide.
Leaves: Gray-green, 3–4 in. (7.5–10 cm.) long, mostly toward the lower half of the plant.
Flowers: Dense clusters, 2–3 in. (5–7.5 cm.) across, of very small funnel-shaped blooms; crimson or white; fragrant. Deadheading encourages a second, lesser flowering.
Season: Summer.
When to plant: Set transplants when available. Cold-hardy zone 3, heat-tolerant zone 9.
Light: Sunny to half-sunny.
Soil: Well drained, moist to on the dry side.
Fertilizer: 5-10-5.
Propagation: Divide established clumps or sow seeds in spring.
Uses: Beds, borders, pots, cut flowers.

CHRYSANTHEMUM
(kriss-ANTH-ee-mum)

Mum; Marguerite; Shasta, Painted, Oxeye, and Montauk Daisies

COMPOSITAE; daisy family

Height/habit: Low to high and shrubby; 1–6 ft. (30–180 cm.) high/wide.

Leaves: Entire, toothed, or pinnate, 1–3 in. (2.5–7.5 cm.) long/wide on stiff or woody stems; notably silver-edged in gold-and-silver mum (*C. pacificum*).

Flowers: Single or double "daisies" from less than 1 in. (2.5 cm.) across to 1 ft. (30 cm.); all colors except blue. Among species worth growing are the Shasta daisy (*C. maximum*); painted daisy, sometimes called pyrethrum (*C. coccineum*); oxeye daisy (*C. leucanthemum*); and Montauk daisy (*C. nipponicum*).

Season: Hardy garden mums (*C. morifolium*) of the North late summer until frost. These also bloom late spring through early summer in Southern gardens. Other species bloom variously spring through fall, zones 3–9. Marguerites (*C. frutescens*) bloom winter through spring in mild regions, through zone 10.

When to plant: Set transplants when available.

Light: Sunny to half-sunny.

Soil: Well drained, evenly moist.

Fertilizer: 5-10-5.

Propagation: Take cuttings or divide roots spring through early summer. Seeds of hardy garden mums started early indoors in late winter flower mid- to late fall.

Uses: Beds, borders, pots, cut flowers.

CIMICIFUGA
(simmy-SIFF-yew-gah)

Bugbane

RANUNCULACEAE; buttercup
family

Height/habit: High (3–8 ft.
[1–2.4 m.]) perennials native
to moist, shaded woodlands,
often seen gracing roadside
ditches from Connecticut to
Georgia and Tennessee.
Leaves: Cut into 3 parts, then
pinnate, 3–12 in. (7.5–30 cm.)
long/wide.
Flowers: Very small in panicles
to 2 ft. (61 cm.) long; some
species more wandlike than
others; white.
Season: Late summer through
fall.
When to plant: Set transplants
when available, ideally in
spring. Cold-hardy zones 3–4,
heat-tolerant zone 8.
Light: Half-shady to shady.
Soil: Well drained, humusy,
moist.
Fertilizer: 5-10-5.
Propagation: Sow seeds in
winter or divide roots of
established clumps in spring.
Uses: Back of beds and borders,
wild and woodland gardens,
at the shady edge of a pond.

CLEMATIS
(KLEHM-ah-tiss)
Clematis
RANUNCULACEAE; buttercup family

Height/habit: Vining or semi-woody and climbing, 3–30 ft. (1–9 m.) high/wide. Exceptions are the bush types, such as *C. heracleifolia.*

Leaves: Compound, divided, often with tendril-forming tips; usually deciduous, though there are exceptions, such as evergreen *C. armandii.*

Flowers: Closed lanterns to open bells, 1–6 in. (2.5–15 cm.) across; some starry or doubled, others flattened; all colors, including blue.

Season: Spring through fall, depending on the clematis, for example: *C. alpina* cultivars typically bloom in spring; *C. montana rubens* early summer; *C. viticella* mid- to late summer; and *C. maximowicziana,* the popular sweet autumn clematis, early fall.

When to plant: Set transplants when available, rootstocks immediately on receipt from nursery. Clematis need a season to take hold. Cold- and heat-tolerant zones 3–9. Prune back in spring the old growth from clematis that bloom on the current season's shoots. Prune out in spring only the dead or straggly growth from any clematis to bloom on wood formed the previous season.

Light: Sunny to half-sunny for the clematis vine, shady for its roots.

Soil: Well drained, well dug, and enlivened by yearly top-dressing with well-rotted compost; add limestone as needed to afford the preferred "sweet," or alkaline, soil.

Fertilizer: 5-10-5.

Propagation: Layer, take stem cuttings, divide, or sow seeds in fall or spring.

Uses: Cover for fence, arbor, trellis, or tepee.

CLERODENDRUM
(klair-oh-DEN-drum)
Glory-bower
VERBENACEAE; verbena family

Height/habit: Bushes or twining vines to 15 ft. (4.5 m.)
high/wide, but much smaller if
grown in pots. The twiners,
such as bleeding-heart vine
(*C. thomsoniae*), are readily
trained on a trellis or arbor and
require only occasional pruning to remove dead wood and
bloomed-out branches.
Leaves: Oval or heart-shaped,
to 10 in. (25 cm.) long/wide,
some giving off a pungent
smell when disturbed.
Flowers: Showy heads to 6 in.
(15 cm.) or more across; white,
pink, rose, blue, or scarlet;
C. fragrans notably fragrant.
Season: Summer through fall
or winter through spring,
depending on the climate and
the species. *C. thomsoniae* is an
outstanding summer per-
former outdoors, but it can also
bloom indoors in winter.
When to plant: Set transplants
when available. *C. bungei* colonizes well along the Gulf Coast.
C. thomsoniae, C. speciossissima,
and numerous other species
are ground-hardy in zone 9;
elsewhere they respond well to
container culture, especially if
placed outdoors in warm
weather. *C. trichotomum,*
whose fragrant white blooms
appear mid- to late summer
and are followed by showy blue
berries, overwinters in the
ground zones 6–7.
Light: Half-sunny to half-shady.
Soil: Humusy, well drained,
moist.
Fertilizer: 14-14-14 timed-
release or 30-10-10.
Propagation: Take root or stem
cuttings in spring or summer.
Uses: Borders, pots, cover for
trellis or arbor.

COREOPSIS
(koh-ree-OPP-siss)
Tickseed
COMPOSITAE; daisy family

Height/habit: Clumps 1–3 ft.
(30–90 cm.) high/wide.
Leaves: Deeply cut and variable
from the base of the plant to
the flowering upper parts;
3–6 in. (7.5–15 cm.) long; very
narrow in the thread-leaved
C. verticillata and its offspring.
Flowers: Single or double
daisies atop wiry, graceful
stems; each flower 1–2 in. (2.5–5
cm.) across; all yellows, also
pink in *C. rosea*. Deadheading
is a boon to longer bloom life
in many plants of this genus.
Season: Late spring through
summer.

When to plant: Set transplants
when available; sow seeds
indoors 8–12 weeks before
warm, planting-out weather
for blooms the same season
from newer hybrid strains.
Widely cold- and heat-tolerant
zones 3–10.
Light: Sunny to half-sunny.
Soil: Well drained, moist; tolerates drought after established.
Fertilizer: 5-10-5.
Propagation: Divide or sow
seeds in spring or fall; alternatively, root airborne plantlets
that form following bloom in
some species.
Uses: Beds, borders, pots,
cut flowers.

DELPHINIUM
(dell-FINN-ee-um)
Perennial Larkspur
RANUNCULACEAE; buttercup family

Height/habit: Among the garden's strongest vertical spire flowers, 3–8 ft. (1–2.4 m.). Staking required for all except the dwarfs.

Leaves: Deeply cut, most clustered in a clump at the base of the plant.

Flowers: Each to 2 in. (5 cm.) across, growing in florets, arranged all around the stems to several feet high. Prompt deadheading of the main spikes, followed by side-dressing the clumps with 5-10-5 fertilizer and watering, results in a bonus second flowering.

Season: Winter through spring in mild-winter regions, such as Southern California and along the Gulf Coast; summer zones 3–7.

When to plant: Set transplants when available, usually fall through winter in mild regions, spring elsewhere. Treat as annuals zones 8 and warmer, though they might possibly grow as perennials zones 3–7. However, they are rarely long-lived under the best of conditions in these zones.

Light: Sunny to half-sunny.

Soil: Well drained, moist.

Fertilizer: 5-10-5.

Propagation: Take cuttings of strong new shoots from the base of a particular variety in spring or sow fresh seeds late summer through early fall.

Uses: Beds, backs of borders, cut flowers.

DIANTHUS
(deye-ANTH-us)

Pink

CARYOPHYLLACEAE; pink family

Height/habit: Mat-forming,
ground-hugging plants 3–8 in.
(7.5–20 cm.) high/wide, with
densely packed, spiky leaves are
later smothered over the top
with flowers, to 2–3 ft. (61–90
cm.) high/wide, some created
for the cut-flower trade, others
naturally higher, notably the
yellow *D. knappii*.

Leaves: Narrow blades or
grasslike, often blue-green or
gray, to 2 in. (5 cm.) long.

Flowers: Single or double, to 3
in. (7.5 cm.) across, often laced
or deeply cut at the edges;
white, pink, rose, red, yellow,
often bicolored; some clove-
scented; *D. plumarius* is cottage
pink. Deadheading encourages
more blooms.

Season: Spring through
summer.

When to plant: Set transplants
when available. Perennials best
zones 4–8. In warmer zones,
especially those with high
humidity, dianthus are sometimes set out as year-old transplants, for blooms that season
as annuals.

Light: Sunny.

Soil: Well drained, moist to on
the dry side.

Fertilizer: 5-10-5.

Propagation: Set stem cuttings
to root in clean, sharp, moist
sand in spring or summer.

Uses: Beds, borders, rock and
wall gardens, pots, cut flowers.

DICENTRA
(deye-CENT-rah)

Bleeding Heart; Turkey Corn; Dutchman's breeches

FUMARIACEAE; fumitory family

Height/habit: Upright, arching clumps, 1–3 ft. (30–90 cm.) high/wide.
Leaves: Intricately cut and divided, 1–3 ft. (30–90 cm.).
Flowers: Nodding, heart- or pantaloon-shaped, each to 1 in. (2.5 cm.), on a graceful raceme; white, pink, rose, burgundy, or purple.
Season: Turkey corn (*D. eximia*) is attractive the longest time, spring through summer. Dutchman's-breeches (*D. cucullaria*) and bleeding heart (*D. spectabilis*) are for spring and early summer.
When to plant: Set transplants when available. Generally grown zones 3–9; the yellow-flowered, tendril-climbing *D. scandens* is for zones 6–9.
Light: Half-sunny to half-shady.
Soil: Humusy, well drained, moist.
Fertilizer: 5-10-5.
Propagation: Divide or sow seeds in fall (those self-sown often yield serendipitous results).
Uses: Beds; borders; rock, wall, and wild gardens; outdoor pots.

DICTAMNUS
(dick-TAM-nuss)

Gas Plant

RUTACEAE; rue family

Height/habit: Self-reliant, upright clumps, 2–4 ft. (61–122 cm.) high/wide.
Leaves: Glossy, lemon-scented, compound, 9–11 leaflets to 3 in. (7.5 cm.) long.
Flowers: To 1 in. (2.5 cm.) across in terminal clusters; white, pink, purplish rose.
Season: Early to midsummer. Leaves often die off by late summer, at which time they may be cut and removed to the compost pile.
When to plant: Set transplants when available. Long-lived in cold climates, best for zones 4–7.
Light: Sunny to partly shady.
Soil: Well drained, moist to on the dry side; tolerates drought after it is established.
Fertilizer: 5-10-5.
Propagation: Take root cuttings in spring or sow seeds in fall.
Uses: Beds, borders.

DIGITALIS
(dij-ih-TAY-liss)

Foxglove

SCROPHULARIACEAE; figwort family

Height/habit: First-year leaves in rosettes, to 1 ft. (30 cm.) high/wide. The second season a flower stalk rises from the center, 2–8 ft. (61–240 cm.) high.
Leaves: Hairy, gray-green, in a basal cluster.
Flowers: Tubular, as in the fingers of a glove; each flower 3 in. (7.5 cm.) long, growing on stalks 1–4 ft. (30–122 cm.) high; white, cream, yellow, pink, rose, or apricot. Prompt deadheading of the main spike results in a beautiful second flowering.
Season: Spring zones 9 and warmer; late spring through summer in cooler regions.
When to plant: Set transplants when available. Digitalis is at best a short-lived perennial, often treated as a biennial. Self-sows satisfactorily under favorable conditions and might even colonize a semiwild area.
Light: Half-sunny to shady.
Soil: Humusy, well drained, moist.
Fertilizer: 5-10-5.
Propagation: Divide roots in early fall or sow seeds in late summer.
Uses: Beds, borders, pots, cut flowers.

ECHINACEA
(eck-ih-NAY-see-ah)

Purple Coneflower

COMPOSITAE; daisy family

Height/habit: Upright to sprawling, 2–4 ft. (61–122 cm.) high/wide.

Leaves: Coarse ovals, mostly at the base, 2–6 in. (5–15 cm.) long.

Flowers: Single daisies 3–5 in. (7.5–12.5 cm.) across, with showy ray flowers surrounding a raised, brown-purple disk; white, pale to dark pink, rosy purple.

Season: Summer to fall.

When to plant: Set transplants when available or sow seeds at the beginning of a growing season, for blooms in a year or so. Cold-hardy zones 3–9.

Light: Sunny to half-sunny.

Soil: Well drained, moist to on the dry side; established plants tolerate drought.

Fertilizer: 5-10-5.

Propagation: Divide or sow seeds. The species *E. purpurea* and *E. pallida*, for example, are smaller and more graceful than the modern cultivars that are larger all around and more assertively upright.

Uses: Beds, borders, pots, cut flowers.

ECHINOPS
(ECK-ih-nopps)

Globe-thistle; Hedgehog Flower

COMPOSITAE; daisy family

Height/habit: Erect, to 5 ft. (1.5 m.) high by 2–3 ft. (61–90 cm.) wide.

Leaves: Coarse, thistlelike, 6–8 in. (15–20 cm.) long; variously spiny, set opposite along pale green to downy white stems.

Flowers: Round, spiny heads (echinops means "hedgehog-like"), 1–2 in. (2.5–5 cm.) across; blue, silvery blue, or white.

Season: Mid- to late summer.

When to plant: Set transplants when available, in clumps of 3 or more. Cold- and heat-tolerant zones 3–9.

Light: Sunny.

Soil: Well drained, moist to on the dry side. Tolerates drought when established.

Fertilizer: 5-10-5.

Propagation: Divide spring or fall or sow seeds for first blooms the second season.

Uses: Borders, backgrounds, large pots, cut flowers.

EPIMEDIUM
(eppy-MEE-dee-um)

Barrenwort

BERBERIDACEAE; barberry family

Height/habit: Spreading-upright, low-growing, 1–1.5 ft. (30–45 cm.) high/wide.

Leaves: Lance- to heart-shaped, 2–5 in. (5–12.5 cm.) long/wide; often burnished red in the spring; variously deciduous or evergreen in climates with mild winters.

Flowers: Delicate, airy, each 1–2 in. (2.5–5 cm.) across; white, violet, pink, red, yellow, purple, or orange, often with spur in contrasting color.

Season: Early to midspring.

When to plant: Set transplants when available. Variously cold-tolerant zones 3–5; heat-tolerant through zone 9.

Light: Half-sunny to half-shady.

Soil: Humusy, well drained, moist.

Fertilizer: 5-10-5.

Propagation: Divide in spring or fall.

Uses: Beds, borders, rock gardens, shady wild gardens, ground cover.

ERYNGIUM
(uhr-IN-jee-um)

Sea Holly

UMBELLIFERAE; parsley or carrot family

Height/habit: Upright to sprawling, 1–4 ft. (30–122 cm.) high by half as wide.

Leaves: Spiny, thistlelike, 6–12 in. (15–30 cm.) long; often heart-shaped at the base, lobed or hand-shaped up toward the flowering parts; green to blue-gray, some with showy white veining.

Flowers: Resemble thistles; 1-in.- (2.5-cm.-) wide cones surrounded by 2–4-in.- (5–10-cm.-) wide bracts; blue to steel-blue and silvery.

Season: Mid- to late summer.

When to plant: Set transplants when available. Cold- and heat-tolerant zones 4–8.

Light: Sunny.

Soil: Well drained, moist to on the dry side.

Fertilizer: 5-10-5.

Propagation: Sow seed in spring or take root cuttings in late winter.

Uses: Borders, cottage gardens, cutting for dried bouquets.

EUPATORIUM
(yew-pah-TOH-ree-um)

Boneset;
Mist Flower;
Hardy Ageratum;
Joe-pye Weed;
White Snakeroot

COMPOSITAE; daisy family

Height/habit: Upright bushes, 2–3 ft. (61–90 cm.); hardy ageratum, or mist flower (*E. coelstinum*), 3–4 ft. (1–1.2 m.); white snakeroot (*E. rugosum*), 8–10 ft. (2.4–3 m.); joe-pye weed (*E. fistulosum*), 6–10 ft. (1.8–3 m.) by half as wide.

Leaves: Lance-shaped, 3–12 in. (7.5–30 cm.) long; opposite or whorled, coarse texture.

Flowers: Fuzzy, growing in rounded or flat-topped clusters, 4–6 in. (10–15 cm.) across, over the tops of the plants; white, blue-violet, red-violet, pinkish lavender.

Season: Late summer through fall.

When to plant: Set transplants when available. Cold-tolerant zones 2–3, heat-tolerant zones 8–9.

Light: Sunny to half-shady.

Soil: Humusy, well drained, moist. Tolerates drought when established.

Fertilizer: 5-10-5.

Propagation: Divide in spring.

Uses: Borders; cottage, meadow, butterfly, and wild gardens; cut flowers; ageratum also for pots.

EUPHORBIA
(yew-FOR-bee-ah)
Cypress Spurge
EUPHORBIACEAE; spurge family

Height/habit: *E. cyparissias* upright to sprawling or spreading, 1–6 ft. (30–180 cm.) high/wide.

Leaves: Narrow, lance- to spear-shaped, in the manner of some long-needled conifers; 1–4 in. (2–10 cm.) long.

Flowers: Inconspicuous in terminal clusters, surrounded by yellowish green bracts, 2–4 in. (5–10 cm.) across, that scintillate in the sun.

Season: Spring through early summer.

When to plant: Set transplants when available. Variously cold-hardy zones 3–8; heat-tolerant zone 9, but not successful with heat and high humidity together. The genus contains thousands of species, some weeds, some ornamentals adapted to nearly every climate and garden.

Light: Sunny to half-shady.

Soil: Well drained, moist to on the dry side; some very drought-tolerant when established.

Fertilizer: 5-10-5.

Propagation: Divide in spring, taking care not to harm the roots. Or sow seed in late winter through early spring.

Uses: Beds, borders, rock gardens, pots.

GAURA
(GARR-ah)

Wild Honeysuckle

ONAGRACEAE; evening-primrose family

Height/habit: Bushy and upright to sprawling, 2–4 ft. (61–122 cm.) high/wide.
Leaves: Lance-shaped, to 3 in. (7.5 cm.) long, mostly toward the base of the plant.
Flowers: Each to 1 in. (2.5 cm.) across, growing mothlike on long, wiry stems; white changing to pink in a day, then disappearing. Cutting back flowered-out stalks encourages more blooms.

Season: Summer through fall.
When to plant: Set transplants when available. Cold- and heat-tolerant zones 6–9; better suited to drier climates than those likely to be humid and hot at the same time.
Light: Sunny.
Soil: Well drained, moist to on the dry side. Tolerates drought when established.
Fertilizer: 5-10-5.
Propagation: Sow seeds in spring. Allow several years for a gaura plant to hit its stride.
Uses: Beds, borders, pots, Xeriscape.

GERANIUM
(juh-RAY-nee-um)
Cranesbill
GERANIACEAE; geranium family

Height/habit: Bushy and upright to trailing/sprawling, 4–24 in. (10–61 cm.) high/wide. Staking or brushing helpful for the higher species.

Leaves: Many-lobed, often toothed and hairy, some evergreen.

Flowers: 5-petaled, saucer-shaped, 1–2 in. (2.5–5 cm.) across; white, pink, rose, violet, blue, purple, often with veining in a contrasting color. Shearing after first flowering encourages a second bloom. Also grown for beaklike seed heads.

Season: Spring, summer, or fall, some in 2 seasons.

When to plant: Set transplants when available. Variously cold-hardy zones 4–5, heat-tolerant zones 8–9.

Light: Sunny to shady, depending on the species and the local conditions; the hotter the summer the more shade.

Soil: Humusy, well drained, moist.

Fertilizer: 5-10-5.

Propagation: Divide or take stem and root cuttings in spring or early fall. Sow seeds in winter for blooms in 2 years.

Uses: Beds, borders, pots, wild and rock gardens.

HELIOPSIS
(hee-lee-OPP-siss)

Oxeye

COMPOSITAE; daisy family

Height/habit: Upright, 3–5 ft. (1–1.5 m.) high/wide. Brush staking as shoots emerge in spring results in self-reliant high plants later on.
Leaves: Coarsely toothed, rounded lance- to egg-shaped, to 5 in. (12.5 cm.) long.
Flowers: Big, brassy single or semidouble daisies, 2–4 in. (5–10 cm.) across; saturated yellow or golden-orange. Deadheading increases bloom and creates a tidy appearance.
Season: Summer into fall.

When to plant: Set transplants when available. Cold- and heat-tolerant zones 4–9.
Light: Sunny.
Soil: Well drained, moist to on the dry side.
Fertilizer: 5-10-5.
Propagation: Divide in spring or fall or sow seeds winter through spring; some cultivars come true from seeds and may flower by the end of their first season.
Uses: Beds, borders (usually in middle or toward the back), large pots, cut flowers.

HELLEBORUS
(hell-lebb-OH-russ)

Christmas Rose; Lenten Rose; Stinking Hellebore

RANUNCULACEAE; buttercup family

Height/habit: Fairly tidy, compact mounds, 1–1.5 ft. (30–45 cm.) high/wide.
Leaves: Palm-shaped, deeply divided, 8–16 in. (20–40 cm.) across, lasting through winter until removed to make way for flowering and new foliage.
Flowers: Nodding bells or cups, 2–4 in. (5–10 cm.) across; white, pink, rose, purple, green.

Season: Winter through spring.
When to plant: Set transplants when available, usually spring. Christmas rose (*H. niger*) and stinking hellebore (*H. foetidus*) generally cold- and heat-tolerant zones 3–9; Lenten rose (*H. orientalis*) zones 5–9.
Light: Half-sunny to shady. The hotter the climate, the more shade helleborus needs.
Soil: Humusy, well drained, moist.
Fertilizer: 5-10-5.
Propagation: Divide or transplant self-sown seedlings in spring.
Uses: Outstanding for shade and wild gardens; also beds, borders, cut flowers.

HEMEROCALLIS
(hem-er-oh-KAY-liss)

Daylily

LILIACEAE; lily family

Height/habit: Grassy clumps, 1–4 ft. (30–122 cm.) high/wide.
Leaves: V-shaped, long, narrow, grasslike, each 1–2 ft. (30–61 cm.) long; deciduous types better in cold-winter regions, evergreen varieties in the South.
Flowers: Single or double, saucers or trumpets, some spidery, 2–8 in. (5–20 cm.) across; all colors except blue. Some are fragrant. Dead-heading does not prolong bloom but it is a morning ritual for most serious daylily growers.

Season: Midspring to early fall. Some daylilies bloom only once a year, but the breeding trend is toward repeat bloomers and even toward those that bloom intermittently over a protracted season. It is the nature of the daylily to open a flower in the morning and close it forever at the end of that day. Modern hybrids may open the evening before and remain into the evening of the following day, or even stay open for two days.
When to plant: Set transplants when available. Daylilies are often sold in pots or right in the field where they can be selected, dug, and moved while in bloom. Cold- and heat-tolerant zones 3–9.
Light: Sunny to half-sunny. Too much shade reduces or rules out bloom in daylilies.

Soil: Well drained, moist to on the dry side. Tolerates drought when established, especially so when not actively budding and blooming.
Fertilizer: 5-10-5.
Propagation: Divide in early spring or immediately following bloom. Seeds started in the spring may give some bloom in the second season.
Uses: Beds, borders, miniatures in pots, ground cover.

HEUCHERA
(HEW-kur-ah)
Coralbells; Alumroot

SAXIFRAGACEAE; saxifrage family

Height/habit: Low, mounding plants, 1–3 ft. (30–90 cm.) high/wide, often with the main mass of foliage concentrated at the lower third of the total height.

Leaves: Rounded to heart-shaped, lobed and scalloped, often toothed; 1–6 in. (2.5–15 cm.) in diameter; usually dark evergreen, except notably dark purple in *H. micrantha* 'Palace Purple' and purple-veined in alumroot (*H. americana* 'Sunset').

Flowers: Tiny, growing in panicles that are 6–12 in. (15–30 cm.) long, carried well above the foliage mass on graceful, hairy stems; white, pink, rose, red, or scarlet. Remove the flowering stems when bloom finishes to play up the tidy aspects of the heuchera plant.

Season: Late spring through early summer, except hairy alumroot (*H. villosa*) in late summer through fall.

When to plant: Set transplants when available. Cold- and heat-tolerant zones 4–9.

Light: Sun to half shade; the hotter the climate, the greater heuchera's need for shade in summer.

Soil: Humusy, well drained, moist.

Fertilizer: 5-10-5.

Propagation: Divide in spring or fall. Sow seeds in spring for nice-sized transplants the following year and blooms the next.

Uses: Beds; borders; pots; shade, rock, and wild gardens.

HOSTA
(HOSS-tah)

Plaintain Lily

LILIACEAE; lily family

Height/habit: Upright, arching clumps or curving mounds, 1–3 ft. (30–90 cm.) high and as wide or wider, with flowers in season rising above.

Leaves: Varying from narrow lance or linear shapes to broad hearts with elegant vein quilting, from 6–12 in. (15–30 cm.) long/wide; all greens, from chartreuse to bluish, also gold and silvery white, in endless variations. Slugs and snails are a perennial problem. Treat as necessary to maintain healthy leaves.

Flowers: Funnel-shaped, 1–3 in. (2.5–7.5 cm.) long; white, pale to violet-blue or lavender; some fragrant, notably *H. plantaginea*. Some growers of the more highly variegated hostas prefer to remove the flowering stalks before they bloom.

Season: Spring until fall for foliage. Late spring through early summer until early fall for flowers—the season depending on the variety. Almost all year in mildest regions, although long, hot, humid summers are not beneficial.

When to plant: Set transplants when available. Often sold in nursery pots fully grown, even in bloom, so that it's possible to create instant effects. Cold- and heat-tolerant zones 3–9.

Light: Sunny in cooler climates to shady in the hottest.

Soil: Humusy, well drained, moist. Surprisingly drought-tolerant when established.

Fertilizer: 14-14-14 timed-release; or side-dress with well-rotted compost.

Propagation: Divide in spring or fall. Hostas can be subdivided fairly rapidly to plant an area with ground cover, but it is also true that they grow best if left undisturbed.

Uses: Beds, borders, pots, wild and shade gardens; leaves and flowers for arranging.

HOUTTUYNIA
(who-TEN-ee-ah)

Houttuynia

SAURURACEAE; lizard's-tail family

Height/habit: Spreading ground cover, 6–18 in. (15–45 cm.) high/wide.
Leaves: Heart-shaped, to 3 in. (7.5 cm.) long/wide; when crushed, yield odor that is unpleasant to some; variegated white, cream, red, and green in the cultivar *H. cordata* 'Chameleon,' also known as 'Variegata.'
Flowers: 2-in. (5-cm.) spikes, inconspicuous, somewhat showier in the double white *H. cordata* 'Flore Pleno.'
Season: Foliage variously attractive depending on the season and the climate, usually midspring through summer.

Grown in the right place, this plant can be quite successful (especially the variegated and the double-flowered types).
When to plant: Set transplants when available. Cold- and heat-tolerant zones 6-9.
Light: Sunny to part shady. Most compact in cooler climate and full sun.
Soil: Humusy, well drained, moist to wet.
Fertilizer: 14-14-14 timed-release.
Propagation: Divide or take cuttings in spring or summer.
Uses: Ground cover for a wet place (can spread to the point of being invasive), pots.

INULA
(INN-yew-lah)

Elecampane

COMPOSITAE; daisy family

Height/habit: Upright or sprawling, reaching 2–6 ft. (61–180 cm.), with masses of coarse leaves toward the base, crowned in season by green-collared and often showy golden daisies.
Leaves: Oblong to elliptical, 6 in. (15 cm.) long, as in *I. hookeri*, to 2 ft. (61 cm.) long, as in *I. helenium*; clustered toward the base, often thinning or disappearing entirely from the flowering stalks.
Flowers: Single daisies, 2–6 in. (5–15 cm.) across; all yellows, from pale to dark; very responsive to deadheading.

Season: Summer through fall.
When to plant: Set transplants when available. Sword-leaf inula (*I. ensifolia*) and *I. helenium* cold- and heat-tolerant zones 3–9; other species zones 4–8, excepting Himalayan elecampane (*I. royleana*), suited only to the cooler zones 3–7.
Light: Sunny.
Soil: Well drained, moist.
Fertilizer: 5-10-5.
Propagation: Divide in spring or fall or sow seeds in spring.
Uses: Beds, borders, wild and meadow gardens, large pots, cut flowers.

IPOMOPSIS
(ipp-oh-MOPP-siss)

Standing Cypress

POLEMONIACEAE; phlox family

Height/habit: Slender, leafy
stalks crowned by torches
of flowers reaching 4–6 ft.
(1.2–1.8 m.).
Leaves: Finely dissected, 4–6 in.
(10–15 cm.) long/wide, growing
in a basal rosette the first year,
on strongly vertical stems in
the second.
Flowers: Tubular, each to
1 in. (2.5 cm.) long, blooming
in profusion; orange-red or
apricot.
Season: Summer: early in hot
climates, later in cool.
When to plant: Set transplants
when available. Seedlings
started the first year bloom the
next and die. Colonizes readily
in the right site and performs
as a self-reliant perennial.
Light: Sunny.
Soil: Well drained, moist to on
the dry side.
Fertilizer: 5-10-5.
Propagation: Sow seeds in
spring or summer.
Uses: Beds, borders, pots,
wild and meadow gardens,
Xeriscape.

IRIS
(EYE-riss)

Flag; Fleur-de-lis

IRIDACEAE; iris family

Height/habit: Upright, tidy fountains of grassy leaves in the highly rated Siberian iris (*I. sibirica*), 2–4 ft. (61–122 cm.) high, nearly as wide; short, perky fans in the native woodland dwarf crested iris (*I. cristata*), 6–9 in. (15–22.5 cm.) high/wide; evergreen clumps to 2 ft. (61 cm.) high/wide in the unfortunately named stinking iris (*I. foetidissima*); leaves odorous when crushed but pale violet flowers are followed by long-lasting, showy red berries.

Leaves: Swordlike or similar to blades of grass, 9–30 in. (22.5–76 cm.) long, mostly 1 in. (2.5 cm.) wide or less; bluish to dark green, some evergreen.

Flowers: Fleur-de-lis-shaped, 2–5 in. (5–12.5 cm.) across; most colors; some fragrant.

Season: Spring through early summer.

When to plant: Set transplants when available. Siberian iris rated cold- and heat-tolerant zones 3–9 ('Caesar's Brother' performs well along the Gulf Coast); *I. foetidissima* is for zones 7–9; *I. cristata* zones 4–8.

Light: Sunny, except part to full shade for *I. cristata*.

Soil: Well drained, moist; on the dry side acceptable after flowering, when established.

Fertilizer: 5-10-5.

Propagation: Divide in early spring or late summer.

Uses: Beds, borders, ground covers, pots.

JASMINUM
(JAZZ-min-um)

Jasmine

OLEACEAE; olive family

Height/habit: Twining or shrubby vines, 5–30 ft. (1.5–9 m.) high/wide.

Leaves: Simple or pinnate, 3–6 in. (7.5–15 cm.) long, often glossy and evergreen. *J. nudiflorum* deciduous and flowers (yellow) while leafless.

Flowers: Borne singly or in clusters, each 1–2 in. (2.5–5 cm.) across; slender tube flaring into corolla with 4–9 lobes; there are also doubles and hose-in-hose types; white or yellow; usually fragrant.

Season: Almost any time of year, depending on the kind of jasmine and weather conditions. *J. polyanthum* blooms white blushed with pink in mild-climate winter through spring, in gardens or cool

greenhouses. 'Maid of Orleans' blooms all year, especially well through warm weather. *J. tortuosum* blooms with starry white flowers all year and will quickly cover a trellis or lace over and around an arbor.

When to plant: Set transplants when available. *J. nudiflorum* cold-hardy zones 6–7, heat-tolerant zones 8–9. Grow tropical and subtropical species in pots or outdoors zones 8–9 and warmer.

Light: Sunny to half-sunny.

Soil: Humusy, well drained, moist.

Fertilizer: 5-10-5.

Propagation: Take cuttings of half-mature wood in spring or summer.

Uses: Cover for trellis, arbor, or tepee.

JUSTICIA
(juss-TIH-see-ah)

Shrimp Plant; King's Crown

ACANTHACEAE; acanthus family

Height/habit: Upright, branching tropical American shrubs, 3–5 (1–1.5 m.) ft. high, capable of spreading to similar width.

Leaves: Oval, hairy, 2–12 in. (5–30 cm.) long and nearly as wide, often with prominent midveins, in opposite pairs along square stems. Foliage can also be boldly textured for interesting contrast.

Flowers: Showy clusters, so dense on shrimp plant (*J. brandegeana*) that its leaves are hidden by bracts of salmon pink, chartreuse, or lemon yellow; appearing as a plume of feathery pink or white at top of king's crown (*J. carnea* and varieties); in yellow king's crown (*J. aurea*), flowers yellow and larger.

Season: Primarily warm-weather plants. Shrimp plant can bloom all year in mild-climate gardens, making an unexpected show at midspring.
When to plant: Set transplants when available. Freshly rooted cuttings form the best flowering plants each new season. Container and bedding plants zones 8 and colder. Zones 9 and warmer they live in the garden through winter, surviving from the roots in all but exceptionally cold years.
Light: Sunny to half-shady; more shade in the hotter climates.
Soil: Humusy, well drained, moist throughout the active growing season.
Fertilizer: 14-14-14 timed-release, 5-10-5 at flowering.
Propagation: Take stem cuttings in spring or summer.
Uses: Pots, beds, borders, cottage gardens.

LAMIUM
(LAY-mee-um)
Dead Nettle
LABIATAE; mint family

Height/habit: Trailing plants to 2 ft. (61 cm.), sprawling in *L. galeobdolon* (yellow flowers), tidier in *L. maculatum* and its cultivated forms, 1–1.5 ft. (30–45 cm.) high/wide.
Leaves: Simple, toothed, set opposite along square stems; often variegated paler green, silvery, or yellow.
Flowers: To 1 in. (2.5 cm.) across, in whorls at the upper leaf axils; white, yellow, pink, or purple.
Season: Flowers late spring through summer. However, light shearing after flowering concentrates energy on the foliage, an important part of lamium's appeal.
When to plant: Set transplants when available.
Light: Half-sunny to half-shady.
Soil: Humusy, well drained, moist.
Fertilizer: 14-14-14 timed-release at the time of planting, possibly 5-10-5 at start of next flowering season.
Propagation: Take stem cuttings spring through early summer; divide spring or fall.
Uses: Ground cover under trees and shrubs, shade or wild gardens, pots.

LAVANDULA
(lah-VAN-dew-lah)

Lavender

LABIATAE; mint family

Height/habit: Small shrubs,
1–3 ft. (30–90 cm.) high/wide.
Leaves: Narrow and spiky or
broader and cut fernlike, 1–2 in.
(2.5–5 cm.) long; grayish to
blue-green.
Flowers: Very small in packed
spikes, 1–3 in. (2.5–7.5 cm.)
long, growing above the foliage;
English lavender (*L. officinalis*)
is true lavender color. French
lavender (*L. stoechas*) has
showy purple bracts.
Season: Spring and again in fall
if cut back after blooming;
year-round in mild climates.
When to plant: Set transplants
when available. English lavender is hardly a stranger to most
gardeners, yet its cold and heat
tolerance as a garden plant is
through zones 7–8—perhaps 9
if the climate is dry. The other
lavenders are grown outdoors
all year zones 8–10, elsewhere
in pots brought indoors at the
threat of freezing weather.
Light: Sunny.
Soil: Well drained, moist to on
the dry side. Tolerates drought
when established.
Fertilizer: 5-10-5.
Propagation: Divide in early
spring; sow seeds in spring
through summer, especially
those of *L. officinalis* 'Lady,' an
All-America Selections winner
that blooms the first year; take
stem cuttings late summer
through early fall.
Uses: Beds, borders, pots,
hedging, cutting fresh or dried.

LIATRIS
(leye-YAY-triss)
Gay-feather
COMPOSITAE; daisy family

Height/habit: 2–6 ft. (61–180 cm.) high and half as wide.

Leaves: Narrow, linear leaves, 6–12 in. (15–30 cm.) long, appear first in a clump, then become gradually smaller and grow farther apart as main stem shoots up.

Flowers: Straight, dense spikes, 6–12 in. (15–30 cm.) long, flowering from the top of the plant down; reddish purple or white.

Season: Late summer through early fall zones 7 and colder; often late spring through early summer in warmer zones.

When to plant: Set transplants when available. Cold-hardy zone 4; heat-tolerant through zone 9 if arid, zone 8 if moist.

Light: Sunny.

Soil: Well drained, moist to on the dry side. Tolerates drought when established.

Fertilizer: 5-10-5.

Propagation: Sow seeds or divide in early spring.

Uses: Beds, borders, wild gardens, pots, cut flowers.

LIGULARIA
(ligg-yew-LAY-ree-ah)

Leopard Plant; Silver Farfugium

COMPOSITAE; daisy family

Height/habit: Choice foliage plants 2–4 ft. (61–122 cm.) high by nearly as wide. *L. przewalskii* (possibly a hybrid with *L. stenocephala*) 'The Rocket' is an example of one with spectacular flowers as well.

Leaves: Rounded hearts, kidney shapes, or toothed lobes, 1–2 ft. (30–61 cm.) across; besides green, they can be purple, as in *L. dentata* ('Desdemona'), spotted and splashed with yellow in leopard plant (*L. tussilaginea* 'Aureo-maculata'), or edged and variegated white in silver farfugium (*L. t.* 'Argentea').

Flowers: Small "daisies" massed dramatically in the 4-ft. (1.2-m.) spires produced by 'The Rocket'; gardeners often remove the buds from leopard plant and silver farfugium since actual flowering detracts from the leaves.

Season: Mid- to late summer for flowers; foliage attractive most seasons.

When to plant: Set transplants when available. Cold- and heat-tolerant zones 4–8, except zones 8 and warmer for leopard plant and silver farfugium.

Light: Half-sunny for flowering types ('The Rocket'), mostly shade for foliage types.

Soil: Humusy, moist to wet.

Fertilizer: 14-14-14 timed-release when planting, 5-10-5 later only to encourage bloom.

Propagation: Divide in spring.

Uses: Bold feature in a wet site with afternoon shade. Leopard plant and silver farfugium do well in large pots in shade.

LOBELIA
(loh-BEE-lee-ah)

Cardinal Flower; Great Blue Lobelia

LOBELIACEAE; lobelia family

Height/habit: Tidy basal rosettes rise into slender flowering columns, 4–6 ft. (1.2–1.8 m.) high by 1 ft. (30 cm.) wide.

Leaves: Egg- to lance-shaped, 4–6 in. (10–15 cm.) long; some have reddish purple foliage and stems.

Flowers: Prominently 3-lobed at the bottom and distinctly spiky at the top, 1–2 in. (2.5–5 cm.) across, in many-flowered spikes; red in cardinal flower (*L. cardinalis*), light blue in great blue lobelia (*L. siphilitica*). Permit seed heads to develop, in the interest of fostering self-sown seedlings.

Season: Mid- to late summer, early fall.

When to plant: Set transplants when available. Cardinal flower cold- and heat-tolerant zones 2–9; great blue lobelia, zones 4–8.

Light: Half-sunny to shady.

Soil: Humusy, well drained, moist to wet.

Fertilizer: 5-10-5.

Propagation: Divide or sow seeds in spring; divide or take stem cuttings midsummer.

Uses: Beds, borders, stream-side, wild and meadow gardens, pots, cut flowers.

LONICERA
(lonn-ISS-er-ah)

Honeysuckle

CAPRIFOLIACEAE; honeysuckle family

Height/habit: Shrubs or vines, from 3 to 80 ft. (1-24 m.) high/wide.

Leaves: Opposite pairs, 1–2 in. (2.5–5 cm.) long; joined together at the base so as to appear they are one with the flowering stem passing through; some blue-green, also evergreen.

Flowers: Tubular, 1–6 in. (2.5–15 cm.), in clusters; white, yellow, pink, purple, rose, or red; some of the most fragrant are *L. fragrantissima*, *L. hildebrandtiana*, *L. japonica*, *L. nitida*, *L. periclymenum* (especially in the variety 'Belgica'), and *L. pileata*.

Season: Spring to fall, some everblooming.

When to plant: Set transplants when available. There are locally adapted varieties having fragrant flowers and acceptable garden manners for almost every cold and heat zone. Zones 5–9 *L. fragrantissima* and *L. periclymenum*; 4–9 *L. japonica*; zone 9 *L. hilde-brandtiana*.

Light: Sunny to half-sunny.

Soil: Well drained, moist to on the dry side.

Fertilizer: 5-10-5.

Propagation: Take stem cuttings or layer spring or summer.

Uses: Ground cover; cover for trellis, arbor, or fence; shrub-bery border; wild and cottage gardens; cut flowers.

LUPINUS
(loo-PEYE-nus)

Lupine; Texas Bluebonnet

LEGUMINOSAE; pea family

Height/habit: Concentrated clumps, 1–2 ft. (30–61 cm.) high/wide.

Leaves: Fingerlike leaflets, 6–12 in. (15–30 cm.) long, silky-hairy in some.

Flowers: Similar to those of butterfly pea, to 1 in. (2.5 cm.) across, densely and orderly packed along high spikes, 1–2 ft. (30–61 cm.) long; all colors, many bicolors, strong in pastels, clear blues, oranges, and pinks.

Season: Spring through summer.

When to plant: Set transplants when available. Cold- and heat-tolerant zones 4–7, although not by nature long-lived under the best of conditions. Often treated as spring-flowering annuals, zones 8–9.

Light: Sunny.

Soil: Well drained, moist to on the dry side.

Fertilizer: 5-10-5.

Propagation: Sow seeds winter through spring; divide roots carefully in early spring.

Uses: Beds, borders, large pots, wild and meadow gardens, cut flowers.

LYCHNIS
(LISH-niss; LIKE-niss)

Campion

CARYOPHYLLACEAE; pink family

Height/habit: Clump-forming
or trailing, 1.5–4 ft. (45–122 cm.)
high/wide.
Leaves: Egg-, linear-, or lance-
shaped, to 6 in. (15 cm.) long;
woolly gray in *L. coronaria* and
L. flos-jovis.
Flowers: Borne singly or clustered, each 1–2 in. (2.5–5 cm.)
across; red scarlet, pink, white,
rose, magenta, or orange.
Season: Summer.

When to plant: Set transplants
when available. Cold- and heat-
tolerant zones 4–8, 9 if not too
hot and humid.
Light: Sunny to partly sunny.
Soil: Well drained, moist.
Fertilizer: 5-10-5.
Propagation: Divide in spring
or fall; alternatively, take basal
cuttings in spring or sow seeds
in late spring.
Uses: Beds, borders, pots,
cut flowers; cottage, wild, or
meadow gardens.

LYSIMACHIA
(leye-sim-ACK-ee-ah)

Loosestrife; Creeping Jennie

PRIMULACEAE; primrose family

Height/habit: Trailing in creeping Jennie (*L. nummularia*) and *L. procumbens*, to 8 in. (20 cm.) high x 2 ft. (61 cm.) wide; upright in gooseneck loosestrife (*L. clethroides*) and the yellow *L. punctata*, 2–3 ft. (61–90 cm.) high by half as wide.

Leaves: Egg- to spear-shaped, 4–6 in. (10–15 cm.) long.

Flowers: Very small but showy in dense spires or open spikes; white or yellow. *L. procumbens* larger, to 1 in. (2.5 cm.) across, yellow, in terminal clusters.

Season: Mostly spring for *L. procumbens*; summer for creeping Jennie and gooseneck and yellow loosestrife.

When to plant: Set transplants when available. Cold- and heat-tolerant zones 3–4 to zones 8–9, except *L. procumbens*, zones 8–9, well-suited to container gardening in cold climates.

Light: Sunny to partly shady.

Soil: Humusy, well drained, moist.

Fertilizer: 5-10-5.

Propagation: Divide or take stem cuttings spring or fall.

Uses: Beds, borders, pots, cut flowers; wild and bog gardens. Inclined to being invasive; beautiful when well managed. Creeping Jennie used primarily for foliage effect as a ground cover or spilling from a hanging basket.

MALVA
(MAL-vah)
Mallow
MALVACEAE; mallow family

Height/habit: Upright, 2–4 ft. (61–122 cm.) high/wide.
Leaves: Lobed or dissected, 6–12 in. (15–30 cm.) across.
Flowers: Distinctively lobed and notched, 1–2 in. (2.5–5 cm.) across; white to rose pink and lavender with purple veins.
Season: Late spring through fall.
When to plant: Set transplants when available. Cold- and heat-tolerant zones 3–4 to 8–9.
Light: Sunny in cooler climates to half-shady in warmer.
Soil: Well drained, moist.
Fertilizer: 5-10-5.
Propagation: Divide in spring or fall; take cuttings of basal shoots in spring.
Uses: Beds, borders, cottage and wild gardens, pots.

MACLEAYA
(mack-LAY-ah)
Plume Poppy
PAPAVERACEAE; poppy family

Height/habit: Upright clumps, 8–10 ft. (2.4–3 m.) high by half as wide. May require staking.
Leaves: Heart-shaped, lobed, to 8 in. (20 cm.) across, undersides covered with white felt.
Flowers: Petals absent, in plumes to 1 ft. (30 cm.) long; creamy, white, buff, or pink (in *M. cordata* 'Flamingo').

Season: Summer until fall.
When to plant: Set transplants when available. Cold- and heat-tolerant zones 4–9.
Light: Sunny to half-sunny.
Soil: Humusy, well drained, moist.
Fertilizer: 5-10-5.
Propagation: Divide in spring or fall; take cuttings of basal shoots in spring.
Uses: Accent, back of border, wild garden. Can be invasive.

MANDEVILLA

(man-duh-VILL-ah)

Mandeville; Chilean Jasmine

APOCYNACEAE; dogbane family

Height/habit: Twining, flowering vines, 5–30 ft. (1.5–9 m.).

Leaves: Elliptic to oblong, 2–6 in. (5–15 cm.) long.

Flowers: Showy funnelforms, 2–4 in. (5–10 cm.) across the face; white, pink, cherry red, or yellow; fragrant in white Chilean jasmine (*M. laxa*).

Season: During warm, frost-free weather, which can include winter in a cold-climate green-house. Well-grown mandevillas often bloom through 3 seasons.

When to plant: Set transplants when available. Cold-hardy zone 10; elsewhere grow as con-tainer plants that can be brought to a warm place when outdoor temperatures drop below 50°F (10°C).

Light: Sunny to half-sunny.

Soil: Humusy, well drained, moist.

Fertilizer: 14-14-14 timed-release; 5-10-5 at flowering time.

Propagation: Take stem cuttings in spring or summer.

Uses: Cover for trellis, fence, or tepee.

MISCANTHUS
(mis-KAN-thus)

Eulalia; Japanese Silver Grass

GRAMINEAE; grass family

Height/habit: Mostly upright and clump-forming, plumes rise above foliage 8–12 ft. (2.4–3.6 m.).

Leaves: Grasslike, arching, 1–2 in. (2.5–5 cm.) across; 6 in. (15 cm.) to 6 ft. (1.8 m.) long.

Flowers: Panicles or plumes, 10–15 in. (25–38 cm.) long; silvery, pale pink to red.

Season: For foliage effect almost all year. Flowers summer through fall.

When to plant: Set transplants when available. Widely and locally adapted, zones 5–9.

Light: Sunny to half-sunny.

Soil: Well drained, moist to on the dry side.

Fertilizer: 5-10-5 or 14-14-14 timed-release.

Propagation: Divide in spring. Most grasses need cutting back in early spring to clear the way for fresh new blades. Leave them standing through winter, however, for visual interest, to catch snow, and as wildlife shelter.

Uses: Beds; borders; pots; background plantings; Xeriscape; cottage, meadow, and wild gardens; seed heads for dried arrangements.

MONARDA
(mohn-ARD-ah)

Bee Balm; Oswego Tea

LABIATAE; mint family

Height/habit: *M. didyma* in upright to sprawling clumps, 2–4 ft. (61–122 cm.) high/wide.
Leaves: Egg-shaped, toothed and pointed, 3–6 in. (7.5–15 cm.) long; scented.
Flowers: Tubular, to 1 in. (2.5 cm.) long, in dense, whorled clusters; white, pink, red, lavender, or purple.

Season: Summer.
When to plant: Set transplants when available.
Light: Sunny to half-sunny.
Soil: Humusy, well drained, moist to wet. Dryness aids mildew.
Fertilizer: 5-10-5.
Propagation: Divide in spring.
Uses: Beds, borders, streamside, pots, wild and bog gardens, cut flowers. Attractive to bees, butterflies, and hummingbirds.

NEPETA
(NEPP-ett-ah)

Catmint
LABIATAE; mint family

Height/habit: Clump, mound, or bushy upright, 1–3 ft. (30–90 cm.) high/wide.
Leaves: Egg-shaped, softly toothed, to 1 in. (2.5 cm.) long.
Flowers: To 1 in. (2.5 cm.) in plentiful spikes; white, bluish lavender, or pale yellow.
Season: Summer.
When to plant: Set transplants when available. Cold- and heat-tolerant zones 3–4 to 8–9. Pale yellow *N. govaniana* is least tolerant of hot summers. *N.* x *faassenii* and cultivars 'Dropmore' and 'Six Hills Giant' best general garden plants.
Light: Sunny to partly shady.
Soil: Well drained, moist.
Fertilizer: 5-10-5.
Propagation: Divide in spring or take cuttings in summer.
Uses: Beds, borders, ground cover, pots.

NEPHROLEPIS
(nee-FROLL-e-pis)

Sword Fern; Boston Fern
POLYPODIACEAE; polypody family

Height/habit: Tidy clumps or in self-reliant colonies, 1–3 ft. (30–90 cm.) high/wide.
Leaves: Narrow arching or drooping fronds, 1–3 ft. (30–90 cm.) long; sometimes feathery in Boston fern (*N. exaltata* var. *bostoniensis*).
Season: Spring through fall; all year zone 10.
When to plant: Set transplants when available.
Light: Half-sunny to shady.
Soil: Humusy, well drained, moist.
Fertilizer: 30-10-10 or 14-14-14 timed-release.
Propagation: Divide in spring or fall.
Uses: Beds; borders; rock, shade, and wild gardens; pots; houseplant.

OENOTHERA
(ee-NOTH-er-ah)

Evening Primrose; Sun Drops

ONAGRACEAE; evening-primrose family

Height/habit: Stocky, upright to bushy, trailing, 1–3 ft. (30–90 cm.) high/wide.
Leaves: Lance-, linear-, or spoon-shaped, often clustered at the base.
Flowers: Cup-shaped, 2–5 in. (5–12.5 cm.) across; white, pink, or yellow.

Season: Summer; *O. speciosa* blooms spring in mild climates and can be invasive in any zone.
When to plant: Set transplants when available. Cold- and heat-tolerant zones 3–4 to 8–9.
Light: Sunny to half-sunny.
Soil: Well drained, moist. Tolerates drought and heat when established.
Fertilizer: 5-10-5.
Propagation: Divide or sow seeds in spring or fall.
Uses: Beds; borders; rock, wild, meadow, and cottage gardens.

PAEONIA
(pay-OH-nee-ah)
Peony
PAEONIACEAE; peony family

Height/habit: Herbaceous types form upright clumps, 1.5–3 ft. (45–90 cm.) high/wide (staking advised). Shrubby, woody, tree peonies grow upright, 6–12 ft. (1.8–3.6 m.) high/wide.

Leaves: Divided into leaflets or appearing palmate, 6–8 in. (15–45 cm.) across; finely cut, fernlike in *P. tenuifolia*.

Flowers: Bowl-shaped, single to double, 2–8 in. (5–20 cm.) across; all colors except blue; fragrant.

Season: Late spring through early summer.

When to plant: Set transplants when available, the roots of herbaceous peonies usually in the fall; set the growth eyes exactly 2 in. (5 cm.) deep in the soil. Cold-tolerant zones 3–4 to 8; not adapted for warmer zones since they afford insufficient hours of winter chilling. Site tree peonies so they are protected from morning sun and harsh northeast winds.

Light: Sunny.

Soil: Humusy, well drained, moist.

Fertilizer: 5-10-5.

Propagation: Divide roots (herbaceous types) in fall; take cuttings of ripe wood (tree peonies) in late fall through winter.

Uses: Beds, borders, edging, cottage gardens, cut flowers.

PAPAVER
(PAPP-ah-ver)
Perennial Poppy
PAPAVERACEAE; poppy family

Height/habit: Basal clumps of coarsely cut, hairy leaves, 1–2 ft. (30–61 cm.) high/wide, all but forgotten under the spectacular flowers, atop stems 24–40 in. (61–100 cm.) high.

Leaves: Dissected or lobed, 6–12 in. (15–30 cm.) long. They die down in summer, after flowering finishes.

Flowers: Bowl- or cup-shaped, 3–6 in. (7.5 –15 cm.) across; all reds and pinks to dark crimson to orange, salmon, and white.

Season: Early summer.

When to plant: Set transplants when available or divide roots late summer through early fall. Cold- and heat-tolerant zones 2–3 to 8; intolerant of hot, humid summers.

Light: Sunny.

Soil: Well drained, moist.

Fertilizer: 5-10-5.

Propagation: Divide in spring or late summer; take root cuttings winter through early spring.

Uses: Beds, borders, cut flowers.

PENSTEMON
(PEN-stem-on)
Beardtongue; Gulf Coast Penstemon
SCROPHULARIACEAE; figwort family

Height/habit: Tidy clumps of basal leaves, 6–12 in. (15–30 cm.) high/wide, except when the spikes of showy flowers appear in season, then 1.5–3 ft. (45–90 cm.) high/wide.

Leaves: Lance-shaped, linear, or rounded, 2–6 in. (5–15 cm.) long, sometimes evergreen.

Flowers: Tubular, 1–2 in. (2.5–5 cm.) long, in spikes above the larger leaves; all colors. Deadheading encourages a second, lesser flowering.

Season: Spring through summer.

PASSIFLORA
(pass-if-LOH-rah)

Passionflower

PASSIFLORACEAE; passionflower family

Height/habit: Small to large tendril-climbing vines, 10–30 ft. (3–9 m.); some native to North America, with fascinating flowers, often followed by showy or edible fruit.

Leaves: Variously lobed or not, some suggesting the shape of a bat wing, others of an outstretched hand, 1–8 in. (2.5–20 cm.) across.

Flowers: Complex, round, with filaments and corona, petals and sepals, 1–6 in. (2.5–15 cm.) across; white, pink, blue, red, greenish yellow, purple, or orange.

Season: Spring through summer; some hybrids ever-blooming in mild climates.

When to plant: Set transplants when available. 'Incense' and others are ground-hardy zones 5 and warmer; some species and cultivars cold-tolerant zones 8–9, thus suited only to pots in colder regions.

Light: Sunny to half-sunny.

Soil: Well drained, moist.

Fertilizer: 5-10-5.

Propagation: Take cuttings or sow seeds winter through spring.

Uses: Cover for trellis, arbor, fence, tepee in flower garden; pots.

When to plant: Set transplants when available. Choose locally adapted species sold nearby; cold- and heat-tolerant zones 3–4 to 8–9. Many are native to high, dry, and cold climates; other species, such as the Gulf Coast penstemon (*P. tenuis*), don't mind muggy heat; they bloom and go to seed before summer.

Light: Sunny.

Soil: Well drained, moist to on the dry side, some more drought-tolerant than others.

Fertilizer: 5-10-5.

Propagation: Divide in spring; take cuttings of nonflowering shoots in summer; sow seeds winter through spring.

Uses: Beds; borders; wild, meadow, and rock gardens; cut flowers.

PEROVSKIA
(per-OFF-skee-ah)
Russian Sage
LABIATAE; mint family

Height/habit: Shrublike, 3–5 ft. (1–1.5 m.) high/wide.

Leaves: Egg-shaped to filigree-cut, to 2 in. (5 cm.) long; often silvery; aromatic.

Flowers: Panicles of tiny blooms resemble cloud formations in the garden; lavender or purplish blue.

Season: Late summer through fall.

When to plant: Set transplants when available. Cut back sharply in the spring to encourage annual renewal. Cold- and heat-tolerant zones 5–9.

Light: Sunny.

Soil: Well drained, moist to on the dry side.

Fertilizer: 5-10-5.

Propagation: Take stem cuttings in summer.

Uses: Beds, borders, cottage gardens.

PHLOX
(FLOX)

Phlox; Moss Pink

POLEMONIACEAE; phlox family

Height/habit: Mat-forming to knee-deep spreaders to high and clump-forming, 3–48 in. (7.5–122 cm.) high, 1 ft. (30 cm.) wide or more.

Leaves: Lance- or oblong-shaped to linear, from less than 1 in. (2.5 cm.) long and needlelike in moss pink (*P. subulata*) to softly leafy, 4–6 in. (10–15 cm.) long.

Flowers: 5-lobed, tubular, to 1 in. (2.5 cm.) across, in clusters or panicles; all colors; summer phlox (*P. paniculata*) notably fragrant.

Season: Spring for native species, summer for garden phlox.

When to plant: Set transplants when available; set summer phlox root crowns while dormant, mid- to late fall. Cold- and heat-tolerant zones 4 to 8–9.

Light: Sunny to half-shady.

Soil: Well drained, moist.

Fertilizer: 5-10-5.

Propagation: Divide in spring or fall; take cuttings in summer. Seeds of hybrid phlox do not produce reliable results; it is best to deadhead phlox before seeds ripen.

Uses: Beds; borders; edging; rock, wild, and cottage gardens; cut flowers.

PHYSOSTEGIA
(feye-soss-TEE-jee-ah)

Obedient Plant

LABIATAE; mint family

Height/habit: Upright clumps, 3–4 ft. (1–1.2 m.) high x half as wide and more; colonizes.
Leaves: Lance-shaped, sharply toothed, 3–5 in. (7.5–12.5 cm.) long, set opposite along noticeably square stems.
Flowers: Tubular, lipped, and lobed, to 1 in. (2.5 cm.) long, in dense spikes; white, pink, purplish pink, lilac-tinged pink.
Season: Mid- to late summer.

When to plant: Set transplants when available. Cold- and heat-tolerant zones 3-9.
Light: Sunny to half–shady.
Soil: Humusy, well drained, moist.
Fertilizer: 5-10-5.
Propagation: Divide spring or fall (helpful for renewing congested clumps after several years); take stem cuttings in spring.
Uses: Beds, borders, wild and cottage gardens, pots, cut flowers, colonizing a moist bank or ditch.

PLATYCODON
(plat-ee-KOH-don)
Balloon Flower

CAMPANULACEAE; bellflower
family

Height/habit: Upright, narrow
to spreading clumps, 6–36 in.
(15–90 cm.) high; slow-growing.
Leaves: Egg-shaped, serrated,
to 3 in. (7.5 cm.) long, growing
in whorls up a smooth stem;
bluish green.
Flowers: Open to 5-pointed,
2-in. (5-cm.) stars growing
from balloon-shaped buds
at the terminals; there are
also doubles; blue, white, or
shell pink.
Season: Summer. Late to
sprout in spring; mark site to
avoid damage.
When to plant: Set transplants
when available. Cold- and heat-
tolerant zones 3–9.
Light: Sunny.
Soil: Well drained, moist.
Fertilizer: 5-10-5.
Propagation: Sow seed or
divide in spring; take basal
cuttings in summer.
Uses: Beds, borders, rock
and cottage gardens, pots,
cut flowers.

POLEMONIUM
(poh-lee-MOH-nee-um)

Jacob's Ladder; Greek Valerian

POLEMONIACEAE; phlox family

Height/habit: Upright to spreading, 1–2 ft. (30–61 cm.) high/wide.

Leaves: Leaflets 8–10 in. (20–25 cm.) long, paired so as to resemble ladder rungs.

Flowers: Cup- or bell-shaped, to 1 in. (2.5 cm.) across, in clusters; blue, lavender, pink, white, or yellow.

Season: Spring through summer.

When to plant: Set transplants when available. Cold- and heat-tolerant zones 3–4 to 8.

Light: Partly sunny to partly shady.

Soil: Humusy, well drained, moist.

Fertilizer: 5-10-5.

Propagation: Divide in spring; sow seeds in fall.

Uses: Bed; borders; woodland, wild, and cottage gardens; pots.

POLYGONATUM
(poh-ligg-oh-NAY-tum)

Solomon's Seal

LILIACEAE; lily family

Height/habit: Arching, unbranched stems set alternately with veined leaves and hung in spring with elegant bell flowers, averaging 2–3 ft. (61–90 cm.) high/wide.

Leaves: Broadly elliptic to lance or oval shapes, .5–6 in. (1.25–15 cm.) long.

Flowers: Resemble bells, .5 in. (1.25 cm.) long, in pairs from the leaf axils; white to greenish or lilac-tinged pink.

Season: Late spring to early summer.

When to plant: Set transplants when available. Cold- and heat-tolerant zones 4–9.

Light: Part to full shade.

Soil: Humusy, well drained, moist.

Fertilizer: 14-14-14 timed-release at planting; 5-10-5 at the start of the following season.

Propagation: Divide in spring or fall; sow seeds in fall.

Uses: Borders; shade, wild, and woodland gardens; ground cover; pots.

POLYGONUM
(poh-LIGG-oh-num)

Knotweed;
Fleece Flower;
Silver Lace Vine;
Mexican Bamboo;
Showy Bistort

POLYGONACEAE; buckwheat family

Height/habit: This genus is also known as *Periscaria*. From trailing to climbing or strongly upright, 6 in. (15 cm.) to 6–15 ft. (1.8–4.5 m.).

Leaves: Heart-shaped or oval, 1–10 in. (2.5–25 cm.) long.

Flowers: Small, reaching just .5 in. (1.25 cm.) across, often in fleecy clusters or sprays of tiny florets; white or pink, to glowing orange-crimson.

Season: Spring through fall for foliage effect, early summer for showy bistort (*P. bistorta* 'Superbum'); late summer through fall for most.

When to plant: Set transplants when available. Cold- and heat-tolerant zones 3–5 and 8–9.

Light: Sunny to partly shady.

Soil: Humusy, well drained, moist.

Fertilizer: 5-10-5.

Propagation: Divide spring or fall. *P. virginiana* (also known as *Tovara virginiana*) in the variegated-leaf variety 'Painter's Palette' produces foliar embryos that may be used to grow new plants.

Uses: Ground cover, wild gardens, pots; silver lace vine (*P. aubertii*) on fences, trellises, arbors. Mexican bamboo (*P. cuspidatum*) grows rapidly as a screen in warm weather, but roots need to be restricted by concrete or other barrier.

POTENTILLA
(poh-ten-TILL-ah)

Cinquefoil

ROSACEAE; rose family

Height/habit: Perennials
and woody plants, 6–36 in.
(15–90 cm.) high/wide.
Leaves: Compound, small,
to 1 in. (2.5 cm.) long.
Flowers: Resembling strawberry flower or a single rose,
5-petaled, about .75 in. (2 cm.)
across, often with showy yellow
stamens; white, yellow, red,
orange, or pink.

Season: Summer through fall.
When to plant: Set transplants
when available. Cold- and heat-
tolerant zones 4–5 to 7–8.
Light: Sunny to partly shady.
Soil: Well drained, moist.
Fertilizer: 5-10-5.
Propagation: Divide in spring
or fall; take basal cuttings in
late spring; sow seeds in spring.
Uses: Beds, borders, rock
gardens, pots.

PRIMULA
(PRIM-yew-lah)

Primrose

PRIMULACEAE; primrose family

Height/habit: Upright clumps or tidy mounds, 6–18 in. (15–45 cm.) high/wide.

Leaves: To 4 in. (10 cm.) long; rounded to lance-shaped, usually in a clump of rosettes. Some people allergic to the essential oils produced by German primrose (*P. obconica*).

Flowers: To 2 in. (5 cm.) across, alone or in clusters, rising directly from the base of the plant or from stems, to multi-levels in some, such as mature German primroses; most colors, including greens and various blues, often elaborately bicolored.

Season: Spring through early summer; winter through spring in mild-climate winters, including greenhouses.

When to plant: Set transplants when available. Cold- and heat-hardy zones 6–8 for *P. beesiana*, candelabra primrose (*P. bulleyana*), Japanese primrose (*P. japonica*), and *P. pulverulenta*, also called candelabra primrose; zones 5 to 8–9 for the mass-marketed *P. polyantha*, or English primroses. German primrose is often perennial in shady, moist gardens in zone 9.

Light: Sunny to half-sunny in cool weather, half-shady to shady at other times.

Soil: Humusy, well drained, moist.

Fertilizer: 5-10-5.

Propagation: Divide after flowering or in early fall; sow fresh seeds in summer.

Uses: Beds; borders; wild, woodland, rock, and cottage gardens; pots; cut flowers.

PULMONARIA
(pull-moh-NAY-ree-ah)

Lungwort

BORAGINACEAE; borage family

Height/habit: Self-reliant clumps 9–12 in. (22.5–30 cm.) high, spreading to twice this measurement.

Leaves: Lance- to heart-shaped, mostly from the base, 8–18 in. (20–45 cm.) long, often spotted silver with hairy stems.

Flowers: Funnel-shaped, 5-lobed, in clusters; blue, pink, red, or white.

Season: Early spring, as the foliage is emerging.

When to plant: Set transplants when available. Cold- and heat-tolerant zones 3–4 to 8.

Light: Partial to full shade.

Soil: Humusy, well drained, moist.

Fertilizer: 14-14-14 timed-release at planting time, with 5-10-5 at the beginning of the following season.

Propagation: Divide in spring or fall.

Uses: Ground cover; beds; borders; pots; wild, woodland, and cottage gardens.

RUDBECKIA
(rudd-BECK-ee-ah)

Coneflower; Black-eyed Susan

COMPOSITAE; daisy family

Height/habit: Upright to sprawling clumps, 2–8 ft. (61–240 cm.) high by one-third to half as wide; staking recommended for higher sorts, such as *R. laciniata*, which reaches 4–8 ft. (1.2–2.4 m.).

Leaves: Rounded to lance-shaped, deeply cut in some, to 6 in. (15 cm.) long.

Flowers: Single or double daisies, 2–4 in. (5–10 cm.) across; yellow with purple-brown to black central disks; respond to deadheading, which prolongs the season.

Season: Summer through fall.

When to plant: Set transplants when available. Cold- and heat-tolerant zones 3–4 to 9.

Light: Sunny.

Soil: Well drained, moist to on the dry side.

Fertilizer: 5-10-5.

Propagation: Divide in spring or fall; sow seeds in spring.

Uses: Beds; back of borders; wild, meadow, and cottage gardens; cut flowers.

RUELLIA
(roo-EE-lee-ah)

Wild Petunia;
Mexican Petunia

ACANTHACEAE; acanthus family

Height/habit: Upright, 6–12 in.
(15–30 cm.) high/wide in
R. brittoniana 'Katie,' much
higher to sprawling, 3–4 ft.
(1–1.2 m.) in the wild
species; high-growing Mexican
petunia (*R. brittoniana*) 4–6 ft.
(1.2–1.8 m.).
Leaves: Lance-shaped, 4–6 in.
(10–15 cm.) long.
Flowers: Tubular, 5-lobed,
1–2 in. (2.5–5 cm.) across; blue-
purple with darker veins.

Season: Spring through fall;
Mexican petunia blooms midsummer through fall. The
flowers open early in the day
and disappear by the afternoon, except in cooler weather.
When to plant: Set transplants
when available. Cold- and heat-
tolerant zones 7–9.
Light: Sunny to half-sunny.
Soil: Well drained, moist.
Fertilizer 5-10-5.
Propagation: Divide or sow
seeds in spring or fall.
Uses: Beds, borders, pots, semiwild gardens; the wild species
can be invasive, but also very
pretty if root run is restricted.

SALVIA
(SAL-vee-ah)

Sage

LABIATAE; mint family

Height/habit: Upright to sprawling, herbaceous to sub-shrubby, 2–8 ft. (61–240 cm.) high/wide.

Leaves: Egg-, oblong-, spoon-, or lance-shaped, 1–8 in. (2.5–20 cm.) long, prominently veined or pebbled in summer; green, gray, bluish, variegated in some; clean-scented.

Flowers: 2-lipped, often from bract of a contrasting color, 1–2 in. (2.5–5 cm.) long; most colors, but strong in blues, pinks, and reds. *S. madrensis*, a fall-flowering yellow species for mild-climate gardens (zones 8–9), gives the effect of forsythia in northern spring landscapes.

Season: Almost all year, zones 8–9 and warmer; concentrated summer for northern favorites, such as silver sage (*S. argentea*), prairie sage (*S. azurea*), mealy-cup sage (*S. farinacea*), and *S.* x *superba*.

When to plant: Set transplants when available. The species mentioned above are cold- and heat-tolerant zones 5–9; zones 7–9 there are a host of native and locally adapted species that make superb garden plants.

Light: Sunny.

Soil: Well drained, moist to on the dry side. Tolerates drought when established.

Fertilizer: 5-10-5.

Propagation: Divide herbaceous perennials or sow seeds in spring; take cuttings in midsummer.

Uses: Beds, borders, pots, wild and cottage gardens, Xeriscape.

SEDUM
(SEE-dum)

Stonecrop

CRASSULACEAE; orpine family

Height/habit: Ground-hugging, mat-forming, to 6 in. (15 cm.) high and twice to several times as wide; upright clumps in *S. spectabile*, *S. telephium*, and their offspring *S.* x 'Autumn Joy,' 15–24 in. (38–61 cm.) high/wide.

Leaves: Fleshy, pointed, cylindrical, oblong, or oval, linear or rounded, .25–6 in. (.63–15 cm.) long; various greens to bluish or gray, often with white or yellow variegation.

Flowers: Starry, tiny, reaching just .5 in. (1.25 cm.) across, in terminal clusters 2–6 in. (5–15 cm.) across; yellow, white, pink, or red to rust.

Season: Late spring, summer through fall, depending on the species. Foliage effective throughout the growing season.

When to plant: Set transplants when available. Cold- and heat-tolerant zones 3–9.

Light: Sunny.

Soil: Well drained, moist to on the dry side. Tolerates drought when established.

Fertilizer: 5-10-5.

Propagation: Divide in spring; take cuttings in summer.

Uses: Beds, borders, ground cover, rock gardens, pots.

SEMPERVIVUM
(sem-per-VEYE-vum)

Houseleek; Live-forever

CRASSULACEAE; orpine family

Height/habit: Ground-hugging foliage in rosettes, 6–12 in. (15–30 cm.) high/wide.

Leaves: Fleshy, to 3 in. (7.5 cm.) long in dense rosettes; various greens, also bronze, red, blue- to gray-green, burgundy, lavender, purple; leaf tips often in contrasting color.

Flowers: Starry, .5–1 in. (1.25–2.5 cm.) across, in dense clusters atop an erect stem above the foliage; rose, red, purple, greenish yellow, or yellowish white.

Season: Summer; foliage attractive throughout the growing season.

When to plant: Set transplants when available. Cold- and heat-tolerant zones 5–9.

Light: Sunny.

Soil: Well drained, moist to on the dry side; drought-tolerant when established.

Fertilizer: 5-10-5.

Propagation: Take offsets in early fall or spring; sow seed in spring.

Uses: Beds, borders, rock and wall gardens, between paving stones, pots.

STACHYS
(STACK-iss)
Lamb's Ears
LABIATAE; mint family

Height/habit: *S. byzantina* mat-forming, 1–1.5 ft. (30–45 cm.) high/wide.

Leaves: Elliptical to oblong, 4–6 in. (10–15 cm.) long; white and woolly.

Flowers: Woolly spikes above or flopping over the leaves; red-purple. Fastidious gardeners often remove the buds before they open, so as to concentrate the plant's energy on the production of decorative foliage.

Season: Leaves spring through fall; often suffers die-out in summer from heat, high humidity, and overhead sprinkling.

When to plant: Set transplants when available. Cold- and heat-tolerant zones 4–8.

Light: Sunny to partly shaded.

Soil: Well drained, moist.

Fertilizer: 5-10-5.

Propagation: Divide in spring or fall.

Uses: Beds, borders, rock gardens, ground cover, pots.

STIGMAPHYLLON
(stig-mah-FILL-on)
Butterfly Vine
MALPIGHIACEAE; malpighia family

Height/habit: Twining evergreen vine to 12 ft. (3.6 m.) or more.

Leaves: Elliptical, 3–4 in. (7.5–10 cm.) long.

Flowers: Resemble butterfly orchids, each to 1.5 in. (3.7 cm.) across, in clusters of 3–7; yellow.

Season: Spring (zones 9–10), summer in cooler zones.

When to plant: Set transplants when available. Cold- and heat-tolerant zones 8–9.

Light: Sunny to half-sunny.

Soil: Well drained, moist to on the dry side.

Fertilizer: 5-10-5.

Propagation: Sow seeds in spring; take stem cuttings in summer.

Uses: Cover for trellis, fence, arbor, or tepee.

SYMPHYTUM
(sim-FEYE-tum)

Comfrey

BORAGINACEAE; borage family

Height/habit: Clump-forming, upright to sprawling, 2–4 ft. (61–122 cm.) high/wide.
Leaves: Coarse, egg- to lance-shaped, 6–10 in. (15–25 cm.) long.
Flowers: Nodding, tubular, to 1 in. (2.5 cm.) long, in branched clusters; yellow, white, blue, or pink.
Season: Spring through summer.

When to plant: Set transplants when available. Cold- and heat-tolerant zones 4–9. Most common is the herb comfrey, *S. officinale*. Showier are *S. caucasicum, S. grandiflorum,* and *S. x uplandicum.*
Light: Sunny to partly shady.
Soil: Humusy, well drained, moist.
Fertilizer: 5-10-5.
Propagation: Divide in spring or fall.
Uses: Beds; borders; wild, woodland, and shade gardens; pots.

THALICTRUM
(thah-LICK-trum)
Meadow Rue

RANUNCULACEAE; buttercup
family

Height/habit: Much-divided
leaves concentrated in the bottom half of the plant with
branching panicles of airy
flowers above, 3–5 ft. (1–1.5 m.)
high x half as wide.
Leaves: Small leaflets, to
1 in. (2.5 cm.); blue-green in
T. aquilegifolium. Foliage is an
asset even before the flowers
appear.
Flowers: Small blooms appear
in fluffy, showy panicles; white,
purple, lilac, or yellow.
Season: Summer.
When to plant: Set transplants
when available. Cold- and
heat-tolerant zones 5–8;
T. dasycarpum zones 5–9.
Light: Sunny to partly shaded.
Soil: Humusy, well drained,
moist.
Fertilizer: 5-10-5.
Propagation: Divide or sow
seeds in spring. Recovers slowly
from root disturbance.
Uses: Beds, borders, woodland
and wild gardens, pots.

THUNBERGIA
(thun-BERJ-ee-ah)

Blue Trumpet Vine

ACANTHACEAE; acanthus family

Height/habit: *T. grandiflora* twining evergreen vine, 20–30 ft. (6–9 m.).

Leaves: Triangular to heart-shaped, toothed, 3–8 in. (7.5–20 cm.) long.

Flowers: Lobed, tubular, to 3 in. (7.5 cm.), blooming in sprays; blue or white.

Season: Fall, winter, spring. Vines frozen back to the ground often return from the roots but take a year to come back into bloom.

When to plant: Set transplants when available. Cold- and heat-tolerant zones 8–10; elsewhere grow as a container plant placed outdoors in warm weather.

Light: Sunny to half-sunny.

Soil: Humusy, well drained, moist.

Fertilizer: 5-10-5.

Propagation: Take stem cuttings in spring or summer.

Uses: Cover for trellis, fence, arbor, or tepee; pots.

TIARELLA
(teye-ah-RELL-ah)

False Mitrewort

SAXIFRAGACEAE; saxifrage family

Height/habit: Mostly basal foliage crowned in spring by delicate flowers, 1–1.5 ft. (30–45 cm.) high/wide.

Leaves: Hairy, lobed, or divided, heart-shaped or triangular, to 3 in. (7.5 cm.), resembling those of the popular (and related) houseplant *Tolmiea*, or pickaback; evergreen except at northern hardiness limits.

Flowers: Small blooms in fuzzy spikes, 8–12 in. (20–30 cm.) long; white to pinkish.

Season: Spring through summer.

When to plant: Set transplants when available. Cold- and heat-tolerant zones 3–4 to 7–8.

Light: Shady to partly shady.

Soil: Humusy, well drained, moist.

Fertilizer: 14-14-14 timed-release at planting time.

Propagation: Divide in spring or fall; sow seed in early spring.

Uses: Beds; borders; ground cover; pots; wild, woodland, and shade gardens.

TRACHELOSPERMUM
(track-ell-OSS-per-mum)

Star Jasmine; Confederate Jasmine

APOCYNACEAE; dogbane family

Height/habit: Evergreen climber by twining stems and aerial rootlets, to 15 ft. (4.5 m.). Often trained as a bush, to 3–4 ft. (1–1.2 m.) high/wide.

Leaves: Oval, 2–3 in. (5–7.5 cm.) long.

Flowers: Starry blooms, to 1 in. (2.5 cm.) across, growing in clusters; white or pale yellow; fragrant.

Season: Spring and intermittently in summer.

When to plant: Set transplants when available. Cold- and heat-tolerant zones 8–9; *T. jasminoides* 'Madison' zones 7–10.

Light: Half-sunny to shady.

Soil: Humusy, well drained, moist.

Fertilizer: 5-10-5.

Propagation: Take cuttings in spring or summer.

Uses: Cover for trellis, fence, arbor, porch, or tepee in border.

TRADESCANTIA
(tradd-ess-KANT-ee-ah)

Spiderwort

COMMELINACEAE; spiderwort family

Height/habit: Clump-forming, upright, 1–2 ft. (30–61 cm.) high/wide.

Leaves: Narrow, similar to blades of grass, to 1 ft. (30 cm.) long.

Flowers: 3-petaled, to 1 in. (2.5 cm.) across, opening in the morning and closing by midafternoon; blue, white, pink, purple, or rose.

Season: Late spring through summer.

When to plant: Set transplants when available. Cold- and heat-tolerant zones 4–9. Cultivated hybrids of *T. ohiensis*, *T. subaspera*, and *T. virginiana*, grouped under *T.* x *andersoniana*, are best suited to the cultivated garden.

Light: Sunny to partly shady.

Soil: Humusy, well drained, moist.

Fertilizer: 5-10-5.

Propagation: Divide in spring.

Uses: Beds, borders, wild, and shade gardens, pots.

TRILLIUM
(TRILL-ee-uh)

Wake-robin

LILIACEAE; lily family

Height/habit: Clump-forming, upright, 1–1.5 ft. (30–45 cm.) high/wide.

Leaves: In groups of 3, rounded to egg-shaped, 3–6 in. (7.5–15 cm.) long; mottled yellow-green or bronze in some.

Flowers: 3-petaled or doubled, upright or nodding, 2–3 in. (5–7.5 cm.) across; white, pink, yellow, purple-red, or maroon.

Season: Spring.

When to plant: Set transplants when available. Cold- and heat-tolerant zones 3–5 to 9.

Light: Partly sunny to shady.

Soil: Humusy, well drained, moist.

Fertilizer: 5-10-5.

Propagation: Divide in early spring or late summer.

Uses: Beds; borders; wild, shade, and woodland gardens.

TROLLIUS
(TROLL-ee-uss)
Globeflower
RANUNCULACEAE; buttercup family

Height/habit: Clumps of basal foliage with flowers above, 1–3 ft. (30–90 cm.) high/wide.
Leaves: Fan-shaped, lobed or divided, 2–6 in. (5–15 cm.) long.
Flowers: Globe-shaped, 1–4 in. (2.5–10 cm.) across; yellow, golden orange, orange-red, or lemon.
Season: Spring through early summer.
When to plant: Set transplants when available. Cold- and heat-tolerant zones 3–5 to 7.
Light: Sunny to partly shady.
Soil: Humusy, well drained, moist to wet.
Fertilizer: 5-10-5.
Propagation: Divide in fall.
Uses: Beds, borders, bog or wild garden, cut flowers.

VERBASCUM
(ver-BASS-kum)

Mullein

SCROPHULARIACEAE; figwort
family

Height/habit: Rosette-forming
in the first season, sending up
spires of bloom in the second,
1–2 ft. (30–61 cm.) wide by 6 ft.
(1.8 m.) high or higher in the
biennial *V. bombyciferum.*
Leaves: Oval to oblong or
broadly lance-shaped, 6–12 in.
(15–30 cm.), often densely
covered with fine hairs. Flowers
5-lobed, 1–2 in. (2.5–5 cm.)
across, in high spikes; white,
yellow, pink, purple, or orange
Deadheading the central
spike as it finishes flowering
encourages secondary spikes.
Season: Spring through
summer.
When to plant: Set transplants
when available. Cold- and heat-
tolerant zones 5–6 to 9.
Light: Sunny.
Soil: Well drained, moist to on
the dry side.
Fertilizer: 5-10-5.
Propagation: Sow seed in
spring; take root cuttings late
winter through early spring.
Uses: Beds, borders, wild
garden, pots.

VERONICA
(ver-ON-ick-ah)

Speedwell

SCROPHULARIACEAE; figwort family

Height/habit: Prostrate, trailing, or mat-forming to upright clumps (staking helps), 6–12 in. (15–30 cm.) to 1.5–3 ft. (45–90 cm.) high/wide.

Leaves: Oblong, egg- to lance-shaped, often toothed, 1–3 in. (2.5–7.5 cm.) long.

Flowers: Saucer-shaped, small, in dense spikes; blue, white, pink, or violet-blue.

Season: Late spring, summer, fall.

When to plant: Set transplants when available. Cold- and heat-tolerant zones 4–8.

Light: Sunny.

Soil: Well drained, moist.

Fertilizer: 5-10-5.

Propagation: Divide in spring or fall; take cuttings in summer.

Uses: Beds, borders, rock and wall gardens, pots.

VIOLA
(veye-OH-lah)
Violet
VIOLACEAE; violet family

Height/habit: Upright to spreading, tufted or stemmed, 4–12 in. (10–30 cm.) high/wide.
Leaves: Rounded, lance-, heart-, or ivy-shaped, 1–2 in. (2.5–5 cm.) across.
Flowers: Single or double, 1–2 in. (2.5–5 cm.) across; blue, lilac, white, violet, yellow, ruby red, mauve purple; some fragrant, notably *V. odorata.*
Season: Winter through spring in mild climates; primarily spring in colder regions.
When to plant: Set transplants when available. Cold- and heat-tolerant zones 3–5 to 8–9. Widely adapted, some becoming outright weeds, others indispensable as edgings and ground covers.
Light: Sunny to partly shady.
Soil: Humusy, well drained, moist.
Fertilizer: 5-10-5.
Propagation: Divide in spring or fall; sow seeds or take cuttings in spring or summer.
Uses: Beds; borders; ground cover; wild, shade, and rock gardens; pots; cut flowers.

VITEX
(VEYE-tex)

Chaste Tree

VERBENACEAE; verbena family

Height/habit: Though technically shrubs or small trees that can reach 10–15 ft. (3–4.5 m.) high/wide, these plants can often be cut to the ground in spring so that relatively small, compact new season's growth produces bloom at a welcome time in the garden.

Leaves: Compound into 5–7 leaflets, to 4 in. (10 cm.) long. Grayish green (variegated white in some) and aromatic.

Flowers: Very small in showy terminal clusters to 4–8 in. (10–20 cm.) long; blue, white, pink, lilac, or lavender; fragrant.

Season: Summer, earlier in warmest zones.

When to plant: Set transplants when available. Cold- and heat-tolerant zones 6–7 to 9–10.

Light: Sunny.

Soil: Well drained, moist. Tolerates drought when established.

Fertilizer: 5-10-5.

Propagation: Take cuttings or layer in spring or summer.

Uses: Beds, back of borders, wild or cottage gardens, pots.

YUCCA
(YUCK-ah)
Spanish Dagger
AGAVACEAE; agave family

Height/habit: Rosette or sword-shaped leaves, above which flowers rise on woody spike, 4–8 ft. (1.2–2.4 m.) high/wide.

Leaves: Narrow daggers, .5 in. (1.25 cm.) wide x up to 3 ft. (90 cm.) long in *Y. glauca*; also varying in succulence and fiber content, from relatively flexuous to quite hard; from blue- to yellow-green, some variegated lengthwise with white to pale yellow; evergreen, but some deciduous.

Flowers: Pyramidal spires of pendant bells 2–4 in. (5–10 cm.) across; white or purple; fragrant.

Season: Spring through summer.

When to plant: Set transplants when available.

Light: Sunny.

Soil: Well drained, moist to on the dry side; very drought-tolerant when established.

Fertilizer: 5-10-5.

Propagation: Take root cuttings or divide spring or fall.

Uses: Beds, borders, Xeriscape, pots, cut flowers.

Chapter Seven:
Troubleshooting Guide for Perennials

The best way to keep a garden trouble-free is to prevent problems from arising in the first place. Ensure that any plants you obtained are as healthy as possible, and keep the garden cleaned of debris and weeds, which provide convenient cover for insects. Even the most diligent gardener experiences problems, however, such as the following:

No blooms. This signals the need for more light, more water or fertilizer, possibly more cold (peonies will not bloom unless they have sufficient hours of chilling in winter, usually in zones 8 and colder). Sometimes this is a sign that the plants have lived for too long in one spot, without replenishment of the soil and without division and thinning out of other plant competition.

Insects clustered on new growth. These are probably aphids and can be knocked off with stiff streams of water from the hose. Or treat with insecticidal soap or Neem tree sprays (a traditional Indian bug repellent).

White insects clustered on main stems from the ground up. These are doubtlessly mealybugs. Spray weekly and thoroughly with insecticidal soap or Neem tree sprays.

Powdery white spots on leaves. Powdery mildew attacks numerous perennials, especially summer phlox. This usually happens late in the summer when nights turn cool and days remain warm and dry. The condition can be treated by applying fungicide.

Tiny white flies around plant; lower leaves moldy. Spray weekly with insecticidal soap or other spray labeled specifically for use against white flies. The plant will outgrow the sooty mold; it cannot be removed.

Generally poor or weak growth. The plant needs more light, water, and nutrients. Avoid planting perennials where the soil is filled with tree and shrub roots. In such situations it may be better to grow selected perennials in containers.

Chapter Eight:
Bringing Perennials Into Your Home

Container-grown perennials are a perfect way of enjoying these plants indoors. Gallon-size or larger service pots can be dressed for indoors by slipping each inside a woven basket, cachepot, or earthen container, with some sheet moss to carpet any bare surface soil.

Perennial flowers and vines are also a seemingly endless source of fragrant blooms and fresh foliage for arrangements. Whether creating a casual bouquet for a milk bottle on the porch or a formal centerpiece for the dining room, here are some delightful suggestions:

❧ Aster with irises, snapdragon, marigold, lily or zinnia

❧ Chrysanthemum with dianthus (a long-lasting combination)

❧ Country-style combinations of delphinium with gerbera, snapdragon, purple coneflower

❧ Irises in Oriental-style ikebana arrangements

❧ Liatris as framework flower in large-scale designs

❧ Phlox with tulips and snapdragons

❧ Coralbells with miniature roses and violets

For everlastings arrangements and potpourri, the following air-dried flowers and seed heads are recommended:

❧ Delphinium for brilliant color in potpourri

❧ False goat's beard for unique texture of dried flowers in potpourri

❧ Peony petals for color and heavenly scent in potpourri

❧ Yarrow with false indigo dried seed heads

❧ Globe thistle with strawflowers

Part Three:
Bulbs

Chapter Nine:
The Bulb Garden

Flowers that grow from corms, tubers, rhizomes, thickened roots, and true bulbs all fall under the umbrella heading of bulbs. Most gardeners consider bulbs to be the most supreme among all flowering plants. So varied are they in size, color, and blooming periods, bulbs alone can easily comprise an elaborate, multiseason garden. At the same time, bulbs fit in nicely with the overall gardening scheme.

Bulbs grow equally well both in the ground and in containers, and gardeners will find types for all kinds of climates. Some are evergreen, but it is the general habit of bulbs to return to the ground for one season yearly, either in winter or summer, depending on each plant's built-in timetable.

Planning and Designing the Bulb Garden
Bulbs growing on their own in the wild form irregularly shaped colonies. Mimicking nature and planting in informal drifts, the gardener can create such a charming scene in his or her own garden, perhaps on a grassy bank. Another possibility is to design formal beds, perhaps edged with dwarf boxwood or dwarf yaupon holly, and to fill them with different bulbs in season. Such a scheme entails discarding each successive round of bulbs when its season has finished.

Of course, many gardeners also choose to fill their beds with bulbs in spring and annuals in summer. By the time the annuals finish in early fall, it is time to plant another round of bulbs. Bulbs also look lovely planted among ground cover plants so that when they're done blooming, the area will not look bare. Remember to plant low-growing bulbs in places where they'll be clearly visible, reserving the taller types for the back of the garden.

Another aesthetic—and practical—design tip to keep in mind is that spring bulbs are uniquely suited to growing in the company of deciduous trees; the bulbs usually bloom and grow leaves before the trees leaf out. The trees have a way of sucking up any extra moisture in summer, which is a boon to resting bulbs. Whether you live in a wet or dry climate, also consider using raised planting beds for bulbs. This makes gardening a lot easier in the long run and gives better results with most kinds of plants.

Soil Preparation

Bulbs adapt to various soil conditions, from soggy or boglike to quite dry. Study the description for each bulb you wish to grow (see Chapter Ten). Cannas and crinums are examples of bulbous plants that grow and bloom in boggy conditions, even standing in water. Tulips, hyacinths, and daffodils and other narcissi are examples of bulbs that need a good supply of moisture from the time roots start expanding in fall until the leaves start yellowing naturally after bloom the following spring or early summer. Thereafter, it is beneficial to keep them quite dry, perhaps even stored out of the ground, for three or four months.

Before you plant bulbs, you need to dig and turn over the soil—at least to the depth of a spade—as well as clear away any weeds or other debris. Add a top-dressing of organic fertilizer and up to 6 inches (15 centimeters) of well-rotted compost. After you've tilled all of this together, the bed is ready for planting.

Buying and Planting Bulbs

Bulbs are sold in all seasons, both locally and through catalogs. When purchasing them, remember that, generally speaking, the larger the bulb, the bigger the blossoms. Just as with buying fruit, steer clear of bulbs that are too soft and mushy or seem to have moldy or bruised areas. On the other hand, if a bulb's outer skin is loose or torn, it is not necessarily damaged—this could even be a sign that root growth will be accelerated.

With all this in mind, it's time to plant the garden. The so-called Dutch, or spring, bulbs are planted in the fall, before the ground freezes in colder regions, up to around the first of the year in the South, in zone 9 and warmer. Narcissi, crocuses, hyacinths, tulips, Dutch irises, and scillas all belong to this category. One loose rule of thumb with spring bulbs is that they should be planted twice as deep as they are long, but check the descriptions in

Chapter Ten for precise measurements before planting.

Then there are the tender, or summer, bulbs, such as gladioli, dahlias, tuberoses, and tigridias. Northern gardeners traditionally plant them in the spring for summer blooms. Before the ground seriously begins to freeze in

the fall, they dig them up and store them indoors. Plant summer bulbs at specific depths according to their needs, not based on the size of the bulb. Consult Chapter Ten for specifics.

To plant bulbs, dig a hole to the specified depth, and be sure to loosen the soil under the bulbs as well. Cover with soil and water well.

Caring for Bulbs Throughout the Seasons

Despite the way they look, always bear in mind that bulbs are living things. Protect them from temperature extremes and be especially careful of their well-being at any time they are out of the ground. Spring-flowering bulbs, in particular, are quite vulnerable to high temperatures and direct sunshine, especially in a poorly ventilated room. Keep them well protected before planting, stored at a temperature below 60°F

(15°C), perhaps in a well-ventilated closet in an open cardboard box. Keep all bulbs away from fruit before planting or during storing periods, as they are damaged by ethylene, released by the ripening fruit.

If the bulb is frost-sensitive, growing in a pot is often the solution. Also, if the bulb needs a season of cold in order to bloom, chilling in the refrigerator is an option—provided it is kept away from fruit, as mentioned above.

At the other end of the bulb season, after flowering finishes, it is an absolute necessity to allow the foliage to grow out and complete its natural season. In many bulbous plants the leaves eventually turn yellow and die to the ground. It is at this point that the plants can be removed without harming their ability to bloom for the coming season. In general, spring-flowering bulbs can stay in the ground year-round (which encourages them to naturalize, especially crocuses, low-growing daffodils, snowdrops, and scillas), while summer-flowering bulbs should be dug up and stored in any climate where there is frost.

When any kind of bulb is resting, think of it not so much as being dormant but semi-

dormant. Adequate fresh air circulation is important to prevent disease problems with such bulbs, and so is maintaining a state of dampness sufficient to prevent harmful drying-out but not to the point of encouraging rot. With the exception of spring-flowering bulbs, which like a cooler temperature, most bulbs can be stored in a well-ventilated closet at temperatures of around 65–70°F (18–21°C).

A word about propagation: Bulbs that bloom in spring are usually divided in summer or fall; bulbs that bloom in summer can be divided in the spring. Many bulbs never need to be divided, except for the purpose of propagation. Others start to die out in the center of the clump and stop blooming. This is a sign that digging and dividing are in order during or immediately following the next resting period.

To propagate bulbs by division, dig them up with a sharpshooter, garden spade, or trowel. Bulblets approximately the size of the bulbs originally planted can be removed and planted separately. Smaller ones may be set in groups of at least three or rowed out in a nursery bed for growing a year or two before being planted in a garden spot.

Bulbs that are content in a location will often colonize, spreading by offsets and sometimes by self-sown seedlings. Seeds of bulb flowers don't always come true, especially not of the highly hybridized Dutch tulips, daffodils, and hyacinths, but the progeny is certainly fun to watch. Such kinds as the rain lilies—zephyranthes and habranthus, for example—seed profusely. They will take root quite nicely in well-prepared garden beds, either permitted to dry and drop seed where they will or harvested just before the capsule dries and breaks open, then planted within a month in shallow drills of moist soil. Friends will appreciate any extras.

The seeds of some bulbs planted one year may not germinate until the following spring or early summer. This is particularly true of

the hardy types that need cold temperatures in winter, such as tulips, narcissi, and many of the true lilies (*Lilium*) and daylilies (*Hemerocallis*).

Essential Tools

Bulbs can be planted with a trowel or garden spade. There are hand-held bulb planters on the market but they do not work as handily as one might hope. A variation with a longer handle designed to be used with the feet works much better. When naturalizing fall-planted spring bulbs, such as crocus and winter aconite, you can use a dibble or crowbar to open up holes efficiently.

Year-round Gardening Calendar

Make note of the bulbs you like, then organize them according to recommended planting times. Write these various dates in your regular datebook/organizer or on a wall calendar. That way they serve as constant reminders of upcoming planting dates and also of bulbs that you'll need to obtain from a specialist or pick up at a local garden center. Here is a calendar of seasonal reminders:

SPRING:

Till and prepare soil in garden beds.

Replant summer bulbs stored over the winter after danger of frost has passed.

Divide bulbs in early spring, before blooming or at time of planting, according to individual instructions in Chapter Ten.

Purchase and plant summer-flowering bulbs.

Mulch with organic matter.

Start a gardening watering schedule, watering soil thoroughly yet infrequently as a conservation measure. To check if soil needs to be watered, see if it feels dry 3 to 4 inches (7.5 to 10 cm.) down.

Bring spring bulb bouquets indoors.

After bulbs have bloomed, remove spent flowers but allow the leaves to develop, then disintegrate naturally.

If you wish, dig and store spring-blooming bulbs after the leaves start to die down.

SUMMER:

Continue weeding, watering, and deadheading.

Purchase and plant fall-blooming bulbs, such as autumn crocus.

Bring summer bulb bouquets indoors.

FALL:

Purchase and plant spring-flowering bulbs (September-October in Northern climates; November until early December in the South).

Bring autumn bulb bouquets indoors.

Divide bulbs after blooming according to individual instructions in Chapter Ten.

Dig and store summer-flowering bulbs before frost.

Mulch to protect garden beds from cold temperatures and lock in soil nutrients over the winter.

WINTER:

Force spring bulbs indoors, using a refrigerator, cool basement, or cold frame for chilling.

Purchase and store summer-flowering bulbs.

Chapter Ten:
The 100 Best Bulbs for Your Garden

ACHIMENES 224 *Nut Orchid;
Hot-water Plant*

ACIDANTHERA 225 *Fragrant Gladiolus*

AGAPANTHUS 226 *Lily of the Nile*

ALBUCA 227 *Sentry-in-the-box*

ALLIUM 228 *Ornamental Onion*

ALPINIA 229 *Shell Ginger*

ALSTROEMERIA 230 *Peruvian Lily*

AMARYLLIS 231 *Belladonna Lily*

ANEMONE 232 *Windflower*

ANIGOZANTHOS 233 *Kangaroo Paw*

ARISAEMA 234 *Jack-in-the-pulpit*

ASPHODELINE 235 *Asphodel*

ASPHODELUS 236 *Silver Rod*

BEGONIA 237 *Tuberous Begonia*

BEGONIA 238 *Hardy Begonia*

BLETILLA 238 *Chinese Ground Orchid*

CALADIUM 239 *Fancy-leaved Caladium*

CAMASSIA 240 *Camass; Wild Hyacinth*

CANNA 241 *Indian Shot*

CHASMANTHE 242 *Pennants*

CHIONODOXA 242 *Glory-of-the-snow*

CLIVIA 243 *Kaffir Lily*

COLCHICUM 244 *Autumn Crocus*

COLOCASIA 245 *Elephant's Ear; Taro*

CONVALLARIA 246 *Lily of the Valley*

CORYDALIS 247 *Fumaria*

CRINUM 248 *Florida Swamp Lily;
Milk-and-wine Lily*

CROCOSMIA 249 *Copper Tip; Montbretia*

CROCUS 249 *Crocus*

CURCUMA 250 *Hidden Ginger*

CYCLAMEN 251 *Persian Violet;
Florists' Cyclamen*

CYRTANTHUS 252 *Miniature Amaryllis*

DAHLIA 253 *Common Dahlia*

DICENTRA	254	Squirrel Corn (D. Canadensis); Dutchman's-Breeches (D. Cucullaria); Turkey Corn (D. Eximia)
DIETES	255	African Iris
ERANTHIS	255	Winter Aconite
EREMURUS	256	Desert Candle; Foxtail Lily
ERYTHRONIUM	257	Dogtooth Violet; Trout Lily
EUCHARIS	258	Amazon Lily; Eucharist Lily
EUCOMIS	259	Pineapple Lily
EUCROSIA	260	Eucrosia
FREESIA	261	Freesia
FRITILLARIA	262	Crown Imperial; Checkered Lily
GALANTHUS	263	Snowdrop
GALTONIA	263	Summer Hyacinth
GLADIOLUS	264	Corn Flag; Sword Lily
GLOBBA	265	Dancing Lady Ginger
GLORIOSA	265	Climbing Lily
GLOXINIA	266	True Gloxinia
HABRANTHUS	267	Rain Lily
HAEMANTHUS	268	White Paintbrush
HEDYCHIUM	268	Butterfly Ginger
HELICONIA	269	Lobster Claws
HIPPEASTRUM	270	Florists' Amaryllis; Dutch Amaryllis
HYACINTHOIDES	271	English Bluebell; Spanish Bluebell
HYACINTHUS	272	Hyacinth
HYMENOCALLIS	273	Spider Lily
IPHEION	273	Spring Starflower
IPOMOEA	274	Sweet Potato Vine
IRIS	274	Dutch, German, Japanese, and Louisiana Irises
KAEMPFERIA	275	Peacock Ginger
KNIPHOFIA	276	Tritoma; Torch Lily; Red-hot Poker
KOHLERIA	277	Isoloma; Tree Gloxinia
LACHENALIA	278	Cape Cowslip
LEDEBOURIA	279	Silver Squill
LEUCOJUM	279	Snowflake
LILIUM	280	Lily
LYCORIS	281	Naked Lady; Hurricane Lily
MUSCARI	282	Grape Hyacinth
NARCISSUS	283	Daffodil; Telephone Flower
NEOMARICA	284	Walking Iris; Twelve Apostles
NERINE	285	Guernsey Lily
ORNITHOGALUM	285	Chincherinchee; Star-of-Bethlehem
OXALIS	286	Lucky Clover; Wood Sorrel
PANCRATIUM	287	Sea Daffodil
PLEIONE	288	Indian Crocus
POLIANTHES	289	Mexican Tuberose
PUSCHKINIA	290	Striped Squill
RANUNCULUS	291	Buttercup
RHODOHYPOXIS	291	Red Star
SCADOXUS	292	Blood Lily
SCHIZOSTYLIS	293	Crimson Flag; River Lily
SCILLA	294	Squill
SEEMANNIA	294	Seemannia
SINNINGIA	295	Florists' Gloxinia
SMITHIANTHA	296	Temple Bells
SPARAXIS	297	Wandflower; Velvet Flower
SPREKELIA	298	Jacobean Lily; Aztec Lily
STERNBERGIA	299	Winter Daffodil; Lily of the Field
TACCA	299	Batflower
TIGRIDIA	300	Mexican Shellflower
TRITONIA	301	Montbretia; Flame Freesia
TROPAEOLUM	301	Tuber Nasturtiums
TULBAGHIA	302	Society Garlic
TULIPA	303	Tulip
VALLOTA	304	Scarborough Lily
VELTHEIMIA	304	Forest Lily
ZANTEDESCHIA	305	Calla Lily
ZEPHYRANTHES	306	Rain Lily
ZINGIBER	307	Ginger

ACHIMENES
(ah-KIM-uh-neez)

Nut Orchid;
Hot-water Plant

GESNERIACEAE; gesneriad family

Height/habit: Bushy, upright to semicascading, 1 ft. (30 cm.) mounds.

Leaves: Simple; ovate, linear, or lanceolate, 1–2 in. (2.5–5 cm.) long, hairy; often olive above, flushed burgundy below.

Flowers: 5-lobed, tubular to funnelform, 1–2 in. (2.5–5 cm.) across, occasionally double; most colors, often with contrasting veins.

Season: Summer until fall, primarily through the longest days.

When to plant: Set scaly rhizomes 1 in. (2.5 cm.) deep, the same distance apart, in starting pots or where they are to grow, late winter through spring, only in warm temperatures (60–80°F [15–26°C]). Despite love of warmth, often proves ground-hardy zone 9 and warmer.

Light: Sunny to half-sunny in spring, more shade in summer.

Soil: Humusy, well drained, moist.

Fertilizer: Alternate 30-10-10 and 15-30-15.

Storage: Store scaly rhizomes barely damp to nearly dry in barely damp to nearly dry peat moss or vermiculite, late fall to early spring, at 50–60°F (10–15°C).

Propagation: By natural increase of scaly rhizomes; or sow seeds in spring or individual scales as "seeds" in warm nursery conditions.

Uses: Beds, borders, pots, hanging baskets.

ACIDANTHERA
(acid-ANTH-er-ah)

Fragrant Gladiolus

IRIDACEAE; iris family

Height/habit: Upright, 12–30 in. (30–76 cm.).

Leaves: Linear, to 1 ft. (30 cm.) long, resembling those of gladiolus.

Flowers: Loose spikes of 2–12, each to 3 in. (7.5 cm.) across; fragrant; white with reddish brown basal blotch.

Season: Late summer through early fall.

When to plant: Set corms 2–4 in. (5–10 cm.) deep, 4–8 in. (10–20 cm.) apart where they are to grow in spring, when weather is warm. Ground-hardy zone 9 and warmer.

Light: Sun a half day or more.

Soil: Well drained, moist.

Fertilizer: 5-10-5.

Storage: Store corms and cormels formed at their base in nearly dry peat moss or vermiculite, from late fall to spring, at 50–60°F (10–15°C).

Propagation: Remove and plant cormels in spring.

Uses: Beds, borders, pots, cut flowers.

AGAPANTHUS
(ag-ah-PANTH-us)

Lily of the Nile

AMARYLLIDACEAE; amaryllis
family

Height/habit: Grasslike
clumps, upright fountain
form, 1–3 ft. (30–90 cm.)
high/wide.

Leaves: Narrow or strap-
shaped, up to 2 in. (5 cm.)
across, 6–24 in. (15–61 cm.)
long, rising in 2 ranks from
a rhizome having fleshy roots.

Flowers: Umbels vary in number from a few to over 100,
appearing atop a wiry to stiff
scape, 1–4 ft. (30–122 cm.)
long; blue or white.

Season: Spring through
summer.

When to plant: Set transplants
when available, ideally established in a container; roots
recover slowly if disturbed.
Grow outdoors all year zone 9
and warmer. In colder regions
maintain indoors when frost
threatens.

Light: Sun half day or more.

Soil: Well drained; moist
spring through summer, dry
side fall through winter.

Fertilizer: 5-10-5.

Storage: Avoid freezing; keep
in sunny place but avoid severe
drying; add water sparingly as
needed to prevent large numbers of leaves from dying.

Propagation: Divide in late
winter or spring from a clump
having several sets of leaves.
Fresh seeds grow readily,
reaching flowering size in
3–5 years.

Uses: Beds, borders in frost-
free climates, pots, cut flowers.

ALBUCA
(al-BEW-kah)

Sentry-in-the-box

LILIACEAE; lily family

Height/habit: Basal rosette of several leaves, 1–2 ft. (30–61 cm.).

Leaves: Concave at the base, to cylindrical or flat, to 1 ft. (30 cm.) long, arising from the bulb.

Flowers: Racemelike spikes, to 2.5 ft. (76 cm.) high, each 1–2 in. (2.5–5 cm.) across; white or pale yellow with pronounced green striping on the outside; fragrant.

Season: Spring through early summer. Foliage disappears around midsummer.

When to plant: Set bulbs 2–4 in. (5–10 cm.) deep, 9–12 in. (22.5–30 cm.) apart in fall or when dormant.

Light: Sun half day or more.

Soil: Well drained; moist spring until flowers finish, gradually drying off.

Fertilizer: 5-10-5.

Storage: Only to protect from freezing in winter at 50–60°F (10–15°C) until planting time.

Propagation: Remove offsets at planting time; seedlings bloom in 3–4 years.

Uses: Beds, borders zones 9–10 and warmer, pots all climates.

ALLIUM
(AL-lee-um)

Ornamental Onion

LILIACEAE; lily family

Height/habit: Grassy to
onionlike clumps, 8–24 in.
(20–61 cm.).

Leaves: Straplike and hollow,
either flat or round, growing
to 1 ft. (30 cm.) long.

Flowers: Loose or tightly
packed heads, 1–6 in.
(2.5–15 cm.) across on bare
stalks above the leaves; lilac
purple, yellow, white, pink,
or blue.

Season: Spring through summer, depending on the variety.

When to plant: Set bulbs or
transplants where they are to
grow in spring or fall, or when
available. Most are perennial
all zones.

Light: Sun half day or more.

Soil: Well drained, moist to on
the dry side.

Fertilizer: 5-10-5.

Storage: Store dormant bulbs
in dry, dark, frost-free place,
at 50–60°F (10–15°C) in peat
moss or vermiculite, in winter
until planting time.

Propagation: Divide clumps
spring or fall. Seedlings bloom
in 3 years.

Uses: Beds, borders, pots,
cutting, drying. Leaves of
A. schoenoprasum are the
edible herb chives.

ALPINIA
(al-PINE-ee-ah)

Shell Ginger

ZINGIBERACEAE; ginger family

Height/habit: Erect clumps 5–10 ft. (1.5–3 m.) high/wide.

Leaves: Appear all along the stalks, each 1–2 ft. (30–61 cm.) long, to 5 in. (12.5 cm.) wide.

Flowers: Bell-shaped in dense clusters to 1 ft. (30 cm.) long; fragrant; white or flushed pink with red and brown details.

Season: Summer.

When to plant: Set transplants when available, ideally spring after the weather is warm and settled. Best for ground planting zone 10 and warmer; roots may survive light frost but recovery to flowering may be slow. Remove canes annually, after they have flowered.

Light: Part sun to part shade.

Soil: Humusy, well drained, generous moisture in summer.

Fertilizer: 5-10-5.

Storage: Only to prevent freezing; in winter in dry peat moss or vermiculite; avoid temperatures below 60°F (15°C).

Propagation: Divide rhizomatous roots in spring.

Uses: Beds, backgrounds, accents, large containers.

ALSTROEMERIA
(al-stroh-MEER-ee-ah)
Peruvian Lily

ALSTROEMERIACEAE;
alstroemeria family

Height/habit: Upright,
1.5–2.5 ft. (45–76 cm.), forming
clumps or colonizing.
Leaves: Linear to lanceolate,
1–5 in. (2.5–12.5 cm.) long,
growing from the base and
all along the stems; whorled
in *A. psittacina*.
Flowers: 1–3 in. (2.5–7.5 cm.)
across in terminal clusters,
resembling the Dutch amaryllis
blossom in miniature; in
A. caryophyllaea, fragrant yellow, orange, or white with red
tips; in *A. psittacina*, dark red
tipped green with brown spots.

Season: Midwinter through
early summer, depending on
the species and climate.
When to plant: Set transplants
when available. Tends to be
dormant in hottest weather,
grows mostly in cooler seasons. *A. pulchella* hardy zone 5
and warmer, with protection
in coldest sections. Seeds
started in a cool greenhouse in
the fall flower after 2–3 seasons.
Light: Sun half day or more.
Soil: Well drained; evenly
moist while in active growth
(cool seasons), drier in summer. Cool (around 50°F
[10°C]) soil in fall and early
winter helps set buds.
Fertilizer: 5-10-5.
Storage: Rest bulbs from
receipt until planting time in
peat moss or vermiculite at
50–60°F (10–15°C).

Propagation: Sow seeds in
summer; divide in spring.
Uses: Beds, borders, pots,
long-lasting cut flower.
A. psittacina can be a useful
(at times striking, on occasion
invasive) ground cover zone 9
and warmer.

AMARYLLIS
(am-ah-RILL-iss)

Belladonna Lily

AMARYLLIDACEAE; amaryllis
family

Height/habit: Upright, self-reliant clumps of leaves fall-winter, 2–3 ft. (60–90 cm.) tall/wide.

Leaves: Straplike, to 18 in. (45 cm.) long.

Flowers: In an umbel atop a naked, reddish scape, 15–30 in. (35–75 cm.) tall, each 3–4 in. (8–10 cm.) long/wide; rose-red to pale pink or near white.

Season: Late summer-early fall.

When to plant: Set the bulb early fall, immediately after flowering, with neck at soil surface. Cold hardy zone 8 and warmer, zone 7 if protected.

Light: Sunny to half-sunny.

Soil: Humus-rich, well-drained, moist except on the dry side late spring-early summer.

Fertilizer: 5-10-5.

Uses: Beds, borders, large pots, cutting.

ANEMONE
(ah-NEM-oh-nee)

Windflower

RANUNCULACEAE; buttercup family

Height/habit: *A. blanda* types 6–8 in. (15–20 cm.). *A. coronaria* varieties form a basal rosette of foliage resembling parsley, then flower on straight stems to 1.5 ft. (45 cm.).

Leaves: Basal, much divided, 1–3 in. (2.5–7.5 cm.) across.

Flowers: Daisylike in *A. blanda*, 1–2 in. (2.5–5 cm.) across. Poppylike in *A. coronaria*, 2–3 in. (5–7.5 cm.) across; white, blue, pink, red, or rose.

Season: Winter through spring. *A. coronaria* grows well outdoors in mild climates.

When to plant: Set tuberous rhizomes 1–2 in. (2.5–5 cm.) deep, 6–12 in. (15–30 cm.) apart in fall. Zone 7 and colder set *A. coronaria* in spring for blooms in summer.

Light: Sunny to partly sunny; more shade for *A. blanda*.

Soil: Humusy, well drained, moist while in active growth.

Fertilizer: 5-10-5.

Storage: Store dormant rhizomes from receipt until planting time in peat moss or vermiculite in a dry and dark place with moderate temperatures (50–70°F [10–21°C]).

Propagation: Sow seeds in late summer or early fall.

Uses: *A. blanda* types carpet ground, often interplanted with tulips, hyacinths, and daffodils; cut flowers.

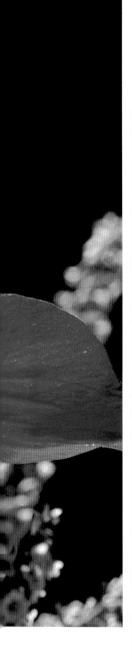

Kangaroo Paw

HAEMODORACEAE; bloodwort family

Height/habit: Clumps with flowering stalks rising 3–5 ft. (1–1.5 m.).

Leaves: Linear or sword-shaped, 1–1.5 ft. (30–45 cm.) long.

Flowers: 1-sided spikes, woolly, 1–3 in. (2.5–7.5 cm.) long; red to yellow to greenish; showy in bloom, unusual.

Season: Late spring through fall; periodically cut back bloomed-out spikes to the ground.

When to plant: Set rootstocks with growth eyes at ground level in spring or early fall; set transplants when available. Winter-hardy zone 9 and warmer.

Light: Sun half day or more.

Soil: Well drained, moist; maintain on the dry side in winter.

Fertilizer: 5-10-5.

Storage: Store rootstocks out of the ground in dry peat moss and moderate temperatures (50–60°F [10–15°C]), as briefly as possible, from receipt until planting time.

Propagation: Divide established clumps in spring or early fall.

Uses: Beds, borders, large containers, cut flowers.

ARISAEMA
(air-iss-EE-mah)

Jack-in-the-pulpit
ARACEAE; aroid family

Height/habit: Erect, 1–2 ft. (30–61 cm.).

Leaves: 1–3 per tuber, divided, 3–5-parted, 9–12 in. (22.5–30 cm.) long.

Flowers: Clublike spadix surrounded by an ornamental spathe; combinations of green, white, and purple-brown.

Season: Late spring through early summer. Leaves attractive in summer; red berries in fall.

When to plant: Set tubers 4–6 in. (10–15 cm.) deep, 1 ft. (30 cm.) apart in fall or early spring. Set transplants when available. North American arisaemas and some from Asia are winter-hardy to zone 5; those from milder climates require wintering in a frost-free place.

Light: Part sun to part shade.

Soil: Humusy, well drained, moist.

Fertilizer: 5-10-5.

Storage: Rest tubers as necessary in dry peat moss, with moderate temperatures (50–60°F [10–15°C]) and darkness until planting time.

Propagation: Remove offsets at transplanting time or sow seeds in spring.

Uses: Beds, borders, wild gardens.

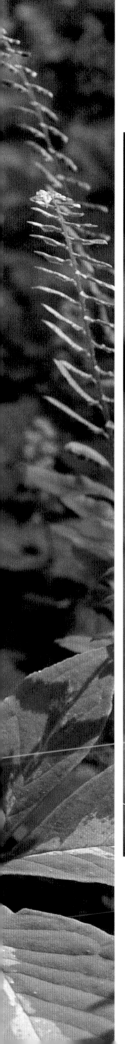

ASPHODELINE
(ass-foh-del-LYE-nee)

Asphodel

LILIACEAE; lily family

Height/habit: Grasslike clumps, 1–1.5 ft. (30–45 cm.) high/wide. Dormant in winter.
Leaves: Linear, to 1 ft. (30 cm.) long.
Flowers: Starry, 1–2 in. (2.5–5 cm.) across, in dense, cylindrical racemes, to 2 ft. (61 cm.) high; yellow; fragrant.
Season: Early to midsummer.
When to plant: Set clumps of thickened roots with growth eyes 1–2 in. (2.5–5 cm.) deep, 6–8 in. (15–20 cm.) apart in early spring or fall. Set transplants when available. Ground-hardy zone 5 and warmer.
Light: Sun half day or more.
Soil: Well drained, moist.
Fertilizer: 5-10-5.
Storage: Store root clumps in dry peat moss, darkness, and moderate temperatures (50–60°F [10–15°C]) from receipt until planting time.
Propagation: Divide at transplanting time or sow seeds in fall or spring.
Uses: Beds, borders, cut flowers.

ASPHODELUS
(ass-FOD-el-us)

Silver Rod

LILIACEAE; lily family

Height/habit: Erect, 2–5 ft. (61–150 cm.).

Leaves: Coarse, grasslike, in clumps, 1–1.5 ft. (30–45 cm.) high/wide. Dormant in winter.

Flowers: Starry, 1–2 in. (2.5–5 cm.) across, in showy, erect spikes 1.5–5 ft. (45–150 cm.) high; white or pink.

Season: Late spring through early summer.

When to plant: Set clumps of thickened roots with the growth eyes 1–2 in. (2.5–5 cm.) deep, 6–8 in. (15–20 cm.) apart in early spring or fall. Set transplants when available. Ground-hardy zones 6–7 and warmer.

Light: Sun half day or more.

Soil: Well drained, moist.

Fertilizer: 5-10-5.

Storage: Store root clumps in dry peat moss, darkness, and moderate temperatures (50–60°F [10–15°C]) from receipt until planting time.

Propagation: Divide at transplanting time or sow seeds in fall or spring.

Uses: Beds, borders, cut flowers.

BEGONIA
(be-GOH-nee-ah)
Tuberous Begonia
BEGONIACEAE; begonia family

Height/habit: *Begonia* x *tuberhybrida* upright or cascading, 1–3 ft. (30–90 cm.).

Leaves: Lightly hairy, angel-wing-shaped, 5 in. (12.5 cm.) long x 3 in. (7.5 cm.) wide; bright green; stalks and stems often flushed reddish copper.

Flowers: Single or double, 2–8 in. (5–20 cm.) across, in a variety of forms, including camellia, rose, carnation, and picotee; most colors except blue.

Season: Summer until early fall. They bloom while days are longest and are not suited to gardens where temperatures rise above 80°F (26°C).

When to plant: Set tubers to root in pots or flats indoors 8–12 weeks before planting-out weather. Upright varieties can be set in beds; most tuberous begonias are grown in containers.

Light: Half sun to half shade; the cooler the temperatures, the more sun they need.

Soil: Humusy, well drained, moist throughout the growing season, dry while dormant.

Fertilizer: 5-10-5.

Storage: Store tubers in nearly dry peat moss and moderate temperatures (50–60°F [10–15°C]) from fall until planting time the next late winter through spring.

Propagation: Sow seeds winter through spring in a warm, moist, bright place; divide tubers, each part with a growth eye, at planting time.

Uses: Beds, borders, pots, hanging baskets.

BEGONIA
(be-GOH-nee-ah)

Hardy Begonia

BEGONIACEAE; begonia family

Height/habit: *B. grandis* upright, 1.5–2.5 ft. (45–76 cm.) high/wide.

Leaves: Angel-wing-shaped, 5 in. (12.5 cm.) long x 3 in. (7.5 cm.) wide; olive above, flushed red below.

Flowers: 1 in. (2.5 cm.) across in drooping cymes; fragrant; pink (white in 'Alba').

Season: Midsummer to fall.

When to plant: Set bulblets 1 in. (2.5 cm.) deep, 8–12 in. (20–30 cm.) apart in spring. Bulblets form annually in the leaf axils. Ground-hardy zone 7 and warmer.

Light: Half sun to half shade.

Soil: Humusy, well drained, moist.

Fertilizer: 5-10-5.

Storage: Place bulblets in dry peat moss, darkness, and moderate temperatures (50–60°F [10–15°C]) during winter until planting time.

Propagation: In spring, plant bulblets formed the previous growing season.

Uses: Beds, borders, ground cover.

BLETILLA
(bleh-TILL-ah)

Chinese Ground Orchid

ORCHIDACEAE; orchid family

Height/habit: Upright, forming good-sized clumps, 8–20 in. (20–50 cm.) high/wide.

Leaves: Narrow, arching, pleated, palmlike, 8–12 in. (20–30 cm.) long.

Flowers: Racemes of 3–12 rise above the leaves, each 1–2 in. (2.5–5 cm.) across; purple or white.

Season: Early to midsummer.

When to plant: Set tuberlike roots 1–2 in. (2.5–5 cm.) deep 6–8 in. (15–20 cm.) apart in fall or early spring. Set transplants when available. Do not disturb unnecessarily; established, crowded clumps bloom best. Ground-hardy zone 8 and warmer.

Light: Half sun to half shade.

Soil: Humusy, well drained, moist while in active growth.

Fertilizer: 5-10-5.

Storage: Store roots briefly in dry peat moss and moderate temperatures (50–60°F [10–15°C]) from receipt until planting time.

Propagation: Divide rootstocks in fall or early spring.

Uses: Beds, borders, wild gardens, pots.

CALADIUM
(kal-LAY-dee-um)

Fancy-leaved Caladium

ARACEAE; aroid family

Height/habit: Upright, rounded clumps, 1–3 ft. (30–90 cm.) high/wide.
Leaves: Arrowhead-shaped, 2–12 in. (5–30 cm.) long by half to two-thirds as wide; lance-leaved cultivars thrive in sun. Leaves typically veined, speckled, or banded with a contrasting color.

Flowers: Mostly hidden by leaves; resemble the calla lily; gardeners usually remove them as soon as the buds appear in order to produce beautiful foliage.
Season: Spring and summer.
When to plant: Set caladium tubers 2–4 in. (5–10 cm.) deep, 6–12 in. (15–30 cm.) apart when soil is warm in spring; tubers can be started indoors in separate pots 8–12 weeks before planting-out weather; sometimes proves ground-hardy zone 9 and warmer.
Light: Sun for lance-leaved cultivars; equal amounts sun and shade for standard large, arrowhead varieties.

Soil: Humusy, well drained, moist while in active growth.
Fertilizer: 5-10-5.
Storage: Store tubers in dry peat moss or vermiculite at 50–60°F (10–15°C) from receipt until planting time.
Propagation: Remove offsets from tubers in spring.
Uses: Beds, borders, pots.

CAMASSIA
(kah-MASS-ee-ah)

Camass; Wild Hyacinth

LILIACEAE; lily family

Height/habit: Upright clumps, 1–1.5 ft. (30–45 cm.) high/wide.
Leaves: Grassy, narrow, tapering, 1–3 ft. (30–90 cm.) long.
Flowers: Dense spikes rising from center of plant; starry, 1–2 in. (2.5–5 cm.) across; blue, white, purple, or cream.
Season: Late spring.
When to plant: Set bulbs 4 in. (10 cm.) deep, 9 in. (22.5 cm.) apart in fall. Ground-hardy zone 5 and warmer.
Light: Sun half day or more.

Soil: Well drained, moist; keep dry during summer resting period.
Fertilizer: 5-10-5.
Storage: Store bulbs in dry peat moss at 50–60°F (10–15°C) until planting time.
Propagation: Divide crowded clumps in fall.
Uses: Beds, borders, cut flowers, perimeter plantings for pond and bog gardens.

CANNA
(KAN-nah)
Indian Shot
CANNACEAE; canna family

Height/habit: Upright clumps, 4–12 ft. (1.2–3.6 m.) high by half as wide.

Leaves: Reminiscent of those of banana; simple, rounded, entire; 1–4 ft. (30–122 cm.) long by about half as wide; often with fine edging of red-brown. In *Canna* x *generalis* 'Striata' the red-margined bright green leaves are feathered and striped with cream yellow.

Flowers: Terminal clusters resembling butterfly ginger but larger; most colors except blue and purple.

Season: Summer in cold climates, spring through fall zone 8 and warmer. Prompt removal of spent flowers increases bloom and enhances appearance. After all the flowers on a stalk have bloomed, it can be cut back to the ground.

When to plant: Set tuberlike rhizomes 5 in. (12.5 cm.) deep, 10 in. (25 cm.) apart when soil is warm in spring. Set transplants when available. Ground-hardy zone 7 and warmer.

Light: Sun half day or more.

Soil: Humusy, well drained, moist during active growing season; pots of cannas can be left standing in saucers of water.

Fertilizer: 5-10-5.

Storage: Store tuberlike rhizomes in dry peat moss at 50–60°F (10–15°C) from light frost season in fall to spring planting.

Propagation: Divide rhizomes in spring or sow seeds indoors 12–16 weeks before warm weather.

Uses: Beds, borders, large pots, perimeter plantings for ponds and bog gardens.

CHASMANTHE
(chaz-MANTH-ee)

Pennants

IRIDACEAE; iris family

Height/habit: Upright clumps, 2–4 ft. (61–122 cm.) high/wide.
Leaves: 1–2 in. (2.5–5 cm.) wide, 1–2 ft. (30–61 cm.) long.
Flowers: Erect spikes growing above the leaves, to 2 in. (5 cm.) long; orange-red with yellow or green.
Season: Spring through early summer.
When to plant: Set the corms 2–4 in. (5–10 cm.) deep, 4–8 in. (10–20 cm.) apart, fall zone 8 and warmer, spring zone 7 and colder.
Light: Sun half day or more.
Soil: Well drained, moist while in active growth.
Fertilizer: 5-10-5.
Storage: Store corms in dry peat moss at 50–60°F (10–15°C) from receipt until planting time.
Propagation: Divide established clumps in spring.
Uses: Beds, borders, pots, cut flowers.

CHIONODOXA
(key-on-oh-DOX-ah)

Glory-of-the-snow

LILIACEAE; lily family

Height/habit: Grassy clumps, 6–8 in. (15–20 cm.) high/wide.
Leaves: Narrow, to 6 in. (15 cm.) long.
Flowers: 4–6 per terminal raceme, each to 1 in. (2.5 cm.) across; blue, white, or pink.
Season: Early spring.
When to plant: Set bulbs 3 in. (7.5 cm.) deep, 2 in. (5 cm.) apart in fall. Ground-hardy zone 5 and warmer.

Light: Sun in spring, shade acceptable at other times.
Soil: Well drained; moist fall through spring, keep on the dry side in summer.
Fertilizer: 5-10-5.
Storage: Store bulbs in dry peat moss at 50–60°F (10–15°C) from receipt until planting time.
Propagation: Divide established clumps in fall.
Uses: Beds, borders, pots; excellent for planting under deciduous trees and shrubs since they do not leaf out until the chionodoxa leaves have done their season's gathering of solar energy.

CLIVIA
(KLYE-vee-ah)
Kaffir Lily
AMARYLLIDACEAE; amaryllis family

Height/habit: Upright, evergreen clumps, 1–2 ft. (30–61 cm.) high/wide.

Leaves: Strap-shaped, 2–3 in. (5–7.5 cm.) wide, 1–1.5 ft. (30–45 cm.) long.

Flowers: Many-flowered umbels atop stiff stalks; each flower to 2 in. (5 cm.) across; apricot, orange, scarlet, rarely yellow.

Season: Winter through spring, depending on climate and treatment. Suited to ground planting zone 10 and warmer.

When to plant: Best to purchase transplants in bloom so you know the color and form are superior.

Light: Half sun to half shade.

Soil: Humusy, well drained; moist, except keep on the dry side in fall and winter.

Fertilizer: 5-10-5.

Storage: Store potted plant in cool (40–60°F [4–15°C]) but not freezing temperatures; keep on the dry side in fall and early winter, but do not let leaves die.

Propagation: Remove offsets in spring or sow seeds as soon as they are ripe. Set each young plant in a 5-in. (12-5 cm.) clay pot and do not transplant to a larger size until it has bloomed, usually within 3 years.

Uses: Pots and cut flowers in all climates; beds zone 10 and warmer.

COLCHICUM
(KOLE-chick-um)

Autumn Crocus

LILIACEAE; lily family

Height/habit: Clumps of spring foliage, to 1 ft. (30 cm.) high/wide.

Leaves: Basal, to 3 in. (7.5 cm.) wide x 1 ft. (30 cm.) long.

Flowers: Clusters, each to 6 in. (15 cm.) across by 10 in. (25 cm.) high; white, purple, or pink; double in 'Waterlily.'

Season: Fall.

When to plant: Set bulbs 2–3 in. (5–7.5 cm.) deep, 4–6 in. (10–15 cm.) apart in late summer or early fall. Ground-hardy zone 6 and warmer.

Light: Sun half day or more.

Soil: Well drained, moist spring and fall; during summer dormancy, keep on the dry side.

Fertilizer: 5-10-5.

Storage: Store in dry peat moss at 50–60˚F (10–15˚C), as briefly as possible, from receipt until planting time.

Propagation: Separate corms at planting time or sow seeds.

Uses: Beds, borders, pots.

COLOCASIA
(koh-low-KAY-see-ah)
Elephant's Ear; Taro
ARACEAE; aroid family

Height/habit: Upright stalks arising directly from the tuber, to 5 ft. (1.5 m.) high/wide.

Leaves: Arrowhead- or shield-shaped, to 3 ft. (1 m.) long by half as wide; prominent veins and satin texture.

Flowers: Calla-type spathe hidden by much taller leaf stalks; pale yellow.

Season: Late spring through summer.

When to plant: Set tubers 4–6 in. (10–15 cm.) deep, 1–1.5 ft. (30–45 cm.) apart when the soil is warm. Ground-hardy zone 8 and warmer.

Light: Half sun to half shade.

Soil: Humusy, well drained; moist during the active growing season.

Fertilizer: 20-20-20 or 5-10-5.

Storage: Rest tubers in dry peat moss at 50–60°F (10–15°C) from fall through winter.

Propagation: Remove offsets from tubers at planting time.

Uses: Beds, borders, pots, accent plants.

CONVALLARIA
(kon-val-LAY-ree-ah)

Lily of the Valley

LILIACEAE; lily family

Height/habit: Dense carpets, to 8 in. (20 cm.), with indefinite diameter.

Leaves: Lanceolate to ovate to elliptic, to 8 in. (20 cm.) long x 2 in. (5 cm.) wide.

Flowers: Very small to .5 in. (1.25 cm.), fragrant nodding bells on a 1-sided raceme, growing among or slightly above the leaves in single or double forms; white or pink.

Season: Late spring through early summer.

When to plant: Set pips (upright rootstock) 1–2 in. (2.5–5 cm.) deep, 6 in. (15 cm.) apart in fall or early spring. Set transplants when available. Divide crowded stands after a few years. Cold-hardy almost everywhere but languishes zone 9 and warmer. Pips potted in fall and subjected to cold temperatures (minor freezing) 8–12 weeks can then be forced into early bloom in a window garden.

Light: Half sun to half shade.

Soil: Humusy, well drained, moist.

Fertilizer: 20-20-20 or 5-10-5.

Storage: Store pips in barely damp peat moss at 40–50°F (4–10°C) from fall through winter until planting time.

Propagation: Divide crowded clumps early spring or fall.

Uses: Beds, borders, rock gardens, ground cover, cut flowers.

CORYDALIS
(koh-RID-ah-liss)

Fumaria

FUMARIACEAE; fumitory family

Height/habit: Upright rosettes, 9–12 in. (22.5–30 cm.) high/wide.

Leaves: Fernlike, 6–12 in. (15–30 cm.) long.

Flowers: Resemble bleeding heart (*Dicentra*), though smaller, in erect racemes of 10–20; rose, purple, pink, white, or yellow.

Season: Early spring through summer. Resilient yellow *C. lutea* blooms constantly from late spring until end of summer.

When to plant: Set root divisions in early spring or fall, growth eyes near soil surface, 6 in. (15 cm.) apart. Grows best zones 5–7. Established plantings self-sow generously.

Light: Half sun to half shade.

Soil: Humusy, well drained, moist.

Fertilizer: 5-10-5.

Storage: Store rootstocks in barely damp peat moss at 40–60°F (4–15°C), as briefly as possible, from receipt until planting time.

Propagation: Divide rootstock clumps in fall or early spring; alternatively, sow seeds or transplant self-sown seedlings.

Uses: Beds, borders, rock or wild gardens, pockets in rock walls.

CRINUM
(KRYE-num)

Florida Swamp Lily; Milk-and-wine Lily

AMARYLLIDACEAE; amaryllis family

Height/habit: Bold, upright, 3–6 ft. (1–1.8 m.) high/wide.
Leaves: Strap- or sword-shaped, to 3 ft. (1 m.) long, arranged in a spiral.

Flowers: Funnelform or spidery, each 3–5 in. (7.5–12.5 cm.) across, a few to many atop a stiff scape, 2–3 ft. (61–90 cm.) high; white, pink, rose, or red and white.
Season: Spring through summer.
When to plant: Set bulbs up to their necks, 1 ft. (30 cm.) apart in spring or fall; set transplants when available. Ground-hardy zones 8–9 and warmer. Favored landscape plant in Florida, along the Gulf Coast and in Southern California.

Light: Sun half day or more.
Soil: Humusy, well drained, moist.
Fertilizer: 20-20-20 or 5-10-5.
Storage: Store bulbs briefly in dry peat moss at 50–60°F (10–15°C) from receipt until planting time.
Propagation: Remove offsets in spring or fall or sow seeds (first flowers in 3–4 seasons).
Uses: Beds, borders, large pots, cut flowers, accent plant; surrounding pond or bog gardens.

CROCOSMIA
(kroh-KAZH-mee-ah)

Copper Tip; Montbretia

IRIDACEAE; iris family

Height/habit: Upright grassy clumps, 2–4 ft. (61–122 cm.) high/wide.

Leaves: Sword-shaped, pleated, resembling those of gladiolus; clustered mostly toward the base, 1–2 ft. (30–61 cm.) long.

Flowers: Borne on wiry, graceful stems standing above the leaves, gracefully curving so that the individual flowers, to 2 in. (5 cm.) across, all face same direction; orange-red or yellow. Cultivar 'Lucifer' is said to have hybrid vigor and will form a remarkable colony in a few years.

Season: Summer.

When to plant: Set corms 2 in. (5 cm.) deep, 6 in. (15 cm.) apart in spring or fall. Set transplants when available. Ground-hardy zone 7 and warmer; in colder regions, apply mulch or other protection.

Light: Full sun to half sun (more shade where summers are hot).

Soil: Well drained, moist.

Fertilizer: 5-10-5.

Storage: Store corms in dry peat moss at 50–60°F (10–15°C) from receipt until planting time.

Propagation: Divide corms in spring or fall or sow seeds in spring.

Uses: Beds, borders, naturalizing, pots, long-lasting cut flower, hummingbird attractant.

CROCUS
(KROH-kuss)

Crocus

IRIDACEAE; iris family

Height/habit: Grassy, 6–12 in. (15–30 cm.).

Leaves: Narrow and linear 4–12 in. (10–30 cm.) long, with a prominent silvery midrib accompanying those that bloom in spring but preceding fall bloomers.

Flowers: Goblets 1–3 in. (2.5–7.5 cm.) across, rising directly from corms; some fragrant; yellow, white, cream, blue, or striped.

Season: Fall (*C. asturicus, C. cancellatus, C. kotschyanus, C. laevigatus, C. longiflorus, C. ochroleucus, C. pulchellus, C. sativus, C. speciosus*); winter through early spring (many species and the large Dutch hybrids).

When to plant: Set corms 3–4 in. (7.5–10 cm.) deep and the same distance apart in late summer through early fall.

Ground-hardy as cold as zone 3 but might not persist in gardens warmer than zone 7. Winter and spring crocuses can be potted in the fall, set to root in a cold (40–50°F [4–10°C]) but not freezing place for 8–12 weeks, then brought inside for early bloom in a cool window.

Light: Sun half day or more.

Soil: Well drained; moist fall through spring and on the dry side in summer.

Fertilizer: 5-10-5.

Storage: Store corms in dry peat moss at 40–50°F (4–10°C) from receipt until planting time.

Propagation: Separate clumps having many corms in fall or sow seeds. Crocuses multiply on their own, eventually forming large colonies.

Uses: Beds, borders, rock gardens, naturalizing, pots.

CURCUMA
(kur-KEW-mah)

Hidden Ginger

ZINGIBERACEAE; ginger family

Height/habit: Tidy, upright clumps, 1.5–2.5 ft. (45–76 cm.) high and half as wide.

Leaves: Long stalks, 1–1.5 ft. (30–45 cm.) tall by one-third as wide.

Flowers: Terminal spike to 8 in. (20 cm.) long; pale yellow cupped bracts; *C. roscoeana* turns fiery orange-scarlet and persists several weeks.

Season: Summer through early fall.

When to plant: Set tubers 2 in. (5 cm.) deep, 6–12 in. (15–30 cm.) apart in warm soil in spring; set transplants when available. Ground-hardy zone 10 and warmer; outstanding for containers in any climate. Dies to ground fall through spring.

Light: Half sun to half shade.

Soil: Humusy, well drained; moist in summer but nearly dry while resting.

Fertilizer: 20-20-20 or 5-10-5.

Storage: Store tubers in dry peat moss at 50–60°F (10–15°C) during winter until planting time.

Propagation: Remove offsets at planting time in spring.

Uses: Beds, borders, pots.

CYCLAMEN
(SIKE-lah-men; SICK-lah-men)

Persian Violet; Florists' Cyclamen

PRIMULACEAE; primrose family

Height/habit: Mounds or rosettes, 4–10 in. (10–25 cm.) high/wide.

Leaves: Heart-, kidney-, or ivy-shaped on wiry stalks arising directly from the tuber, each 1–2 in. (2.5–5 cm.) across, often with contrasting veins or pronounced silver variegation on green.

Flowers: Inverted/reflexed, 1–3 in. (2.5–7.5 cm.) across; some with sweet fragrance; red, rose, pink, violet, purple, or white.

Season: Winter through spring. Regular and miniature forms of florists' cyclamen (*C. indicum*) tolerate cold to about 28°F (-2°C) and can be used zone 9 and warmer for color where impatiens bloom in warm weather. Other species are hardy zone 5 and warmer and bloom during winter mild spells or spring.

When to plant: Set transplants when available, usually spring, fall, or winter.

Light: Part sun to part shade.

Soil: Humusy, well drained; moist while in active growth, on the dry side at other times.

Fertilizer: 5-10-5 or 14-14-14.

Storage: Store florists' cyclamen tubers in their pots, nearly dry, in moderate temperatures (60–70°F [15–21°C]) late spring until late summer, when it is time to repot and activate growth for a new flowering season.

Propagation: Sow seeds from winter through spring for flowers in 12–18 months after planting.

Uses: Beds, borders, pots.

CYRTANTHUS
(sur-TANTH-us)

Miniature Amaryllis

AMARYLLIDACEAE; amaryllis family

Height/habit: Grassy clumps, 8–15 in. (20–38 cm.).
Leaves: Narrow, to 1 ft. (30 cm.) long.
Flowers: Nodding, fragrant clusters at the end of stems to 1 ft. (30 cm.) high, each a narrow funnel flaring at the apex into 6 petals; white, pink, yellow, or orange-red.
Season: Summer or winter, sometimes fall or spring.
When to plant: Set dormant bulbs with the tips at soil level 6–12 in. (15–30 cm.) apart in fall or spring; set transplants when available. Ground-hardy zone 9 and warmer.
Light: Sun half day or more.
Soil: Humusy, well drained; moist during active season, on the dry side while resting.
Fertilizer: 5-10-5 or 14-14-14.
Storage: Store bulbs in dry peat moss at 55–65°F (13–18°C) from receipt until planting time.
Propagation: Divide at planting time or sow seeds. Like many amaryllids this one does best if set in a fairly large pot and left undisturbed for several years. Many offsets will form and there will be an extraordinary number of flowers.
Uses: Beds, borders, pots, cut flowers.

DAHLIA
(DAL-ee-ah)
Common Dahlia
COMPOSITAE; daisy family

Height/habit: Bushy, upright (with staking), 4–8 ft. (1.2–2.4 m.) high and half as wide.

Leaves: Compound, dark green, in pairs along hollow, jointed, smooth stems 1–2 in. (2.5–5 cm.) long.

Flowers: Daisylike but in at least 15 recognized classes: single, mignon, orchid-flowering, anemone-flowering, collarette, duplex, peony-flowering, incurved cactus, recurved or straight cactus, semicactus, formal decorative, informal decorative, ball, miniature, and pompon; 1–12 in. (2.5–30 cm.) across; most colors except blue, often bicolored.

Season: Midsummer to fall frost.

When to plant: When weather is warm and settled in spring, set each tuber in planting hole 6 in. (15 cm.) deep, 2–3 ft. (61–90 cm.) apart; cover initially with 2–3 in. (5–7.5 cm.) soil; after growth commences, fill remainder of hole. Ground-hardy in warmer regions, but tubers multiply so rapidly that plants go into decline unless dug and divided every year or two. Best performance where summers are mildly hot and there is a protracted fall season with cool but not freezing temperatures.

Light: Sun half day or more.

Soil: Humusy, well drained; moist throughout the growing season.

Fertilizer: 5-10-5 or 14-14-14.

Storage: Rest tubers in dry peat moss at 50–60°F (10–15°C) from fall through spring.

Propagation: Divide clumps in spring; be sure that each tuber is separated with a portion of the neck and a growing eye.

Uses: Beds, borders, large containers, cut flowers.

DICENTRA
(deye-SENT-rah)

Squirrel Corn
(D. CANADENSIS)

Dutchman's-Breeches
(D. CUCULLARIA)

Turkey Corn
(D. EXIMIA)

Height/habit: Upright basal rosettes 1–2 ft. (30–61 cm.) high/wide.

Leaves: Compound, much cut, 10–18 in. (25–45 cm.) long/wide.

Flowers: Racemes of nodding, irregular, 1–2 in. (2.5–5 cm.) long, often 2-spurred at the base; greenish white or purple-tinged (D. canadensis), white with yellow tips (D. cucullaria), white or lavender pink to dark purplish red (D. eximia).

Season: Spring (D. canadensis, D. cucullaria); spring through summer (D. eximia).

When to plant: Set tubers or fleshy rhizomes in fall, 1–2 in. (2.5–5 cm.) deep; set transplants when available. Cold-hardy to zone 4 but not suited to zone 9 and warmer.

Light: Half sun to half shade.

Soil: Humusy, well drained, moist.

Fertilizer: 5-10-5 or 14-14-14.

Storage: Store in dry peat moss and moderate temperatures (50–70°F [10–21°C]) until planting time.

Propagation: Divide established clumps late summer through fall; also by self-sown seedlings.

Uses: Beds, borders, wild or rock gardens.

DIETES
(deye-EE-teez)

African Iris

IRIDACEAE; iris family

Height/habit: Grassy clumps
to 2 ft. (61 cm.) high/wide.
Leaves: Linear to sword-
shaped in 2 ranks, 2–2.5 ft.
(61–76 cm.) long, evergreen.
Flowers: Hover like butterflies
above the leaves, 2–4 in.
(5–10 cm.) across; lemon
yellow with dark brown basal
spot (*D. bicolor*) or white with
yellow or brown spots and
blue markings (*D. vegeta*).
Season: Summer; old bloom
stalks often flower again.
When to plant: Set transplants
when available. Winter-hardy
zone 9 and warmer. Elsewhere
containerize and bring indoors
during freezing weather.
Light: Full sun to half sun.
Soil: Well drained, moist.
Fertilizer: 5-10-5.
Storage: Store upright in
barely damp peat moss, as
briefly as possible, until
planting time.
Propagation: Divide established clumps in fall or spring.
Uses: Beds, borders, pots.

ERANTHIS
(ee-RANTH-iss)

Winter Aconite

RANUNCULACEAE; buttercup
family

Height/habit: 3–6 in. (7.5–15
cm.).
Leaves: Solitary, lobed, peltate
leaf, to 2 in. (5 cm.) across;
stands rufflike atop each stem.
Flowers: Single, cupped, 1–2 in.
(2.5–5 cm.) across; bright
yellow.
Season: During winter thaws
or earliest spring; disappears
by late spring.

When to plant: Set bulbs 3–4
in. (7.5–10 cm.) deep, 3 in. (7.5
cm.) apart as soon as they are
available in fall. Cold-hardy
zone 6 but not recommended
zone 9 and warmer.
Light: Half sun to half shade.
Soil: Well drained; moist
through spring, on the dry side
in summer.
Fertilizer: 5-10-5.
Storage: Store in damp peat
moss at 40–50°F (4–10°C), as
briefly as possible, until planting time.
Propagation: By normal
increase, usually self-sown
seedlings.
Uses: Wild or rock gardens.

EREMURUS
(air-ee-MEW-russ)

Desert Candle; Foxtail Lily

LILIACEAE; lily family

Height/habit: Raceme rises 4–6 ft. (1.2–1.8 m.).

Leaves: Strap-shaped and narrow, to 15–20 in. (38–50 cm.) long, in tufts or rosettes; basal foliage to 2 ft. (61 cm.) high/wide.

Flowers: Showy, blooming profusely in small bell shapes on long spikes; orange, pink, white, or yellow.

Season: Late spring through early summer.

When to plant: Set the fleshy roots in fall, with the growth eye 4–6 in. (10–15 cm.) deep 1.5–2 ft. (45–61 cm.) apart. Winter-hardy zone 7 and warmer but not suited to the mild, humid Gulf Coast.

Light: Sun half day or more.

Soil: Well drained; moist in spring, on the dry side throughout summer.

Fertilizer: 5-10-5.

Storage: Store roots in dry peat moss at 50–60°F (10–15°C), as briefly as possible, from receipt until planting time.

Propagation: Sow seeds as soon as they ripen in summer or divide roots in fall.

Uses: Back of border or as accent in a rock garden; cut flowers.

ERYTHRONIUM
(air-ee-THROW-nee-um)

Dogtooth Violet;
Trout Lily

LILIACEAE; lily family

Height/habit: Slender flower stalks rise to 1 ft. (30 cm.) from a pair of basal leaves.

Leaves: Tongue-shaped, 6–12 in. (15–30 cm.) long; often mottled purple, brown, or white.

Flowers: Lilylike, 1–2 in. (2.5–5 cm.) across; white, pink, yellow, rose, purple, cream, sometimes with contrasting color in the throat.

Season: Spring.

When to plant: Set the small corms 3 in. (7.5 cm.) deep, 6 in. (15 cm.) apart, in fall and leave undisturbed as long as possible. Since these American natives are on the preservation lists of numerous states, purchase corms certified to have originated in a nursery. Ground-hardy zone 5 and warmer but not suited to warm, humid Gulf Coast gardens.

Light: Half sun to half shade; ideal under deciduous trees.

Soil: Humusy, deep, well drained, moist.

Fertilizer: 5-10-5 or 14-14-14 to help them become established.

Storage: Store corms in dry peat moss at 50–60°F (10–15°C), as briefly as possible, from receipt until planting time.

Propagation: Remove bulb offsets or sow seeds in fall.

Uses: Wild or rock gardens, beds, borders.

EUCHARIS
(YEW-kah-riss)

Amazon Lily; Eucharist Lily

AMARYLLIDACEAE; amaryllis family

Height/habit: Clumps of dark green leaves resembling those of spathiphyllum (peace lily, or closet plant), 1–2 ft. (30–61 cm.) high/wide.

Leaves: Rise directly from the bulb, first a slender stalk, then reaching 6 in. (15 cm.) wide by twice as long. After a season the oldest die down naturally.

Flowers: To 4 in. (10 cm.) across, several atop each smooth stalk, 1.5–2 ft. (20–61 cm.) high; white with touches of green in the throat; lemon-scented flowers resemble daffodils.

Season: Spring in Southern gardens; at various times during the year for potted specimens, which can be alternatively pushed to promote leaf production, then dried out for a few weeks, followed by regular watering and fertilizer, which promotes a round of bloom.

When to plant: Set dormant bulbs with the neck slightly exposed, 6–12 in. (15–30 cm.) apart, when available; potted specimens with leaves are a better investment. Ground-hardy zone 10 and warmer, elsewhere best grown in a pot.

Light: Half sun to half shade.

Soil: Humusy, well drained; moist, except on the dry side after a season of leaf production.

Fertilizer: 5-10-5 or 14-14-14.

Storage: Store bulbs in dry peat moss at 50–60°F (10–15°C), as briefly as possible, from receipt until planting time.

Propagation: Divide established clumps at repotting time in early spring.

Uses: Beds, borders, pots, cut flowers.

EUCOMIS
(yew-KOH-miss)

Pineapple Lily

LILIACEAE; lily family

Height/habit: Basal rosettes 1–2 ft. (30–61 cm.) high/wide with flower stalks rising slightly higher.

Leaves: Strap-shaped, wavy-edged, 1–2 ft. (30–61 cm.) long, 2–3 in. (5–7.5 cm.) wide.

Flowers: Dense raceme or spike along the upper third of the scape, 1–1.5 ft. (30–45 cm.) high, crowned by a leafy rosette, reminiscent of a pineapple; creamy to greenish with thin purple edging.

Season: Mid- to late summer.

When to plant: Set the bulbs 1 in. (2.5 cm.) deep, 8–12 in. (20–30 cm.) apart in spring, after the weather is warm and settled. Ground-hardy zone 8 and warmer. Elsewhere treat as gladiolus.

Light: Sun half day or more.

Soil: Humusy, moist, well drained.

Fertilizer: 5-10-5 or 14-14-14.

Storage: Store bulbs in dry peat moss at 50–60°F (10–15°C) during freezing weather.

Propagation: Remove offsets in spring or sow seeds.

Uses: Beds, borders, pots, cut flowers.

EUCROSIA
(yew-KROH-zee-ah)

Eucrosia

AMARYLLIDACEAE; amaryllis family

Height/habit: Tidy clumps, 1–1.5 ft. (30–45 cm.) high/wide.

Leaves: Narrow stalks arise from the bulb, then flare to 2–3 in. (5–7.5 cm.) wide by 6–8 in. (15–20 cm.) long; also rounded.

Flowers: Distinguished by long yellow stamens extending noticeably beyond the corolla tube, up to a dozen atop each scape, 1–2 in (2.5–5 cm.) across; reddish orange.

Season: Fall or early winter; also blooms at various times under the regimen set out for *Eucharis*, a closely related plant.

When to plant: Set bulbs or transplants when available; position so that the neck of the bulb is just above the soil, 6–12 in. (15–30 cm.) apart. Ground-hardy zone 10 and warmer; elsewhere grow in pots.

Light: Half sun to half shade.

Soil: Humusy, well drained; moist while in bloom; on the dry side during the summer resting period.

Fertilizer: 5-10-5 or 14-14-14.

Storage: Store bulbs in dry peat moss at 60°F (15°C), as briefly as possible, until planting time.

Propagation: Divide established clumps or sow seeds in fall or spring.

Uses: Beds, borders, pots, cut flowers.

Freesia

IRIDACEAE; iris family

Height/habit: Small clumps, 1–1.5 ft. (30–45 cm.) high/wide.
Leaves: Sword-shaped and grassy, 6–18 in. (15–45 cm.) long, to 1 in. (2.5 cm.) wide.
Flowers: Borne on distinctive 1-sided spikes, tubular, each to 2 in. (5 cm.) long; single or double; white, yellow, pink, red, lavender, purple, orange, or blue; whites and yellows most dependably fragrant.
Season: Winter in mild climate, cool window, or greenhouse; summer in cold climates having relatively cool summers.
When to plant: Set corms 2 in. (5 cm.) deep, 2 in. (5 cm.) apart in early fall for indoor pots or in the ground (mild climates); in cold regions set corms outdoors in spring, as with gladiolus. Ground-hardy zone 9 and warmer. Common white freesia naturalizes best along the Gulf Coast.
Light: Sun half day or more.
Soil: Well drained; moist while in active growth, on the dry side during other seasons.
Fertilizer: 5-10-5 or 14-14-14.
Storage: Store corms in dry peat moss at 50–60°F (10–15°C) from receipt until planting time.
Propagation: Remove offsets or sow seeds in fall or spring.
Uses: Beds, borders, pots, cut flowers.

FRITILLARIA
(frit-ill-LAY-ree-ah)

Crown Imperial; Checkered Lily

LILIACEAE; lily family

Height/habit: Crown imperial (*F. imperialis*) types produce a strong, upright stalk 3–4 ft. (1–1.2 m.), crowned by flowers, with a tuft of leaves on top; checkered lily (*F. meleagris*) types much smaller, graceful, 1–1.5 ft. (30–45 cm.).

Leaves: Lance-shaped in crown imperial, to 6 in. (15 cm.) long; narrow and linear in checkered lily, 3–6 in. (7.5–15 cm.) long.

Flowers: Nodding bells, to 2 in. (5 cm.) across, clustered at the top of the stalk in crown imperial; solitary or up to 3 atop a wiry stem in checkered lily; scarlet to orange or yellow in crown imperial (with skunklike odor that is compensated for by beauty of blooms); veined or checkered reddish purple to white in checkered lily.

Season: Spring.

When to plant: Set bulbs in fall: larger ones (crown imperial) 4–6 in. (10–15 cm.) deep, 1 ft. (30 cm.) apart; smaller ones (checkered lily) 3–4 in. (7.5–10 cm.) deep, 6 in. (15 cm.) apart. Ground-hardy zones 5–9; rarely successful after the first season.

Light: Sun half day or more.

Soil: Well drained; moist while in active growth, on the dry side during other seasons.

Fertilizer: 5-10-5 or 14-14-14.

Storage: Store bulbs in dry peat moss at 40–50°F (4–10°C) from receipt until planting time.

Propagation: Remove offsets in fall.

Uses: Beds, borders, cut flowers.

GALANTHUS
(gay-LANTH-us)
Snowdrop
AMARYLLIDACEAE; amaryllis family

Height/habit: Short, erect, 6–8 in. (15–20 cm.).
Leaves: 2–3 from each bulb, 4–6 in. (10–15 cm.) long.
Flowers: Dangling bells, 1–2 in. (2.5–5 cm.) long; white, often with distinctive green markings between the petals.
Season: Winter thaws or earliest spring.
When to plant: Set bulbs 2–4 in. (5–10 cm.) deep, 2–4 in. (5–10 cm.) apart in early fall. Ground-hardy zones 2–3 and farther south; short-lived zones 8–9 and warmer.
Light: Full sun to part shade.
Soil: Well drained, moist.
Fertilizer: 5-10-5.
Storage: Store bulbs in dry peat moss at 40–50°F (4–10°C), as briefly as possible, from receipt until planting time.
Propagation: Divide bulb clumps in early fall.
Uses: Beds, borders, wild and rock gardens, cut flowers.

GALTONIA
(gal-TOH-nee-ah)
Summer Hyacinth
LILIACEAE; lily family

Height/habit: Resembling gladiolus, erect, 3–4 ft. (1–1.2 m.).
Leaves: Sword-shaped, to 1 ft. (30 cm.) long.
Flowers: Bells, 1 in. (2.5 cm.) long, appear along upper half of a straight stalk; white; fragrant.
Season: Late summer through early fall in cold climates, spring through early summer along the Gulf Coast.
When to plant: Set bulbs 6 in. (15 cm.) deep, 6–12 in. (15–30 cm.) apart in spring. Ground-hardy zone 5 with deep winter mulch, elsewhere to zones 9–10.
Light: Full sun to part shade.
Soil: Well drained, moist.
Fertilizer: 5-10-5.
Storage: Store bulbs in dry peat moss at 50–60°F (10–15°C), as briefly as possible, from receipt until planting time.
Propagation: Remove offsets or seeds in spring.
Uses: Beds, borders, cut flowers.

GLADIOLUS
(glad-ee-OH-luss)

Corn Flag;
Sword Lily

IRIDACEAE; iris family

Height/habit: Clumps; spikes reach 2–6 ft. (61–180 cm.).
Leaves: Sword-shaped, erect, grassy; 1–2 ft. (30–61 cm.) long.
Flowers: Open from bottom up on a 1-sided spike; quite stiffly presented in large-flowered hybrids; much smaller (about 1.5 in. [3.7 cm.] long) and more graceful in the species and hardy types; *G. tristis* fragrant; almost all colors.
Season: Spring and fall in mild-winter, hot-summer gardens; summer elsewhere.

When to plant: Spring through early summer in cold climates; at almost any time the corms are available in mild-winter areas. Set corms 3–6 in. (7.5–15 cm.) deep, the same distance apart.
Light: Sun half day or more.
Soil: Well drained, moist.
Fertilizer: 5-10-5.
Storage: Store corms in dry peat moss at 50–60°F (10–15°C) from fall through winter until planting time.
Propagation: Remove cormlets or sow seeds in spring.
Uses: Beds, borders, pots, cut flowers.

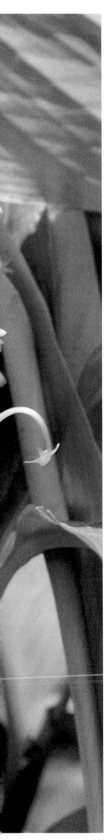

GLOBBA
(GLOB-bah)
Dancing Lady Ginger
ZINGIBERACEAE; ginger family

Height/habit: Upright clumps 1.5–2 ft. (20–61 cm.) high/wide.
Leaves: Lance-shaped, to 8 in. (20 cm.) long x 2 in. (5 cm.) wide; bright green.
Flowers: Appear in pendant racemes; yellow with reflexed purple bracts.
Season: Summer through early fall.
When to plant: Set tubers 2 in. (5 cm.) deep, 2 in. (5 cm.) apart in spring, or when the soil is warm. Ground-hardy zone 9 and warmer. Elsewhere, grow in pots and bring inside during winter.
Light: Half sun to half shade.
Soil: Humusy, well drained; moist while in active growth, quite dry when dormant.
Fertilizer: 5-10-5.
Storage: Store roots from fall through winter in dry peat moss at 60°F (15°C); alternatively, dry in the pots where they are established.
Propagation: Divide in spring.
Uses: Beds, borders, pots.

GLORIOSA
(gloh-ree-OH-sah)
Climbing Lily
LILIACEAE; lily family

Height/habit: Tendril-climbing to 6 ft. (1.8 m.).
Leaves: Lance-shaped, extending into a long tip that acts as a climbing tendril.
Flowers: Recurved, often wavy edged, to 3 in. (7.5 cm.) across; red, yellow, apricot, or bicolored.
Season: Spring, summer, or fall, depending on the species and growing conditions.
When to plant: Set tubers 2 in. (5 cm.) deep, 1 ft. (30 cm.) apart (or in sufficiently large pots to accommodate their long cigar shape) in spring or summer. Ground-hardy zone 9 and warmer.
Light: Sun half day or more.
Soil: Humusy, well drained; moist during the active growing season.
Fertilizer: 5-10-5.
Storage: Store tubers in dry peat moss at 60°F (15°C) from fall through winter until planting time.
Propagation: Remove offsets and tuber divisions or sow seeds in spring.
Uses: For ornamenting fences, trellises, lattice structures; cut flowers.

GLOXINIA
(glox-IN-ee-ah)
True Gloxinia
GESNERIACEAE; gesneriad family

Height/habit: Bushy or upright, 1–2 ft. (30–61 cm.).

Leaves: Ovate, hairy, to 3–4 in. (7.5–10 cm.) long.

Flowers: Funnel- to bell-shaped, 1–2 in. (2.5–5 cm.) long; rose pink with red spots, lavender with purple throat.

Season: Summer through early fall.

When to plant: Set scaly rhizomes 1–2 in. (2.5–5 cm.) deep, 3–4 in. (7.5–10 cm.) apart in spring, or when the soil is warm. Ground-hardy zone 10 and warmer; elsewhere, grow potted.

Light: Half sun to half shade.

Soil: Humusy, well drained; moist while active, nearly dry while resting.

Fertilizer: 5-10-5.

Storage: Store scaly rhizomes in dry peat moss at 50–60°F (10–15°C) from fall through winter until planting time.

Propagation: By natural increase of the rhizomes; alternatively, sow individual scales as "seeds" in warm nursery conditions.

Uses: Beds, borders, mostly in pots.

HABRANTHUS
(hay-BRANTH-us)

Rain Lily

AMARYLLIDACEAE; amaryllis family

Height/habit: Grassy clumps, 8–12 in. (20–30 cm.) high/wide.

Leaves: Narrow blades, 8–12 in. (20–30 cm.) long.

Flowers: Trumpet-shaped, 2–3 in. (5–7.5 cm.) across; pale to dark pink and rose, yellow, copper, or white.

Season: Summer or autumn, often following rain that ends a period of dry weather.

When to plant: Set bulbs 1–2 in. (2.5–5 cm.) deep, 3–6 in. (7.5–15 cm.) apart in spring; set transplants as available. Ground-hardy zone 9 and warmer. Elsewhere, grow in pots or dig before frost.

Light: Sun to half shade.

Soil: Well drained, moist to on the dry side.

Fertilizer: 5-10-5.

Storage: Store in dry peat moss at 50–60°F (10–15°C) only from receipt until planting time.

Propagation: Remove offsets in spring or summer, or sow seeds as soon as they are ripe.

Uses: Beds, borders, wild and rock gardens, pots.

HAEMANTHUS
(hay-MANTH-us)
White Paintbrush
AMARYLLIDACEAE; amaryllis family

Height/habit: Upright, to 1 ft. (30 cm.).

Leaves: Broad straps, 8–10 in. (20–25 cm.) long x 3–4 in. (7.5–10 cm.) wide in most haemanthus; finely haired in white paintbrush (*N. albiflos*).

Flowers: Appear in a dense umbel, 2–3 in. (5–7.5 cm.) wide, with protruding yellow stamens; white in white paintbrush, scarlet red in others (see also *Scadoxus*).

Season: Fall through winter, or following 2–3 months of dryness.

When to plant: Set bulbs with the tips exposed, 1 ft. (30 cm.) apart; set transplants when available. Disturb established haemanthus as little as possible. Winter-hardy zone 9 and warmer.

Light: Sun half day or more.

Soil: Humusy, well drained; moist, except on the dry side from fall through winter.

Fertilizer: 5-10-5.

Storage: Store in dry peat moss at 50–60°F (10–15°C), as briefly as possible, until planting time. Do not deprive evergreen species of light.

Propagation: Remove offsets when active growth begins.

Uses: Beds, borders, pots.

HEDYCHIUM
(heh-DICK-ee-um)
Butterfly Ginger
ZINGIBERACEAE; ginger family

Height/habit: Upright, 3–10 ft. (1–10 m.), forming colonies of about the same width.

Leaves: Broadly lance-shaped, to 10–24 in. (25–61 cm.) long x 4–10 in. (10–25 cm.) wide.

Flowers: 2–3 in. (5–7.5 cm.) across in spikes at the top of each leafy, bamboolike stalk; fragrant; white, orange, coral red, or pale yellow.

Season: Summer through fall.

When to plant: Set rhizomes at beginning of warm season, 1–3 in. (2.5–7.5 cm.) deep, 1–2 ft. (30–61 cm.) apart; set transplants when available. Ground-hardy zone 9 and warmer.

Light: Half sun to half shade.

Soil: Humusy, well drained, moist.

Fertilizer: 5-10-5.

Storage: Store rhizomes in dry peat moss at 50–60°F (10–15°C), as briefly as possible, from receipt until planting time.

Propagation: Divide bulbs in spring.

Uses: Beds, borders, pots; exceptional for partly shaded summer gardens in hot climates.

HELICONIA
(hell-ick-OH-nee-ah)

Lobster Claws

HELICONIACEAE; heliconia family

Height/habit: Erect, 10–15 ft. (3–4.5 m.), forming colonies. Dwarfs only 1.5 ft. (45 cm.).

Leaves: Paddle-shaped on long stalks, each 2–4 ft. (61–122 cm.) long; reminiscent of bird of paradise (*Strelitzia*) and banana (*Musa*).

Flowers: Bloom from colorful, boat-shaped bracts, 5–10 in. (12.5–25 cm.) long; variously erect or pendulous; yellow, orange, or red.

Season: Summer through fall, or during any warm period.

When to plant: Set transplants when available. Hardy zone 10 and warmer.

Light: Half sun to half shade.

Soil: Humusy, well drained, moist.

Fertilizer: 5-10-5.

Storage: Not feasible; evergreen leaves need light, warmth (60°F [10–15°C]), and moisture.

Propagation: Divide at beginning of summer.

Uses: Beds, borders, pots, cut flowers.

HIPPEASTRUM
(hip-pee-AST-rum)

Florists' Amaryllis; Dutch Amaryllis

AMARYLLIDACEAE; amaryllis family

Height/habit: Upright, 1–4 ft. (30–122 cm.), forming colonies.
Leaves: Strap-shaped, 1–4 ft. (30–122 cm.) long, 1–4 in. (2.5–10 cm.) wide; variously evergreen or deciduous.

Flowers: Trumpets, single or double, 2–10 in. (5–25 cm.) across; some fragrant; most colors except true blue.
Season: Fall through winter if newly purchased, otherwise winter through spring.
When to plant: Set bulbs with the neck and some shoulder above ground, 1–2 ft. (30–61 cm.) apart, in fall through winter or as available. Ground-hardy zone 8 and warmer.
Light: Sun half day or more.
Soil: Humusy, well drained; moist, except one season of

dryness, usually fall through winter.
Fertilizer: 5-10-5, 14-14-14.
Storage: Store bulbs in dry peat moss at 50–60°F (10–15°C) from receipt until planting time. Do not deprive evergreen types of light or dry off to the point of yellowing all the leaves.
Propagation: Remove offsets at repotting time or sow seeds as soon as ripe.
Uses: Beds, borders, pots, cut flowers.

HYACINTHOIDES
(high-ah-sin-THOY-deez)

English Bluebell;
Spanish Bluebell

LILIACEAE; lily family

Height/habit: Upright 1–1.5 ft. (30–45 cm.); at first in tidy clumps, later colonizing.

Leaves: Strap-shaped to 1 ft. (30 cm.) long, rising directly from the base.

Flowers: Erect racemes, each to 2 in. (5 cm.) across, bell-like; fragrant; blue, white, or pink. Sometimes also known as *Scilla* and *Endymion*.

Season: Late spring.

When to plant: Set bulbs 2–4 in. (5–10 cm.) deep, 4–6 in. (10–15 cm.) apart in fall. Ground-hardy zone 5 and warmer.

Light: Half sun to half shade.

Soil: Well drained; moist fall through spring, dryness acceptable in summer.

Fertilizer: 5-10-5.

Storage: Store bulbs in dry peat moss at 40–50°F (4–10°C) from receipt until planting time.

Propagation: Remove offsets at fall planting time.

Uses: Beds, borders, wild gardens, cut flowers. Often interplanted with hostas and hardy ferns.

HYACINTHUS
(high-ah-SINTH-us)

Hyacinth

LILIACEAE; lily family

Height/habit: Upright, 8–18 in.
(20–45 cm.).
Leaves: Strap-shaped, rising
directly from the base, 8–14 in.
(20–35 cm.) long x 1–2 in.
(2.5–5 cm.) wide.
Flowers: Appear in dense
racemes at the top of a succulent stalk; single or double,
each to 1 in. (2.5 cm.) across;
fragrant; most colors, including outstanding blues.

Season: Spring. Much favored
for forcing into winter bloom
indoors.
When to plant: Set bulbs
4–6 in. (10–15 cm.) deep,
6–8 in. (15–20 cm.) apart in
fall. Cold-hardy zone 6 and
warmer but not reliable for
repeat performance zone 8
or warmer.
Light: Sun half day or more.
Soil: Well drained, moist.
Fertilizer: 5-10-5.
Storage: Store bulbs in dry
peat moss at 40–50°F (4–10°C)
from receipt until planting
time.

Propagation: Remove offsets.
Uses: Beds, borders, pots,
cut flowers, forcing.

HYMENOCALLIS
(high-men-OCK-al-liss)
Spider Lily
AMARYLLIDACEAE; amaryllis family

Height/habit: Upright, 1–3 ft. (30–90 cm.).
Leaves: Strap-shaped, 1–2 ft. (30–61 cm.) long, 1–2 in. (2.5–5 cm.) wide.
Flowers: Long, spidery petals grow from a daffodil-like cup, each to 5–6 in. (12.5–15 cm.) across; fragrant; white.
Season: Summer.
When to plant: Set bulbs 4–6 in. (10–15 cm.) deep, 6–8 in. (15–20 cm.) apart in spring; set transplants when available. Ground-hardy zone 9 and warmer. Elsewhere, dig and bring inside before hard frost in autumn.
Light: Sun half day or more.
Soil: Humusy, well drained; moist to wet while in active growth.
Fertilizer: 5-10-5.
Storage: Store bulbs in dry peat moss at 50–60°F (10–15°C) from receipt until planting time.
Propagation: Divide bulbs in spring.
Uses: Beds, borders, pots, cut flowers.

IPHEION
(IF-fee-on)
Spring Starflower
AMARYLLIDACEAE; amaryllis family

Height/habit: Grassy clumps, 6–8 in. (15–20 cm.), rapidly colonizing.
Leaves: Narrow, strap-shaped, 6–8 in. (15–20 cm.) long, smelling of onion.
Flowers: Star-shaped, 1–2 in. (2.5–5 cm.) across, standing slightly above the leaves; white tinged blue or lavender.
Season: Spring.
When to plant: Set bulbs 1–2 in. (2.5–5 cm.) deep, 2–4 in. (5–10 cm.) apart in fall. Ground-hardy zone 6 and warmer. Colonizes freely through zone 9.
Light: Sun to half shade.
Soil: Well drained; moist fall through spring, dryness acceptable in summer.
Fertilizer: 5-10-5.
Storage: Store bulbs in dry peat moss at 40–50°F (4–10°C) from receipt until planting time.
Propagation: Remove offsets at fall planting time or sow seeds.
Uses: Beds, borders, rock and wild gardens.

IPOMOEA
(ipp-oh-MEE-ah)
Sweet Potato Vine
CONVOLVULACEAE; morning-glory family

Height/habit: Trailing, stem-rooting vine.
Leaves: Variously oval, triangular, or digitately lobed, to 3 in. (7.5 cm.) long, blackish green in the cultivar 'Blackie.'
Flowers: Inconspicuous.
Season: Summer until frost.
When to plant: At beginning of warm weather, set root cuttings or tubers or tuber pieces with eyes 1–2 in. (2.5–5 cm.) deep, 6–8 in. (15–20 cm.) apart. Ground-hardy zone 9 and warmer.
Light: Sun to half shade.
Soil: Humusy, well drained, moist.
Fertilizer: 5-10-5.
Storage: Store tubers in dry peat moss at 50–60°F (10–15°C) from receipt until planting time.
Propagation: Divide tubers at planting time or propagate from cuttings.
Uses: Beds, borders, ground cover, hanging baskets.

IRIS
(EYE-riss)
Dutch, German, Japanese, and Louisiana Irises
IRIDACEAE; iris family

Height/habit: Grassy, upright, 8–48 in. (20–122 cm.).
Leaves: Narrow spears, about 9–12 in. (22.5–30 cm.) long.
Flowers: Similar to a fleur-de-lis, consisting of 3 standards and 3 falls, 1–8 in. (2.5–20 cm.) across; often fragrant; all colors, many bicolors and blends (especially with Japanese iris [*I. kaempferi*]).
Season: Spring.
When to plant: Set corms, rhizomes, or divisions in late summer or fall; set transplants as available. Set corms 2–4 in. (5–10 cm.) deep, 4–6 in. (10–15 cm.) apart. Gardeners often set rhizomes and divisions in groups of 3, in order to produce a big show beginning the second season. German iris (*I. germanica*) handsome in clumps. Cold-hardy zone 6 and warmer; Louisiana iris (*I. fulva* and others) favored in zone 8 and warmer, especially along the Gulf Coast.
Light: Sun to half shade.
Soil: Humusy, well drained; moist, except on the dry side following the blooming season.
Fertilizer: 5-10-5.
Storage: Store corms in dry peat moss at 40–50°F (4–10°C) from receipt until planting time.
Propagation: Divide or sow seeds.
Uses: Beds, borders, ground cover, containers, cut flowers. Dutch iris (*I. xiphium*) forced for winter bloom.

KAEMPFERIA
(kamp-FEAR-ee-ah)
Peacock Ginger
ZINGIBERACEAE; ginger family

Height/habit: Leafy ground cover, to 1.5 ft. (45 cm.).

Leaves: Broadly oval to rounded, 8–10 in. (20–25 cm.) long/wide; highly variegated in *K. roscoeana*, resembling taffeta fabric.

Flowers: Bloom for 1 day, appearing from the base of the leaves or on upright stalks, each 1–3 in. (2.5–7.5 cm.) across; lavender blue or yellow.

Season: Summer.

When to plant: Set tubers 1 in. (2.5 cm.) deep, 8–12 in. (20–30 cm.) apart at the beginning of warm weather. Set transplants when available. Ground-hardy zone 9 and warmer.

Light: Half to full shade.

Soil: Humusy, well drained; moist, except on the dry side in winter.

Fertilizer: 5-10-5.

Storage: Store tuberous roots in dry peat moss at 50–60°F (10–15°C) from fall through winter until planting time. Potted kaempferias can be left in their containers, kept dry and moderately warm through their winter dormancy.

Propagation: Divide in spring.

Uses: Beds, borders, ground cover, pots.

KNIPHOFIA
(nipp-HOH-fee-ah)

Tritoma;
Torch Lily;
Red-hot Poker

LILIACEAE; lily family

Height/habit: Grassy clumps; flowers rise high above, to 4 ft. (1.2 m.).

Leaves: Long, narrow spears, 1–1.5 ft. (30–45 cm.) long.

Flowers: Tubular with noticeable stamens, densely packed at the top of rigid, showy stalks, 10 in. (25 cm.) long; yellow, cream, chartreuse, orange, or red.

Season: Summer.

When to plant: Set rhizomatous roots or transplants in spring, at the beginning of the growing season, with the eyes barely covered 1.5 ft. (45 cm.) apart. Ground-hardy zone 6; heat-tolerant through zones 9–10.

Light: Sun half day or more.

Soil: Well drained, moist to on the dry side.

Fertilizer: 5-10-5.

Storage: Store roots in dry peat moss at 40–50°F (4–10°C) from receipt until planting time.

Propagation: Divide in spring or sow seeds.

Uses: Beds, borders, pots, cut flowers.

KOHLERIA
(koh-LEAR-ee-ah)

Isoloma; Tree Gloxinia

GESNERIACEAE; gesneriad family

Height/habit: Bushy, self-branching, 1–2.5 ft. (30–76 cm.) high/wide.

Leaves: Ovate, 1–2 in. (2.5–5 cm.) long, velvety-hairy to the touch, growing along upright stems.

Flowers: Numerous nodding bells, 1–2 in. (2.5–5 cm.) across; orange, red, yellow, or pink.

Season: Summer or at any season if potted and provided with sufficient warmth, humidity, and light; tip cuttings often bloom in fluorescent-light gardens when quite tiny.

When to plant: Set scaly rhizomes 1–2 in. (2.5–5 cm.) deep, 2–4 in. (5–10 cm.) apart at the beginning of a warm season. Ground-hardy zone 10 and warmer.

Light: Half sun to half shade.

Soil: Humusy, well drained; moist, except on the dry side while resting.

Fertilizer: 5-10-5.

Storage: Store scaly rhizomes in dry peat moss at 50–60°F (10–15°C) from fall through winter until planting time.

Propagation: Divide rhizomes at planting time or sow seeds.

Uses: Beds, borders, pots.

LACHENALIA
(lack-en-NAY-lee-ah)
Cape Cowslip
LILIACEAE; lily family

Height/habit: Fleshy leaves appear in a basal rosette, resembling hyacinth, to 1 ft. (30 cm.).

Leaves: Strap-shaped, green or with silvery variegation, 6–12 in. (15–30 cm.) long.

Flowers: Nodding, tubular, to 1 in. (2.5 cm.), in racemes above the leaves; yellow, scarlet, often green-tipped.

Season: Winter through spring.

When to plant: Set bulbs 2 in. (5 cm.) deep, 4–6 in. (10–15 cm.) apart in fall. Ground-hardy zone 9 and warmer.

Light: Sun half day or more.

Soil: Well drained; moist fall through spring, dry during summer rest.

Fertilizer: 5-10-5.

Storage: Store bulbs in dry peat moss at 50–60°F (10–15°C) in summer through planting time.

Propagation: Remove offsets at planting time or sow seeds.

Uses: Beds, borders, pots, cut flowers.

LEDEBOURIA
(led-eh-BOO-ree-ah)

Silver Squill

LILIACEAE; lily family

Height/habit: Clump-forming bulbous plant, 6–8 in. (15–20 cm.) high/wide.
Leaves: Succulent straps, 2–4 in. (5–10 cm.) long x 1 in. (2.5 cm.) wide; silver spotted, olive green above, wine red below.
Flowers: Quite small in slender racemes 6–8 in. (15–20 cm.) long; green and blue. Sometimes known as *Scilla violacea.*
Season: Winter for flowers; leaves attractive at most times.

When to plant: Set bulbs 1 in. (2.5 cm.) deep, 2–4 in. (5–10 cm.) apart in fall; set transplants when available. Ground-hardy zone 10 and warmer; elsewhere this makes an outstanding houseplant.
Light: Sun half day or more.
Soil: Well drained, moist to on the dry side.
Fertilizer: 5-10-5.
Storage: Store in dry peat moss at 50–60°F (10–15°C), as briefly as possible, from receipt until planting time.
Propagation: Remove offsets in spring or summer.
Uses: Beds, borders, rock gardens, pots, houseplant.

LEUCOJUM
(LEW-koh-jum)

Snowflake

AMARYLLIDACEAE; amaryllis family

Height/habit: Grassy clumps to 1 ft. (30 cm.) high/wide.
Leaves: Narrow straps, 8–16 in. (20–40 cm.) long.
Flowers: Nodding bells, to 1 in. (2.5 cm.) across; white, green-tipped.
Season: Early spring for *L. vernalis*; late spring for *L. aestivum*; fall for *L. autumnale.*
When to plant: Set bulbs 2–4 in. (5–10 cm.) deep, 4–6 in. (10–15 cm.) apart in fall; set transplants when available. Ground-hardy zones 4–5 and warmer. *L. aestivum* colonizes in gardens along the Gulf Coast zone 9 and warmer; *L. autumnale* does better zone 8 and colder.
Light: Sun to half shade.
Soil: Well drained; moist; after flowering and foliage development, dryness is acceptable.
Fertilizer: 5-10-5.
Storage: Store bulbs in dry peat moss at 40–60°F (4–15°C), as briefly as possible, from receipt until planting time.
Propagation: Remove offsets at planting time. Leucojums are best left undisturbed indefinitely.
Uses: Beds, borders, wild gardens, cut flowers.

LILIUM
(LIL-e-um)
Lily
LILIACEAE; lily family

Height/habit: Upright stalks clothed by many leaves and crowned by numerous flowers, 1–8 ft. (30–240 cm.).

Leaves: Narrow, 3–5 in. (7.5–12.5 cm.) long.

Flowers: Trumpets or reflexed petals, 2–8 in. (5–20 cm.) wide; fragrant; white, pink, rose, red, orange, yellow, lavender, often with contrasting spots or margins.

Season: Spring until early fall, depending on the lineage.

When to plant: Set bulbs 6–8 in. (15–20 cm.) deep, 8–12 in. (20–30 cm.) apart in fall or early spring. Ground-hardy zone 6 and warmer. Bermuda Easter lily (*L. longifolium*) and Formosa lily (*L. formosanum*) thrive along Gulf Coast and other mild regions (zone 9 and warmer).

Light: Sun to half shade.

Soil: Humusy, well drained, moist.

Fertilizer: 5-10-5.

Storage: Store bulbs in dry peat moss at 40–50°F (4–10°C), as briefly as possible, from receipt until planting time.

Propagation: Remove offsets at planting time or sow seeds.

Uses: Beds, borders, pots, cut flowers.

LYCORIS
(leye-KOH-riss)

Naked Lady; Hurricane Lily

AMARYLLIDACEAE; amaryllis family

Height/habit: Foliage, 1–1.5 ft. (30–45 cm.), followed by flower stalks, 15–30 in. (38–76 cm.).

Leaves: Narrow straps, to 1 ft. (30 cm.) long; appear in spring and die down in summer, followed by flowers.

Flowers: Spidery-looking, each to 2 in. (5 cm.) across; bloom in umbels atop a rigid scape; red, pink, yellow, or white.

Season: Late summer early fall.

When to plant: Set the bulbs 2–4 in. (5–10 cm.) deep, 6 in. (15 cm.) apart in late summer or fall; set transplants when available in spring. *L. squamigera* is ground-hardy zone 5 and warmer, the others zone 8 and warmer. *L. radiata* has naturalized in gardens throughout the Southeastern United States.

Light: Sun to half shade.

Soil: Well drained; moist, except summer dryness acceptable.

Fertilizer: 5-10-5.

Storage: Store bulbs in dry peat moss at 50–60°F (10–15°C) from receipt until planting time.

Propagation: Remove offsets at planting time in the fall.

Uses: Beds, borders, pots, cut flowers.

MUSCARI
(moos-KAH-ree)

Grape Hyacinth

LILIACEAE; lily family

Height/habit: Grassy leaves stay close to the ground with flowers rising just above on slender, erect spikes, 6–10 in. (15–25 cm.).

Leaves: Long, narrow, grassy, to 8–10 in. (20–25 cm.), appearing in fall and persisting through the spring blooming season.

Flowers: Urn-shaped and tiny, .75 in. (2 cm.) across; bloom in fragrant spires; blue, purple, or white.

Season: Early to midspring. Excellent for forcing earlier in pots indoors.

When to plant: Set bulbs 2–4 in. (5–10 cm.) deep, 4–6 in. (10–15 cm.) apart in early fall. Ground-hardy zone 5 and warmer; might not return in zone 9 and warmer.

Light: Sun to half shade.

Soil: Well drained, moist, except summer dryness acceptable.

Fertilizer: 5-10-5.

Storage: Store bulbs in dry peat moss at 40–50°F (4–10°C) from receipt until planting time.

Propagation: Remove offsets at planting time or sow seeds.

Uses: Beds, borders, pots, cut flowers, forcing.

NARCISSUS
(nar-SISS-us)

Daffodil; Telephone Flower

AMARYLLIDACEAE; amaryllis family

Height/habit: Grassy clumps, 6–18 in. (15–45 cm.) high/wide.
Leaves: Narrow, grasslike, 6–18 in. (15–45 cm.) long.
Flowers: Shallow to deep cups surrounded by petals, single or double; tubes 1–2 in. (2.5–5 cm.) long; fragrant; white, yellow, orange, or pink.
Season: Primarily spring in cold climates; fall through winter and early spring zone 9 and warmer. Can be forced indoors ahead of outdoor blooming season.
When to plant: Set bulbs 4–6 in. (10–15 cm.) deep, 3–6 in. (7.5–15 cm.) apart in early fall.
Light: Sun to half shade.
Soil: Well drained; moist, except summer dryness acceptable.
Fertilizer: 5-10-5.
Storage: Store bulbs in dry peat moss at 40–50°F (4–10°C) only from receipt until planting time.
Propagation: Remove offsets at planting time.
Uses: Beds, borders, wild and rock gardens, forcing, cut flowers.

NEOMARICA
(nee-oh-mah-REEK-ah)

Walking Iris;
Twelve Apostles

IRIDACEAE; iris family

Height/habit: Grassy clumps
1–1.5 ft. (30–45 cm.) high/wide.
Leaves: Flat swords, 1 in.
(2.5 cm.) wide x 1–1.5 ft.
(30–45 cm.) long; flowers
occur at the tip of a leaflike
spike that follows the production of 12 leaves in a fan.
Flowers: Irislike, fleeting, to
2 in. (5 cm.) across; white
with touches of brown, blue,
or yellow.
Season: Spring through summer; various seasons when
grown as a houseplant.
When to plant: Set rhizomes
in spring, barely covered with
soil, 1 ft. (30 cm.) apart; set
transplants when available.
Hardy zone 9 and warmer.
Light: Sun to half shade.
Soil: Well drained, moist.
Fertilizer: 5-10-5, 14-14-14.
Storage: Store briefly in damp
soil at 50–60°F (10–15°C);
cut back the leaves to 4–5 in.
(10–12.5 cm.) to reduce
transpiration.
Propagation: Root offsets that
form following flowering on
each bloom stalk.
Uses: Beds, borders, pots,
hanging baskets, houseplant.

NERINE
(neh-REYE-nee)

Guernsey Lily

AMARYLLIDACEAE; amaryllis
family

Height/habit: Grassy clumps,
1–1.5 ft. (30–45 cm.) high/wide.
Leaves: Narrow blades, 1–1.5 ft.
(30–45 cm.) long, appearing
before, during, or after flowers
bloom.
Flowers: Umbels atop a scape;
spidery, each 2–3 in. (5–7.5
cm.) across; pink, magenta,
red, rose, or scarlet.
Season: Fall.
When to plant: Set bulbs
2–4 in. (5–10 cm.) deep,
4–6 in. (10–15 cm.) apart in
late summer or early fall; set
transplants when available.
Ground-hardy zone 8 and
warmer.

Light: Sun half day or more.
Soil: Well drained; moist,
except on the dry side in
summer.
Fertilizer: 5-10-5.
Storage: Store bulbs in dry
peat moss at 50–60°F (10–15°C)
only from receipt until
planting time.
Propagation: Remove offsets
at planting time.
Uses: Beds, borders, pots,
cut flowers.

ORNITHOGALUM
(or-nith-OGG-al-um)

Chincherinchee;
Star-of-Bethlehem

LILIACEAE; lily family

Height/habit: Basal clumps
of grassy foliage with flowers
rising considerably above,
1–2 ft. (30–61 cm.).
Leaves: Thick, linear to lanceolate, 1–1.5 ft. (30–45 cm.) long.
Flowers: Racemes 1–1.5 ft.
(30–45 cm.) high bear many
fragrant flowers, each 1–2 in.
(2.5–5 cm.) wide; white.
Season: Spring through
summer.
When to plant: Set bulbs
2–4 in. (5–10 cm.) deep,
4–8 in. (10–20 cm.) apart in

fall. Ground-hardy zone 8
and warmer. Elsewhere can
be grown as a potted plant.
Light: Sun half day or more.
Soil: Well drained, moist.
Fertilizer: 5-10-5.
Storage: Store bulbs in dry
peat moss at 50–60°F (10–15°C)
from receipt until planting
time.
Propagation: Remove offsets
at planting time.
Uses: Beds, borders, pots,
outstanding cut flowers.

OXALIS
(OX-al-iss)

Lucky Clover;
Wood Sorrel

OXALIDACEAE; oxalis family

Height/habit: Low, ground-covering plants, 3–6 in. (7.5–15 cm.).

Leaves: Small, to .5 in. (1.25 cm.); resemble clover, often with a contrasting zone of color.

Flowers: Delicate, shallow trumpets, each to 1 in. (2.5 cm.) across, in clusters atop a slender, wiry scape; red, pink, yellow, white, rose, or lavender.

Season: Spring through fall, depending on the species; winter in mild climates (zone 9 and warmer).

When to plant: Set bulbs or rhizomes 1–2 in. (2.5–5 cm.) deep, 4–6 in. (10–15 cm.) apart in fall or spring; transplants when available. Wild, weedy oxalis grows almost every-where. Cultivated sorts are showier and ground-hardy zone 8 and warmer.

Light: Sun to half shade.

Soil: Well drained; moist, except dryness acceptable during dormancy.

Fertilizer: 5-10-5.

Storage: Store in dry peat moss at 50–60°F (10–15°C) from receipt until planting time.

Propagation: Remove offsets at planting time.

Uses: Beds, borders, rock and wild gardens, pots, hanging baskets.

PANCRATIUM
(pan-CRAY-shum)

Sea Daffodil

AMARYLLIDACEAE; amaryllis family

Height/habit: Basal foliage rosettes topped by umbels, to 3 ft. (1 m.).
Leaves: Evergreen, linear, to 2.5 ft. (76 cm.) long.
Flowers: Resemble daffodils but more spidery, to 3 in. (7.5 cm.) across; white; fragrant.
Season: Summer.
When to plant: Set bulbs 4–6 in. (10–15 cm.) deep, 6–8 in. (15–20 cm.) apart in fall or spring; transplants when available. Ground-hardy zone 8 and warmer; elsewhere dig and bring inside before hard freezing in the fall, or grow as a container plant.
Light: Sun half day or more.
Soil: Humusy, well drained; moist, except on the dry side fall through winter.
Fertilizer: 5-10-5.
Storage: Store bulbs in dry peat moss at 50–60°F (10–15°C) from receipt until planting time.
Propagation: Remove offsets in spring.
Uses: Beds, borders, pots, cut flowers.

PLEIONE
(ply-OH-nee)

Indian Crocus

ORCHIDACEAE; orchid family

Height/habit: Small orchid, to
8 in. (20 cm.).

Leaves: Plicate (fanlike), lance-
shaped, 4–8 in. (10–20 cm.)
long.

Flowers: Resemble a small,
showy cattleya orchid, to 3 in.
(7.5 cm.) across; lavender pink,
rose, white, or yellow.

Season: Spring.

When to plant: Set transplants
when available for outdoor
gardens zone 10 and warmer.
Elsewhere, pleiones need to be
brought indoors at the first
hint of freezing weather.
(There is always a large exhibit
of pleiones at the Chelsea
Flower Show in London, held
annually during the third week
of May.)

Light: Sun to half shade.

Soil: Use a purchased mix
labeled for epiphytic orchids.
Pot in a shallow pan with special drainage cuts.

Fertilizer: 14-14-14.

Storage: Quite cool (40–50°F
[4–10°C]) and on the dry side
in fall through winter, but
not to the point of freezing in
their pots.

Propagation: Remove offsets
in spring.

Uses: Mostly in pots.

POLIANTHES
(polly-ANTH-eez)

Mexican Tuberose

AGAVACEAE; agave family

Height/habit: Basal rosettes from which rise the tall spikes of flowers, to 2.5 ft. (76 cm.).

Leaves: Succulent, grassy, each to 1.5 ft. (45 cm.) long.

Flowers: Single or double, each 1–2 in. (2.5–5 cm.) across, growing from spikes; fragrant; white with touches of pink, especially in the double-flowered variety.

Season: Late summer through fall.

When to plant: Set the tuberous rootstock 2–4 in. (5–10 cm.) deep, 6–12 in. (15–30 cm.) apart in spring. Ground-hardy zone 9 and warmer. Elsewhere, dig before fall killing frost and place in a protected place. Single-flowered species naturalize better in mild-climate gardens than do the doubles.

Light: Sun half day or more.

Soil: Well drained; moist, except dry during winter dormancy.

Fertilizer: 5-10-5.

Storage: Store in dry peat moss at 50–60°F (10–15°C) from fall to winter until planting time.

Propagation: Remove offsets at planting time. For best results, however, leave each rootstock intact from year to year.

Uses: Beds, borders, pots, cut flowers.

PUSCHKINIA
(push-KIN-ee-ah)

Striped Squill

LILIACEAE; lily family

Height/habit: Basal rosettes grow upright, to 6 in. (15 cm.).
Leaves: Strap-shaped, linear, to 6 in. (15 cm.) long.
Flowers: Short spikes, bell-like, each to 1 in. (2.5 cm.) across; porcelain blue often with greenish stripe.
Season: Spring.
When to plant: Set bulbs 2–4 in. (5–10 cm.) deep, 4–6 in. (10–15 cm.) apart in fall.

Ground-hardy zone 4 and warmer but not reliable for return seasons zone 8 and warmer.
Light: Sun to half shade.
Soil: Well drained; moist, except summer dryness acceptable.
Fertilizer: 5-10-5.
Storage: Store bulbs in dry peat moss at 40–50°F (4–10°C) from receipt until planting time.
Propagation: Remove offsets at planting time.
Uses: Beds, borders, pots.

RANUNCULUS
(rah-NUNK-yew-lus)

Buttercup

RANUNCULACEAE; buttercup
family

Height/habit: Basal foliage
resembling parsley, above
which the flowers appear,
to 15 in. (38 cm.).
Leaves: Dissected, cut, 8–10 in.
(20–25 cm.) long/wide.
Flowers: Double, many
rounded, overlapping petals,
2–3 in. (5–7.5 cm.) across; most
colors except blue.
Season: Spring.
When to plant: Set tubers
2–4 in. (5–10 cm.) deep, 4–6 in.
(10–15 cm.) apart in fall (spring
zone 7 and colder).

Light: Sun half day or more.
Soil: Well drained, moist.
Fertilizer: 5-10-5.
Storage: Place tubers in dry
peat moss at 50–60°F (10–15°C)
from receipt until planting
time. They sprout more
quickly if soaked 24 hours in
water at room temperature
immediately before planting.
Propagation: Divide at planting time.
Uses: Beds, borders, cut
flowers.

RHODOHYPOXIS
(rho-doh-high-POX-iss)

Red Star

HYPOXIDACEAE; hypoxis family

Height/habit: Short, grasslike
plants from a rhizome
with fleshy roots, 3–4 in.
(7.5–10 cm.) high/wide.
Leaves: Basal, 3–4 in.
(7.5–10 cm.) long; ribbed
with silky hairs.
Flowers: Starry, 6–petaled,
to 1 in. (2.5 cm.) across; white,
rose, pink, or crimson.
Season: Spring through early
summer.

When to plant: Set transplants
when available; rhizomes 1 in.
(2.5 cm.) deep, 3 in. (7.5 cm.)
apart in fall. Ground-hardy
zone 8 and warmer.
Light: Sun to half sun.
Soil: Well drained, moist.
Fertilizer: 5-10-5.
Storage: Store bulbs in dry
peat moss at 40–50°F (4–10°C),
as briefly as possible, from
receipt until planting time.
Propagation: Divide or sow
seeds in spring.
Uses: Rock garden or pots.

SCADOXUS
(skad-OX-us)
Blood Lily

AMARYLLIDACEAE; amaryllis
family

Height/habit: A red-spotted
stalk rises from each bulb to
6–8 in. (15–20 cm.), at which
point the leaves unfurl, causing
the plant to reach 1–1.5 ft.
(30–45 cm.).

Leaves: Rounded, lanceolate,
6–10 in. (15–25 cm.) long.

Flowers: Appear in a ball in
groups of up to 100, each to
1 in. (2.5 cm.) across, atop a
stiff scape; coral pink, salmon,
or crimson; sometimes
known as *Haemanthus.*

Season: Spring through
summer.

When to plant: Set bulbs 2 in.
(5 cm.) deep, 6–12 in. (15–30
cm.) apart at the beginning of
warm weather; set transplants
in pots as available. Ground-
hardy zone 9 and warmer.

Light: Sun to half sun.

Soil: Well drained, moist,
except quite dry during winter
dormancy.

Fertilizer: 5-10-5.

Storage: Store bulbs in dry
peat moss at 50–60°F (10–15°C)
from fall through winter until
planting time.

Propagation: Remove offsets
at planting time.

Uses: Beds, borders, pots,
cut flowers.

SCHIZOSTYLIS
(sky-zoh-STYLE-iss)

Crimson Flag; River Lily

IRIDACEAE; iris family

Height/habit: Grassy evergreen clumps 2–2.5 ft. (61–76 cm.) high/wide.
Leaves: Sword-shaped, narrow, 12–15 in. (30–38 cm.) long.
Flowers: Slender stalks bear 6–14 starry blossoms to 2 in. (5 cm.) across; scarlet red.
Season: Summer through fall.

When to plant: Set rhizomes 1 in. (2.5 cm.) deep, 8–12 in. (20–30 cm.) apart in spring; set transplants when available. Ground-hardy zone 9 and warmer; elsewhere, grow in containers or dig before frost and winter as for gladiolus.
Light: Sun half day or more.
Soil: Well drained, moist.
Fertilizer: 5-10-5.
Storage: Store bulbs in dry peat moss at 50°F (10°C), as briefly as possible, from receipt until planting time.
Propagation: Divide or sow seeds spring or fall.
Uses: Beds, borders, pots.

SCILLA
(SILL-ah)
Squill
LILIACEAE; lily family

Height/habit: Fleshy foliage from the base, 6–12 in. (15–30 cm.) high/wide.
Leaves: To 6 in. (15 cm.) long, grasslike in some species.
Flowers: Nodding bells or dense clusters of stars, each to 1 in. (2.5 cm.) across; blue, dark purplish blue, or lavender.
Season: Early spring.
When to plant: Set bulbs 2–4 in. (5–10 cm.) deep, 4–8 in. (10–20 cm.) apart in the fall. Siberian squill (*S. siberica*) ground-hardy zone 4 and warmer but might not return after the first season zone 9 and warmer. Peruvian squill (*S. peruviana*), also called Cuban lily, is ground-hardy zone 9 and warmer and makes a fine pot specimen.
Light: Sun half day or more.
Soil: Well drained; moist, except summer dryness acceptable.
Fertilizer: 5-10-5.
Storage: Store bulbs in dry peat moss at 40–50°F (4–10°C) from receipt until planting time.
Propagation: Remove offsets at planting time.
Uses: Beds, borders, ground cover, pots, cut flowers.

SEEMANNIA
(see-MANN-ee-ah)
Seemannia
GESNERIACEAE; gesneriad family

Height/habit: Upright, bushy, 1.5–2.5 ft. (45–76 cm.) high/wide.
Leaves: Lightly covered with hairs, lance-shaped, 2–3 in. (5–7.5 cm.) long.
Flowers: Tubular, about 1 in. (2.5 cm.) long; bloom in great profusion; orange-red.
Season: Warm weather or any season in a warm greenhouse.
When to plant: Set scaly rhizomes 1–2 in. (2.5–5 cm.) deep, 4–6 in. (10–15 cm.) apart at the beginning of warm growing season. Ground-hardy zone 10 and warmer.
Light: Half sun to half shade.
Soil: Humusy, well drained, moist.
Fertilizer: 5-10-5.
Storage: Store scaly rhizomes in dry peat moss at 50–60°F (10–15°C) from fall through winter until planting time.
Propagation: Break up larger rhizomes at planting time.
Uses: Beds, borders, pots.

SINNINGIA
(sin-IN-jee-ah)
Florists' Gloxinia
GESNERIACEAE; gesneriad family

Height/habit: Compact rosettes of foliage surrounding large numbers of flowers that grow from the center, to about 4 in. (10 cm.).

Leaves: Succulent, hairy, veined, and quilted, 6–12 in. (15–30 cm.) long/wide.

Flowers: Upright or outward-facing, single or double, 1–4 in. (2.5–10 cm.) across; some fragrant; most colors except yellow and orange.

Season: When outdoor weather is warm or at almost any time in a warm greenhouse or indoor fluorescent-light garden.

When to plant: Set tubers rounded side down, hollowed-out side up, not more than 1 in. (2.5 cm.) deep, 1 ft. (30 cm.) apart at the beginning of a warm growing season. Hardy outdoors zone 10 and warmer; elsewhere, tubers must be brought inside when there is danger of frost.

Light: Half sun to half shade. Ideal porch plants where there is bright, indirect light and protection from rain and wind.

Soil: Humusy, well drained; moist, except quite dry during the season of rest (usually fall through winter).

Fertilizer: 5-10-5.

Storage: Store tubers in dry peat moss at about 60°F (15°C) from fall through winter until planting time.

Propagation: Divide tubers at planting time; alternatively, sow seeds or take leaf cuttings.

Uses: Beds, borders, pots. There are miniatures, such as *S. pusilla*, that thrive in a terrarium or bubble bowl.

SMITHIANTHA
(smith-ee-ANTH-ah)
Temple Bells
GESNERIACEAE; gesneriad family

Height/habit: Upright, 2–3 ft. (61–90 cm.) high/wide.

Leaves: Densely haired, crenate, heart-shaped, to 4–5 in. (10–12.5 cm.) across; often marbled reddish brown.

Flowers: Nodding or outward-facing tubular bells, each to 1 in. (2.5 cm.) across; bloom in great numbers; yellow, orange-red.

Season: Summer or at almost any time in a warm, humid indoor garden.

When to plant: Set scaly rhizomes 2 in. (5 cm.) deep, 4–8 in. (10–20 cm.) apart at the beginning of warm weather. Ground-hardy zone 10 and warmer.

Light: Half sun to half shade.

Soil: Humusy, well drained, moist.

Fertilizer: 5-10-5.

Storage: Store scaly rhizomes in dry peat moss at 50–60°F (10–15°C) from fall through winter until planting time.

Propagation: Break apart large scaly rhizomes at planting time.

Uses: Beds, borders, pots.

SPARAXIS
(spah-RAX-iss)

Wandflower; Velvet Flower

IRIDACEAE; iris family

Height/habit: Grassy clumps, to 1 ft. (30 cm.) high/wide.

Leaves: Narrow swords in 2 ranks along the stem, to 1 ft. (30 cm.) long.

Flowers: Several along a wiry stalk, each to 2 in. (5 cm.) across; vivid colors and combinations, including yellow, scarlet, purplish black, orange, and crimson.

Season: Spring.

When to plant: Set corms 3–4 in. (7.5–10 cm.) deep, 4–8 in. (10–20 cm.) apart in fall (mild climates) or in spring zone 6 and colder.

Light: Sun half day or more.

Soil: Well drained, moist, except quite dry during summer rest.

Fertilizer: 5-10-5.

Storage: Store corms in dry peat moss at 50–60°F (10–15°C) from receipt until planting time.

Propagation: Remove offsets at planting time or sow seeds.

Uses: Beds, borders, pots, cut flowers.

SPREKELIA
(spreh-KEE-lee-ah)

Jacobean Lily; Aztec Lily

AMARYLLIDACEAE; amaryllis family

Height/habit: Grassy clumps to 12–15 in. (30–38 cm.) high/wide.

Leaves: Narrow, linear, to 1 ft. (30 cm.) long, appearing after the flowers.

Flowers: 1 per 1-foot- (30-cm-) long stalk, to 5 in. (12.5 cm.) across; intense crimson.

Season: Early summer.

When to plant: Set bulbs 2–4 in. (5–10 cm.) deep, 4–8 in. (10–20 cm.) apart in spring. Ground-hardy zone 9 and warmer; elsewhere, treat as gladiolus. Rather notorious for not blooming after the first season.

Light: Sun half day or more.

Soil: Well drained, moist, except quite dry fall through winter.

Fertilizer: 5-10-5.

Storage: Store bulbs in dry peat moss at 50–60°F (10–15°C) from fall through winter until planting time.

Propagation: Remove offsets at planting time or sow seeds.

Uses: Beds, borders, pots, cut flowers.

STERNBERGIA
(stern-BERJ-ee-ah)

Winter Daffodil; Lily of the Field

AMARYLLIDACEAE; amaryllis family

Height/habit: Grassy clumps, to 1 ft. (30 cm.) high/wide.
Leaves: Narrow, linear, to 1 ft. (30 cm.) long.
Flowers: Crocuslike, to 2 in. (5 cm.) across; bright golden yellow.
Season: Fall.
When to plant: Set bulbs 4 in. (10 cm.) deep, 8–12 in. (20–30 cm.) apart in late summer. Ground-hardy zone 7 and warmer, zone 6 if protected.
Light: Sun half day or more.
Soil: Well drained; moist, except summer dryness acceptable.
Fertilizer: 5-10-5.
Storage: Store bulbs in dry peat moss at 50–60°F (10–15°C) from receipt until planting time.
Propagation: Remove offsets at planting time or sow seeds. Excellent colonizer in many situations.
Uses: Beds, borders, rock gardens, pots.

TACCA
(TACK-ah)

Batflower

TACCACEAE; tacca family

Height/habit: Leafy clumps to 2 ft. (61 cm.) high/wide.
Leaves: Olive green, quilted, 1.5–2 ft. (20–61 cm.) long.
Flowers: Curiously batlike, 4–6 in. (10–15 cm.) across, with a spreading bract and long, whiskerlike filaments; maroon to black.
Season: Spring through summer; any season in a warm, humid greenhouse.
When to plant: Set transplants when available. Root-hardy zone 10 and warmer; else-where, treat as a container plant that can be moved indoors when temperatures drop below 50°F (10°C).
Light: Half sun to half shade.
Soil: Humusy, well drained, moist.
Fertilizer: 5-10-5.
Storage: Rest rootstock in dry peat moss at 50–60°F (10–15°C) from fall through winter until planting time.
Propagation: Remove offsets in spring.
Uses: Beds, borders, pots.

TIGRIDIA
(teye-GRID-ee-ah)

Mexican Shellflower

IRIDACEAE; iris family

Height/habit: Upright leaves above which the flowers appear, rising to 1.5–2 ft. (20–61 cm.).

Leaves: Ribbed, narrow swords, 8–12 in. (20–30 cm.) long, on erect stems rising from corms.

Flowers: Last only for 1 day. Cupped with spreading segments in groups of 3, to 3 in. (7.5 cm.) across; brilliant yellows, oranges, pinks, or reds with contrasting spots.

Season: Late spring through summer.

When to plant: Set corms 4–6 in. (10–15 cm.) deep, 6–8 in. (15–20 cm.) apart in spring. Ground-hardy zone 9 and warmer.

Light: Sun half day or more.

Soil: Well drained, moist.

Fertilizer: 5-10-5.

Storage: Store corms in dry peat moss at 50–60°F (10–15°C) from fall through winter until planting time.

Propagation: Plant cormlets separately or sow seeds for blooms the next season in spring.

Uses: Beds, borders, pots.

TRITONIA
(try-TOH-nee-ah)
Montbretia; Flame Freesia
IRIDACEAE; iris family

Height/habit: Grassy clumps with flowers hovering above, 1–1.5 ft. (30–45 cm.) high/wide.
Leaves: Narrow swords, to 1.5 ft. (45 cm.).
Flowers: Bell- to cup-shaped, each 1–2 in. (2.5–5 cm.) across, on wiry stems; yellow, orange, or coral.
Season: Fall, winter, spring, early summer, depending on planting time and local temperatures.
When to plant: Set corms 2–4 in. (5–10 cm.) deep, 4–8 in. (10–20 cm.) apart when available; fall in mild climates, spring in colder regions. Ground-hardy zone 9 and warmer.

Light: Sun half day or more.
Soil: Well drained; moist, except summer dryness acceptable.
Fertilizer: 5-10-5.
Storage: Store corms in dry peat moss at 40–50°F (4–10°C) from receipt until planting time.
Propagation: Separate clumps at beginning of growing season.
Uses: Beds, borders, pots, cut flowers.

TROPAEOLUM
(tropp-ee-OH-lum)
Tuber Nasturtiums
TROPAEOLACEAE; nasturtium family

Height/habit: *T. tuberosum* and *T. tricolorum* are climbers, 5–15 ft. (1.5–4.5 m.).
Leaves: Rounded, 5- or 6-lobed, to 1 in. (2.5 cm.) across, on wiry stems.
Flowers: Tubular, to 1 in. (2.5 cm.) long; scarlet, purple, red, or yellow.
Season: Spring through summer.
When to plant: Set tubers 1–2 in. (2.5–5 cm.) deep, 1 ft. (30 cm.) apart in spring. Ground-hardy zone 8 and warmer.

Light: Sun half day or more.
Soil: Well drained, moist.
Fertilizer: 5-10-5.
Storage: Store tubers in dry peat moss at 50–60°F (10–15°C) from fall through winter until planting time.
Propagation: Divide at planting time.
Uses: Trailing over shrubbery or brush, on small trellis or tepee, spilling from hanging baskets.

TULBAGHIA
(tull-BAY-ghee-ah)

Society Garlic

AMARYLLIDACEAE; amaryllis
family

Height/habit: Grassy clumps,
1–1.5 ft. (30–45 cm.) high/wide.
Leaves: Linear, glaucous, to
1 ft. (30 cm.) long. Variegated
lengthwise in *T. violacea*
'Tricolor,' which is green,
cream, and bronze.
Flowers: Umbels of 20–40,
each to 1 in. (2.5 cm.) across,
atop a slender scape to 2 ft.
(61 cm.) long; fragrant in
T. fragrans but somewhat
overpowered by the oniony
smell of the plant itself; lilac
to lavender purple.

Season: Spring through
summer through fall.
When to plant: Set transplants
when available, ideally in
spring. Ground-hardy zone 9
and warmer.
Light: Sun half day or more.
Soil: Well drained; moist,
except summer dryness
acceptable.
Fertilizer: 5-10-5.
Storage: Store bulbs in dry
peat moss at 50–60°F (10–15°C)
from receipt until planting
time.
Propagation: Divide or sow
seeds in spring.
Uses: Beds, borders, pots,
cut flowers.

TULIPA
(TEW-lip-ah)

Tulip

LILIACEAE; lily family

Height/habit: Upright, 4–36 in.
(10–90 cm.).
Leaves: Glaucous, succulent,
grassy to wide, 4–12 in.
(10–30 cm.) long x .5–4 in.
(1.25–10 cm.) wide.
Flowers: Single or double,
1–8 in. (2.5–20 cm.) wide; all
colors between (and including)
white and black.
Season: Spring.
When to plant: Set bulbs
4–8 in. (10–20 cm.) deep,
6–10 in. (15–25 cm.) apart
in fall zone 8 and warmer.
Ground-hardy just about
everywhere but not depend-
able for repeat bloom
zone 8 and warmer.
Light: Sun half day or more.
Soil: Well drained; moist,
except summer dryness
desirable.
Fertilizer: 5-10-5.
Storage: Store bulbs in dry
peat moss at 40–50°F (4–10°C)
until planting time. For zone 8
and warmer, it is common
practice to refrigerate (not
freeze) tulip bulbs from the
time they arrive in the fall
until planting the last week
of December.
Propagation: Remove offsets
at planting time or sow seeds
(not practical except in cold
temperate regions, basically
zone 6 and colder).
Uses: Beds, borders, pots,
cut flowers.

VALLOTA
(val-LOT-ah)

Scarborough Lily

AMARYLLIDACEAE; amaryllis
family

Height/habit: Clumps of
evergreen leaves, 1.5–2 ft.
(20–61 cm.) high/wide.
Leaves: Strap-shaped, 1–1.5 ft.
(30–45 cm.) long, reddish at
the edges and on the undersides.
Flowers: Funnel-shaped, to
3-in. (7.5 cm.) across, in a
cluster at the top of a hollow
stalk the size of a pencil; scarlet.
Season: Summer through fall.
When to plant: Set bulbs with
the neck and some shoulder
above the soil, 6–12 in. (15–30
cm.) apart at any season; set
transplants when available.

Hardy zone 10 and warmer,
elsewhere grow as a container
plant and bring inside when
frost threatens.
Light: Sun half day or more.
Soil: Humusy, well drained,
moist; avoid severe drying
even during the cool winter
rest.
Fertilizer: 5-10-5.
Storage: Store bulbs in dry
peat moss at 50°F (10°C), as
briefly as possible, from receipt
until planting time.
Propagation: Remove offsets
at planting time, but note:
Established, undisturbed bulbs
produce the most flowers.
Uses: Beds, borders, pots,
cut flowers.

VELTHEIMIA
(vel-THEEM-ee-ah)

Forest Lily

LILIACEAE; lily family

Height/habit: Showy flowers
rise from basal foliage rosette,
to about 2 ft (61 cm.).
Leaves: Wavy-margined,
somewhat succulent, 6–8 in.
(15–20 cm.) long x 2 in.
(5 cm.) wide.
Flowers: Tubular, nodding,
1–2 in. (2.5–5 cm.) long,
clustered symmetrically at the
top of a sturdy stalk; chartreuse
to pink and dusty red, often
green-tipped.
Season: Winter or spring.
When to plant: Set bulbs in
fall, the tips just exposed,
8–12 in. (20–30 cm.) apart.

Ground-hardy zone 9 and
warmer; elsewhere grow as
a container plant and protect
from freezing. A cool start-up
season fall through winter
leads to a perfect flower show
winter through early spring.
Light: Sun half day or more.
Soil: Well drained, moist,
except dry in summer during
dormancy.
Fertilizer: 5-10-5.
Storage: Store bulbs in dry
peat moss at 50–60°F (10–15°C)
from receipt until planting
time.
Propagation: Remove offsets
at planting time or sow seeds.
Uses: Beds, borders, pots,
cut flowers.

ZANTEDESCHIA
(zant-eh-DEE-shuh)

Calla Lily

ARACEAE; aroid family

Height/habit: Upright in clumps, 1–3 ft. (30–90 cm.) high/wide.

Leaves: Arrowhead- or lance-shaped, 6–8 in. (15–20 cm.) long, to half as wide; spotted translucent white in some.

Flowers: Curving, petal-like spathe, 2–8 in. (5–20 cm.) long; white, yellow, pink, rose, or apricot.

Season: Winter through spring for white callas; often spring through summer for the yellows and pastels.

When to plant: Set white tubers late summer through early fall, the others winter through spring, 2 in. (5 cm.) deep, 4–6 in. (10–15 cm.) apart. Maintain warm to moist conditions thereafter. Ground-hardy zone 9 and south; else-where, grow in pots or dig and bring inside before hard frost.

Light: Half sun to half shade.

Soil: Well drained, moist to wet. While growing actively a pot of callas can be left standing in a saucer of water.

Fertilizer: 5-10-5, 14-14-14.

Storage: Store tubers in dry peat moss at 50–60°F (10–15°C) from receipt until planting time.

Propagation: Divide at beginning of growing season or sow seeds.

Uses: Beds, borders, pots, cut flowers.

ZEPHYRANTHES
(zeff-er-ANTH-eez)

Rain Lily

AMARYLLIDACEAE; amaryllis
family

Height/habit: Grassy clumps,
6–18 in. (15–45 cm.) high/wide.
Leaves: Evergreen or
deciduous; narrow, some
thin as coarse grass, 6–18 in.
(15–45 cm.) long.
Flowers: Funnel-shaped,
1–3 in. (2.5–7.5 cm.) across;
white, yellow, pink, or rose.
Season: Summer through
fall, mostly in response to
signficant rainfall, as common
name implies.
When to plant: Set bulbs
2–4 in. (5–10 cm.) deep, 4–8 in.
(10–20 cm.) apart in spring.
Use transplants when available. They are easy to dig and
replant. Ground-hardy zone 7
and warmer, especially popular along the Gulf Coast.
Light: Sun to half shade.
Soil: Well drained; moist to on
the dry side.
Fertilizer: 5-10-5.
Storage: Store bulbs briefly
in dry peat moss at 50–60°F
(10–15°C), from receipt until
planting time.
Propagation: Remove offsets
or sow seeds from spring
through summer.
Uses: Beds, borders, rock and
wild gardens, pots.

ZINGIBER
(ZING-ib-er)

Ginger

ZINGIBERACEAE; ginger family

Height/habit: Upright rhizomatous perennial, to 3 ft. (1 m.).

Leaves: To 1 ft. (30 cm.) long x 1–2 in. (2.5–5 cm.) wide; smell strongly of ginger when disturbed.

Flowers: Dense cone-shaped spikes to 3 in. (7.5 cm.) long; yellowish green spotted yellow.

Season: Summer until cold weather.

When to plant: Set rhizome rootstocks 2–4 in. (5–10 cm.) deep, 6–12 in. (20–30 cm.) apart in spring; or set transplants at the beginning of warm weather. Ground-hardy zone 9 and warmer; elsewhere, maintain as large container plants.

Light: Half sun to half shade.

Soil: Humusy, well drained, moist.

Fertilizer: 5-10-5, 14-14-14.

Storage: Store tuberous roots in dry peat moss at 50–60°F (10–15°C) from receipt until planting time.

Propagation: Divide tuberous roots in spring.

Uses: Beds, borders, ground cover in part shade, pots.

Chapter Eleven

Troubleshooting Guide for Bulbs

*S*ubjected to being in storage and living in the garden for many years, bulbs undergo a great deal. Sometimes, things go awry. Here are common problems and advice for how to handle them.

Bulb shriveled up and dry or soggy and possibly foul smelling.

Indicates the bulb has succumbed to some extreme stress such as freezing or overheating, drying, or waterlogging. Discard.

Little green bugs clustered on new shoots, especially flower buds.

Indicates aphids, also known as plant lice. Rub off with fingers or wash away with water sprays. Usually not serious.

Bulbs have been in garden for several years. Originally they bloomed, now there are few if any flowers.

Indicates a need for digging, dividing, and resetting the bulbs. Before doing any of this, refurbish the soil by adding up to 6 inches (15 centimeters) of well-rotted compost and a dusting of organic fertilizer, then till or fork together with the endemic soil.

Summer bulbs planted in the spring have grown spindly leaves on weak stems; there are no flowers.

This indicates planting in poorly prepared soil and in a site that is too shaded. With a few exceptions, such as the gingers, bulbs need four hours or more of sunlight a day during the time of year when they put most of their energies into growing.

Bulbs have lots of healthy leaves but no flowers.

This may indicate a too rich soil or an excess of nitrogen. Apply a fertilizer labeled specifically for flowering plants, 15-30-15 for example. This could also indicate that spring bulbs in pots have been forced in temperatures too warm, thus preventing the flower buds from developing.

Bulb foliage streaked with yellow, progresses slowly, then collapses.

This indicates a bulb that has disintegrated from one or more stresses, such as over-heating while in transit or after it was planted. Conversely, the planting might have been over- or underwatered at a critical stage.

Chapter Twelve:
Bringing Bulbs Into Your Home

Bulbs provide some of the flower world's loveliest and most fragrant blooms. One of their nicest attributes is that gardeners can bring them indoors to bloom in pots weeks or months ahead of their normal appearance outdoors, a process known as forcing.

One of the most common methods of forcing involves containers with drainage holes. Partially fill the pot with soil. Place the bulb on top, pointed (nose) side up so that they're just about even with the rim. Then add soil until it almost covers the bulbs. Water well and keep soil moist. Place in refrigerator, a root cellar, or outdoor cold frame (covered with mulch). The temperature must be about 40–50° F (4–10°C). After about twelve to fifteen weeks, bring them into the house to bloom, preferably in indirect sunlight. You can stagger the process to have bulbs throughout the bleakest times of winter.

Gardeners can also force some bulbs in containers without drainage holes. 'Paperwhite' narcissi are good candidates, available in several look-alike cultivars that in their natural order bloom early, midseason, and late, thus making it possible to have fresh, fragrant indoor blooms from about October until March. To do so, place 1–2 in. (2.5–5 cm.) of gravel in a low container. Add bulbs, pointed side up, and anchor with a little more gravel. Add water. They will bloom at room temperature (60–65°F [15–18°C] is ideal). Keep them in a window until the time they are about to flower.

Hydroponic forcing is another easy method that involves chilling the plants in a cellar or in the refrigerator as noted previously. Dutch and Roman hyacinths respond well to this treatment. They look lovely grown in specially shaped hyacinth glasses, which cradle each bulb so that water reaches only the base. If this container is clear, you can observe the emergence and growth of the white roots. Aside from hyacinth glasses, small pilsner glasses work well for hydroponic forcing.

Of course, you can always bring in bulb arrangements from the garden. Here are some suggestions, mixing in other types of plants from the home plot and the florist:

- Snowdrops with early-blooming tulips
- Iris with poppies and anemones
- Star-of-Bethlehem with gerbera daisies
- Iris, kangaroo paw, Kaffir lily, or agapanthus in ikebana arrangements
- Freesia or lily of the valley with miniature roses
- Gladioli and dahlias
- Anemones with brodiaea.

For everlastings arrangements and potpourri, the following air-dried flowers and seed heads are recommended:

- Alliums with gladiolus leaves
- Ranunculus, roses, and poppy seed heads
- Daffodil petals for bright potpourri color
- Grape hyacinth blossoms for subtle scent in potpourri
- Iris blossoms for light violet scent and color in potpourri
- Whole lily flowers as elegant topping for potpourri

Part Four:
Trees and
Shrubs

Chapter Thirteen:
The Woody Plant Garden

Within this grouping are the major plants used in making beautiful yards, gardens, and parks. Grouped together under the heading of woody plants, they all actually produce wood and have buds that survive above ground during the winter months. These plants give us shade and shelter, while also offering the ornamental value of beautiful flowers, showy or edible fruits, and exquisite varieties of foliage. Even when they are relatively short-lived, trees and shrubs stay around for at least a couple of decades.

Planning and Designing the Woody Plant Garden

Since woody plants may not mature for several years, they are often the first elements added to a new landscape. From the outset, the gardener should consider if there will be headroom for a tree or shrub as it matures, as well as if its roots could spread to encroach upon walls, foundations, and paving. Chapter Fourteen indicates the mature height and width of each plant and facilitates landscape design with the future in mind.

The right tree or shrub in the right place will require little pruning and no extraordinary amount of irrigation during normal times of drought. Thorny types—such as barberry, rose, and pyracantha—are best reserved for barrier or perimeter plantings and are not practical choices near walkways or other places where there is heavy foot traffic.

Many homes have foundation plantings that look tidy at first—but without rigorous pruning and knowing management, they soon grow up to hide the walls and hang over the windows, casting a pall throughout the home. This is not to say that all foundation plantings are wrong, only to suggest that in many situations the house would look better with clean space all around and the usual front-yard plantings moved to the perimeter of the yard. It then becomes possible to create flower gardens between the dwelling and the property lines, to turn these once public spaces into private retreats. Consider, too, that planting deciduous trees on the east and west sides of your house gives you sun-filtering shade in summer while allowing light in during the winter.

All kinds of hedge and screen plants are also contained within the woody class, and these are included here along with trees and shrubs. Some can be as low as 1 foot (30 centimeters) high, while others tower at 12 feet (3.6 meters). They can be clipped into precise shapes or left to grow into natural shapes.

Nothing adds so much to the visual impact of a woody plant or ground cover as using it in multiples rather than dotted about here and there. Instead of a few ground-hugging evergreens for coloring in under trees and shrubs or in shaded areas where nothing else will grow, consider using just about any tree or shrub in this way by repeating them en masse over a sizable area to create a thicket.

On large or rural properties, mixed hedges or windbreaks up to 50 feet (15 meters) wide

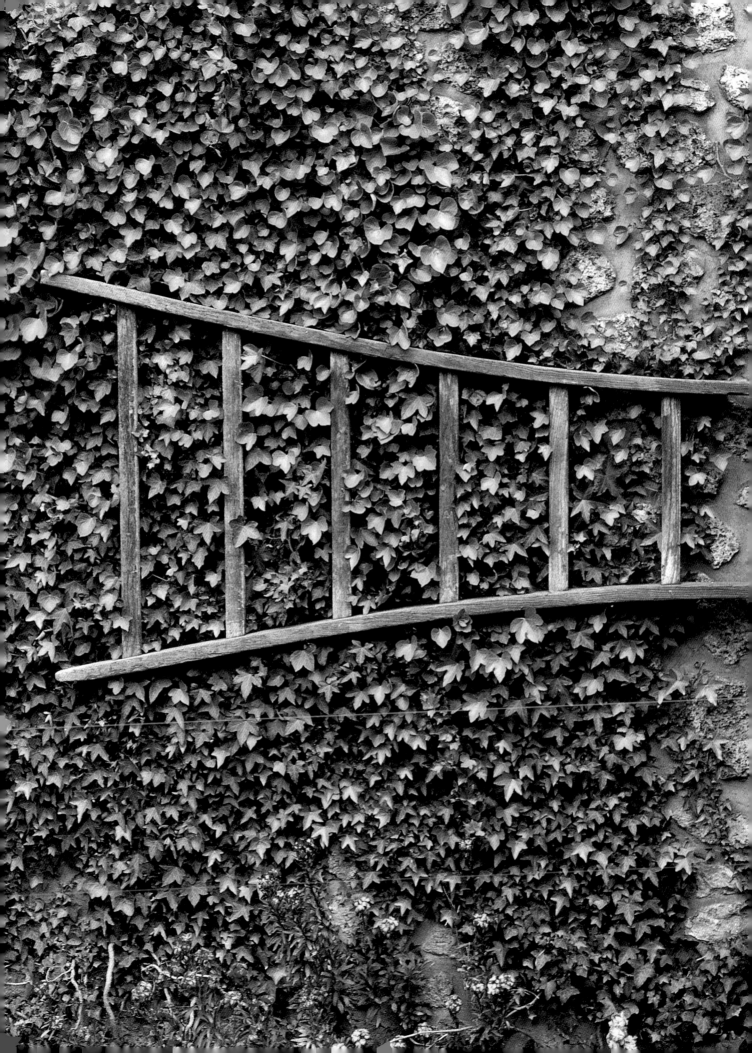

by many times as long are an excellent choice. These act as safe havens for wildlife and provide gardeners and flower arrangers with an endless source of delight.

Mixed shrubbery borders have great potential in large and small spaces, in city gardens as well as those in the country. If you wish to have four seasons of visual interest, make a detailed plan using graph paper, using each square to represent a given amount of space on your lot. Factor in the approximate space needed for each shrub you wish to grow. Also consider the light needs for each plant. The International Society of Arboriculture recommends planting the tree a distance of half its height from houses or other structures.

Another option is planting a single specimen of tree lining both sides of a walk or driveway to create an allée. These can serve as giant hedges through which one can walk or drive, thus adding certain grandeur and even mystery to surprisingly small parcels of land.

Soil Preparation

Since woody plants by nature take time to become established and reach maturity, it makes sense to start them off with well-prepared soil. Almost all of them do best on a well-drained site; numerous kinds appreciate a constant supply of water and therefore thrive by the side of a stream or pond. These are noted in the individual plant discussions in the chapter that follows.

It is wise to spend more time making sure the endemic soil and any added to the planting hole mesh with the original container soil. Toward this end, the rootball of a container plant usually needs some pruning, perhaps slashing with a knife several times up the sides or pulling out the rootball with both hands from the bottom—a kind of filleting process. This helps the roots spread out into the new soil.

To further amend the soil, add a sprinkling of timed-release fertilizer pellets, such as

14-14-14, into the planting hole—even organic gardeners admit to doing this at planting time.

Buying and Planting Woody Plants

A practical approach to buying woody plants is to purchase container specimens on a regular basis from local nurseries and garden centers, always selecting plants just coming into bloom or showing colorful berries. After a couple of years of buying and planting regularly, the border will begin to move smoothly from one season to another, with no significant lapses when nothing looks promising.

Botanic gardens and arboretums are an important source for worthwhile, often unusual woody plants. If there is one in your area, inquire about membership and how you can participate in any distribution of worthy plants. Specialty mail-order nurseries are another impressive source for the best in woody plants; the names and addresses for some are listed in the Resources section of this book.

For many woody plants, which for simplicity's sake will be referred to in this section as trees, you'll have a choice of three different types: container-grown, balled-and-burlapped (B&B), and bare root. (B&B trees are increasingly rare at nurseries nowadays, however.) Before buying, make sure the trunks are relatively strong and capable of fully supporting the plant once in the ground. In overall shape, the tree should be well balanced. For bare-root trees, look for uniform, hearty growth emanating from all areas around the main root. If you opt for a B&B tree, make sure that the roots are not upsurging from the rootball, which indicates that they are too tightly packed. The rootball should be firm and compact.

When purchasing container-grown trees, the same applies: Check to see that the roots are not circling the surface of the container or coming out of the drainage holes. Containers generally range from 3 to 5 gallons (11.4 to 19 liters), though some are larger.

When planting, remember that your hole should be twice or three times as wide as the original rootball. As far as depth is concerned, it is almost never advisable to set a woody plant more deeply into the ground than it was growing previously in the container. Dig the planting hole deeply enough so that the plant is at about the same depth, or slightly higher, than it was growing originally.

With bare-root trees, place the roots in the hole and fan them out. When planting a B&B tree, if it's encased in actual burlap cloth, leave it in place and simply remove the ties (if the "burlap" is another material that will not decompose, remove it). With container-grown trees, remove the tree from the container in the same way that you might remove a cake from a pan. Trim off any gnarled roots and place in the hole.

Then refill the hole and water. A great many trees are drought-tolerant after they become established; but early after planting, deep, slow watering is essential to their taking hold in a strong, reassuring way.

Sowing seeds, taking cuttings, layering, and dividing are some of the ways to propagate trees, shrubs, and ground covers. Seeds may or may not produce offspring exactly like the

plant from which they were harvested. In the directions for individual plants in the chapter that follows, unless otherwise noted, instructions for sowing seeds are intended for outdoors, usually in some sort of protected seed frame. A frame allows the gardener to maintain evenly moist soil and to distinguish easily between desired seedlings and weeds. The seeds of woody plants from temperate zones often require a period of chilling before they can sprout, which is why fall and winter are often the recommended planting times.

Cuttings yield new plants exactly like the parent from which they were taken. Those made in the spring and early summer are often referred to as softwood and green wood; those from midsummer into early fall are called half-ripe and semiripe. Hardwood cuttings taken in fall and winter work especially well for deciduous species. It is beneficial to reduce the size of larger leaves by one-half to two-thirds so that the cutting has less top growth to support while it is establishing a set of roots.

Another way to produce new plants exactly like the parent is by layering, which usually takes place in early spring. The process is simple. It can be done by pulling a branch down toward the ground until it can be buried with at least one or two sets of leaf nodes below the soil surface. The leafy tip should stick out of the ground. Place a brick or rock on top to hold everything in place. Rooting occurs in one season, after which you can sever the new plant from the parent and transplant it.

Air-layering is a slight variation on this process whereby the gardener wraps a handful of moist sphagnum moss around a set of leaf nodes of a branch and then seals the moss and branch with plastic. This procedure usually commences in late spring after leaf development. After several weeks or months, new roots will grow into the moss. At this time—often as late as fall—the plant can be severed and transplanted.

Professionals, as well as home orchardists, use bud grafts to propagate new cultivars. This activity takes place in winter through early spring and involves inserting a bud on stock and allowing them to grow as one. A complicated process, it is not recommended for amateurs.

Inspect large trees regularly, especially after windstorms, to be sure all branches are intact.

Many experts recommend pruning in late winter through early spring, as trees heal more quickly at this time of year. However, some trees, such as oaks and honey locusts, do not

Caring for Woody Plants
Throughout the Seasons

This plant group is remarkably carefree on any given day. Low ground covers often can benefit from tidying up and removing large leaves and wind-blown trash. If there is a serious drought, any water that can possibly be spared should go toward saving the woody plants perceived as most valuable or the most difficult to replace.

Most woody plants benefit from an organic mulch 2 to 4 inches (5 to 10 centimeters) deep over their root run, which saves water, moderates soil-root temperatures, and reduces the number of weeds that must be pulled.

respond well to pruning at this time of year; if in doubt, consult with your local nursery. The purpose of pruning is to remove damaged or dead limbs and branches that weaken the healthy parts of the tree and to shape the growth of the tree. Make angled, precise cuts.

Essential Tools

A shovel, not to mention a strong back, are necessary to dig planting holes. Another basic is a pair of sharp pruners with by-pass blades, for cutting wood up to pencil thickness; long-handled pruners or loppers, for cutting growth up to .5 inch (1.25 centimeters) in diameter; and a pruning saw, for branches up to 3 to 4 inches

(7.5 to 10 centimeters) in diameter. Larger projects may require a power chain saw or the hired services of a professional.

Hedges are most ideally clipped with hand-powered shears, but most gardeners don't have the time or strength and prefer to use electric- or gasoline-powered hedge trimmers.

Year-round Gardening Calendar

Use this season-by-season calendar to organize your gardening schedule for woody plants.

SPRING:
At the beginning of the growing season, apply a fertilizer.

Begin watering whenever soil feels dry at a few inches down. When you do water, water well.

Before new leaves are out, inspect dormant branches for signs of scale insects. If detected, spray using a dormant or horticultural oil treatment.

This is a good time for planting—though trees and shrubs planted in fall have more time to make roots in their new home before bud break occurs.

Fertilize established plants by side-dressing; follow label directions. Inspect for aphids and treat as described in Chapter Fifteen.

Woody plants that bloom on the current year's growth typically need pruning early. Wait to prune those that bloom in spring or early summer on growth produced the previous year.

Bring in branches of spring-flowering shrubs and trees to enjoy.

SUMMER:
This is also an ideal time for planting container shrubs and trees, but they will need lots of water if the weather turns hot and dry.

Around the 4th of July it is usually appropriate to make a light application of fertilizer, 5-10-5 for flowering types, 14-14-14 timed-release

or 30-10-10 for foliage and all kinds needing acid soil.

Water deeply in times of drought.

Bring in branches of summer-flowering shrubs and trees to enjoy.

FALL:
An ideal season for setting out most container plants: The ground is warm, less likely to be waterlogged than in spring, and air temperatures are gradually decreasing, so the transplant directs energy toward establishing roots rather than making new top growth. If any newly planted trees or shrubs are in a windswept location, be sure to stake securely. Wrap trunks with burlap, or set up burlap screens to shield broadleaf evergreens from harsh northeast winds and direct sun early in the day.

Mulch with organic matter (leaf litter, pine straw, shredded bark and twigs, peat moss, and wood chips) at the base of trees and shrubs at this time.

Late fall through early winter is the time to enjoy evergreens and berried branches indoors.

WINTER:
Begin designing your border, hedge, or allée.

Early in the season is the time to side-dress around shrubs with several inches of well-rotted compost or cow manure. By spring this will have broken down into the surface soil, so that plenty of nutrients will be available to the plants and conditions will be conducive to growing.

Immediately after heavy snows, inspect the garden; use a broom to knock off any branch-threatening accumulations. In late winter through spring, bring in flowering branches of shrubs and trees.

In late winter through early spring, prune sparingly.

Chapter Fourteen:
The 100 Best Trees, Shrubs, and Ground Covers

ABELIA	326	Abelia
ACER	327	Japanese Maple
AESCULUS	328	Horse Chestnut; Scarlet Buckeye; Yellow Buckeye
ARDISIA	328	Coralberry; Spiceberry; Marlberry
BERBERIS	329	Barberry
BETULA	330	Birch
BUDDLEIA	331	Buddleia; Fountain Butterfly Bush; Summer Lilac
BUXUS	332	Box
CALLICARPA	333	Beautyberry
CALLISTEMON	333	Bottlebrush
CALYCANTHUS	334	Chinese Spicebush; Carolina Allspice
CAMELLIA	335	Camellia
CARYOPTERIS	336	Bluebeard
CEANOTHUS	336	California Lilac
CEPHALANTHUS	337	Buttonbush
CERCIS	338	Eastern Redbud; Judas Tree; Raceme Redbud
CHAENOMELES	339	Japanese Flowering Quince
CHIONANTHUS	340	Fringetree
CODIAEUM	341	Croton
CORNUS	342	Dogwood; Bunchberry; Cornelian Cherry
CORYLOPSIS	343	Winter Hazel
COTINUS	344	Smoketree
COTONEASTER	345	Cotoneaster; Rock Spray
CRATAEGUS	346	Hawthorn
CYDONIA	347	Quince
CYTISUS	348	Broom
DAPHNE	349	Daphne; Garland Flower
DELONIX	350	Royal Poinciana
DEUTZIA	351	Deutzia
ELAEAGNUS	352	Russian Olive; Silverberry; Gumi
ENKIANTHUS	352	Bellflower; Enkianthus
ERYTHRINA	353	Coral Tree; Coral Bean; Cardinal Spear

EUONYMUS	354	*Dwarf Burning Bush; Strawberry Bush; Cork Bush; Wintercreeper; Evergreen Euonymus*
EXOCHORDA	355	*The Bride*
FAGUS	356	*Beech*
FEIJOA	357	*Pineapple Guava*
FORSYTHIA	357	*Forsythia*
FOTHERGILLA	358	*Witch Alder*
FRANKLINIA	359	*Franklin Tree*
FUCHSIA	360	*Fuchsia*
GARDENIA	360	*Gardenia; Cape Jasmine*
GINKGO	361	*Ginkgo; Maidenhair Tree*
HALESIA	362	*Silver Bell; Snowdrop Tree*
HAMAMELIS	363	*Witch Hazel*
HAMELIA	363	*Fire Bush; Hummingbird Bush*
HEDERA	364	*Ivy*
HIBISCUS	365	*Texas Star; Swamp Mallow; Confederate Rose; Chinese Hibiscus; Rose of Sharon*
HYDRANGEA	366	*Hydrangea*
ILEX	366	*Holly; Winterberry; Yaupon*
INDIGOFERA	367	*Indigo*
ITEA	368	*Holly-leaf Itea; Sweetspire*
KALMIA	369	*Mountain Laurel; Calico Bush*
KERRIA	370	*Japanese Rose; Variegated Kerria*
KIRENGESHOMA	371	*Kirengeshoma*
KOELREUTERIA	372	*Golden-rain Tree; Flamegold-rain Tree*
LABURNUM	372	*Golden-chain Tree*
LAGERSTROEMIA	373	*Crape Myrtle*
LIGUSTRUM	374	*Privet; Golden Vicary*
LINDERA	375	*Spicebush*
LIRIODENDRON	375	*Tulip Tree*
MAGNOLIA	376	*Cucumber Tree; Ear-leaved Umbrella Tree; Bull Bay; White Yulan; Magnolia*
MAHONIA	377	*Oregon Grape; Japanese Mahonia*
MALUS	378	*Crab Apple*
MITRIOSTIGMA	379	*African Gardenia*
NANDINA	380	*Heavenly Bamboo*
NERIUM	381	*Oleander*
OSMANTHUS	382	*Sweet Olive; Tea Olive; Orange-flowered Sweet Olive; Chinese Holly-leaved Olive*
OXYDENDRUM	383	*Sourwood; Sorrel Tree*
PACHYSANDRA	383	*Allegheny Spurge; Japanese Spurge*
PAULOWNIA	384	*Empress Tree*
PERNETTYA	384	*Chilean Myrtle*
PHILADELPHUS	385	*Mock Orange*
PHOTINIA	386	*Photinia*
PIERIS	387	*Andromeda*
PINUS	387	*Pine*
PITTOSPORUM	388	*Japanese Pittosporum*
PLUMERIA	389	*Singapore Plumeria; Frangipani*
PODOCARPUS	390	*Southern Yew; Japanese Yew*
PONCIRUS	390	*Hardy Orange*
POPULUS	391	*Poplar; Quaking Aspen*
PRUNUS	392	*Almond; Apricot; Cherry; Plum; Cherry Laurel*
PYRACANTHA	393	*Scarlet Firethorn*
PYRUS	394	*Pear*
QUERCUS	395	*Oak*
RHODODENDRON	395	*Azalea Types: Gable Hybrids, Ghent, Glenn Dale Hybrid, Indian, Knap Hill, Kurume, and Mollis*
RHODODENDRON	396	*Rhododendron Hybrid Types: Catawba, Caucasian, Fortune, and Griffithianum*
ROSA	396	*Rose*
ROSMARINUS	397	*Rosemary*
ROYSTONEA	398	*Florida Royal Palm*
SALIX	399	*Willow; Purple Osier*
SAMBUCUS	399	*Elder*
SPIRAEA	400	*Spirea*
STEWARTIA	401	*Silky Camellia; Stewartia*
SYRINGA	402	*Lilac*
TAMARIX	403	*Athel Tamarisk; Salt Tree; Tamarisk*
TIBOUCHINA	403	*Glory Bush; Princess Flower*
VIBURNUM	404	*Viburnum; Nannyberry; Cranberry Bush; Japanese Snowball; Black Haw*
VINCA	405	*Trailing Vinca; Running Myrtle*
WEIGELA	406	*Common Weigela*
WISTERIA	407	*Wisteria*

ABELIA
(ab-BEE-lee-ah)
Abelia

CAPRIFOLIACEAE; honeysuckle family

Height/habit: Upright to cascading, 3–8 ft. (1–2.4 m.) high/wide, mostly in a range of 3–5 ft. (1–1.5 m.).

Leaves: Dimpled, oval, .5–1 in. (1.25–2.5 cm.) long; bronzy red at first, changing to glossy green in glossy abelia (*A.* x *grandiflora*); variously evergreen, deciduous, or semievergreen .

Flowers: Bell-like or tubular, to 1.5 in. (3.7 cm.) long, clustered at the axils and tips; white to pinkish white, lavender pink; *A. chinensis* fragrant. *A.* x *grandiflora* 'Edward Goucher' flowers profusely with purplish pink blooms.

Season: Summer into fall; after the flowers drop, coppery or reddish sepals remain indefinitely.

When to plant: Set transplants when available. Cold- and heat-tolerant zones 6–8 to 9–10.

Light: Sunny to partly shady.

Soil: Humusy, well drained, moist.

Fertilizer: 5-10-5 or 14-14-14 timed-release.

Pruning: Winter through spring, cut some of the oldest stems to the ground; shearing not recommended.

Propagation: Take cuttings in summer.

Uses: Specimen, borders, hedge, ground cover, cutting.

Japanese Maple

ACERACEAE; maple family

Height/habit: *A. palmatum* small, gracefully branched tree, to 20 ft. (6 m.) high/wide.

Leaves: Palmately lobed into 5–11 parts, some lacily cut, 2–4 in. (5–10 cm.) long; all greens to purplish, bronze, or red.

Flowers: Inconspicuous.

Season: Foliage outstanding spring through fall.

When to plant: Set transplants when available. Cold- and heat-tolerant zones 5–9.

Light: Sunny (cooler climates) to partly shady (warmer).

Soil: Humusy, well drained, moist.

Fertilizer: 5-10-5 in spring, again early to midsummer. Soil too alkaline or salty causes brown leaf tips.

Pruning: In summer, emphasize tree's natural planed surfaces or encourage weeping form if at water's edge; cut frost-damaged wood 4 in. (10 cm.) into healthy wood.

Propagation: Take green-wood cuttings in summer, hardwood cuttings fall through winter.

Uses: Decorative understory tree for accent, especially in Japanese garden; containers; bonsai.

AESCULUS
(ESK-kew-luss)

Horse Chestnut; Scarlet Buckeye; Yellow Buckeye

HIPPOCASTANACEAE; buckeye family

Height/habit: Mound-forming shrubs and small trees 12–20 ft. (3.6–6 m.) high/wide, in the case of dwarf horse chestnut and the scarlet or yellow buckeyes (*A. parviflora* and *A. pavia*, respectively), to major shade trees, 75–100 ft. (22.7–30 m.) high/wide, as with red horse chestnut and standard horse chestnut (*A. x carnea* and *A. hippocastanum*, respectively).
Leaves: Compound, palmlike, 6–10 in. (15–25 cm.) across.
Flowers: Small, in showy panicles, to 8 in. (20 cm.) long; pink to dark red, greenish yellow, white, or yellow; white and fragrant in California buckeye (*A. californica*).
Season: Flowers spring through summer, followed by interesting fruit and winter branches.
When to plant: Set transplants when available. Cold- and heat-tolerant zones 3–5 to 9.
Light: Sunny to partly sunny.
Soil: Well drained, moist to on the dry side, slightly acidic.
Fertilizer: 5-10-5.
Pruning: Cut dead or broken branches any time; in general, prune before or after bloom.
Propagation: Sow newly harvested, ripe seeds in fall; layer or propagate from buds in spring.
Uses: Shade or understory trees; also for flowers and interesting fruit.

ARDISIA
(ar-DEE-zee-ah)

Coralberry; Spiceberry; Marlberry

MYRSINACEAE; myrsine family

Height/habit: Upright evergreen shrub, to 4 ft. (1.2 m.) high/wide in coralberry, sometimes also called spiceberry (*A. crenata*); evergreen ground cover shrub, 6–18 in. (15–45 cm.) high/wide in marlberry (*A. japonica*).
Leaves: Elliptic, crenate in coralberry, 3–4 in. (7.5–10 cm.) long; marlberry available in several forms having variegated leaves.

Flowers: Small, .25 in. (.63 cm.) across, in terminal or axillary cymes; white to pinkish; followed by berries that turn shiny, bright red and last well into the next flowering period.
Season: Spring for spiceberry, fall for marlberry; berries winter through spring.
When to plant: Set transplants when available. Cold- and heat-tolerant zones 6 (marlberry) to 9 (both species).
Light: Half-sunny to half-shady.
Soil: Humusy, well drained, moist.
Fertilizer: 5-10-5.
Pruning: Remove dead growth late winter through spring.
Propagation: Sow seeds winter through spring; take cuttings of half-ripened wood summer through fall.
Uses: Borders, ground cover, container.

BERBERIS
(BURR-burr-iss)

Barberry

BERBERIDACEAE; barberry family

Height/habit: Deciduous or evergreen spiny shrubs, 1–8 ft. (30–240 cm.) high/wide. Among outstanding garden types are the evergreen species Magellan barberry (*B. buxifolia*), Chilean barberry (*B. darwinii*), wintergreen barberry (*B. julianae*), and hybrid barberry (*B.* x *stenophylla*). Deciduous species include chalk-leaf barberry (*B. dictyophylla*) and Japanese barberry (*B. thunbergii*). There is also a semievergreen barberry (*B.* x *mentorensis*).

Leaves: Simple, to 1 in. (2.5 cm.) long; various greens, reds, or yellows.

Flowers: Small, bell-like, in umbels; yellow, orange; fruit red, purple, bluish black, or salmon.

Season: Flowers in spring; fruit colorful fall through winter.

When to plant: Set transplants when available. Cold- and heat-tolerant zones 4–6 to 9.

Light: Sunny to partly sunny.

Soil: Well drained, moist; deciduous types more drought-tolerant.

Fertilizer: 5-10-5.

Pruning: Remove dead growth and control size and shape winter through spring.

Propagation: Sow seeds fall through winter; take softwood cuttings in summer.

Uses: Borders, hedge, bonsai.

BETULA
(BET-yew-lah)

Birch

BETULACEAE; birch family

Height/habit: Large deciduous trees, 65–95 ft. (19.7–2 .8 m.), often with showy bark. Among noteworthy types are the Chinese paper birch (*B. albo-sinensis*); river birch (*B. nigra*); monarch birch (*B. maximow-icziana*); carol, canoe, or paper birch (*B. papyrifera*); and the European birch (*B. pendula*).

Leaves: Oval to triangular, to 4 in. (10 cm.) long/wide.

Flowers: Catkins, 1–4 in. (2.5–10 cm.) long, males forming in the fall, persisting to spring, at which time the females appear.

Season: Always attractive.

When to plant: Set container transplants when available; otherwise, in spring with a ball of soil about the main roots. Cold- and heat-tolerant zones 2–5 to 7–8; river birch, zone 9.

Light: Sunny.

Soil: Well drained, moist.

Fertilizer: 14-14-14 timed-release at planting time.

Pruning: Remove dead or storm-damaged wood, cutting to the basal collar, whenever necessary.

Propagation: Sow seeds fall through winter.

Uses: Specimen, set in the open so that form and bark can be appreciated; bonsai.

Buddleia; Fountain Butterfly Bush; Summer Lilac

LOGANIACEAE; logania family

Height/habit: Deciduous or evergreen shrubs or small trees, mostly 6–15 ft. (1.8–4.5 m.) high/wide. Excellent choices include the deciduous species fountain butterfly bush (*B. alternifolia*) and summer lilac (*B. davidii*), the semievergreen ball-flowered buddleia (*B. globosa*), and the evergreen South African buddleia (*B. auriculata*).

Leaves: Lance-shaped, 4–12 in. (10–30 cm.) long.

Flowers: Small, less than .5 in. (1.25 cm.), in dense, spikelike clusters, to 1 ft. (30 cm.) long; most colors; fragrant; attractive to hummingbirds and butterflies.

Season: Spring on previous year's growth in fountain butterfly bush; summer through fall for South African buddleia, fountain butterfly bush; summer through fall for South African buddleia, summer lilac, and ball-flowered buddleia. Prompt deadheading prolongs bloom and tidies appearance.

When to plant: Set transplants when available. Cold- and heat-tolerant zones 6–7 to 9–10.

Light: Sunny to half-sunny.

Soil: Humusy, well drained, moist.

Fertilizer: 5-10-5 or 14-14-14 timed-release.

Pruning: Cut back hard in spring before bloom; prune fountain butterfly bush after spring bloom.

Propagation: Take cuttings spring through fall.

Uses: Beds; borders; cottage, butterfly, and hummingbird gardens; containers.

BUXUS
(BUCKS-us)

Box

BUXACEAE; box family

Height/habit: Evergreen shrubs;
Japanese box (*B. microphylla*)
grows 3–6 ft. (1–1.8 m.)
high/wide; common box
 (*B. sempervirens*) reaches small
tree size, 25 ft. (7.5 m.). Korean
box (*B. microphylla* var.
koreana), grows 1.5 ft. (45 cm.)
high, spreading to 4–5 ft.
(1.2–1.5 m.) wide.

Leaves: Obovate to elliptic or
lance-shaped, to 1 in. (2.5 cm.)
long.

Flowers: Axillary clusters;
inconspicuous.

Season: Always attractive.
When to plant: Set transplants
when available. Cold- and heat-
tolerant zones 4–7 to 9; Korean
box most cold-hardy.
Light: Sunny to partly shady.
Soil: Well drained, moist.
Fertilizer: 14-14-14 timed-
release.
Pruning: Prune late spring, after
new growth has formed; also
clean out dead leaves and twigs.
To rejuvenate old box, reduce
in stages as older wood could
resist forming new shoots.
Propagation: Take cuttings late
summer.
Uses: Hedge, borders, containers, bonsai.

CALLICARPA
(kal-ick-AR-pah)

Beautyberry

VERBENACEAE; verbena family

Height/habit: Deciduous shrubs, 4–9 ft. (1.2–2 .7 m.) high/wide. Noteworthy are American beautyberry (*C. americana*) and the smaller beautyberry (*C. dichotoma*).
Leaves: Elliptic to oval, 3–9 in. (7.5–22.5 cm.) long x half as wide, arranged at distant intervals along the stems.
Flowers: Very small but numerous in 1.5-in. (3.7-cm.) clusters above the leaf axils; pale blue to pink; followed by purple, blue, or white fruit.
Season: Best berry color late summer through fall.

When to plant: Set transplants when available. Cold- and heat-tolerant zones 6–7 to 9.
Light: Sunny to partly shady.
Soil: Humusy, well drained, moist.
Fertilizer: 5-10-5.
Pruning: Remove any dead wood and shape in spring. New growth will bloom and fruit the same year.
Propagation: Sow seeds fall through winter; take cuttings or layer in summer.
Uses: Beds; borders; specimen; containers; underplanting in shaded areas, such as among pine trees.

CALLISTEMON
(kal-iss-TEEM-on)

Bottlebrush

MYRTACEAE; myrtle family

Height/habit: Evergreen shrubs or small trees, generally 6–8 ft. (1.8–2.4 m.) but capable of growing to 30 ft. (9 m.). Noteworthy are lemon bottlebrush (*C. citrinus*) and narrow-leafed bottlebrush (*C. linearis*).
Leaves: Narrow and lanceolate, to 4 in. (10 cm.) long; bronze when young.
Flowers: Showy heads or spikes, 2–4 in. (5–10 cm.) long, the stamens protruding so as to resemble the filaments of a bottlebrush; scarlet red.
Season: Spring through fall.

When to plant: Set transplants when available. Cold- and heat-tolerant zones 8–10; all zones for dwarf varieties in containers.
Light: Sunny.
Soil: Well drained, moist to on the dry side.
Fertilizer: 14-14-14 timed-release.
Pruning: Clean out any dead growth in spring; cutting back hard every third year promotes vigorous blooming.
Propagation: Sow seeds in spring; take semiripe cuttings late summer.
Uses: Beds, borders, specimen, espalier, containers (dwarf varieties), butterfly garden.

CALYCANTHUS
(kal-ee-KANTH-us)

Chinese Spicebush; Carolina Allspice

CALYCANTHACEAE; calycanthus family

Height/habit: Deciduous shrubs 4–10 ft. (1.2–3 m.) high/wide; spicily aromatic leaves, flowers, and fruits.
Leaves: Elliptic to oval, 5–8 in. (12.5–20 cm.) long.
Flowers: Flat or like small water lilies, to 2 in. (5 cm.) across; Carolina allspice (*C. floridus*) reddish brown, fragrant; Chinese spicebush (*C. chinensis*) noted for creamy white flowers.

Season: Late spring through summer.
When to plant: Set transplants when available. Cold- and heat-tolerant zones 5–9.
Light: Sunny (cooler climates) to half-shaded (warmer climates).
Soil: Humusy, well drained, moist.
Fertilizer: 5-10-5 or 14-14-14.
Pruning: Remove dead growth and generally thin shrub (favoring young wood) late winter through early spring.
Propagation: Sow seeds. Take cuttings, layer, or remove suckers spring through summer.
Uses: Beds, borders, specimen, containers.

CAMELLIA
(kah-MEE-lee-ah)

Camellia

THEACEAE; tea family

Height/habit: Evergreen shrubs
to small trees, slow-growing,
ultimately reaching 8–15 ft.
(2.4–4.5 m.) high/wide.
Especially outstanding are
common camellia (*C. japonica*),
compact Chinese camellia
(*C. saluenensis*), netted camellia
(*C. reticulata*), and sasanqua
camellia (*C. sasanqua*).
Leaves: Oval to elliptic, 2–5 in.
(5–12.5 cm.) long.
Flowers: Single, double, formal,
and informal, 1–4 in. (2.5–10
cm.) across; most colors except
blue; sasanqua camellia notably
fragrant, as well as *C. rusticana*
x *C. lutchuensis* 'Fragrant Pink,'
C. reticulata 'Kramer's
Supreme,' and *C. sasanqua*
'Chansonette.'
Season: Fall to spring; for
longest season, select varieties
indicated as early-, midseason-,
and late-flowering.
When to plant: Set transplants
when available. Heat- and cold-
tolerant zones 7–8 to 9–10.
Suited to containers all zones.
Light: Partly sunny (cooler
climates) to partly shady
(most gardens).
Soil: Humusy, well drained,
moist.
Fertilizer: 5-10-10 labeled for
use on camellias; side-dressing
with cottonseed meal is an
organic treatment.
Pruning: Clip to maintain
shape and clean out all dead
leaves and twiggy growths in
spring after blooming.
Propagation: Sow seeds, take
cuttings, or layer in spring.
Uses: Beds, borders, specimen,
bonsai.

CARYOPTERIS
(karry-OPP-ter-iss)

Bluebeard

VERBENACEAE; verbena family

Height/habit: Rounded decidu-ous shrubs, 3–5 ft. (1–1.5 m.) high/wide. Especially notewor-thy is *Caryopteris* x *clandonensis*.
Leaves: Lance-shaped with toothed margins, 3–5 in. (7.5–12.5 cm.) long; leaf reverses silvery gray.
Flowers: Tiny, to .3 in. (.9 cm.) long, in showy clusters; blue.
Season: Late summer through fall.

When to plant: Set transplants when available. Cold- and heat-tolerant zones 5 (with protec-tion) to 9.
Light: Sunny to half-sunny.
Soil: Humusy, well drained, moist.
Fertilizer: 5-10-5 or 14-14-14.
Pruning: Cut back to green wood in spring; blooms appear on the same season's growth.
Propagation: Take cuttings summer through fall; sow seeds in spring.
Uses: Borders, containers, cottage and butterfly gardens.

CEANOTHUS
(see-ah-NO-thus)

California Lilac

RHAMNACEAE; buckthorn family

Height/habit: *C. thrysiflorus* evergreen shrub or tree, 2 ft. (61 cm.) high/wide in dwarf forms, up to 20–30 ft. (6–9 m.) high/wide.
Leaves: Oblong, to 2 in. (5 cm.) long.
Flowers: Small, growing in showy clusters at the branch tips; blue.
Season: Spring.

When to plant: Set transplants when available. Cold- and heat-tolerant zone 8; can be containerized in cooler zones and brought to a protected place in freezing weather.
Light: Sunny to half-sunny.
Soil: Well drained, moist to on the dry side.
Fertilizer: 5-10-5 or 14-14-14.
Pruning: After flowering, prune to within 4 in. (10 cm.) of the base of flowered growths.
Propagation: Take cuttings in summer; sow seeds in winter.
Uses: Wall shrub, espalier, specimen.

CEPHALANTHUS
(seff-al-ANTH-us)

Buttonbush

RUBIACEAE; madder family

Height/habit: *C. occidentalis* a deciduous shrub, 5–15 ft. (1.5–4.5 m.) high/wide.
Leaves: Glossy, oval-, elliptic-, or lance-shaped, to 6 in. (15 cm.) long.
Flowers: Small, to 1 in. (2.5 cm.) across, growing in showy globes; greenish white; fragrant.
Season: Summer.

When to plant: Set transplants when available. Cold- and heat-tolerant zones 4–9.
Light: Sunny to partly shady.
Soil: Well drained, moist to swampy.
Fertilizer: 5-10-5 or 14-14-14.
Pruning: Prune in early spring to maintain shape.
Propagation: Sow seeds or take mature wood cuttings in fall; take green-wood cuttings in spring.
Uses: Beds, borders, specimen.

CERCIS
(SUR-sis)

Eastern Redbud; Judas Tree; Raceme Redbud

LEGUMINOSAE; pea family

Height/habit: Deciduous shrubs or small trees, 15–40 ft. (4.5–12.1 m.) high by two-thirds as wide; frequently multi-trunked. Noteworthy are Eastern redbud (*C. canadensis*), Judas tree (*C. siliquastrum*), Chinese Judas tree (*C. chinensis*), and raceme redbud (*C. racemosa*).

Leaves: Kidney- or heart-shaped, with 2 upper lobes forming above both sides of the leaf stem, to 5 in. (12.5 cm.) wide; yellow fall color.

Flowers: Small, pealike, borne in dense clusters to 1 in. (2.5 cm.) across spaced around entire branch at regular intervals; white through pink, magenta, rose purple; followed by seed-pods resembling immature English pea pods.

Season: Early spring, before the new leaves. Old branches, to 20 years and more, have been known to flower, along with the main trunk.

When to plant: Set young transplants when available. Cold- and heat-tolerant zones 5–6 to 9–10.

Light: Sunny to partly shady.

Soil: Sandy, well drained, moist.

Fertillzer: 5-10-5 or 14-14-14.

Pruning: Cut only to shape or remove dead wood.

Propagation: Sow seeds, take cuttings, or layer summer through fall.

Uses: Borders, wild and shade gardens, understory tree, specimen, cutting to enjoy fresh or dried, bonsai.

CHAENOMELES
(kee-NOM-el-eez)

Japanese Flowering Quince

ROSACEAE; rose family

Height/habit: *C. speciosa* a deciduous, mostly spiny, shrub, 3–4 ft. (1–1.2 m.) to 10 ft. (3 m.) high/wide.

Leaves: Ovate to oblong, 1–4 in. (2.5–10 cm.) long.

Flowers: Resemble those of the apple, 1–2 in. (2.5–5 cm.) wide, single or double; scarlet, pink, white, apricot, coral, and most reds.

Season: Early spring, mostly before the new leaves.

When to plant: Set transplants when available. Cold- and heat-tolerant zones 5–9.

Light: Sunny.

Soil: Well drained, moist, not too alkaline.

Fertilizer: 14-14-14 timed-release.

Pruning: Any branches in need of pruning and not removed for forcing or fresh flowers can be cut after bloom time; cut side growths back to 2 or 3 buds; aim toward a bush that is fairly open through the center in order to show off the blooms.

Propagation: Sow seeds, take cuttings, layer, or graft summer through fall.

Uses: Beds, borders, cottage gardens, fan-shaped espalier, containers, bonsai, cutting (branches force well for winter bloom).

CHIONANTHUS
(kee-oh-NANTH-us)

Fringetree

OLEACEAE; olive family

Height/habit: Deciduous, multi trunked, large shrubs or small trees, easily 10–25 ft. (3–7.5 m.) high/wide.

Leaves: Ovate to elliptic, to 4 in. (10 cm.) long; showy yellow fall color.

Flowers: Fringelike, 4-petaled, in clusters to 6 in. (15 cm.) long; white followed by inedible blue fruits, in grapelike clusters.

Season: Spring.

When to plant: Set transplants when available. Cold- and heat-tolerant zones 5–8 for Chinese fringetree (*C. retusa*), 3–9 for common fringetree (*C. virginicus*).

Light: Sunny.

Soil: Humusy, well drained, moist.

Fertilizer: 14-14-14 timed-release at planting; 5-10-5 as general boost at beginning of growing season.

Pruning: Remove dead wood in spring.

Propagation: Sow seeds in spring; take semiripe shoots in early summer.

Uses: Background, specimen, hedgerow.

CODIAEUM
(koh-DEE-um)
Croton
EUPHORBIACEAE; spurge family

Height/habit: *C. variegatum* var. *pictum* a bold tropical shrub, 6–12 ft. (1.8–3.6 m.) high/wide; grows to height of small tree in warmest climes.

Leaves: Linear to oval-lanceolate with smooth or undulating margins, leathery, 6–12 in. (15–30 cm.) long; all greens, reddish or cordovan, creamy to golden yellow, orange, rose pink, or apricot.

Flowers: Unusual, drooping racemes, to 8 in. (20 cm.) long; white.

Season: Best growth occurs in warm weather.

When to plant: Set transplants when available. Suited to planting in the ground zones 10–12; elsewhere container specimens can be placed outdoors in frost-free temperatures.

Light: Sunny to half-sunny.

Soil: Humusy, well drained, moist.

Fertilizer: 14-14-14 timed-release.

Pruning: Prune only to remove dead wood, usually spring at the beginning of active growth.

Propagation: Air-layer the most colorful branches spring through summer; take cuttings in high humidity and with bottom heat (in greenhouse, with soil-heating cables, or with electric blankets/sheets placed under pots and flats) winter through spring.

Uses: Colorful foliage accents for beds, borders, or background; specimen; container; cutting.

CORNUS
(KORN-us)

Dogwood; Bunchberry; Cornelian Cherry

CORNACEAE; dogwood family

Height/habit: Deciduous ground covers, multistemmed shrubs, and small trees, for example: bunchberry (*C. canadensis*) to 9 in. (22.5 cm.) high, spreading by woody rhizomes; red-osier dogwood (*C. sericea*) to 10 ft. (3 m.) high, forming colonies to 10–12 ft. (3.6 m.) wide; and Chinese dogwood (*C. kousa* var. *chinensis*) to 30 ft. (9 m.) high/wide.

Leaves: Oval to elliptic, 1–6 in. (2.5–15 cm.) long; excellent fall color.

Flowers: Small, but set off by showy, colorful bracts to 3 in. (7.5 cm.) across, before or after the leaves; white, pink, rose, red, or yellow.

Season: Spring through early summer.

When to plant: Set transplants when available; if root disturbance is involved, best early spring or late fall. Cold- and heat-tolerant zones 4-9, red-osier to zone 2, evergreen yellow-flowered dogwood (*C. capitata*) only zones 9–10.

Light: Sunny to half-shady.

Soil: Humusy, well drained, moist, acidic.

Fertilizer: 14-14-14 timed-release.

Pruning: Trees and ground covers need little cutting. Shrubby cornus, such as red-osier, grown for winter bark color need cutting back sharply in spring to induce growth for next cold season.

Propagation: Sow seeds, take cuttings, layer, or graft summer through fall.

Uses: Ground cover, borders, specimen, stream or pond banks, bonsai, cutting.

CORYLOPSIS
(korry-LOP-sis)

Winter Hazel

HAMAMELIDACEAE; witch-hazel family

Height/habit: Deciduous shrubs, 6–8 ft. (1.8–2.4 m.) high/wide. *C. pauciflora* and *C. spicata*, both called witch hazel, particularly noteworthy.
Leaves: Roundish, 2–4 in. (5–10 cm.) long; tinged pink at first, then bright green.
Flowers: Short, nodding clusters or drooping spikes, to 2 in. (5 cm.) long; yellow; fragrant.
Season: Early spring, before forsythia.

When to plant: Set transplants when available. Cold- and heat-tolerant zones 6–8.
Light: Sunny to half-sunny.
Soil: Humusy, well drained, moist.
Fertilizer: 14-14-14 timed-release at planting; 5-10-5 as spring side-dressing.
Pruning: Little needed.
Propagation: Sow seeds or take cuttings summer through fall.
Uses: Beds, borders, cottage gardens, specimen, containers, bonsai, cutting.

COTINUS
(koh-TEE-nus)
Smoketree
ANACARDIACEAE; cashew family

Height/habit: *C. coggygria* a deciduous shrub or small tree, to 15 ft. (4.5 m.) high/wide.

Leaves: Elliptic, to 3 in. (7.5 cm.) long; blue-green in summer, yellow-orange-red in fall; 'Rubrifolia' has dark purple foliage.

Flowers: Much-branched panicles, to 8 in. (20 cm.) long, hairy pedicels; purplish, "smoky."

Season: Early to midsummer.

When to plant: Set transplants when available. Cold- and heat-tolerant zones 5–6 to 8.

Light: Sunny.

Soil: Well drained, moist.

Fertilizer: 14-14-14 timed-release.

Pruning: Little needed by smoketree; purple-leaved forms may be pruned back hard in early spring to induce strong shoots with large leaves.

Propagation: Sow seeds, layer, or take root cuttings (for faithful replicas of desirable fruiting plants) in spring.

Uses: Border, specimen, wild or prairie gardens, bonsai.

COTONEASTER
(koh-toh-nee-AST-er)

Cotoneaster; Rock Spray

ROSACEAE; rose family

Height/habit: Variously ever-green, as with Dammer ever-green (*C. dammeri*), semiever-green, as with box-leaved cotoneaster (*C. buxifolius*), or deciduous shrub, such as pointy-leaved cotoneaster (*C. apiculatus*), from ground covers like rock spray (*C. horizontalis*) that reach 1 ft. (30 cm.) high and twice as wide after several years, to high, arching branches reaching 20 ft. (6 m.), including *C. rehderi*. Other noteworthy species include creeping cotoneaster (*C. adpressa*), spreading coton-easter (*C. divaricata*), small-leaved cotoneaster (*C. micro-phylla*), and willow-leaved cotoneaster (*C. salicifolia*).
Leaves: Round to elliptic, .5–1 in. (1.25–2.5 cm.) long.
Flowers: Small (to .25 in. [.63 cm.]), borne singly or in clusters, some showy; white, pink, reddish; berries bright red.
Season: Spring flowers, fall through winter fruit, all-year branch structure.
When to plant: Set transplants when available. Cold- and heat-tolerant zones 4–6 to 9, although not well adapted to hot, humid zones.
Light: Sunny to half-shady for high-pruned trees.
Soil: Well drained, moist to slightly dry.
Fertilizer: 14-14-14 timed-release.
Pruning: Remove dead parts in spring. Low-growers are ill suit-ed to placement next to walks since cutting them back results in unattractive stubs.
Propagation: Take cuttings or layer spring through summer; sow seeds in fall.
Uses: Ground cover, rock gardens, specimen, container, bonsai, cutting.

CRATAEGUS
(krah-TEE-jus)

Hawthorn

ROSACEAE; rose family

Height/habit: Deciduous, spiny shrubs or small trees, 20–30 ft. (6–9 m.) high/wide. Especially good performers are Arnold hawthorn (*C. arnoldiana*), Kansas hawthorn (*C. cocciniodes*), cockspur thorn (*C. crusgallii*), hybrid hawthorn (*C. x lavalleii*), Eastern hawthorn (*C. mollis*), May haw (*C. opaca*), English hawthorn (*C. oxyacantha*), Washington hawthorn (*C. phaenopyrum*), and green haw (*C. viridis*).

Leaves: Often lobed, 2–4 in. (5–10 cm.) long; brilliant fall color in some, ranging from yellow to scarlet, red, orange, and bronze shades.

Flowers: Similar to apple blossoms, single or double, in showy clusters, to 2 in. (5 cm.) across; white, pink, cerise, carmine, crimson, or purple; fruit ornamental as well as edible, *C. opaca* 'Louisiana Choice' notably good for making jelly.

Season: Flowers late spring through early summer, fruit and foliage color in fall.

When to plant: Set transplants when available. Cold- and heat-tolerant zones 4–6 to 9; it is important to purchase a crataegus known to be locally adapted.

Light: Sunny.

Soil: Well drained, moist.

Fertilizer: 14-14-14 timed-release at planting time, 5-10-5 thereafter.

Pruning: Train trees and remove dead wood early spring through summer.

Propagation: Layer in summer; sow seeds fall through winter. Seedlings of natives can sometimes be transplanted in spring.

Uses: Hedges, ornamental trees, windbreaks and hedgerows, espalier, bonsai, cutting.

CYDONIA
(sigh-DOH-nee-ah)

Quince

ROSACEAE; rose family

Height/habit: Common quince (*C. oblonga*) a small deciduous tree, to 20 ft. (6 m.) high by two-thirds as wide.

Leaves: Oval to oblong, to 4 in. (10 cm.) long.

Flowers: Similar to apple blossoms, to 2 in. (5 cm.) across; white to pink; fruit apple- or pear-shaped, 3–4 in. (7.5–10 cm.) in diameter, bright yellow.

Season: Flowers spring, fruit late summer through fall.

When to plant: Set transplants when available, allowing 20 ft. (6 m.) between trees. Cold- and heat-tolerant zones 4–8; *C. sinensis* to zone 9.

Light: Sunny.

Soil: Well drained, moist.

Fertilizer: 5-10-5.

Pruning: Remove surplus branches late winter through spring; little needed.

Propagation: Take hardwood cuttings fall through winter.

Uses: Shade, specimen, fruit, bonsai.

CYTISUS
(SIT-ih-sus)
Broom
LEGUMINOSAE; pea family

Height/habit: Deciduous or persistent-leaved shrubs, upright or fountainlike, 1–10 ft. (30–300 cm. [3 m.]) high/wide. Spike broom (*C. nigricans*), purple broom (*C. purpureus*), and Scotch broom (*C. scoparius*) especially good performers.

Leaves: Simple or trifoliate, .5–.75 in. (1.25–2 cm.) long.

Flowers: Pealike, to 1 in. (2.5 cm.) across, growing in dense clusters or scattered along the stems; white, yellow, orange, red, or purplish; often fragrant.

Season: Spring through summer.

When to plant: Set transplants when available; disturb roots as little as possible. Cold- and heat-tolerant zones 5–7 to 8–9.

Light: Sunny.

Soil: Well drained, moist to on the dry side; locally adapted species drought-tolerant when established.

Fertilizer: 5-10-5. Yellowish leaves could indicate soil too alkaline; apply chelated iron or 30-10-10.

Pruning: Immediately after flowering, cut back new wood by two-thirds; cutting into old wood not advised as it rarely breaks into vigorous new growth.

Propagation: Sow newly ripened seeds summer through fall; take 2–4-in.- (5–10 cm.-) long cuttings in summer.

Uses: Specimen, borders, cottage or rock gardens, cutting.

DAPHNE
(DAFF-nee)

Daphne; Garland Flower

THYMELACEAE; mezereum family

Height/habit: Small deciduous and evergreen shrubs, 1–4 ft. (1.2 m.) high/wide. Deciduous garden favorites include Caucasus daphne (*D. caucasica*), lilac daphne (*D. genkwa*), and February daphne (*D. mezereum*). Evergreen choices include garland flower (*D. cneorum*) and winter daphne (*D. odora*).

Leaves: Oblong to lance-shaped, 2–3 in. (5–7.5 cm.) long.
Flowers: Small, .5 in. (1.25 cm.) across, in dense terminal heads; white, rose pink, lilac, purple, or pink; fragrant.
Season: Late winter through spring.
When to plant: Set transplants when available. Cold- and heat-tolerant zones 4–8.
Light: Sunny to partly sunny.
Soil: Humusy, well drained, moist; slightly acidic.
Fertilizer: 14-14-14 timed-release.

Pruning: Cut only to shape or to remove dead wood after flowering.
Propagation: Sow seeds fall through winter; take cuttings or layer in spring.
Uses: Beds, borders, specimen, container, espalier, cottage and rock gardens, bonsai, cutting.

DELONIX
(dee-LON-ix)

Royal Poinciana

LEGUMINOSAE; pea family

Height/habit: *D. regia* a wide-branching tree, to 40 ft. (12.1 m.) high/wide or more.
Leaves: Fernlike, pinnate, growing to 2 ft. (61 cm.) long.
Flowers: To 4 in. (10 cm.) wide, appearing in clusters; bright scarlet or yellow.
Season: Summer.

When to plant: Set transplants when available. Limited to frost-free gardens, zone 10; could live some years if in protected site zone 9.
Light: Sunny.
Soil: Well drained, moist.
Fertilizer: 5-10-5.
Pruning: Shape in winter; remove weak or dead wood after flowering.
Propagation: Sow seeds spring through summer.
Uses: Specimen, lawn, shade.

DEUTZIA
(DEWT-zee-ah)

Deutzia

SAXIFRAGACEAE; saxifrage family

Height/habit: Low to medium, spreading, mostly deciduous shrubs, 3–8 ft. (1–2.4 m.) high/wide. Best choices are semidwarf deutzia (*D. crenata*), *D.* x *elegantissima* 'Rosealind,' slender or spreading deutzia (*D. gracilis*), *D.* x *hybrida* 'Contraste,' *D. scabra* 'Pride of Rochester,' and early deutzia (*D.* x *rosea* 'Grandiflora'). *D. crenata* 'Nakata' is a ground cover.

Leaves: Slender, curving, oblong- to lance-shaped, 2–3 in. (5–7.5 cm.) long, slightly hairy.

Flowers: Tubular, 5-lobed, to 1 in. (2.5 cm.) across, growing in clusters; white, pink, or rose pink.

Season: Late spring to early summer.

When to plant: Set transplants when available. Cold- and heat-tolerant zones 4–5 to 8; semidwarf deutzia zones 6–9.

Light: Sunny to half-sunny.

Soil: Well drained, moist.

Fertilizer: 5-10-5.

Pruning: As soon as the flowers fade, cut back to strong new shoots. Periodically remove 1 or 2 stems to the ground to simulate young shoots.

Propagation: Sow newly ripened seeds, take cuttings, or layer summer through fall.

Uses: Beds, borders, specimen, ground cover, bonsai.

ELAEAGNUS
(el-ee-AG-nus)

Russian Olive; Silverberry; Gumi

ELAEAGNACEAE; oleaster family

Height/habit: Shrubs or small trees, deciduous or evergreen, 6–20 ft. (1.8–6 m.) high/wide. Among deciduous choices are Russian olive (*E. angustifolia*), silverberry (*E. commutata*), Gumi (*E. multiflora*), and silver elaeagnus (*E. umbellata*). Thorny elaeagnus (*E. pungens*) is evergreen.

Leaves: Elliptic, 3–4 in. (7.5–10 cm.) long, covered with silver to brown scales, resulting in a silver-and-gold effect; variegated creamy to yellow in some cultivars.

Flowers: Inconspicuous, .5–1 in. (1.25–2.5 cm.), borne on stems below the leaves; white or yellow; very fragrant; followed by yellow, pink, or red fruit.

Season: Flowers in spring; fruit, summer through fall; plants attractive in all seasons.

When to plant: Set transplants when available. Cold- and heat-tolerant zones 3–4 to 9, with the exception of thorny elaeagnus, zones 6–10.

Light: Sunny to shady.

Soil: Humusy, well drained, moist.

Fertilizer: 14-14-14 timed-release.

Pruning: Deciduous types can be cut back hard in early spring; cut thorny elaeagnus as necessary from spring through early summer or fall through winter, using the cut branches for flower arrangements; promptly remove any plain green shoots appearing on a variegated plant.

Propagation: Sow seeds or take hardwood cuttings fall through winter; layer spring through summer.

Uses: Borders, specimen, espalier, containers, hedge, seaside gardens, bonsai, cutting.

ENKIANTHUS
(enk-ee-ANTH-us)

Bellflower Enkianthus

ERICACEAE; heath family

Height/habit: *E. campanulatus* a deciduous shrub, 15–30 ft. (1.5–9 m.) high/wide.

Leaves: Elliptic to ovate, to 3 in. (7.5 cm.) long, in whorls at the branch tips; brilliant scarlet fall color.

Flowers: Bell-like, resembling lily of the valley, to .5 in. (1.25 cm.) long, in drooping clusters; white to pale yellowish to orange and red with dark red veins; followed by smooth orange-yellow fruit.

Season: Late spring to early summer.

When to plant: Set transplants when available. Cold- and heat-tolerant zones 5–7.

Light: Half-sunny to half-shady.

Soil: Humusy, well drained, moist, acidic.

Fertilizer: 14-14-14 timed-release.

Pruning: Only cut to size and shape immediately after flowering.

Propagation: Sow seeds, take cuttings, or layer summer through fall.

Uses: Borders, specimen, espalier, bonsai.

ERYTHRINA
(airy-THREYE-nah)

Coral Tree; Coral Bean; Cardinal Spear

LEGUMINOSAE; pea family

Height/habit: Thorny subshrubs 6–12 ft. (1.8–3.6 m.) high/wide, to full-grown trees 40–60 ft. (12.1–18.2 m) high/wide. Excellent showy choices are hybrid coral tree (*E.* x *bidwillii*); cockspur coral tree (*E. crista-galli*); *E. flabelliformis*; and coral bean, also known as cardinal spear (*E. herbacea*).

Leaves: Composed of 3 leaflets united to a single stem, to 3 in. (7.5 cm.) long or more.
Flowers: Similar to those of butterfly pea, spreading or folding, 1–5 in. (2.5–12.5 cm.) across, growing in erect racemes to 2 ft. (61 cm.); red, orange, pink, or rose.
Season: Late spring through summer.
When to plant: Set transplants when available. Cold- and heat-tolerant zones 7–8 to 10. Herbaceous types treated as root-hardy perennials at the colder limits, more shrublike in the tropics.

Light: Sunny.
Soil: Well drained, moist to on the dry side; becomes drought-tolerant with age.
Fertilizer: 5-10-5.
Pruning: Cut back to healthy green wood or all the way to the ground, as appropriate, in spring. Flowers appear on new growth.
Propagation: Sow seeds spring through summer; take woody cuttings summer through fall.
Uses: Hedgerow, borders, accent.

EUONYMUS
(yew-ON-ee-mus)

Dwarf Burning Bush; Strawberry Bush; Cork Bush; Wintercreeper; Evergreen Euonymus

CELASTRACEAE; staff-tree family

Height/habit: Deciduous or evergreen shrubs and small trees, 1.5 ft. (45 cm.) to 20 ft. (6 m.) high/wide. Fine deciduous choices are dwarf burning bush (*E. alata* 'Compacta') and strawberry bush (*E. americana*). Wintercreeper (*E. fortunei*) and evergreen euonymus (*E. japonicus*) retain their leaves year-round.

Leaves: Ovate-, elliptic- or lance-shaped, 1–3 in. (2.5–7.5 cm.) long; some evergreens notably variegated silvery to bright golden yellow; fall color outstanding in dwarf burning bush. Bare winter branches noteworthy in cork bush, also known as winged euonymus (*E. alata*).

Flowers: Small, inconspicuous, in axillary cymes; green, purple; showy fruits may be pink, orange, or red.

Season: Attractive all year.

When to plant: Set transplants when available. Cold- and heat-tolerant zones 3–5 to 9; *A. alata* and varieties zones 3–8.

Light: Sunny to half-sunny.

Soil: Humusy, well drained, moist; deciduous types can be drought- and wind-tolerant.

Fertilizer: 5-10-5.

Pruning: Prune deciduous types only to remove dead wood or in winter if they form clipped hedge; remove from variegated types any branches that revert to plain green leaves.

Propagation: Take cuttings summer through fall.

Uses: Borders, accent, hedge, ground cover, seaside gardens, espalier, bonsai, cutting.

EXOCHORDA
(ex-oh-KOR-dah)

The Bride

ROSACEAE; rose family

Height/habit: *E. macrantha* a deciduous, weeping shrub, to 4 ft. (1.2 m.) high/wide.
Leaves: Rounded, 1–2 in. (2.5–5 cm.) across.
Flowers: Showy, 1–2 in. (2.5–5 cm.) across, growing in loose clusters; white.
Season: Spring.
When to plant: Set transplants when available. Cold- and heat-tolerant zones 5–9.
Light: Sunny to half-sunny.
Soil: Well drained, moist to wet.
Fertilizer: 5-10-5.
Pruning: To rejuvenate old, neglected plants cut back hard in early spring.
Propagation: Sow newly ripened seeds or take cuttings summer through fall.
Uses: Borders, accent, cottage gardens.

FAGUS
(FAY-gus)

Beech

FAGACEAE; beech family

Height/habit: Stately deciduous trees, 80–100 ft. (24–30 m.) high/wide.

Leaves: Serrated—though less so in the European beech (*F. sylvatica*)—to ovate, to 4 in. (10 cm.) long; American beech (*F. grandifolia*) turns clear yellow in fall. Also worth growing is weeping beech (*F. sylvatica* 'Pendula').

Flowers: Males in drooping heads, inconspicuous.

Season: Attractive all year.

When to plant: Set transplants when available. Do not disturb taproot. Cold- and heat-tolerant zones 3–5 to 9.

Light: Sunny to half-sunny.

Soil: Humusy, well drained, moist, acidic.

Fertilizer: 14-14-14 timed-release.

Pruning: Cut only to remove dead or damaged wood.

Propagation: Sow seeds fall through winter. Containerize seedlings to prevent taproot from becoming deeply established in the ground.

Uses: Shade, windbreak, clipped hedge, bonsai.

FEIJOA
(fay-JOH-uh)
Pineapple Guava
MYRTACEAE; myrtle family

Height/habit: *F. sellowiana* an evergreen shrub or small tree, to 225 ft. (68 m.) high/wide.
Leaves: Elliptic to oblong, to 3 in. (7.5 cm.) long, green above, woolly beneath.
Flowers: Cup-shaped, to 1.5 in. (3.7 cm.) across, 4 petals fleshy, eaten in salads; white outside, purplish red inside, with dark red stamens; edible fruit 2–3 in. (5–7.5 cm.) long, green tinged red, tasting of guava.
Season: Flowers in spring; fruit follows in 4–7 months.

When to plant: Set transplants when available. Cold- and heat-tolerant zones 8–10.
Light: Sunny.
Soil: Humusy, well drained, moist.
Fertilizer: 5-10-5.
Pruning: Control and guide growth in spring.
Propagation: Sow seeds or take cuttings spring through summer; graft named varieties winter through spring.
Uses: Borders, specimen, hedge, espalier, edible fruit, containers.

FORSYTHIA
(for-SITH-ee-ah)
Forsythia
OLEACEAE; olive family

Height/habit: Deciduous shrubs of loosely spreading form, 1.5 ft.(45 cm.) to 10 ft. (3 m.) high/wide. Excellent choices are border forsythia (*F. x intermedia*), weeping forsythia (*F. suspensa*), and green-stem forsythia (*F. viridissima*).
Leaves: Often 3-lobed, to 6 in. (15 cm.) long.
Flowers: Precede the leaves, 1 in. (2.5 cm.) across, growing in clusters around the branches; every shade of yellow from pale to bright to dark.
Season: Early spring.

When to plant: Set transplants when available. Cold- and heat-tolerant zones 4–8, green-stem zones 5–9. Protracted cold below zero can kill flower buds.
Light: Sunny.
Soil: Well drained, moist.
Fertilizer: 5-10-5.
Pruning: To control growth, remove some branches for forcing in winter, others while coming into bloom; when flowering finishes, cut back to the ground some of the oldest branches.
Propagation: Take cuttings of green wood or ground-layer the tips spring through summer.
Uses: Borders, unclipped hedge, espalier, containers (dwarfs), bonsai, cutting.

FOTHERGILLA
(foth-uhr-GILL-ah)

Witch Alder

HAMAMELIDACEAE; witch-hazel family

Height/habit: Deciduous, spreading shrubs, 3–10 ft. (1–3 m.) high/wide. Of note are Eastern dwarf witch alder (*F. gardenii* 'Eastern Form') and American witch alder (*F. major*).

Leaves: Round to oval, 3–4 in. (7.5–10 cm.) long; long-lasting red color in fall.

Flowers: Precede the leaves; feathery tufts or cylindrical spikes, comprised of bundled filaments or stamens; white.

Season: Blooms in spring, foliage color in fall.

When to plant: Set transplants when available. Cold- and heat-tolerant zones 5–8.

Light: Sunny to partly sunny.

Soil: Humusy, well drained, moist.

Fertilizer: 5-10-5.

Pruning: Little needed.

Propagation: Layer spring through fall; it can take 2 years to strike roots.

Uses: Borders, specimen.

FRANKLINIA
(frank-LIN-ee-ah)

Franklin Tree

THEACEAE; tea family

Height/habit: *F. alatamaha* a small, deciduous tree, 20–30 ft. (6–9 m.) high.
Leaves: Oblong, 4–6 in. (10–15 cm.) long, clustered at the tips of new growth; turning scarlet in fall.
Flowers: Open flat from round buds, 3–4 in. (7.5–10 cm.) across, with yellow stamens prominent in center; creamy white.
Season: Flowers late summer, often coinciding with changing leaf colors.

When to plant: Set transplants when available. Cold- and heat-tolerant zones 4–9.
Light: Sunny to partly shady.
Soil: Humusy, well drained, moist, acidic.
Fertilizer: 14-14-14 or 5-10-5.
Pruning: Little needed.
Propagation: Sow seeds spring through summer; they bloom in up to 7 years; take half-ripe cuttings summer through fall.
Uses: Specimen for garden, lawn, or patio; companion for azaleas and rhododendrons.

FUCHSIA
(FEW-shuh)

Fuchsia

ONAGRACEAE; evening-primrose family

Height/habit: Deciduous to evergreen shrubs (depending on climate and growing conditions), from tidy shrublets to upright bushes, tree-form standards, or hanging baskets, 1–15 ft. (30–450 cm. [4.5 m.]) high/wide. Well worth growing are common fuchsia (*F.* x *hybrida*), hummingbird fuchsia (*F. magellanica*), and honeysuckle fuchsia (*F. triphylla* 'Gartenmeister Bohnstedt').

Leaves: Oval, from .5 in. (1.25 cm.) to 6–7 in. (15–17 cm.) long.

Flowers: Hanging, solitary, or bunched, single or double, 1–4 in. (2.5–10 cm.) across; all colors except oranges and yellows, often strikingly bicolored.

Season: Spring through summer.

When to plant: Set transplants when available. Cold- and heat-hardy in a fairly narrow range, around zone 8, but grown elsewhere as tender perennials, wintered in a frost-free place.

Light: Sunny (cooler climates) to shady.

Soil: Humusy, well drained, moist; dry side acceptable in winter.

Fertilizer: 14-14-14 timed-release.

Pruning: Remove any dead wood in spring; for baskets, bushes, and tree-form standards, cut back by half to two-thirds at the beginning of the new season.

Propagation: Take cuttings spring through summer; sow seeds winter through spring.

Uses: Borders, containers, hanging garden, window boxes, espalier, bonsai.

GARDENIA
(gar-DEE-nee-ah)

Gardenia; Cape Jasmine

RUBIACEAE; madder family

Height/habit: Evergreen shrublets or shrubs, 1–10 ft. (30–300 cm. [3 m.]) high/wide.

Leaves: Leathery, lance-shaped to ovate, to 4 in. (10 cm.) long.

Flowers: Single extended tubes in single gardenia (*G. thunbergia*), doubled in common gardenia, also known as Cape jasmine (*G. jasminoides*), 2–3 in. (5–7.5 cm.) across; velvety white; fragrant.

Season: Spring through summer through fall, depending on variety and climate.

When to plant: Set transplants when available. Cold- and heat-tolerant zones 8–9 to 10; in colder zones place containers outdoors in warm weather.

Light: Sunny to half-sunny.

Soil: Humusy, well drained, moist, acidic.

Fertilizer: 30-10-10 or 14-14-14 timed-release.

Pruning: Little needed, only to remove dead branches or to thin out twiggy cross-branching from interior of the plant.

Propagation: Take cuttings spring through summer or in winter with bottom heat (in greenhouse, with soil-heating cables, or with electric blankets/sheets placed under pots and flats).

Uses: Borders, specimen, containers, tree-form standard, bonsai, cutting.

GINKGO
(GINK-go)

Ginkgo; Maidenhair Tree

GINKGOACEAE; ginkgo family

Height/habit: *G. biloba* deciduous tree, to 120 ft. (36.4 m.) high.

Leaves: Distinctly fanned into 2 lobes, to 2 in. (5 cm.) across, reminiscent of maidenhair fern; turning rapidly golden in fall, then falling all at once into a glowing carpet.

Flowers: Male (staminate) and female (pistillate) on separate plants; female flowers in loose catkins followed by oval fruit, greenish golden when ripe and smelling of rancid butter, edible, considered a delicacy by some.

Season: Satisfactory at all times.

When to plant: Set transplants when available. Cold- and heat-tolerant zones 3–9. Unless the fruit is desired, male clones are recommended, such as 'Compacta,' 'Fairmount,' 'Fastigiata,' 'Lakeview,' 'Old Gold,' and 'Saratoga.'

Light: Sunny.

Soil: Well drained, moist.

Fertilizer: 14-14-14 timed-release.

Pruning: Little needed, except to shape or remove dead parts. Staking helps young trees.

Propagation: Take cuttings from males or sow seeds fall through winter.

Uses: Shade, street, lawn, specimen, bonsai.

HALESIA
(hay-LEE-zee-ah)

Silver Bell; Snowdrop Tree

STYRACACEAE; storax family

Height/habit: Deciduous trees, 40–50 ft. (12.1–15 m.) high/wide.
Leaves: Oval to oblong, 4–8 in. (10–20 cm.) long.
Flowers: Pendulous, bell-shaped, .75–1 in. (2–2.5 cm.) long, set along the branches; white or, rarely, pink.
Season: Spring.
When to plant: Set transplants when available. Cold- and heat-tolerant zones 4–5 to 8–9.
Light: Sunny (cool climates) to partly shady/protected (hotter climates).

Soil: Humusy, well drained, moist.
Fertilizer: 14-14-14 timed-release.
Pruning: Immediately after flowering, oldest flowered shoots may be removed to encourage new ones and attractive form.
Propagation: Layer or take root cuttings spring through summer; sow seeds in fall.
Uses: Borders, background, woodland and cottage gardens, cutting.

HAMAMELIS
(ham-am-MEEL-iss)

Witch Hazel

HAMAMELIDACEAE; witch-hazel family

Height/habit: Deciduous shrubs or trees, 6–30 ft. (1.8–9 m.) high/wide. Hybrid witch hazel (*H.* x *intermedia*), Japanese witch hazel (*H. japonica*), Chinese witch hazel (*H. mollis*), Dwarf Ozark witch hazel (*H. vernalis*), and common witch hazel (*H. virginiana*) are all excellent choices.
Leaves: Roundish, 4–6 in. (10–15 cm.) long; fall color yellow or orange.
Flowers: Ribbonlike, to 1 in. (2.5 cm.) long, in dense clusters; yellow, orange, or red; fragrant.
Season: Late winter through earliest spring, with the exception of common witch hazel, which blooms in late fall.
When to plant: Set transplants when available. Cold- and heat-tolerant zones 4–5 to 8.
Light: Sunny to half-shady.
Soil: Humusy, well drained, moist.
Fertilizer: 14-14-14 timed-release at planting or 5-10-5.
Pruning: Little needed, except for long branches that extend beyond the general outline of the bush; do so at flowering time so as to enjoy the cut branches indoors.
Propagation: Layer in summer; sow seeds in fall.
Uses: Borders, cottage gardens, screening, specimen, espalier, bonsai.

HAMELIA
(ham-EE-lee-ah)

Fire Bush; Hummingbird Bush

RUBIACEAE; madder family

Height/habit: *H. patens*, called both fire bush and hummingbird bush, an evergreen shrub or small tree, to 25 ft. (7.5 m.).
Leaves: Elliptic to ovate, to 6 in. (15 cm.) long; green to golden in summer, glowing red in fall.
Flowers: Tubular, to 1 in. (2.5 cm.) long, growing in terminal clusters; reddish orange. Attractive to both butterflies and hummingbirds.
Season: Summer through fall; foliage color persists in mild-winter climates.
When to plant: Set transplants when available, usually spring through summer. Cold- and heat-tolerant zones 9–10.
Light: Sunny to half-sunny.
Soil: Humusy, well drained, moist.
Fertilizer: 14-14-14 timed-release, 5-10-5 or 15-30-15 at onset of bloom season.
Pruning: Cut back to green wood in late spring; even if killed to the ground, the root-stocks often survive and send up new shoots that bloom the same season.
Propagation: Take cuttings spring through summer.
Uses: Beds, borders, containers, hedge, butterfly and hummingbird gardens.

HEDERA
(HED-der-ah)

Ivy

ARALIACEAE; aralia family

Height/habit: Evergreen vines becoming shrublike with age, size (length) dictated by the site and method of training, as well as by the variety or cultivar.

Leaves: Distinctly lobed and pointed, .5–4 in. (1.25–10 cm.) long; various greens, also variegated gold, white, creamy, or silver.

Flowers: Inconspicuous; appear only on mature ivies, followed by berries.

Season: Attractive at most times.

When to plant: Set transplants when available. Cold- and heat-tolerant zones 8–10 for Algerian ivy (*H. canariensis*), 4–9 for smaller-leaved English ivy (*H. helix*).

Light: Sunny to shady.

Soil: Humusy, well drained, moist.

Fertilizer: 14-14-14 timed-release.

Pruning: Only to remove dead growth or to curtail any that is overextended.

Propagation: Set tip cuttings to root in clean, moist medium in bright light and moderate temperatures (50–70°F [10–21°C]).

Uses: Ground cover; wall climber; mature form as shrub specimen, espalier, and topiary; bonsai; cutting.

HIBISCUS
(high-BISK-us)

Texas Star; Swamp Mallow; Confederate Rose; Chinese Hibiscus; Rose of Sharon

MALVACEAE; mallow family

Height/habit: Upright herbaceous or woody shrubs to small trees, 3–15 ft. (1–4.5 m.) high/wide. Of note for the garden are Texas star (*H. coccineus*), swamp mallow (*H. moscheutos* 'Disco Belle,' 'Southern Belle'), Confederate rose (*H. mutabilis*), Chinese hibiscus (*H. rosa-sinensis*), fringe-petalled hibiscus (*H. schizopetalus*), and rose of Sharon (*H. syriacus*).
Leaves: Palmate, ovate to elliptic, heart-shaped, or triangular with lobes, 1–6 in. (2.5–15 cm.); tropical species glossy or shiny.

Flowers: Cups or saucers, 2–10 in. (5–25 cm.) across, appearing at the branch tips on new wood; most colors.
Season: Spring through summer; Chinese hibiscus most of the year in frost-free climates.
When to plant: Set transplants when available. Cold- and heat-tolerant zones 5–9 for swamp mallow and rose of Sharon, 9–10 for the tropical species.
Light: Sunny.
Soil: Humusy, well drained, moist, acidic.
Fertilizer: 7-2-7 or 10-2-4 for Chinese hibiscus; 14-14-14 for general growth boost.
Pruning: Remove dead wood or prune to guide and train in spring—it may be necessary to cut it to the ground.
Propagation: Sow seeds, take cuttings, or layer spring through summer.
Uses: Beds, borders, specimen, screening, containers, cutting.

HYDRANGEA
(high-DRAIN-jee-uh)

Hydrangea

SAXIFRAGACEAE; saxifrage family

Height/habit: Mostly deciduous shrubs or climbers, 6 to 20 ft. (1.8–6 m.) high/wide or more. Climbing hydrangea (*H. anomala* var. *petiolaris*), hills-of-snow (*H. arborescens*), French hydrangea (*H. macrophylla*), peegee hydrangea (*H. paniculata* var. *grandiflora*), and Snow Queen oakleaf hydrangea (*H. quercifolia* 'Snow Queen') are excellent garden choices.

Leaves: Roundish to ovate or similar to oak leaf, 4–6 in. (10–15 cm.) long; some varieties variegated silvery white.

Flowers: Dense clusters, few or many showy; lacy fertile flowers surrounded by sterile; white, blue, pink, purplish mauve, or white turning pale green in peegee hydrangea.

Season: Spring through summer through fall, depending on the species and the local weather.

When to plant: Set transplants when available. Cold- and heat-tolerant zones 4–6 to 8–9.

Light: Sunny to partly shady.

Soil: Humusy, well drained, moist; acidic for blue flowers in the colored strains of French hydrangea.

Fertilizer: 14-14-14 timed-release; 30-10-10 for more acidity.

Pruning: Remove old shoots from French hydrangea after flowering. Hydrangeas that bloom on current season's growth can be cut back as sharply as needed in early spring.

Propagation: Take cuttings or layer summer through fall.

Uses: Beds, borders, specimen, hedge, wall or fence cover, containers, seaside and cottage gardens, cutting.

ILEX
(EYE-lex)

Holly; Winterberry; Yaupon

AQUIFOLIACEAE; holly family

Height/habit: Evergreen or deciduous shrubs or trees, 1–80 ft. (30–240 cm. [24 m.]) high/wide. Among evergreen favorites are English holly (*I. aquifolium*), Chinese holly (*I. cornuta*), Japanese holly (*I. crenata*), American holly (*I. opaca*), and yaupon (*I. vomitoria*). Winterberry (*I. verticillata*) is deciduous.

Leaves: Often tipped with spines 1.5–3 in. (3.7–7.5 cm.) long; various greens, often variegated creamy or yellow.

Flowers: Male (staminate) and female (pistillate) on different plants, inconspicuous; white or greenish; followed by berries in range of colors.

Season: Attractive all year.

When to plant: Set transplants when available. Cold- and heat-tolerant zones 3–7 to 9.

Light: Sunny.

Soil: Humusy, well drained, moist.

Fertilizer: 14-14-14 or 5-10-5.

Pruning: Trim lightly as growth begins in spring; also remove any dead branches or tips damaged by winter. To rejuvenate old hollies, cut back sharply in spring. Holly hedges need shearing midsummer. Cuttings removed for holiday decorations count also as pruning.

Propagation: Take cuttings of deciduous types in summer and hardwood cuttings of evergreen types fall through winter.

Uses: Beds, borders, screening, specimen, hedge, espalier, tree-form standard, bonsai, cutting.

INDIGOFERA
(in-dig-GOFF-er-ah)

Indigo

LEGUMINOSAE; pea family

Height/habit: Deciduous shrubs or perennial herbs 5–6 ft. (1.5–1.8 m.) high/wide. Popular choices are pink indigo (*I. amblyantha*), Asian indigo (*I. kirilowii*), and Chinese indigo (*I. potaninii*).

Leaves: Odd-numbered leaflets, often 5–7 or 9–11, to 6 in. (15 cm.) long.

Flowers: Gracefully drooping clusters, 5–7 in. (12.5–17 cm.) long; lilac pink, rose, lilac purple, or white.

Season: Spring through summer.

When to plant: Set transplants when available. Cold- and heat-tolerant zones 5–9.

Light: Sunny to half-shady.

Soil: Humusy, well drained, moist.

Fertilizer: 14-14-14 or 5-10-5.

Pruning: Cut back hard in early spring; new shoots form graceful, vigorous bushes with plenty of blooms.

Propagation: Take cuttings spring through summer.

Uses: Beds, borders, specimen, containers, cottage gardens.

ITEA
(eye-TEE-ah)

Holly-leaf Itea; Sweetspire

SAXIFRAGACEAE; saxifrage family

Height/habit: Deciduous, as with sweetspire (*I. virginica*), and evergreen, as with holly-leaf itea (*I. ilicifolia*), shrubs or small trees, 8–18 ft.(2.4–5.5 m.) high/wide.

Leaves: Hollylike in holly-leaf itea, to 4 in. (10 cm.) long; finely toothed, to 3 in. (7.5 cm.) long, in sweetspire, turning brilliant red in fall.

Flowers: Tiny, growing in drooping clusters to 1 ft. (30 cm.) long in holly-leaf tea; upright to 6 in. (15 cm.) long and fragrant in sweetspire; white to greenish white.

Season: Summer.

When to plant: Set transplants when available. Cold- and heat-tolerant zones 5–9.

Light: Sunny to shady.

Soil: Well drained, moist.

Fertilizer: 14-14-14 or 5-10-5.

Pruning: Little needed except to remove winter-damaged growth in spring.

Propagation: Divide in spring or take softwood cuttings in summer; sow seeds fall through spring.

Uses: Beds; borders; background; woodland, wild, or cottage gardens; cutting.

KALMIA
(KAL-mee-ah)

Mountain Laurel; Calico Bush

ERICACEAE; heath family

Height/habit: *K. latifolia*, known as both mountain laurel and calico bush, an evergreen shrub, 6–8 ft. (1.8–2.4 m.) high/wide, eventually thicket-forming, to 15 ft. (4.5 m.) high/wide.

Leaves: Elliptic, glossy, 2–5 in. (5–12.5 cm.) long; warning: poisonous if ingested.
Flowers: Cupped, starry, to 1 in. (2.5 cm.) across, appearing in showy, terminal clusters; white, pink, rose, red, or maroon; often bi-colored.
Season: Late spring through early summer; foliage attractive all year.

When to plant: Set transplants when available. Cold- and heat-tolerant zones 4–8; marginally in zone 9 if climate is not too hot and humid in the summer and soil not too alkaline.
Light: Partly sunny to partly shady.
Soil: Humusy, well drained, moist, acidic.
Fertilizer: 14-14-14 timed-release; chelated iron in case of chlorosis (yellowed leaves with green veins).
Pruning: Only cut to remove dead wood or for flower arrangements.

Propagation: Layer spring through summer; sow seeds fall through winter; green-wood cuttings under glass winter through spring.
Uses: Borders; massed plantings; cottage, shade, woodland, or wild gardens; cutting.

KERRIA
(KEHR-ee-ah)

Japanese Rose; Variegated Kerria

ROSACEAE; rose family

Height/habit: Deciduous shrub, roselike but unarmed, gracefully rounded or fountain form, 5–8 ft. (1.5–2.4 m.) high/wide.
Leaves: Simple ovals, often toothed, to 4 in. (10 cm.) long; mixed pleasingly with white in the variegated kerrias: *K. japonica* 'Picta,' *K. j.* 'Superba,' and *K. j.* 'Variegata.'
Flowers: Resemble roses, as common name implies, to 2 in. (5 cm.) across; single (as with Japanese rose, *K. japonica*) or double (as with double Japanese rose, *K. j.* 'Pleniflora'); yellow.
Season: Spring, sporadically in summer. Bare twigs bright green in the winter landscape.

When to plant: Set transplants when available. Cold- and heat-tolerant zones 4–9.
Light: Sunny to half-shady.
Soil: Humusy, well drained, moist.
Fertilizer: 14-14-14 timed-release or rose fertilizer.
Pruning: Immediately after flowering, cut out as much old wood as possible, back to strong new shoots, even if this means pruning to the ground. Remove completely green shoots from variegated sorts.
Propagation: Take softwood cuttings in summer, hardwood cuttings fall through winter; layer or divide roots in spring.
Uses: Beds, borders, informal hedge, wild garden, cutting.

KIRENGESHOMA
(kihr-en-geh-SHOW-mah)

Kirengeshoma

SAXIFRAGACEAE; saxifrage family

Height/habit: *K. palmata* an herbaceous perennial 3–4 ft. (1.2 m.) high/wide that gives the garden effect of a deciduous shrub.

Leaves: Palmately lobed, toothed, to 9 in. (22.5 cm.) long on purplish stems.

Flowers: Nodding, trumpet-shaped, growing in terminal and axillary cymes, to 5 in. (12.5 cm.) long; yellow.

Season: Mid- to late summer.

When to plant: Set transplants when available, ideally in spring. Cold- and heat-tolerant zones 6–8.

Light: Half-sunny to half-shady.

Soil: Humusy, well drained, moist.

Fertilizer: 14-14-14 timed-release.

Pruning: Remove all dead parts or cut to the ground in early spring; flowers appear on new shoots.

Propagation: Divide roots or sow seeds in spring.

Uses: Beds; borders; specimen; shade, wild, or cottage gardens.

KOELREUTERIA
(kel-roo-TEHR-ee-ah)

Golden-rain Tree; Flamegold-rain Tree

SAPINDACEAE; soapberry family

Height/habit: Deciduous trees, 15–40 ft. (4.5–12.1 m.) high/wide. Especially rewarding to grow are *K. bipinnata* and *K. paniculata*, both called golden-rain tree, as well as flamegold-rain tree (*K. elegans*).
Leaves: Pinnate, 1–2 ft. (30–61 cm.) long; oval leaflets, sometimes toothed.
Flowers: Terminal panicles, 1–1.5 ft. (30–45 cm.) long; yellow; fragrant. Followed by long-lasting seed capsules that turn rose, dark red, pinkish bronze, or chartreuse.
Season: Flowers in summer, decorative seed capsules in fall.

When to plant: Set transplants when available. *S. paniculata* cold- and heat-tolerant zones 6–9, the others zones 7–8 to 10.
Light: Sunny.
Soil: Well drained, moist to on the dry side; drought-tolerant when established.
Fertilizer: 14-14-14 timed-release at planting; 5-10-5 before flowering.
Pruning: Remove all dead wood and shape late winter through early spring.
Propagation: Sow seeds spring through summer; transplant self-sown seedlings in spring.
Uses: Light shade, street, terrace, lawn; for screening if planted thicket-style.

LABURNUM
(lab-BURN-um)

Golden-chain Tree

LEGUMINOSAE; pea family

Height/habit: Ornamental deciduous shrubs to 15–20 ft. (4.5–6 m.). Trained as single-trunked trees, grow to 30 ft. (9 m.) high. Excellent choices are common golden-chain tree (*L. anagyroides*) and Voss hybrid golden-chain tree (*L.* x *watereri* 'Vossii').
Leaves: Cloverlike, to 3 in. (7.5 cm.) long.
Flowers: Wisterialike clusters, 8–15 in. (20–38 cm.) long; yellow.
Season: Late spring through summer.
When to plant: Set transplants when available. Cold- and heat-tolerant zones 5–7.

Light: Sunny to half-shady; protect from afternoon sun in hotter climates.
Soil: Well drained, moist.
Fertilizer: 14-14-14 timed-release at planting, 5-10-5 thereafter.
Pruning: Remove suckers faithfully if training to single-trunk tree-form standard. Late winter through early spring remove any dead or damaged growth.
Propagation: Sow seeds in fall.
Uses: Borders, background, espalier, arbor, bonsai.

LAGERSTROEMIA
(lay-gur-STREEM-ee-ah)

Crape Myrtle

LYTHRACEAE; loosestrife family

Height/habit: *L. indica* a decid-uous shrub or small tree, to 20–35 ft. (6–10.5 m.) high/wide. Dwarf types to 3 ft. (1 m.) high/wide.

Leaves: Elliptic, 1–3 in. (2.5–7.5 cm.) long; yellow to scarlet in fall.

Flowers: Frilly, to 1 in. (2.5 cm.) across, with prominent yellow stamens in large, showy clus-ters; pink, red, rose, coral, lavender, or white. Prompt deadheading promotes more bloom.

Season: Summer through early fall.

When to plant: Set transplants when available. Cold- and heat-tolerant zones 7–9. Often man-aged as container plants in colder zones.

Light: Sunny.

Soil: Well drained, moist.

Fertilizer: 14-14-14 timed-release initially, 5-10-5 there-after; 30-10-10 or chelated iron in the event of chlorosis (yel-lowish leaves).

Pruning: Remove all dead wood in spring before new leaves appear. Blooms appear on new growth. Keep suckers and water shoots removed from the base, trunks, and main branches of trees.

Propagation: Sow seeds winter through spring; take cuttings in summer.

Uses: Border, screen, lawn, light shade, specimen, bonsai, con-tainers (dwarf types), ground cover (dwarf types).

LIGUSTRUM
(lig-GUST-rum)
Privet;
Golden Vicary
OLEACEAE; olive family

Height/habit: Deciduous, semi-
to evergreen shrubs, rarely
small trees, 10–15 ft. (3–4.5 m.)
high/wide. Best deciduous
choices include amur privet
(*L. amurense*), border privet
(*L. obtusifolium*), variegated
privet (*L. sinense* 'Variegatum'),
and golden vicary (*L. x
vicaryi*). Glossy Chinese privet
(*L. lucidum*) and wax-leaved
privet (*L. japonicum*) are
evergreen.

Leaves: Ovate to elliptic, 2–4 in.
(5–10 cm.) long; variegated silvery white or golden yellow in
some selections.

Flowers: Very small in dense
panicles; white; unpleasantly
scented.

Season: Flowers in spring or
summer.

When to plant: Set transplants
when available. Cold- and heat-
tolerant zones 5–7 to 9–10.

Light: Sunny to shady.

Soil: Moist, well drained.

Fertilizer: 14-14-14 timed-
release.

Pruning: Formal privet hedges
need clipping several times
each season. Specimens need
little pruning except to remove
dead twigs and branches.

Propagation: Take cuttings
spring through summer; sow
seeds in fall; plant also grows
from self-sown seedlings.

Uses: Clipped or informal
hedges, screens, borders, shade,
seaside and city gardens, topiary, bonsai.

LINDERA
(lin-DEER-ah)

Spicebush

LAURACEAE; laurel family

Height/habit: *L. obtusiloba* deciduous shrub to 15 ft. (4.5 m.) high by one-third to one-half as wide. All parts have a spicy fragrance.
Leaves: Broad ovals, to 5 in. (12.5 cm.) across; fall color is clear yellow.
Flowers: Tiny, in dense clusters; male (staminate) and female (pistillate) on separate plants; greenish yellow.
Season: Flowers early spring, before the leaves; oblong scarlet berries persist on branches of female plant after leaves are gone.
When to plant: Set transplants when available. Larger plants intolerant of root disturbance. Cold- and heat-tolerant zones 6–9.
Light: Sunny (cooler regions) to partly shaded.
Soil: Well drained, moist.
Fertilizer: 5-10-5 or 14-14-14 timed-release.
Pruning: Remove dead wood in spring.
Propagation: Take softwood cuttings spring through summer; sow newly ripe seeds fall through winter.
Uses: Borders, background, accent, shade, butterfly and wild gardens, cutting.

LIRIODENDRON
(lihr-ee-oh-DEN-dron)

Tulip Tree

MAGNOLIACEAE; magnolia family

Height/habit: *L. tulipifera* a fast-growing deciduous tree, 60–80 ft. (18–24 m.) high, spreading to 40 ft. (12.1 m.) in a pyramidal crown.
Leaves: Lyre-shaped, 5–6 in. (12.5–15 cm.) long/wide; bright yellow-green, turning yellow or yellow-brown in fall.
Flowers: Tulip-shaped, to 2 in. (5 cm.) across; yellowish green with orange at the base; often not appearing until the tree is 10 years old.
Season: Flowers late spring.
When to plant: Set container transplants when available, ideally in spring. Avoid root disturbance. Cold- and heat-tolerant zones 4–9.
Light: Sunny.
Soil: Well drained, moist.
Fertilizer: 14-14-14 timed-release.
Pruning: Remove dead wood in spring; remove suckers from the base or water shoots from any branch in summer.
Propagation: Layer or graft cultivars spring through summer; sow seeds fall through winter.
Uses: Shade; lawn; roadside; butterfly garden; spreading roots discourage gardening under tulip tree.

MAGNOLIA
(mag-NO-lee-ah)

Cucumber Tree; Ear-leaved Umbrella Tree; Bull Bay; White Yulan; Magnolia

MAGNOLIACEAE; magnolia family

Height/habit: Ornamental shrubs to large trees, deciduous or evergreen, 10–80 ft. (3–24 m.). Noteworthy deciduous species include cucumber tree (*M. acuminata*), ear-leaved umbrella tree (*M. fraseri*), white yulan (*M. denudata*), star magnolia (*M. kobus* var. *stellata*), large-leaved cucumber tree (*M. macrophylla*), Siebold magnolia (*M. sieboldii*), and saucer magnolia (*M. x soulangiana*). Bull bay (*M. grandiflora*) is evergreen.

Leaves: Entire, often glossy, variously ovate, elliptic, lanceolate, obovate, or oblanceolate, 6–36 in. (15–90 cm.) long.

Flowers: Cups, saucers, or stars; 3–12 in. (7.5–30 cm.) across; pink, red, white, rose, or yellow; fragrant.

Season: Spring or summer.

When to plant: Set transplants when available. Cold- and heat-tolerant zones 5–6 to 9.

Light: Sunny to half-shady.

Soil: Well drained, moist, acidic.

Fertilizer: 14-14-14 timed-release; chelated iron to treat chlorosis (yellowish foliage).

Pruning: After flowering, remove any unwanted growth, usually taking the branch to the basal collar at its point of origination.

Propagation: Sow seeds or take hardwood cuttings fall through winter; take softwood cuttings in summer.

Uses: Specimen, lawn, garden, shade, espalier, bonsai, cutting.

MAHONIA
(mah-HOH-nee-ah)

Oregon Grape; Japanese Mahonia

BERBERIDACEAE; barberry family

Height/habit: Upright broadleaf evergreen shrubs, 3–10 ft. (1–3 m.) high/wide. *M. aquifolium* and *M. bealei*, both called Oregon grape, as well as Japanese mahonia (*M. japonica*), recommended species.

Leaves: Pinnate, spiny-toothed, 3–16 in. (7.5–40 cm.) long.
Flowers: Small in drooping racemes, 3–6 in. (7.5–15 cm.) long; yellow; fragrant.
Season: Midspring to early summer; showy bluish to purplish black fruit fall through winter.
When to plant: Set transplants when available. Cold- and heat-tolerant zones 6–9.
Light: Partly sunny to partly shady.
Soil: Humusy, well drained, moist, acidic.
Fertilizer: 14-14-14 timed-release; chelated iron to treat chlorosis (yellowish foliage).

Pruning: Little needed; remove dead growth late winter through spring. Bare branches extending awkwardly may be removed to the ground at the same time.
Propagation: Layer or take suckers spring through summer; sow seeds or take hardwood cuttings fall through winter.
Uses: Borders, informal hedge, specimen, shade and Japanese gardens, containers.

MALUS
(MAY-luss)

Crab Apple

ROSACEAE; rose family

Height/habit: Deciduous shrubs or small trees, 15–45 ft. (4.5–13.6 m.) high. Fine choices are Arnold crab apple (*M.* x *arnoldiana*), carmine crab apple (*M.* x *atrosanguinea*); Siberian crab apple (*M. baccata*), Japanese flowering crab apple (*M. floribunda*), common apple (*M. pumila* and *M. sylvestris*), cherry crab apple (*M.* x *robusta*), and Sargent crab apple (*M. sargentii*).

Leaves: Serrate- or smooth-edged, ovate or elliptic, 1–4 in. (2.5–10 cm.) long.
Flowers: Cupped or saucerlike, single or double, about 1 in. (2.5 cm.) across, growing in clusters; pink, white, rose, red, or crimson; some fragrant. Followed by edible or inedible though highly decorative fruits, from brightest red to golden yellow.
Season: Flowers in spring, light green foliage in summer; brightly colored fruit in fall, lasting well into winter on the ornamentals.
When to plant: Set transplants when available. Cold- and heat-tolerances zones 3–5 to 8; may succeed zone 9.

Light: Sunny.
Soil: Well drained, moist.
Fertilizer: 14-14-14 timed-release initially, 5-10-5 thereafter.
Pruning: Cut back after winter but before buds swell. Remove dead wood and shorten laterals by one-third on 2-year-old trees.
Propagation: Grow species from seeds sown fall through winter; grow named selections by grafting on a suitably related stock winter through spring.
Uses: Lawn, border, specimen, shade, orchard, espalier, bonsai, cutting.

MITRIOSTIGMA
(mit-ree-oh-STIG-mah)
African Gardenia
RUBIACEAE; madder family

Height/habit: *M. axillare* an upright evergreen shrub, 3–5 ft. (1–1.5 m.) high/wide.

Leaves: Elliptic, to 4 in. (10 cm.) long; dark green.

Flowers: Funnelform, 5-lobed, 3 or more together, borne at the leaf axils, to .5 in. (1.25 cm.) wide; white blushed bronzy pink on the outside; fragrant.

Season: Everblooming in moderate to warm climates with night lows of 50–60°F (10–15°C), days 70°F (21°C) or higher.

When to plant: Set transplants when available. Cold- and heat-tolerant zones 9 and warmer; elsewhere maintain as a container plant, placing outdoors in warm weather.

Light: Half-sunny to half-shady.

Soil: Humusy, well drained, moist.

Fertilizer: 30-10-10 applied with water; 14-14-14 timed-release.

Pruning: Prune at any time to remove dead wood—especially spring or summer to encourage branching.

Propagation: Take cuttings in spring or summer.

Uses: Cottage garden, border, containers.

NANDINA
(nan-DEE-nah)

Heavenly Bamboo

BERBERIDACEAE; barberry family

Height/habit: *N. domestica* an evergreen shrub 1–8 ft. (30–240 cm.) high; canelike stems.

Leaves: Narrow, pinnate on pendulous stem; leaflets to 1.5 in. (3.7 cm.) long, reduced to threadlike forms in some selections; turning bronze or red in cold weather.

Flowers: Small, appearing in clusters, to 1 ft. (30 cm.) long; white; succeeded by bright red berries.

Season: Flowers in spring; berries fall through winter.

When to plant: Set transplants when available. Cold- and heat-tolerant zones 6–9.

Light: Sunny to shady.

Soil: Well drained, moist. Established nandinas tolerate considerable drought.

Fertilizer: 14-14-14 timed-release; chelated iron in the event of chlorosis (yellowish leaves).

Pruning: Thin out oldest stems to the base in early spring; cut out any dead growth; remove dead or winter-damaged leaves.

Propagation: Divide in spring; sow seeds in fall.

Uses: Informal hedge, borders, specimen, shade or Japanese gardens, containers, bonsai.

NERIUM
(NEER-ee-um)
Oleander
APOCYNACEAE; dogbane family

Height/habit: *N. oleander* an evergreen shrub or small tree, to 20 ft. (6 m.).

Leaves: Narrow, willowlike, 6–10 in. (15–25 cm.) long.

Flowers: Single or double trumpets, 1–2 in. (2.5–5 cm.) across, growing in showy, terminal, branching clusters; white, yellow, rose, red, coral, or salmon; some bicolored; fragrant.

Season: Spring through summer.

When to plant: Set transplants when available. Cold- and heat-tolerant zones 8–10; elsewhere grow in containers that can be moved inside for winter.

Light: Sunny.

Soil: Well drained, moist to on the dry side. Established oleanders in the ground are exceedingly tolerant of drought and vehicular air pollution.

Fertilizer: 14-14-14 timed-release; chelated iron in the event of chlorosis (yellowish leaves).

Pruning: Cut back after spring bloom or throughout the season as a means of control; flowers appear at the tips of new shoots. The sap and all other parts of the oleander plant are poisonous.

Propagation: Take cuttings spring through fall.

Uses: Beds, borders, background, screening, specimen, containers, seaside gardens, tree-form standard, informal hedge.

OSMANTHUS
(oz-MANTH-us)

Sweet Olive; Tea Olive; Orange-flowered Sweet Olive; Chinese Holly-leaved Olive

OLEACEAE; olive family

Height/habit: Evergreen shrubs and trees, 20–30 ft. (6–9 m.).
Leaves: Oval-shaped in sweet olive, also called tea olive (*O. fragrans*), to 4 in. (10 cm.) long; hollylike, elliptic to oblong and 2–3 in. (5–7.5 cm.) long in Chinese holly-leaved olive (*O. heterophyllus*).
Flowers: Small, to .5 in. (1.25 cm.), growing in clusters at the leaf axils; white to creamy; fragrant. Orange-flowered sweet olive (*O. f. forma aurantiacus*) particularly beautiful.

Season: Fall through winter through spring.
When to plant: Set transplants when available. Cold- and heat-tolerant zones 7–8 to 10. Elsewhere grow as container specimen that can be wintered in a cool place protected from hard freezing.
Light: Sunny to half-sunny.
Soil: Well drained, moist.
Fertilizer: 14-14-14 timed-release.
Pruning: Remove any dead parts and shape tree late winter through spring; formal hedges and topiaries may require several shearings each growing season.
Propagation: Take cuttings of half-ripe wood in late summer.
Uses: Specimen, fragrance gardens (sweet olive), clipped hedge (Chinese holly-leaved olive), topiary, espalier, containers, bonsai.

OXYDENDRUM
(oxy-DEN-drum)

Sourwood; Sorrel Tree

ERICACEAE; heath family

Height/habit: *O. arboreum*, called both sourwood and sorrel tree, is deciduous and slow-growing, reaching 50–60 ft. (15.1–18.2 m.).

Leaves: Oblong to lanceolate, to 8 in. (20 cm.) long; outstanding fall color.

Flowers: Small, growing in pendulous panicles, 8–10 in. (20–25 cm.) long; white; fragrant. Succeeded by dried silvery capsules, decorative fall through winter.

Season: An outstanding year-round performer.

When to plant: Set transplants when available. Cold- and heat-tolerant zones 5–9.

Light: Sunny to half-shady.

Soil: Well drained, moist.

Fertilizer: 14-14-14 timed-release.

Pruning: Little needed beyond routine maintenance.

Propagation: Sow seeds fall through winter.

Uses: Specimen, lawn, street, shade gardens.

PACHYSANDRA
(pak-iss-SAND-rah)

Allegheny Spurge; Japanese Spurge

BUXACEAE; boxwood family

Height/habit: Evergreen ground covers, 6–12 in. (15–30 cm.) high, spreading to form dense cover if rooted cuttings or divisions are set on 8-in. (20-cm.) centers. Best choices are Allegheny spurge (*P. procumbens*) and Japanese spurge (*P. terminalis*).

Leaves: Obovate, toothed above the middle, 2–4 in. (5–10 cm.) long, clustered at the tips.

Flowers: Inconspicuous, growing in short spikes 1 in. (2.5 cm.) long; greenish white. Succeeded by white berries.

Season: Foliage attractive most seasons.

When to plant: Set transplants when available. Water well to establish. Cold- and heat-tolerant zones 4–9.

Light: Half-sunny to shady.

Soil: Humusy, well drained, moist.

Fertilizer: 14-14-14 timed-release.

Pruning: Prune only to remove dead growth at any time.

Propagation: Divide in spring; take cuttings in summer.

Uses: Ground cover under trees, on banks, around large shrubs.

PAULOWNIA
(pow-LOH-nee-ah)

Empress Tree

SCROPHULARIACEAE; figwort family

Height/habit: *P. tomentosa* a deciduous tree, 40–60 ft. (12.1–18.2 m) high.
Leaves: Broadly oval, 3-lobed, to 1 ft. (30 cm.) or more; densely matted beneath with short, woolly hairs.
Flowers: Lobed pouches, to 2 in. (5 cm.) across, in showy pyramidal panicles to 1 ft. (30 cm.) long; violet-blue.
Season: Spring, as leaves begin to unfold.
When to plant: Set transplants when available. Cold- and heat-tolerant zones 6–9.
Light: Sunny to half-sunny.
Soil: Humusy, well drained, moist.
Fertilizer: 14-14-14 timed-release.
Pruning: Remove any dead wood in early spring; for any major cutting, wait until immediately after flowering. If frozen to the ground, cut back hard in spring; new shoots will reach 12 ft. (3.6 m.) that season, with leaves to 1.5 ft. (45 cm.) across.
Propagation: Sow seeds or take root cuttings in spring.
Uses: Specimen, lawn, garden, park.

PERNETTYA
(per-NETT-ee-ah)

Chilean Myrtle

ERICACEAE; heath family

Height/habit: *P. mucronata* an evergreen shrub, 2–3 ft. (61–90 cm.) high/wide.
Leaves: Densely set on much-branched shrub, oval-shaped, to 1 in. (2.5 cm.) long; lightly toothed, tipped with sharp spine.
Flowers: Numerous, nodding, about .25 in. (.63 cm.) long; white, pink, or red.
Season: Spring through early summer.
When to plant: Set transplants when available. Narrowly cold- and heat-tolerant zones 7–8; ideal in cool, moist regions, free of temperature extremes.
Light: Sunny.
Soil: Humusy, well drained, moist, acidic.
Fertilizer: 14-14-14 timed-release; chelated iron in response to chlorosis (yellowish foliage).
Pruning: Little needed; remove any long, straggly growths when full of berries so they can be enjoyed indoors.
Propagation: Take cuttings of half-ripe wood or suckers or layer in summer; sow seeds in fall.
Uses: Specimen, border, rock gardens.

PHILADELPHUS
(fil-ad-DELF-us)
Mock Orange
SAXIFRAGACEAE; saxifrage family

Height/habit: Deciduous shrubs with curving or drooping branches, 4–12 ft. (1.2–3.6 m.) high/wide. Good choices are common mock orange (*P. coronarius*), *P. lewisii* 'Waterton,' and dwarf mock orange (*P. microphyllus*).

Leaves: Oval, lanceolate, or elliptic, 1–5 in. (2.5–12.5 cm.) long.

Flowers: Cup- or saucer-shaped, single or double, 1–2 in. (2.5–5 cm.) across, single or clustered; white; some fragrant.

Season: Late spring early summer.

When to plant: Set transplants when available. Cold- and heat-tolerant zones 4–9.

Light: Sunny.

Soil: Well drained, moist.

Fertilizer: 14-14-14 timed-release.

Pruning: After flowering, prune to shape; new wood will produce next year's flowers.

Propagation: Sow seeds in spring; take softwood cuttings or layer in spring.

Uses: Borders, screening, informal hedge, background, specimen.

PHOTINIA
(foh-TIN-ee-ah)

Photinia

ROSACEAE; rose family

Height/habit: Deciduous
(*P. villosa*) or evergreen
(*P. glabra* and *serrulata*) grow
to size of shrubs or trees,
8–30 ft. (2.4–9 m.).
Leaves: Oblong, glossy, 3–8 in.
(7.5–20 cm.) long; tips red as
new growth develops.

Flowers: Small, growing in
clusters, 4–6 in. (10–15 cm.)
long; white; followed by bright
red fruit.
Season: Year-round performers.
When to plant: Set transplants
when available. Cold- and heat-
tolerant zones 5–7 to 9–10; use
locally adapted species.
Light: Sunny to half-sunny.
Soil: Humusy, well drained,
moist.
Fertilizer: 14-14-14 timed-
release.

Pruning: Little needed. Cut
back long straggly branches
on *P. villosa* in fall. For *P.
glabra*, cut back after flowering in spring; this promotes
young red-tipped leaves.
Propagation: Sow seeds, take
softwood cuttings, or layer
spring through summer.
Uses: Foliage effect, specimen,
lawn, landscape, Japanese
garden, screening, hedge,
containers.

PIERIS
(PYE-er-iss)

Andromeda

ERICACEAE; heath family

Height/habit: Erect, broadleaf evergreen shrubs or small trees, 10–30 ft. (3–9 m.), often much smaller. Recommended are mountain andromeda (*P. floribunda*), scarlet andromeda (*P. forestii*), and Japanese andromeda (*P. japonica*).
Leaves: Obovate to oblanceolate, 3–6 in. (7.5–15 cm.) long; whorled, glossy green, leathery; brilliant red, pink, or glowing burgundy-cordovan in the new growth of some cultivars.
Flowers: Small, waxy, .5-in (1.25-cm.) urns, growing in pendulous, long-lasting clusters, to 6 in. (15 cm.) long; white.
Season: Spring from budding time.

When to plant: Set transplants when available. Cold- and heat-tolerant zones 5–8.
Light: Partly sunny to partly shady.
Soil: Humusy, well drained, moist, acidic.
Fertilizer: 14-14-14 timed-release; chelated iron in the event of chlorosis (yellowish foliage).
Pruning: Little needed except for spring cleanup; later, cut out only odd branches that stick out beyond the shrub's outline.
Propagation: Take cuttings or layer in summer; sow seeds in fall.
Uses: Borders, screen, informal hedge, specimen, shade, woodland garden, containers, bonsai.

PINUS
(PEE-nus)

Pine

PINACEAE; pine family

Height/habit: Evergreen trees bearing true cones, to 100 ft. (30 cm.) high/wide. *P. densiflora* 'Pendula' particularly noteworthy.
Leaves: Needlelike or overlapping scales 2–4 in. (5–10 cm.) long.
Flowers: Inconspicuous, except for the large amount of pollen produced by some.
Season: Flowers in spring; cones grow in summer, mature in fall. Foliage attractive in all seasons, often taking on a different hue during coldest weather.
When to plant: Set transplants when available. Cold- and heat-tolerant most zones, depending on individual adaptability; it is a wise policy with conifers to purchase from a local nursery known to sell only locally adapted species.
Light: Sunny.

Soil: Well drained, moist; some drought-tolerant when established.
Fertilizer: 14-14-14 timed-release.
Pruning: Trim dead wood at any time. Cuttings for house garlanding can often comprise entire pruning for the year. Hedge can be clipped after the first flush of new growth in spring.
Propagation: Take cuttings of horticultural varieties fall through winter; alternatively, sow seeds in protected frames outdoors before winter freeze, for germination in a year or two.
Uses: Beds, borders, background, hedgerow, windbreak, ground cover, espalier, bonsai, cutting.

PITTOSPORUM
(pit-TOSP-or-um)

Japanese Pittosporum

PITTOSPORACEAE; pittosporum family

Height/habit: *P. tobira* a broadleaf evergreen shrub that branches naturally into a layered shrub, to 10 ft. (3 m.) high/wide.

Leaves: Whorled, leathery, lustrous, to 4 in. (10 cm.) long; white-and-silver variegation in some.

Flowers: To .5 in. (1.25 cm.) across, growing in clusters; white or pale yellow; fragrant.

Season: Late spring through early summer.

When to plant: Set transplants when available. Water deeply to establish. Cold- and heat-tolerant zones 8–10.

Light: Sunny to half-sunny.

Soil: Humusy, well drained, moist, acidic.

Fertilizer: 14-14-14 timed-release.

Pruning: Little needed, except for spring cleanup; sometimes sheared or cut back as a means of control or to encourage more branching.

Propagation: Take green-wood cuttings in late summer.

Uses: Informal hedge, screening, Japanese garden, lawn specimen.

PLUMERIA
(ploo-MEER-ee-ah)

Singapore Plumeria; Frangipani

APOCYNACEAE; dogbane family

Height/habit: Evergreen Singapore plumeria (*P. obtusa*) or deciduous frangipani (*P. rubra*) grow to size of shrubs or trees, 6–12 ft. (1.8–3.6 m.) high/wide— more in zone 10, where they can live in the ground all year.
Leaves: Oblong to lanceolate, 4–6 in. (10–15 cm.) long.
Flowers: Tubular, 1–3 in. (2.5–7.5 cm.) across, in clusters at the tips; from white and cream through pale to dark yellow; also reds, pinks, and intriguing blends; fragrant.
Season: Summer through fall.
When to plant: Set transplants when available. Cold- and heat-tolerant zones 9–12; suited to container culture in colder regions.
Light: Sunny.
Soil: Well drained; moist to on the dry side in the active season, on the dry side while semi-dormant fall through winter.
Fertilizer: 5-10-5 or fertilizer labeled for Chinese hibiscus.
Pruning: None required.
Propagation: Take cuttings spring through summer; sow seeds in spring.
Uses: Borders, accent, specimen, containers (large and heavy to counterbalance the plumeria's tendency toward top-heaviness).

PODOCARPUS
(poh-doh-KARP-us)

Southern Yew; Japanese Yew

PODOCARPACEAE; podocarpus family

Height/habit: *P. macrophyllus*, known as Southern yew and Japanese yew, is evergreen, upright, and columnar, growing to 20 ft. (6 m.) high x 7 ft. (2.1 m.) across; specimen trees to 50 ft. (15 m.) high.
Leaves: Narrow, to 4 in. (10 cm.) long; new light green leaves age to dark green.
Flowers: Inconspicuous.
Season: Foliage attractive all year.
When to plant: Set transplants when available. Cold- and heat-tolerant zones 8–10.
Light: Sunny to partly shady.
Soil: Humusy, well drained, moist.
Fertilizer: 14-14-14 timed-release.
Pruning: Clip hedges after the first flush of spring growth, again if needed in a long season. Little needed for podocarpus in general, except to remove dead or broken branches as they appear.
Propagation: Sow seeds or transplant self-sown seedlings spring through summer.
Uses: Hedge, screening, vertical accent, containers, espalier, bonsai.

PONCIRUS
(pon-SYE-rus)

Hardy Orange

RUTACEAE; rue family

Height/habit: *P. trifoliata* a deciduous, spiny shrub or tree growing to 15 ft. (4.5 m.) high.
Leaves: Trifoliate and citruslike, to 3 in. (7.5 cm.) long.
Flowers: Appearing before the leaves and growing to 2 in. (5 cm.) across; white; fragrant.
Season: Flowers in spring; apricotlike fruit in fall; exudes a wonderful scent when picked on a cool fall day, then brought into a warm room.
When to plant: Set transplants when available. Cold- and heat-tolerant zones 5–9.
Light: Sunny.
Soil: Humusy, well drained, moist, acidic.
Fertilizer: 14-14-14 timed-release.
Pruning: Maintain overall shape with minimal cutting; hedges can be clipped late spring through early summer; tree-form standards sheared 2 or 3 times from spring to midsummer.
Propagation: Sow newly ripened seeds fall through winter; alternatively, transplant self-sown seedlings at any season, taking care to coddle the roots until they are re-established.
Uses: Impenetrable hedgerow or clipped hedge, tree-form standard, specimen, cottage and country gardens.

POPULUS
(POP-yew-lus)

Poplar;
Quaking Aspen

SALICACEAE; willow family

Height/habit: Deciduous trees, 50–100 ft. (15–30 m.) or more, most needing a large space where the water-thirsty roots will not overtake the pavement or cultivated garden. Lombardy poplar (*P. nigra* var. *italica*) lives just 25 years.

Leaves: Oval to rounded, linear, or lobed, 3–6 in. (7.5–15 cm.) long; bright yellow fall color in some.

Flowers: Catkins appear in spring before leaves; 2–6 in. (5–15 cm.) long, male (staminate) and female (pistillate) on separate trees.

Season: Attractive in all seasons.

When to plant: Set transplants when available. Cold- and heat-tolerant zones 2–4 to 8. White poplar (*P. alba*) ranges zones 3–8, while columnar poplar (*P.* x *berolinensis*) and cottonwood poplar (*P. deltoides*) only to zone 3; quaking aspen (*P. tremuloides*) to zone 2. Canadian poplar (*P.* x *canadensis*) to zone 4.

Light: Sunny.

Soil: Moist, well drained.

Fertilizer: 14-14-14 timed-release.

Pruning: Except for dead or damaged wood, do cuts for formulative or corrective training of tree in winter while it is dormant.

Propagation: Take cuttings spring through summer; sow newly harvested seeds or transplant self-sown seedlings in fall.

Uses: Windbreaks, screening, large landscape specimen.

PRUNUS
(PROON-us)

Almond; Apricot; Cherry; Plum; Cherry Laurel

ROSACEAE; rose family

Height/habit: Usually deciduous woody plants, 4–60 ft. (1.2–18.2 m.). Among favorites are flowering almond (*P. triloba*), Japanese cherry (*P. serruluta*), Japanese plum (*P. salicina*), peach (*P. persica*), Japanese fragrant apricot (*P. mume*), beach plum (*P. maritima*), cherry laurel (*P. laurocerasus*), plum (*P. domestica*), sour cherry (*P. cerasus*), flowering plum (*P. cerasifera* var. *atropurpurea*, sweet cherry (*P. avium*), and almond (*P. amygdalus*).

Leaves: Alternate, simple, toothed, 2–6 in. (5–15 cm.) long; copper- and purple-leaved in some varieties.

Flowers: Cupped or saucerlike, single or double, 1 in. (2.5 cm.) across; white, pink, rose, or red; some fragrant. Followed by fruit, some edible, others ornamental; yellow, red, purple, or black.

Season: Flowers in spring; fruit summer through fall.

When to plant: Set transplants when available. Cold- and heat-tolerant zones 2–6 to 8–9; best to purchase plants known to be locally adapted.

Light: Sunny.

Soil: Well drained, moist.

Fertilizer: 14-14-14 timed-release initially, 5-10-5 thereafter.

Pruning: Best done while in bloom. For flowering almonds, following flowering, cut the young wood back to within 2 or 3 buds of the old branches.

Propagate: Sow seeds fall through winter; by budding late winter through spring; cuttings under glass fall through winter.

Uses: Specimen, border, hedgerow, espalier, bonsai.

PYRACANTHA
(pye-rah-KANTH-ah)

Scarlet Firethorn

ROSACEAE; rose family

Height/habit: *P. coccinea* a variously upright or sprawling evergreen shrub, 12–15 ft. (3.6–4.5 m.) high/wide.
Leaves: Linear to oblong or lanceolate, toothed, often bristle-tipped, 1–2 in. (2.5–5 cm.) long.
Flowers: Small, growing on year-old shoots in clusters 1–2 in. (2.5–5 cm.) across; white. Followed by showy fruit colored red, golden, orange, or scarlet.
Season: Year-round performers; fruit most showy fall through early winter.
When to plant: Set transplants when available. Cold- and heat-tolerant zones 6–7 to 9. Cultivars 'Thornless' and 'Kasan' can take more cold, to zone 5.
Light: Sunny to half-shady.

Soil: Well drained, moist to on the dry side.
Fertilizer: 14-14-14 timed-release initially, rose fertilizer subsequently.
Pruning: Soon after flowering, trim and groom; tie in new espalier shoots as appropriate; cut back wayward or superfluous growth, taking care to preserve as many of the developing fruit clusters as possible. Late summer, remove secondary shoots that are obscuring the fruit clusters; direct sunlight produces the most colorful and abundant fruit. Use heavy gloves and wear sturdy clothing to protect against the pyracantha's needle-sharp thorns.
Propagation: Take half-ripe cuttings summer through fall; sow seeds fall through winter.
Uses: Impenetrable hedgerow and wildlife safe haven, screening, outstanding for espalier or bonsai.

PYRUS
(PYE-rus)

Pear

ROSACEAE; rose family

Height/habit: Large shrubs or trees, deciduous or evergreen, 30–50 ft. (9–15 m.) high/wide. Among fine choices are common pear (*P. communis*), Bradford ornamental pear (*P. calleryana* 'Bradford'), ornamental pear (*P. ussuriensis*), and evergreen pear (*P. kawakamii*).

Leaves: Long and narrow to ovate, 2–5 in. (5–12.5 cm.) long. Brilliant scarlet fall color in ornamental pear.

Flowers: Appearing before or with leaves; small, growing in showy clusters; white or near-white.

Season: Early spring.

When to plant: Set transplants when available. Cold- and heat-tolerant zones 4–5 to 8–9; evergreen pear zones 8–9. Ornamental pear hardiest of all, to zone 4.

Light: Sunny.

Soil: Well drained, moist.

Fertilizer: 14-14-14 initially, rose fertilizer subsequently.

Pruning: Remove weak or crossing branches and thin crowded growth in winter. Bonsai and espaliers require appropriate trimming later, until early summer.

Propagation: Sow seeds fall through winter; bud or graft winter through spring.

Uses: Specimen, street, lawn, garden, espalier, bonsai.

QUERCUS
(KWURK-us)

Oak

FAGACEAE; beech family

Height/habit: Evergreen and deciduous shrubs and trees, 10–100 ft. (3–30 m.). Varied choices include the deciduous species white oak (*Q. alba*), scarlet oak (*Q. coccinea*), and red oak (*Q. rubra*). Evergreen types include California live oak (*Q. agrifolia*) and live oak (*Q. virginiana*).

Leaves: Usually lobed and deeply cut, 5–9 in. (12.5–22.5 cm.) long. Outstanding fall color, some persisting into winter.

Flowers: Inconspicuous, males in a long catkin, females short and spiky.

Season: Year-round performers.

When to plant: Set transplants when available. Cold- and heat-tolerant 4–9 to 8–10; select locally adapted oaks.

Light: Sunny.

Soil: Well drained, moist. Some oaks drought-tolerant.

Fertilizer: 14-14-14 timed-release.

Pruning: Cut back in winter to guide growth, develop strong central leader, and ensure well-placed main branches; also in winter, thin out old trees to increase light on the ground; remove any winter-damaged branches in spring.

Propagation: Sow seeds spring through fall.

Uses: Specimen, street, lawn, garden, hedgerow or wind-break, seaside, screening, espalier, bonsai.

RHODODENDRON
(roh-doh-DEN-dron)

Azalea Types: Gable Hybrids, Ghent, Glenn Dale Hybrid, Indian, Knap Hill, Kurume, and, Mollis

ERICACEAE; heath family

Height/habit: Deciduous or evergreen shrubs, 3–8 ft. (1–2.4 m.) high/wide.

Leaves: Smooth-margined, from fingernail-sized to 3–5 in. (7.5–12.5 cm.) long, whorled into clusters at the branch tips.

Flowers: Funnel-shaped, single, double, or hose-in-hose, 1–3 in. (2.5–7.5 cm.) across, appearing in showy clusters; most colors; some fragrant.

Season: Primarily spring but in some climates azaleas bloom nearly every day of the year.

When to plant: Set transplants when available. Cold- and heat-tolerant zones 5–9.

Light: Sunny to half-shady.

Soil: Humusy, well drained, moist, acidic.

Fertilizer: 14-14-14 timed-release; chelated iron in the event of chlorosis (yellowish leaves).

Pruning: Little needed, except to remove weak or dead wood; cut back immediately after flowering to control or direct growth. Since azaleas bud and grow out in a 5-spoke radial pattern, routinely pinching back 2 out of the 5 results in a pleasing layered effect.

Propagation: Take cuttings or sow seeds spring through summer.

Uses: Beds, borders, screening, informal hedge, specimen, shade, wild and cottage gardens, tree-form standard, bonsai.

RHODODENDRON
(rho-doh-DEN-dron)

Rhododendron Hybrid Types: Catawba, Caucasian, Fortune, and Griffithianum

ERICACEAE; heath family

Height/habit: Broadleaf evergreen shrubs or small trees, 10–30 ft. (3–9 m.) high/wide.
Leaves: Oblong to obovate, leathery, glossy, to 10 in. (25 cm.) long, whorled toward the branch tips; reverses covered with brown hairs in some.
Flowers: Bell-shaped, to 3 in. (7.5 cm.) across, in showy clusters; most colors. Deadheading immediately after bloom promotes more flowering the next year.
Season: Spring through early summer.

When to plant: Set transplants when available. Cold- and heat-tolerant zones 4–8; selected cultivars zone 9 without long, hot, humid summers.
Light: Half-sunny to half-shady.
Soil: Humusy, well drained, moist, acidic.
Fertilizer: 14-14-14 timed-release; chelated iron in the event of chlorosis (yellowish leaves).
Pruning: Little needed except routine spring tidying. During winter through early spring, old shrubs can be rejuvenated by cutting branches back hard to old wood, resulting in more vigorous flowering specimens 2 or 3 years later.
Propagation: Take 2–3-in.-(5–7.5-cm.-) long green-wood cuttings in early summer; cut off up to two-thirds of each leaf to reduce transpiration.
Uses: Borders, screening, informal hedge, shade and wild gardens, public gardens, and parks.

ROSA
(ROH-zah)

Rose

ROSACEAE; rose family

Height/habit: Deciduous, thorny shrubs, from ground covers to climbers, 1–30 ft. (30–900 cm. [9 m.]) high/wide.
Leaves: Many pinnate, 3–6 in. (7.5–15 cm.) long; new shoots reddish bronze in some.
Flowers: Cup- or saucer-shaped, single or double, 1–6 in. (2.5–15 cm.) across, borne singly or in clusters; all colors except true blue; many fragrant; followed by colorful hips in some species. Deadheading recommended for modern hybrids. Cluster-flowered landscape roses need little attention.
Season: All year in mild climates; summer through fall elsewhere. Note: Some roses bloom once a year; others intermittently or constantly.

When to plant: Set transplants when available. Cold- and heat-tolerant zones 3–5 to 8–9; important to select locally adapted roses.
Light: Sunny to half-sunny.
Soil: Well drained, moist.
Fertilizer: 14-14-14 timed-release or any rose fertilizer.
Pruning: Remove all dead wood late winter through early spring. Wait to do serious pruning on all once-a-year bloomers until they finish flowering, usually by early summer; remove to the ground some of the oldest canes to boost vigorous new shoots for next season's flowers.
Propagation: Take green-wood cuttings summer through fall; take hardwood cuttings fall through winter; sow seeds fall through winter.
Uses: Beds, borders, informal hedges, hedgerows, screening, arbors, trellises, fences, cottage gardens, containers, tree-form standards.

ROSMARINUS
(rohz-mah-RYE-nus)

Rosemary

LABIATAE; mint family

Height/habit: *R. officinalis* an evergreen shrub, variously upright, bushy, or cascading, depending on the variety, to 4–6 ft. (1.2–1.8 m.) high/wide.
Leaves: Linear, narrow, .5–1 in. (1.25–2.5 cm.) long.
Flowers: Typical mint with prominent lip, to .5 in. (1.25 cm.); blue, white, or pink.
Season: Year-round performer; flowers spring through summer or during almost any season.
When to plant: Set transplants when available. 'Arp' and 'Hilltop' cold- and heat-tolerant zones 7–9; other rosemaries zones 8–9. In Gulf Coast areas with hot, humid summers, rosemary does better if containerized and could benefit from being moved to more shade at height of summer.
Light: Sunny.
Soil: Well drained, moist to on the dry side.
Fertilizer: 14-14-14 timed-release.
Pruning: Remove dead growth and shape in spring; shearing can be repeated after the main flowering.
Propagation: Take cuttings in summer; layer spring through summer.
Uses: Beds; edging; borders; herb, cottage, and rock gardens; containers; tree-form standard; topiary; and bonsai.

ROYSTONEA
(roy-STOH-nee-ah)

Florida Royal Palm

PALMAE; palm family

Height/habit: Evergreen trees, 60–100 ft. (18–30 m.) high.
Leaves: Long plumes or fan-shaped, 1–6 ft. (30–180 cm.).
Flowers: Often in showy or curious drooping panicles; becoming brightly colored, light green, golden, or red.
Season: All-year performers.

When to plant: Set transplants when available. Cold- and heat-tolerant zones 9–10.
Light: Sunny to half-sunny.
Soil: Well drained, moist.
Fertilizer: 14-14-14 timed-release.
Pruning: Prune to remove dead parts at any time.
Propagation: Sow seeds spring through summer.
Uses: Specimen, street, or lawn tree; shade, desert, seaside, or tropical gardens.

SALIX
(SAY-lix)
Willow; Purple Osier

SALICACEAE; willow family

Height/habit: Vary from deciduous shrubs to towering trees, from prostrate to 75 ft. (22.7 m.) high. Best choices include weeping willow (*S. babylonica*), white willow (*S. alba*), goat willow (*S. caprea*), pussy willow (*S. discolor*), laurel willow (*S. pentandra*), purple osier (*S. purpurea*), *S. alba* 'Vitellaniana,' and *S. sacalinensis* 'Sekka.'

Leaves: Lanceolate to oblong, 4–6 in. (10–15 cm.) long.

Flowers: Very small, in catkins, male and female on separate plants.

Season: Early spring for pussy willows; winter for those having colorful bark, such as *S. alba* 'Vitellaniana' and purple osier; weeping willows picturesque in all seasons.

When to plant: Set transplants when available. Variously cold- and heat-tolerant zones 4–5 to 8–9.

Light: Sunny.

Soil: Well drained, moist to wet.

Fertilizer: 14-14-14 timed-release.

Pruning: Prune trees while young to ensure strong leader and well-spaced branches. For kinds with colorful winter bark, cut back hard in early spring, within 1 or 2 buds of old wood. For kinds with catkins, thin out as the leaves are unfolding, cutting some of the oldest canes to the ground.

Propagation: Take green-wood cuttings in summer.

Uses: Trees as specimens in large landscapes, parks, public gardens, sides of streams or ponds; shrubs as ground cover, screening, informal hedge, specimen, borders, cutting for pussy willows or basket weaving; other types suited to bonsai.

SAMBUCUS
(sam-BEW-kus)
Elder

CAPRIFOLIACEAE; honeysuckle family

Height/habit: Deciduous shrubs and small trees, 12–15 ft. (3.6–4.5 m.) to 40 ft. (12.1 m.) high. Sweet elder (*S. canadensis*) and English golden elder (*S. racemosa* 'Plumosa-aurea') are good choices.

Leaves: Elliptic- to lance-shaped leaflets, to 6 in. (15 cm.) long.

Flowers: Very small in flat clusters to 10 in. (25 cm.) across; very lacy, large, and similar to Queen Anne's lace; white; followed by red or black fruit.

Season: Flowers spring through summer.

When to plant: Set transplants when available. Cold- and heat-tolerant zones 4–9.

Light: Sunny.

Soil: Humusy, well drained, moist.

Fertilizer: 14-14-14 timed-release.

Pruning: Prune for general maintenance in early spring; if grown for colorful leaves, cut back in spring to 1 or 2 buds from the old wood.

Propagation: Sow seeds, take cuttings or suckers, or transplant self-sown seedlings spring through summer.

Uses: Borders, specimen, background, hedgerow, screening, wild gardens.

SPIRAEA
(spye-REE-ah)

Spirea

ROSACEAE; rose family

Height/habit: Deciduous shrubs, 2–8 ft. (61–240 cm.) high/wide. Excellent varieties include Japanese white spirea (*S. albiflora*), garland spirea (*S. x arguta*), Anthony Waterer spirea (*S. x bumalda* 'Anthony Waterer'), Japanese spirea (*S. japonica* 'Rubberima'), bridal wreath spirea (*S. prunifolia*), and Vanhoutte spirea (*S. x vanhouttei*).

Leaves: Simple or lobed, oblong, elliptic, or lanceolate, 1–4 in. (2.5–10 cm.) long, some toothed.

Flowers: Small, 2–4 in. (5–10 cm.) across, flat or rounded growing in showy clusters; white, pink, or crimson.

Season: Spring or summer.

When to plant: Set transplants when available. Cold- and heat-tolerant zones 4–5 to 8–9.

Light: Sunny to partly sunny.

Soil: Well drained, moist.

Fertilizer: 14-14-14 timed-release initially, 5-10-5 subsequently.

Pruning: Prune kinds that bloom in spring on wood from the previous season after flowering, cutting to evident new shoots; for kinds that bloom late summer on wood produced currently, cut back in spring to within 2 or 3 buds from the old wood.

Propagation: Sow seeds, take cuttings, or layer spring through summer.

Uses: Border, informal hedge, cottage gardens, bonsai.

STEWARTIA
(stew-ART-ee-ah)

Silky Camellia; Stewartia

THEACEAE; tea family

Height/habit: Deciduous shrubs or trees, 8–30 ft. (2.4–9 m.) high/wide. Recommended are silky camellia (*S. malacodendron*), as well as Japanese stewartia (*S. pseudocamellia*) and Chinese stewartia (*S. sinensis*).

Leaves: Alternate, simple, toothed, ovate to elliptic, 3–6 in. (7.5–15 cm.) long; fall color.
Flowers: Saucerlike, 2–4 in. (5–10 cm.) across; white with showy stamens, bluish, purple, or orange-yellow.
Season: Summer.
When to plant: Set transplants when available; disturb the roots as little as possible. Cold- and heat-tolerant zones 5–7 to 8–9.
Light: Partly sunny to partly shady.
Soil: Humusy, moist, well drained, acidic.

Fertilizer: 14-14-14 timed-release; chelated iron in the event of chlorosis (yellowish leaves).
Pruning: Little needed except for tidying up after winter.
Propagation: Sow seeds, take softwood cuttings, or layer in summer.
Uses: Borders, specimen, lawn, woodland or wild gardens, bonsai.

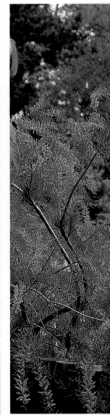

SYRINGA
(sihr-RIN-gah)

Lilac

OLEACEAE; olive family

Height/habit: Deciduous shrubs or small trees, 6–30 ft. (1.8–9 m.) high/wide. Gorgeous choices include Japanese tree lilac (*S. amurensis* var. *japonica*), small-leaved lilac (*S. microphylla*), lacy Persian lilac (*S.* x *persica* var. *laciniata*), Preston Hybrid lilac (*S.* x *prestoniae* 'Babella'), and classic old-fashioned lilac *(S. vulgaris)*.

Leaves: Mostly simple, oval- or heart-shaped, 1–7 in. (2.5–17 cm.) long.

Flowers: Small, growing in showy panicles or loose clusters, 3–10 in. (7.5–25 cm.) long; most colors except bright yellows, reds, and oranges; fragrant.

Season: Late spring to early summer.

When to plant: Set transplants when available. Cold- and heat-tolerant zones 3–6 to 8; needs winter chilling.

Light: Sunny.

Soil: Well drained, moist, neutral to alkaline.

Fertilizer: 14-14-14 timed-release. Fireplace ashes often used as side-dressing in spring for alkalizing effect.

Pruning: Remove flower trusses as soon as they fade; remove any weak growth from the bush interior. Cut back high-growing 1-and 2-year shoots by one-half to two-thirds immediately after flowering. Rejuvenate old lilacs by cutting to the ground in early spring all weak branches. Train new shoots; may not bloom for 3 years.

Propagation: Take cuttings or layer in summer; grow from stratified seeds or graft in spring.

Uses: Borders, specimens, informal hedge, screening, cottage gardens, tree-form standard, bonsai, cutting.

TAMARIX
(TAM-ah-rix)

Athel Tamarisk; Salt Tree; Tamarisk

TAMARICACEAE; tamarisk family

Height/habit: Deciduous shrubs or trees, 15–30 ft. (1.5–9 m.) high/wide. Recommended are athel tamarix, or salt tree (*T. aphylla*), and tamarisk (*T. pentandra*).
Leaves: Alternate, scalelike, 2–3 in. (5–7.5 cm.) long.
Flowers: Feathery racemes, 1–2 in. (2.5–5 cm.) long; pink.
Season: Spring through summer through fall.
When to plant: Set transplants when available. Cold- and heat-tolerant zones 5–9.
Light: Sunny.
Soil: Well drained, moist to on the dry side; neutral to alkaline pH.
Fertilizer: 14-14-14 timed-release.
Pruning: If plant flowers in spring, cut back immediately thereafter; if it flowers late summer through fall, prune back hard in late winter. These are tough plants that can go neglected and still put on a show.
Propagation: Sow seeds or take cuttings spring through summer.
Uses: Border, specimen, screening, informal hedge, seaside garden, windbreak, bonsai.

TIBOUCHINA
(tib-ooh-KEE-nah)

Glory Bush; Princess Flower

MELASTOMACEAE; melastoma family

Height/habit: *T. urvilleana* a semievergreen shrub, 5–10 ft. (1.5–3 m.) high/wide.
Leaves: Oblong to ovate, 2–4 in. (5–10 cm.) long, with distinctive lengthwise veins and soft, hairy undersides; turning golden and scarlet in chilly but not freezing fall weather.
Flowers: Saucerlike, 2–5 in. (5–12.5 cm.) across, growing singly or in groups of 3; blue-purple with prominent pink stamens.
Season: Summer through fall.
When to plant: Set transplants when available. Cold- and heat-tolerant zones 9–10; grow as a container specimen elsewhere and protect from killing frost.
Light: Sunny.
Soil: Well drained, moist, acidic.
Fertilizer: 14-14-14 timed-release.
Pruning: Cut back hard in late winter through early spring. Flowers appear at the tips of new growth, so frequent pinching out early results in more flowering branches later.
Propagation: Take half-ripe cuttings in summer; cut the leaf tips back by half or more to reduce transpiration.
Uses: Beds, borders, cottage gardens, specimen, container, tree-form standard.

VIBURNUM
(vye-BURN-um)

Viburnum; Nannyberry; Cranberry Bush; Japanese Snowball; Black Haw

CAPRIFOLIACEAE; honeysuckle family

Height/habit: Chiefly deciduous shrubs and trees, 5–30 ft. (1.5–9 m.) high/wide. Best choices are English hybrid viburnum (*V.* x *carlcephalum*), *V.* x *carlesii*, nannyberry (*V. lentago*), European cranberry bush (*V. opulus*), Japanese snowball (*V. plicatum*), black haw (*V. prunifolium*), and American cranberry (*V. trilobum*).

Leaves: Ovate, elliptic, or 3-lobed, to 4 in. (10 cm.) long.

Flowers: Showy clusters, ball-shaped ("snowball"), fertile flowers in flat clusters surrounded by larger, sterile flowers, 3–6 in. (7.5–15 cm.) across; white, creamy, or pinkish; many are fragrant.

Season: Spring through early summer; followed by showy red fruit in many species.

When to plant: Set transplants when available. Cold- and heat-tolerant zones 3–7 to 8–10.

Light: Sunny to partly shady.

Soil: Humusy, well drained, moist.

Fertilizer: 14-14-14 timed-release.

Pruning: Little needed. If growth dense and crowded, thin out in winter.

Propagation: Grow from stratified seeds in spring; take softwood cuttings and layer in summer; take hardwood cuttings fall through winter.

Uses: Borders, specimen, informal hedge, screening, hedgerow, woodland garden.

VINCA
(VIN-kah)

Trailing Vinca; Running Myrtle

APOCYNACEAE; dogbane family

Height/habit: Creeping or trailing evergreens, 3–6 ft. (1–1.8 m.) high/wide. Trailing vinca (*V. major*) and running myrtle (*V. minor*) good choices.

Leaves: Ovate to oblong, to 2 in. (5 cm.) long; variegated silvery or gold in some varieties.
Flowers: Pinwheels, 1–2 in. (2.5–5 cm.) across; blue, white, pink, or purple.
Season: Spring.
When to plant: Set transplants when available. Running myrtle cold- and heat-tolerant to zone 4; trailing vinca zones 7–9.
Light: Sunny to shady.

Soil: Humusy, well drained, moist. Water generously to establish.
Fertilizer: 14-14-14 timed-release.
Pruning: Tidy up in spring by removing all dead growth.
Propagation: Take cuttings, divide, or layer spring through summer.
Uses: Ground cover, containers (spilling over sides).

WEIGELA
(wye-JEE-lah)

Common Weigela

CAPRIFOLIACEAE; honeysuckle
family

Height/habit: *W. florida* a
deciduous shrub with curving,
spreading branches, 8–10 ft.
(2.4–3 m.) high/wide.

Leaves: Elliptic or obovate, to
4 in. (10 cm.) long; a variegated
form is cultivated.

Flowers: Funnel-shaped, about
1 in. (2.5 cm.) long, growing in
compound clusters; pink, rose,
rose purple, ruby red.

Season: Late spring through
summer.

When to plant: Set transplants
when available. Cold- and heat-
tolerant zones 4–9.

Light: Sunny.

Soil: Well drained, moist.

Fertilizer: 14-14-14 timed-
release at planting, 5-10-5
thereafter.

Pruning: When the flowers
fade, cut back the previous
year's growth to new shoots
already apparent.

Propagation: Take semiripe
cuttings in summer.

Uses: Borders, specimen,
screening, informal hedge,
parks, background on large
properties, bonsai.

(wiss-TEER-ee-ah)

Wisteria

LEGUMINOSAE; pea family

Height/habit: Deciduous, woody, twining vines, 20–50 ft. (6–15 m.) long. Rigorous pruning can also produce a tree-form standard, 10–15 ft. (3–4.5 m.) high. Two fine types are Japanese wisteria (*W. floribunda*) and Chinese wisteria (*W. sinensis*).

Leaves: Compound, 13–19 leaflets, each to 3 in. (7.5 cm.) long.

Flowers: Single or double, pealike, in pendulous clusters, 1–1.5 ft. (30–45 cm.) long; purple, white, pink, red, or blue; fragrant; succeeded by dangling, velvety pods, 6–7 in. (15–17 cm.) long, lasting into winter.

Season: Primarily spring.

When to plant: Set transplants when available. Grafted plants known to have flowered are preferred to seed-grown or wild-harvested stock. Cold- and heat-tolerant zones 4–5 to 9.

Light: Sunny.

Soil: Well drained, moist.

Fertilizer: 14-14-14 initially, 5-10-5 subsequently.

Pruning: Cut back laterals to 5 or fewer leaflets in late summer, often again at early to midwinter; this encourages flowering spurs. In mild-climate gardens, wisteria often needs maintenance pruning on a biweekly basis in summer to control shape and size and encourage flowering.

Propagation: Sow seeds, take cuttings, layer, or graft in spring.

Uses: Cover for trellis, lattice, arbor, pergola, or fence; bonsai.

Chapter Fifteen:
Troubleshooting Guide for Woody Plants

Though generally easy to care for, woody plants sometimes experience problems. Here are some of the most common:

No blooms. Signals the need for more light, water, or fertilizer, and possibly more cold—lilacs, for example, require a certain number of hours of winter chilling, otherwise they will not bloom even though the plants may linger on for some years. Another possibility is that the plant needs more phosphorus (represented by the middle number in fertilizer NPK ratios, 15-30-15) and less nitrogen. Tree-form wisterias surrounded by a lawn that regularly gets a high-nitrogen fertilizer often do not bloom unless they are root-pruned or an area of turf is cut out around them equal to the branch spread; in this case, apply a low- or no-nitrogen fertilizer such as 1-6-5 or 0-6-5.

Insects clustered on new growth. Probably aphids, which often cluster on the tips of new shoots, especially after they have been given fertilizer with lots of available nitrogen. Wash off with strong streams of water; they will abate in due course, rarely causing permanent damage or requiring any serious pesticide treatment. Knock off with stiff streams of water from the hose. Can also be treated by spraying with insecticidal soap or Neem tree solution.

White or brown "bumpy" insects. Indicative of mealybugs or brown scale. Remove as many by hand as possible. Spray weekly and thoroughly with insecticidal soap, Neem tree solution, or horticultural oil.

Powdery white spots on leaves. Powdery mildew attacks some woody plants, especially crape myrtle early and lilacs late. Can be treated by applying fungicide or ignored. Crape myrtles often have powdery mildew early in the season (when nights are cool, days are warm). It is beneficial to treat them with a fungicide since the problem occurs early in their growth cycle; not needed for lilacs since they do not succumb to powdery mildew until they have done most of their work for the year.

Generally poor or weak growth. This indicates a need for more light, more water, and more nutrients. Avoid planting small shrubs where the soil is already laced with the roots of large trees. Ground covers can be established in these conditions, but first prepare pockets of cultivated soil.

Spider mites. Spider mites are often troublesome in hot, dry weather; spray under leafy shrubs and trees with strong streams of water. This discourages the mites.

Chapter Sixteen:
Bringing Woody Plants Into Your Home

Flowering and berry-covered branches make magnificent accents in the home. With a minimum of arranging, they add a note of drama to just about any room in the house, whether displayed in large floor vases or woven into swags and wreaths.

Woody cut branches remain fresher for a longer period of time if the lowermost inch (2.5 centimeter) or two is split with a knife or pounded with a mallet, then plunged immediately into deep water and left several hours or overnight to condition before being placed in a flower arrangement. Sometimes, branches look better if some or all of the leaves are stripped away, for example to reveal the wispy yellow flowers of fall witch hazel or the purple berries on a branch of callicarpa.

A most rewarding aspect of having one's own shrubbery border and garden with ornamental trees is that the branches of many can be cut during a winter warm spell, brought inside, and set to flower and leaf out early in vases of water. They last longest in cool, bright

places, away from hot, direct sun rays and any currents from the heating system. Favorites include pussy willow, witch hazel, forsythia, flowering quince, flowering peach, flowering cherry, apple, crab apple, pear, flowering almond, lilac, and redbud.

Here are some other delightful ways to use woody plants indoors:

᭥ Delicate flowers of spring-blooming trees and shrubs floated in decorative bowls of water, perhaps inter-mingled with votives

᭥ Scarlet fall sassafras leaves with dried field grasses

᭥ Yellow and orange fall ginkgo leaves with mountain ash berries

᭥ Whole purple lilac blossoms in spring potpourri

᭥ Fragrant petals of damask and cabbage roses or whole miniature roses in potpourri

The Art of Bonsai
Another facet of enjoying woody plants is training them in the ancient manner of Japanese bonsai, developed centuries earlier in China and known there as penjing. This can be a fascinating pursuit that leads the

practitioner to traveling in the Far East in search of visual images and hard goods—such as tools, trays, and pots—that help bring the art to life.

Bonsai, pronounced *bone-sigh* with even stress on both syllables, means literally "tray planting." The process involves root- and top-pruning to produce a dwarfed but vital plant. As practiced originally, the plants used were from moderate temperate climates; these types need moderate winter chilling, around 28°F (-2°C), in order to grow and flower radiantly. Since World War II, bonsai growers have embraced the vast flora of the tropics and subtropics, making it possible for apartment dwellers to grow bonsai successfully indoors year-round, in windows or under fluorescent lights.

Gardeners can also purchase bonsai in various stages of training. The plants range from months to centuries old. The only way to learn the art is to practice it, usually after observing a bonsai master at work. There are also well-illustrated manuals and videos covering all aspects of the pursuit. Local bonsai clubs are an ideal way to participate in this unique expression of art in the garden. Good candidates for miniaturization include maple, cedar, crab apple, and ginkgo.

The most fundamental law of bonsai is that the subjects are living and therefore require almost as devoted and consistent care as a household pet. This means daily or even twice-daily watering during the warmest, hottest seasons of the year.

Bonsai grow best and look their most picturesque if set on high tables or shelves outdoors. A traditional method is to stack concrete blocks on end for supports with 2-x-12-foot (61-x-360-centimeter) wood planks on top for sturdy shelving. You can also make garden display tables from wood or metal painted a mute or earthen color, in keeping with the hues of bonsai containers.

Bibliography

Bailey, Liberty Hyde, and Ethel Zoe Bailey; revised and expanded by the staff of the L.H. Bailey Hortorium. 1976. *Hortus Third*. New York: Macmillan Publishing Co.

Bailey, Ralph; McDonald, Elvin; Good Housekeeping Editors. 1972. *The Good Housekeeping Illustrated Encyclopedia of Gardening*. New York: Book Division, Hearst Magazines.

Graf, Alfred Byrd. 1992. *Hortica*. New Jersey: Roehrs Co.

Greenlee, John. 1992. *The Encyclopedia of Ornamental Grasses*. Pennsylvania: Rodale Press.

Heriteau, Jacqueline, and Charles B. Thomas. 1994. *Water Gardens*. Boston/New York: Houghton Mifflin Co.

Hobhouse, Penelope, and Elvin McDonald, Consulting Editors. 1994. *Gardens of the World: The Art & Practice of Gardening*. New York: Macmillan Publishing Co.

Hobhouse, Penelope. 1994. *On Gardening*. New York: Macmillan Publishing Co.

McDonald, Elvin. 1993. *The New Houseplant: Bringing the Garden Indoors*. New York: Macmillan Publishing Co.

McDonald, Elvin. 1995. *The Color Garden Series: Red, White, Blue, Yellow*. San Francisco: Collins Publishers.

McDonald, Elvin. 1995. *The Traditional Home Book of Roses*. Des Moines: Meredith Books.

Mulligan, William C. 1992. *The Adventurous Gardener's Sourcebook of Rare and Unusual Plants*. New York: Simon & Schuster.

Mulligan, William C. 1995. *The Lattice Gardener*. New York: Macmillan Publishing Co.

River Oaks Garden Club. 1989. Fourth Revised Edition. *A Garden Book for Houston*. Houston: Gulf Publishing Co.

Royal Horticultural Society, The; Clayton, John, revised by John Main. Third Edition. 1992. *Pruning Ornamental Shrubs*. London: Cassell Educational Ltd.

Scanniello, Stephen, and Tania Bayard. 1994 *Climbing Roses*. New York: Prentice Hall.

Schinz, Marina, and Gabrielle van Zuylen. 1991. *The Gardens of Russell Page*. New York: Stewart, Tabori & Chang.

Sedenko, Jerry. 1991. *The Butterfly Garden*. New York: Villard Books.

Sunset Books and Sunset Magazine. 1995. *Sunset Western Garden Book*. Menlo Park: Sunset Publishing Co.

Woods, Christopher. 1992. *Encyclopedia of Perennials*. New York: Facts On File, Inc.

Yang, Linda. 1995. *The City & Town Gardener: A Handbook for Planting Small Spaces and Containers*. New York: Random House.

Jacques Amand
P.O. Box 59001
Potomac, MD 20859
free catalog; all kinds of bulbs

Amaryllis, Inc.
P.O. Box 318
Baton Rouge, LA 70821
free list; hybrid Hippeastrum

Antique Rose Emporium
Rt. 5, Box 143
Brenham, TX 77833
catalog $5; old roses, also perennials, ornamental grasses

Appalachian Gardens
Box 82
Waynesboro, PA 17268
catalog $2; uncommon
woodies

The Banana Tree, Inc.
715 Northampton St.
Easton, PA 18042
catalog $3; seeds of exotics

B & D Lilies
330 "P" St.
Port Townsend, WA 98368
catalog $3; garden lilies

Beaver Creek Nursery
7526 Pelleaux Rd.
Knoxville, TN 37938
catalog $1; uncommon
woodies

Kurt Bluemel
2740 Greene Lane
Baldwin, MD 21013
catalog $2; ornamental grasses,
perennials

Bluestone Perennials
7237 Middle Ridge
Madison, OH 44057
free catalog; perennials

Borboleta Gardens
15980 Canby Ave., Rt. 5
Faribault, MN 55021
catalog $3; bulbs, tubers,
corms, rhizomes

Bovees Nursery
1737 S.W. Coronado
Portland, OR 97219
catalog $2; uncommon
woodies

Brand Peony Farms
P.O. Box 842
St. Cloud, MN 56302
free catalog; peonies

Breck's
6523 N. Galena Rd.
Peoria, IL 61632
free catalog; all kinds
of bulbs

Briarwood Gardens
14 Gully Lane, R.F.D. 1
East Sandwich, MA 02537
list $1; azaleas,
rhododendrons

Brudy's Tropical Exotics
P.O. Box 820874
Houston, TX 77282
catalog $2; seeds,
plants of exotics

W. Atlee Burpee Co.
300 Park Ave.
Warminster, PA 18974
free catalog; seeds, plants, bulbs,
supplies, wide selection

Busse Gardens
5873 Oliver Ave., S.W.
Cokato, MN 55321
catalog $2; perennials

Camellia Forest Nursery
125 Carolina Forest
Chapel Hill, NC 27516
list $1; uncommon
woodies

Canyon Creek Nursery
3527 DIY Creek Rd.
Oroville, CA 95965
catalog $2; silver-leaved plants

Carroll Gardens
Box 310
Westminster, MD 21158
catalog $2; perennials,
woodies, herbs

Coastal Gardens
4611 Socastee Blvd.
Myrtle Beach, SC 29575
catalog $3; perennials

The Cummins Garden
22 Robertsville Rd.
Marlboro, NJ 07746
catalog $2; azaleas,
rhododendrons, woodies

The Daffodil Mart
Rt. 3, Box 794
Gloucester, VA 23061
list $1; Narcissus specialists,
other bulbs

Daylily World
P.O. Box 1612
Sanford, FL 32772
catalog $5; all kinds of
Hemerocallis

deJager Bulb Co.
Box 2010
So. Hamilton, MA 01982
free list; all kinds of bulbs

Tom Dodd's Rare Plants
9131 Holly St.
Semmes, AL 36575
list $1; trees, shrubs,
extremely select

Far North Gardens
16785 Harrison Rd.
Livonia, MI 48154
catalog $2; primulas,
other perennials

Flora Lan Nursery
9625 Northwest
Roy Forest Grove, OR 97116
free catalog; uncommon
woodies

Forest Farm
990 Tetherow Rd.
Williams, OR 97544-9599
catalog $3; uncommon
woodies in small sizes

Fox Hill Farm
P.O. Box 7
Parma, MI 49269
catalog $1; all kinds of herbs

Howard B. French
Box 565
Pittsfield, VT 05762
free catalog; bulbs

Gardens of the Blue Ridge
Box 10
Pineola, NC 28662
catalog $3; wildflowers
and ferns

D.S. George Nurseries
2515 Penfield Rd.
Fairport, NY 14450
free catalog; clematis

Girard Nurseries
Box 428
Geneva, OH 44041
free catalog; uncommon
woodies

Glasshouse Works
Greenhouses
Church St., Box 97
Stewart, OH 45778
catalog $2; exotics for
containers

Gossler Farms Nursery
1200 Weaver Rd.
Springfield, OR 97477
list $2; uncommon
woodies

Greenlee Ornamental Grasses
301 E. Franklin Ave.
Pomona, CA 91766
catalog $5; native and
ornamental grasses

Greer Gardens
1280 Goodpasture Island Rd.
Eugene, OR 97401
catalog $3; uncommon
woodies, especially
Rhododendron

Grigsby Cactus Gardens
2354 Bella Vista Dr.
Vista, CA 92084
catalog $2; cacti and
other succulents

Growers Service Co.
10118 Crouse Rd.
Hartland, MI 48353
list $1; all kinds of bulbs

Heirloom Old Garden Roses
24062 N.E. Riverside Dr.
St. Paul, OR 97137
catalog $5; old garden, English,
and winter-hardy roses

Holbrook Farm and Nursery
Box 368
Fletcher, NC 28732
free catalog; woodies and
other select plants

J.L. Hudson, Seedsman
P.O. Box 1058
Redwood City, CA 94064
catalog $1; nonhybrid flowers,
vegetables

Jackson and Perkins
1 Rose Lane
Medford, OR 97501
free catalog; roses, perennials

Kartuz Greenhouses
1408 Sunset Dr.
Vista, CA 92083
catalog $2; exotics
for containers

Klehm Nursery
Rt. 5, Box 197 Penny Rd.
So. Barrington, IL 60010
catalog $5; peonies,
Hemerocallis, hostas,
perennials

M. & J. Kristick
155 Mockingbird Rd.
Wellsville, PA 17365
free catalog; conifers

Lamb Nurseries
Rt. 1, Box 460B
Long Beach, WA 98631
catalog $1; perennials

Las Pilitas Nursery
Star Rt., Box 23
Santa Margarita, CA 93453
catalog $6; California natives

Lauray of Salisbury
432 Undermountain Rd.
Rt. 41
Salisbury, CT 06068
catalog $2; exotics
for containers

Lilypons Water Gardens
6800 Lilypons Rd.
P.O. Box 10
Buckeystown, MD 21717
catalog $5; aquatics

Limerock Ornamental Grasses
R.D. 1, Box 111
Port Matilda, PA 16870
list $3

Logee's Greenhouses
141 North St.
Danielson, CT 06239
catalog $3; exotics for
containers

Louisiana Nursery
Rt. 7, Box 43
Opelousas, LA 70570
catalogs $3–$6;
uncommon woodies,
perennials

Lowe's Own Root Roses
6 Sheffield Rd.
Nashua, NH 03062
list $5; old roses

McClure & Zimmerman
Box 368
Friesland, WI 53935
free catalog; all kinds of bulbs

Mellinger's
2310 W. South Range Rd. North
Lima, OH 44452
free catalog; all kinds of plants

Merry Gardens
Upper Mechanic St., Box 595
Camden, ME 04843
catalog $2; herbs,
pelargoniums, cultivars
of Hedera helix

Milaegerls Gardens
4838 Douglas Ave.
Racine, WI 53402
catalog $1; perennials

Moore Miniature Roses
2519 E. Noble Ave.
Visalia, CA 93292
catalog $1; all kinds of
miniature roses

Niche Gardens
1111 Dawson Rd.
Chapel Hill, NC 27516
catalog $3; perennials

Nichols Garden Nursery
1190 N. Pacific Highway
Albany, OR 97321
free catalog; uncommon
edibles, flowers, herbs

Nor'East Miniature Roses
Box 307
Rowley, MA 01969
free catalog

North Carolina State University
Arboretum
Box 7609
Raleigh, NC 27695
Propagation guide for woody
plants and lists of plants in
the arboretum, $10; member-
ship permits participation in
worthy plant propagation
and dissemination.

Oakes Daylilies
8204 Monday Rd.
Corryton, TN 37721
free catalog; all kinds
of Hemerocallis

Geo. W. Park Seed Co.
Box 31
Greenwood, SC 29747
free catalog; all kinds of seeds,
plants, and bulbs

Plants of the Southwest
Agua Fria, Rt. 6,
Box 11A
Santa Fe, NM 87501
catalog $3.50

Roses of Yesterday and Today
802 Brown's Valley Rd.
Watsonville, CA 95076
catalog $3 third class,
$5 first; old roses

Roslyn Nursery
211 Burrs Lane
Dix Hills, NY 11746
catalog $3; woodies, perennials

John Scheepers, Inc.
P.O. Box 700
Bantam, CT 06750
free catalog; all kinds of bulbs

Seymour's Selected Seeds
P.O. Box 1346
Sussex, VA 23884-0346
free catalog; English
cottage garden seeds

Shady Hill Gardens
821 Walnut St.
Batavia, IL 60510
catalog $2; 800 different
Pelargonium

Shady Oaks Nursery
112 10th Ave. S.E.
Waseca, MN 56093
catalog $2.50; hostas, ferns,
wildflowers, shrubs

Siskiyou Rare Plant Nursery
2825 Cummings Rd.
Medford, OR 97501
catalog $2; alpines

Anthony J. Skittone
1415 Eucalyptus
San Francisco, CA 94132
catalog $2; unusual bulbs,
especially from South Africa

Sonoma Horticultural Nursery
3970 Azalea Ave.
Sebastopol, CA 95472
catalog $2; azaleas,
rhododendrons

Spring Hill Nurseries
110 W. Elm St.
Tipp City, OH 45371
free catalog; perennials,
woodies, roses

Steffen Nurseries
Box 184
Fairport, NY 14450
catalog $2; clematis

Sunnybrook Farms Homestead
9448 Mayfield Rd.
Chesterland, OH 44026
catalog $2; perennials, herbs

Surry Gardens
P.O. Box 145
Surry, ME 04684
free list; perennials, vines,
grasses, wild garden

Terrapin Springs Nursery
Box 7454
Tifton, GA 31793
list $1; uncommon
woodies

Thompson & Morgan
Box 1308
Jackson, NJ 08527
free catalog; all kinds
of seeds

Transplant Nursery
1586 Parkertown Rd.
Lavonia, GA 30553
catalog $1; azaleas,
rhododendrons

Twombly Nursery, Inc.
163 Barn Hill Rd.
Monroe, CT 06468
list $4; uncommon
woodies

Van Engelen, Inc.
Stillbrook Farm
313 Maple St.
Litchfield, CT 06759
free catalog; all kinds
of bulbs

Andre Viette Farm & Nursery
Rt. 1, Box 16
Fishersville, VA 22939
catalog $3; perennials,
ornamental grasses

Washington Evergreen Nursery
Box 388
Leicester, NC 28748
catalog $2; conifers

Wayside Gardens
One Garden Lane
Hodges, SC 29695
free catalog; all kinds
of bulbs, woodies,
perennials, vines

We-Du Nursery
Rt. 5, Box 724
Marion, NC 28752
catalog $2; uncommon
woodies, perennials

White Flower Farm
Box 50
Litchfield, CT 06759
catalog $5; woodies,
perennials, bulbs

Whitman Farms
3995 Gibson Rd., N.W.
Salem, OR 97304
catalog $1; woodies,
edibles

Winterthur Plant Shop
Winterthur, DE 19735
free list; uncommon woodies

Gilbert H. Wild and Son, Inc.
Sarcoxie, MO 64862
catalog $3; perennials, peonies,
iris, Hemerocallis

Woodlanders
1128 Colleton Ave.
Aiken, SC 29801
catalog $2; woodies,
hardy Passiflora

Yucca Do
P.O. Box 655
Waller, TX 77484
catalog $3; woodies, perennials

Credits

Thanks especially to these gardeners and institutions for providing the subject matter for my photographs of annuals:

Jean Atwater, Spokane, WA

Geo. J. Ball Seed Co., West Chicago, IL

Berkshire Botanical Garden, Stockbridge, MA

British Columbia, University of, Botanic Garden, Vancouver, BC

Brooklyn Botanic Garden, Brooklyn, NY

Burpee Seed Co., Warminster, PA

Butchart Gardens, Victoria, BC

Chelsea Flower Show, London, England

Clause Seed Co., Bretigny-sur-Orge, France

Cook's Garden, Londonderry, VT

Goldsmith Seeds, Gilroy, CA

Karen Park Jennings, Greenwood, SC

Michael Kartuz, Vista, CA

Logee's Greenhouses, Danielson, CT

Longwood Gardens, Kennett Square, PA

Georgia and Eugene Mosier, Sewickley Heights, PA

Meadowbrook Farms, J. Liddon Pennock, Jr., Meadowbrook, PA

Mercer Arboretum and Botanic Gardens, Humble, TX

Minnesota, University of, Landscape Arboretum, Canhassen, MN

Natchez, MS, private garden

National Wildflower Research Center, Austin, TX

George W. Park Seed Co., Inc., Greenwood, SC

Peckerwood Gardens, Waller, TX

Pier 39, San Francisco, CA

Roger's Nursery and Garden Center, Corona del Mar, CA

Sissinghurst Castle Garden, Kent, England

South Coast Botanic Garden, Peninsula, CA

Strybing Arboretum, San Francisco, CA

Sluis & Groot, Enkhausen, Holland

Wave Hill Gardens, Bronx, NY

Thanks to the gardeners and institutions who permitted me to photograph perennial flowers and gardens:

American Horticultural Society, River Farm, Alexandria, VA

Antique Rose Emporium, Brenham, TX

Atlanta Botanic Garden, Atlanta, GA

Jean Atwater, Spokane, WA

Ernesta and Fred Ballard, Philadelphia, PA

Berkshire Botanic Garden, Stockbridge, MA

Bourton House and Gardens, England

British Columbia, University of, Botanic Garden, Vancouver, BC

Brooklyn Botanic Garden, Brooklyn, NY

Francis Cabot, La Malbaie, Quebec

Conservatory Garden in Central Park, New York, NY

Mr. and Mrs. Stuart Crowner, Pasadena, CA

Denmans Garden, John Brooks, England

Dixon Gallery and Gardens, Memphis, TN

C. Z. Guest, Old Westbury, NY

Joshua's Native Plants and Garden Antiques, Houston, TX

Lamb Nurseries, Spokane, WA

Live Oak Gardens, New Iberia, LA

Logee's Greenhouses, Danielson, CT

Longue Vue Gardens, New Orleans, LA

Longwood Gardens, Kennett Square, PA

Frederick and Mary Ann McGourty, Norfolk, CT

Mercer Arboretum and Botanic Gardens, Humble, TX

Lynden and Leigh Miller, Sharon, CT

Minnesota, University of, Landscape Arboretum, Canhassen, MN

Minnesota, University of, School of Business, St. Paul, MN

Montreal Botanic Garden, Montreal, Quebec

National Wildflower Research Center, Austin, TX

The New York Botanical Garden, Bronx, NY

Old Westbury Gardens, Old Westbury, NY

Geo. W. Park Seed Co., Inc., Greenwood, SC

Peckerwood Gardens, Waller, TX

Pier 39, San Francisco, CA

Planting Fields Arboretum, Oyster Bay, NY

Plum Creek Farm, Sharon, CT

Royal Botanical Garden at Kew, London, England

George Schoellkopf, CT

Sissinghurst Castle Gardens, Kent, England

Strybing Arboretum, San Francisco, CA

Wakehurst Gardens, England

Thanks to all the gardeners and institutions who provide the subject matter for my photography, especially these for bulbs:

American Horticultural Society, River Farm, Alexandria, VA

Atlanta Botanic Garden, Atlanta, GA

Ernesta and Fred Ballard, Philadelphia, PA

Breck's Bulbs, Peoria, IL

British Columbia, University of, Botanic Garden, Vancouver, BC

Burpee Seed Co., Warminster, PA

Brooklyn Botanic Garden, Brooklyn, NY

Butchart Gardens, Victoria, BC

Central Park, New York, NY

Chelsea Flower Show, London, England

Chicago Botanic Garden, Chicago, IL

Dorado Beach Hotel, Puerto Rico

El Junque (Rain Forest), Puerto Rico

Betsy Feuerstein, Memphis, TN

Lincoln and Helen Foster, Falls Village, CT

Great Dixter Gardens, England

Golden Gate Park Conservatory, San Francisco, CA

C.Z. Guest, Old Westbury, NY

Hope Hendler, New York, NY

Hidcote Manor Gardens, Gloucestershire, England

Hortus Bulborum, Holland

Michael Kartuz, Vista, CA

Keukenhof Gardens, Lisse, Holland

Live Oak Gardens, New Iberia, LA

Logee's Greenhouses, Danielson, CT

Longue Vue Gardens, New Orleans, PA

Longwood Gardens, Kennett Square, PA

Los Angeles State and County Arboretum, Arcadia, CA

Odette McMurrey, Houston, TX

James K. McNair, San Francisco, CA

Mercer Arboretum and Botanic Gardens, Humble, TX

Montreal Botanical Garden, Montreal, Quebec

Georgia and Eugene Mosier, Sewickley Heights, PA

The New York Botanical Garden, Bronx, NY

Old Westbury Gardens, Old Westbury, NY

Peckerwood Gardens, Waller, TX

Phipps Conservatory, Pittsburgh, PA

Adele Pieper, Houston, TX

Duncan and Kathy Pitney, NJ

Plum Creek Farm, Sharon, CT

Roger's Nursery, Corona Del Mar, CA

Royal Botanical Garden at Kew, London, England

Josephine Shanks, Houston, TX

Sissinghurst Castle Gardens, Kent, England

Strybing Arboretum, San Francisco, CA

Special thanks to these gardeners and institutions where I photographed the trees and other woody plants chosen for this book:

Stanley and Gunvor Adelfang, Huntsville, AL

American Horticultural Society, River Farm, Alexandria, VA

Barnsley House, Rosemary Verey, Gloucestershire, England

Ernesta and Fred Ballard, Philadelphia, PA

British Columbia, University of, Botanic Garden, Vancouver, BC

Brooklyn Botanic Garden, Brooklyn, NY

Francis Cabot, La Malbaie, Quebec

Central Park, New York, NY

Great Dixter Gardens, England

Thomas Dodd Nurseries, Semmes, AL

C. Z. Guest, Old Westbury, NY

Hickey-Robertson, The Farm, Nelsonville, TX

Hidcote Manor Gardens, Gloucestershire, England

Jardins des Plantes, Paris, France

Joe Kirkpatrick, Memphis, TN

Leonardslee Gardens, England

Logee's Greenhouses, Danielson, CT

Longwood Gardens, Kennett Square, PA

Bonny and David Martin, Memphis, TN

Mercer Arboretum and Botanic Gardens, Humble, TX

Mohonk Mountain House, New Paltz, NY

Moody Gardens, Galveston, TX

Georgia and Eugene Mosier, Sewickley Heights, PA

National Wildflower Research Center, Austin, TX

The New York Botanical Garden, Bronx, NY

Mr. and Mrs. Dave Pendarvis, Lake Charles, LA

Mr. and Mrs. Duncan Pitney, NJ

Planting Fields Arboretum, Oyster Bay, NY

Geo. W. Park Seed Co., Inc., Greenwood, SC

Mrs. J. Pancoast Reath, PA

Virginia Robinson Gardens, Beverly Hills, CA

Royal Botanical Gardens at Kew, London, England

Victor Salmones, Acapulco, Mexico

Sissinghurst Castle Gardens, Kent, England

Susan Turner, Baton Rouge, LA

Upton House Gardens, England

Wakehurst Gardens, England

William T. Wheeler, New York, NY

Index

A

Abelia, 326
Abelmoschus, 26
Abutilon, 27, 110
Acanthaceae, 101, 164, 192, 198
Acanthus family, 101, 164, 192, 198
Acer, 327
Aceraceae, 327
Achillea, 126
Achimenes, 224
Acidanthera, 225
Aconite, 127
Aconitum, 127
Aesculus, 328
African Daisy, 30
African Gardenia, 379
African Iris, 255
Agapanthus, 226, 310
Agavaceae, 207, 289
Agave family, 207, 289
Ageratum, 28
Aizoaceae, 52
Ajuga, 127
Albuca, 227
Alchemilla, 128
Allegheny Spurge, 383
Allium, 228, 310
Almond, 392, 410
Alpinia, 229
Alstroemeria, 230
Alstroemeriaceae, 230
Alstroemeria family, 230
Alumroot, 159
Amaranthaceae, 28, 38, 60
Amaranth family, 28, 38, 60
Amaranthus, 28, 110
Amaryllidaceae, 226, 243, 248, 252, 258, 260, 263, 267–68, 270, 273, 279, 281, 283, 285, 287, 292, 298–99, 302, 304, 306
Amaryllis, 231
Amaryllis family, 226, 243, 248, 252, 258, 260, 263, 267–68, 270, 273, 279, 281, 283, 285, 287, 292, 298–99, 302, 304, 306
Amazon Lily, 258
Anacardiaceae, 344
Andromeda, 387
Anemone, 121, 129, 232, 310

Angel's Trumpet, 49
Anigozanthos, 233
Annual Aster, 37
Annual Candytuft, 65
Annual Chrysanthemum, 40
Annual Dahlia, 49
Annual Delphinium, 44
Annual Flax, 70
Annual garden. *See also specific plants*
    bringing into your home, 110
    buying and planting, 18–20
    caring for, 22
    defined, 14
    planning and designing, 14–17, 22
    soil preparation, 18, 22
    tools, 22
    troubleshooting guide, 108
    year-round calendar, 22
Annual Phlox, 89
Annual Sage, 96
Annual Sunflower, 61
Annual Vinca, 38
Antirrhinum, 29
Apocynaceae, 38, 174, 200, 381, 389, 405
Apple, 410
Apricot, 392
Aquifoliaceae, 366
Aquilegia, 130
Arabis, 130
Araceae, 234, 239, 245, 305
Araliaceae, 364
Aralia family, 364
Arctotis, 30
Ardisia, 328
Arisaema, 234
Aristolochiaceae, 133
Aroid family, 234, 239, 245, 305
Artemisia, 131
Aruncus, 132
Asarum, 133
Asclepiadaceae, 134
Asclepias, 134
Asphodel, 235
Asphodeline, 235
Asphodelus, 236
Aster, 135, 210
Astilbe, 136
Athel Tamarisk, 403

Aurinia, 136
Autumn Crocus, 244
Azalea, 395
Aztec Lily, 298

B

Bachelor's Button, 39, 110
Balloon Flower, 185
Balsam family, 66
Balsaminaceae, 66
Bamboo stakes, 22, 122
Baptisia, 121, 137
Barberry, 314, 329
Barberry family, 152, 329, 377, 380
Barrenwort, 152
Bartonia, 75
Basil, 84
Basket-of-gold Alyssum, 136
Batflower, 299
Beardtongue, 86, 117, 180
Beautyberry, 333
Bedding Geranium, 85
Bee Balm, 118, 176
Beech, 356
Beech family, 356, 395
Begonia, 31, 237–38
Begoniaceae, 31, 237–38
Begonia family, 31, 237–38
Belamcanda, 32
Belladonna Lily, 231
Bellflower, 140
Bellflower Enkianthus, 352
Bellflower family, 140, 185
Berberidaceae, 152, 329, 377, 380
Berberis, 329
Bergenia, 138
Betula, 330
Betulaceae, 330
Birch, 330
Birch family, 330
Birthwort family, 133
Blackberry Lily, 32, 110
Black-eyed Susan, 94, 191
Black-eyed-Susan Vine, 101
Black Haw, 404
Blanketflower, 57
Blazing Star, 75
Bleeding Heart, 117–18, 148
Bletilla, 238

Bloodflower, 134
Blood Lily, 292
Bloodwort family, 233
Bluebeard, 336
Blue Daisy, 56
Blue Lace Flower, 103
Blue Trumpet Vine, 198
Boneset, 153
Bonsai, 410–11. *See also under Uses*
Borage, 33
Borage family, 33, 62, 78, 190, 196
Boraginaceae, 33, 62, 78, 190, 196
Borago, 33
Boston Fern, 177
Bottlebrush, 333
Bougainvillea, 139
Bouquets. *See under Uses*
Box, 214, 332
Box family, 332
Boxwood family, 383
Brachycome, 33
Brassica, 34
Brodiaea, 310
Broom, 348
Browallia, 35
Buckeye family, 328
Buckthorn family, 336–37
Buckwheat family, 187
Buddleia, 331
Bud grafts, 321
Bugbane, 143
Bugleweed, 127
Bulb garden. *See also specific plants*
    bringing into your home, 310
    buying and planting, 217
    caring for, 217–21
    planning and designing, 214
    propagation, 218–21
    soil preparation, 217
    tools, 221
    troubleshooting guide, 308
    year-round calendar, 221
Bulb planters, 221
Bull Bay, 376
Bunchberry, 342
Bush Violet, 35
Busy Lizzie, 66

Buttercup, 291
Buttercup family, 44, 82, 127, 129–30, 143–44, 146, 157, 197, 202, 232, 255, 291
Butterfly Flower, 99
Butterfly gardens. *See under Uses*
Butterfly Ginger, 268
Butterfly Pea, 42
Butterfly Vine, 195
Butterfly Weed, 134
Buttonbush, 337
Buxaceae, 332, 383
Buxus, 332

C

Caladium, 239
Calendula, 36, 110
Calico Bush, 369
California Lilac, 336–37
California Poppy, 54
Calla Lily, 305
Callicarpa, 333, 410
Callistemon, 333
Callistephus, 37
Calycanthaceae, 334
Calycanthus, 334
Calycanthus family, 334
Camass, 240
Camassia, 240
Camellia, 335
Campanula, 140
Campanulaceae, 140, 185
Campion, 117, 171
Candy Lily, 32
Candytuft, 110
Canna, 217, 241
Cannaceae, 241
Canna family, 241
Caparaceae, 42
Cape Cod weeder, 121
Cape Cowslip, 278
Cape Jasmine, 360
Cape Jewels, 79
Caper family, 42
Caprifoliaceae, 169, 326, 399, 404, 406
Capsicum, 37
Cardinal Climber, 67
Cardinal Flower, 169
Cardinal Spear, 353

Carex, 140
Carnation, 50
Caroline Allspice, 334
Carpet Bugle, 127
Carpetweed family, 52
Carrot family, 46, 88, 103, 152
Caryophyllaceae, 50, 147, 171
Caryopteris, 336
Cashew family, 344
Castor Bean, 93
Catawba, 396
Catharanthus, 38
Cathey, Henry M., 117
Catmint, 177
Caucasian, 396
Ceanothus, 336–37
Celastraceae, 354
Celosia, 38, 110
Centaurea, 39
Centranthus, 141
Cephalanthus, 337
Cercis, 338
Chaenomeles, 339
Chasmanthe, 242
Chaste Tree, 206
Checkered Lily, 262
Chelsea Flower Show (London), 288
Cherry, 392, 410
Cherry Laurel, 392
Cherry Pie, 62
Chilean Bellflower, 83
Chilean Jasmine, 174
Chilean Myrtle, 384
China Aster, 37, 110
Chincherinchee, 285
Chinese Ground Orchid, 238
Chinese Hibiscus, 365
Chinese Holly-leaved Olive, 382
Chinese Parsley, 46
Chinese Spicebush, 334
Chionanthus, 340
Chionodoxa, 242
Christmas Rose, 157
Chrysanthemum, 22, 40, 110, 118, 142, 210
Cilantro, 46
Cimicifuga, 143
Cineraria, 99
Cinquefoil, 188
Clarkia, 41

Clematis, 144
Cleome, 42
Clerodendrum, 145
Climbing Lily, 265
Clitoria, 42
Clivia, 243
Cockscomb, 38
Codiaeum, 341
Colchicum, 244
Coleus, 43
Colocasia, 245
Columbine, 117, 130
Comfrey, 196
Commelinaceae, 200
Common Dahlia, 253
Common Weigela, 406
Common Zinnia, 107
Compositae, 28, 30, 33, 36–37, 39–40, 46–47, 49, 53, 56–59, 61–63, 74, 91, 94, 97, 99–100, 102, 106–7, 126, 131, 135, 142, 145, 150–51, 153, 157, 161, 167–68, 191, 253
Compost, 18, 118, 217, 308, 322
Coneflower, 118, 191
Confederate Jasmine, 200
Confederate Rose, 365
Consolida, 44
Container garden scheme, 117–18
Containerizing, 18
Containers, 117–18, 210. *See also under Uses*
Convallaria, 246
Convolvulaceae, 45, 67, 274
Convolvulus, 45
Copper Tip, 249
Coral Bean, 353
Coralbells, 118, 159, 210
Coralberry, 328
Coral Tree, 353
Coreopsis, 46, 145
Coriander, 46
Coriandrum, 46
Cork Bush, 354
Cornaceae, 342
Cornelian Cherry, 342
Corn Flag, 264
Cornflower, 39
Cornus, 342
Corydalis, 247

Corylopsis, 343
Cosmos, 22, 47, 110
Cotinus, 344
Cotoneaster, 345
Cottage garden scheme, 117. *See also under Uses*
Crab Apple, 378, 410
Cranberry Bush, 404
Cranesbill, 156
Crape Myrtle, 373, 408
Crassulaceae, 193–94
Crataegus, 346
Creeping Jennie, 172
Creeping Zinnia, 97
Crimson Flag, 293
Crinum, 217, 248
Crocosmia, 249
Crocus, 217–18, 221, 249
Croton, 341
Crowbar, 221
Crown Imperial, 262
Cruciferae, 34, 65, 73–74, 130, 136
Cuban Lily, 294
Cucumber Tree, 376
Cucurbita, 48
Cucurbitaceae, 48
Cultivator, three-pronged, 121
Cup Flower, 81
Curcuma, 250
Cuttings, 318
Cyclamen, 251
Cydonia, 347
Cyperaceae, 140
Cypress Spurge, 154
Cyrtanthus, 252
Cytisus, 348

D

Daffodil, 217–18, 283, 310
Dahlberg Daisy, 53
Dahlia, 49, 110, 217, 253, 310
Daisy family, 28, 30, 33, 36–37, 39–40, 46–47, 49, 53, 56–59, 61–63, 74, 91, 94, 97, 99–100, 102, 106–7, 126, 131, 135, 142, 145, 150–51, 153, 157, 161, 167–68, 191, 253
Dammer Evergreen, 345
Dancing Lady Ginger, 265
Daphne, 349

Datura, 49
Daylily, 114, 117, 158, 221
"Deadheading," 110
Dead Nettle, 165
Delonix, 350
Delphinium, 117, 146, 210
Denver, Colorado, Water
    Department, 117
Desert Candle, 256
Deutzia, 351
Dianthus, 50, 147, 210
Dibble, 221
Dicentra, 148, 254
Dictamnus, 148
Didiscus, 103
Dietes, 255
Digitalis, 149
Dipsacaceae, 98
Dogbane family, 38, 174, 200,
    381, 389, 405
Dogtooth Violet, 257
Dogwood, 342
Dogwood family, 342
Dolichos, 51
Dorotheanthus, 52
Dusty Miller, 39, 99
Dutch Amaryllis, 270
Dutch Hyacinth, 310
Dutch Iris, 217, 274
Dutchman's-Breeches, 148, 254
Dutch Tulip, 218
Dwarf Burning Bush, 354
Dwarf Crested Iris, 163
Dwarf Morning Glory, 45
Dyssodia, 53

E

Ear-leaved Umbrella Tree, 376
Eastern Redbud, 338
Echinacea, 150
Echinops, 121, 151
Edging Lobelia, 72
Elaeagnaceae, 352
Elaeagnus, 352
Elder, 399
Elecampane, 161
Elephant's Ear, 245
Emilia, 53
Empress Tree, 384
English Bluebell, 271

Enkianthus, 352
Epimedium, 152
Eranthis, 255
Eremurus, 256
Ericaceae, 352, 369, 383–84,
    387, 395–96
Eryngium, 152
Erythrina, 353
Erythronium, 257
Eschscholzia, 54
Espalier. See under Uses
Ethylene, 218
Eucharis, 258
Eucharist Lily, 258
Eucomis, 259
Eucrosia, 260
Eulalia, 175
Euonymus, 354
Eupatorium, 153
Euphorbia, 55, 154
Euphorbiaceae, 55, 93, 154, 341
European Pasqueflower, 129
Eustoma, 71
Evening Primrose, 117, 178
Evening-primrose family,
    41, 155, 178, 360
Evergreen Euonymus, 354
Everlasting, 62–63, 106
Everlasting Bachelor's Button, 60
Everlastings arrangements,
    110, 210, 310
Exochorda, 355

F

Fagaceae, 356, 395
Fagus, 356
False Goat's Beard, 136, 210
False Indigo, 137, 210
False Mitrewort, 199
Fancy-leaved Caladium, 239
Farewell-to-spring, 41
Feijoa, 357
Felicia, 56
Fertilizer
    for annual gardens, 18
    for bulb gardens, 217
    general considerations, 11
    for perennial gardens, 118,
        208
    for woody plants, 317, 408

0-6-5: 408
1-6-5: 408
5-10-5: 26, 28–83, 85–107, 118,
    122, 126–30, 132–38, 140–59,
    161–98, 200–207, 225–87,
    289–307
5-10-10: 335
7-2-7: 365
10-2-4: 365
10-10-10: 84, 88
12-12-17: 139
14-14-14: 118, 145, 160–61, 165,
    168, 174–75, 177, 187, 190,
    199, 251–54, 257–62, 270,
    284, 288, 305, 307, 317, 322,
    326, 330–34, 336–46, 349,
    352, 356, 359–88, 390–407
15-30-15: 27, 108, 224, 308,
    363, 408
20-20-20: 245–46, 248, 250
30-10-10: 27, 136, 145, 177, 224,
    322, 360, 366, 373, 379
Figwort family, 29, 76, 79, 86,
    103, 149, 180, 203–4, 384
Fire Bush, 363
Flag, 163
Flame Freesia, 301
Flamegold-rain Tree, 372
Flax family, 70
Fleece Flower, 187
Fleur-de-lis, 163
Flora's Paintbrush, 53
Florida Royal Palm, 398
Florida Swamp Lily, 248
Florists' Amaryllis, 270
Florists' Cyclamen, 251
Florists' Gloxinia, 295
Flossflower, 28
Flowering Cabbage, 34
Flowering Maple, 27
Flowering Okra, 26
Flowering Tobacco, 80, 110
Flowers, 8. See also specific
    plants
Flox, 89, 183
Forcing, 310
Forest Lily, 304
Forget-me-not, 78
Forsythia, 357, 410
Fortune, 396
Fothergilla, 358

Fountain Butterfly Bush, 331
Four-o'clock, 76
Four-o'clock family, 76, 139
Foxglove, 117, 149
Foxtail Lily, 256
Fragrant Gladiolus, 225
Frangipani, 389
Franklinia, 359
Franklin Tree, 359
Freesia, 261, 310
Fringetree, 340
Fritillaria, 262
Fuchsia, 360
Fumaria, 247
Fumariaceae, 148, 247
Fumitory family, 148, 247
Fungicide, 208

G

Gable Hybrids, 395
Gaillardia, 57
Galanthus, 263
Galtonia, 263
Gardenia, 360
Garden Petunia, 88
Garden Verbena, 104
Garland Flower, 349
Gas Plant, 148
Gaura, 155
Gay-feather, 118, 167
Gazania, 58
Gentian family, 71
Gentianiaceae, 71
Geraniaceae, 85, 156
Geranium, 156
Geranium family, 85, 156
Gerbera, 59, 210, 310
German Iris, 274
Gesneriaceae, 224, 266, 277,
    294–96
Gesneriad family, 224, 266, 277,
    294–96
Ghent, 395
Gilia, 60
Ginger, 307
Ginger family, 229, 250, 265,
    268, 275, 307
Ginkgo, 361, 410
Ginkgoaceae, 361
Ginkgo family, 361

Gladiolus, 110, 217, 264, 310
Glenn Dale Hybrid, 395
Globba, 265
Globe Amaranth, 60, 110
Globeflower, 202
Globe Gilia, 60
Globe-thistle, 151, 210
Gloriosa, 265
Gloriosa Daisy, 94
Glory-bower, 145
Glory Bush, 403
Glory-of-the-snow, 242
Gloxinia, 266
Goat's Beard, 132
Godetia, 41
Golden-chain Tree, 372
Golden Cup, 64
Golden-rain Tree, 372
Golden Vicary, 374
Gomphrena, 60
Gourd, 48
Gourd family, 48
Gramineae, 175
Grape Hyacinth, 282
Grass family, 175
Great Blue Lobelia, 169
Greek Valerian, 186
Griffthianum, 396
Guernsey Lily, 285
Gulf Coast Penstemon, 180
Gumi, 352

H

Habranthus, 218, 267
Haemanthus, 268
Haemodoraceae, 233
Halesia, 362
Hamamelidaceae, 343, 358, 363
Hamamelis, 363
Hamelia, 363
Hardy Ageratum, 153
Hardy Begonia, 238
Hardy Orange, 390
Hawthorn, 346
Heath family, 352, 369, 383–84, 387, 395–96
Heavenly Bamboo, 380
Hedera, 364
Hedgehog Flower, 151
Hedges. *See under Uses*

Hedge trimmers, 322
Hedychium, 268
Height/habit, 8. *See also specific plants*
Helianthus, 61
Helichrysum, 62
Heliconia, 269
Heliconiaceae, 269
Heliconia family, 269
Heliopsis, 122, 157
Heliotrope, 62, 110
Heliotropium, 62
Helipterum, 63
Helleborus, 157
Hemerocallis, 158, 221
Herbaceous border scheme, 117
Herbaceous Peony, 121
Heuchera, 159
Hibiscus, 365
Hidden Ginger, 250
Hills of Snow, 366
Hippeastrum, 270
Hippocastanaceae, 328
Holly, 366
Holly family, 366
Holly-leaf Itea, 368
Honeysuckle, 169
Honeysuckle family, 169, 326, 399, 404, 406
Horse Chestnut, 328
Hosta, 160
Hot-water Plant, 224
Houseleek, 194
Houttuynia, 161
Hummingbird Bush, 363
Hummingbird gardens. *See under Uses*
Hunnemannia, 64
Hurricane Lily, 281
Hyacinth, 217–18, 272, 310
Hyacinthoides, 271
Hyacinthus, 272
Hydrangea, 366
Hymenocallis, 273
Hypoxidaceae, 291
Hypoxis family, 291

I

Iberis, 65
Iceland Poppies, 84

Ice Plant, 52
Ikebana arrangements, 210, 310
Ilex, 366
Immortelle, 106
Impatiens, 66
Indian, 395
Indian Crocus, 288
Indian Shot, 241
Indigo, 367
Indigofera, 367
Insecticidal soap, 208, 408
Insects, 108, 208, 308, 408
International Society of Arboriculture, 317
Inula, 161
Ipheion, 273
Ipomoea, 67, 274
Ipomopsis, 162
Iridaceae, 32, 163, 225, 242, 249, 255, 261, 264, 274, 284, 293, 297, 300–301
Iris, 163, 210, 274, 310
Iris family, 32, 163, 225, 242, 249, 255, 261, 264, 274, 284, 293, 297, 300–301
Isoloma, 277
Itea, 368
Ivy, 364

J

Jack-in-the-pulpit, 234
Jacobean Lily, 298
Jacob's Ladder, 186
Japanese Anemone, 129
Japanese Flowering Quince, 339
Japanese gardens. *See under Uses*
Japanese Iris, 274
Japanese Mahonia, 377
Japanese Maple, 327
Japanese Pittosporum, 388
Japanese Rose, 370
Japanese Silver Grass, 175
Japanese Snowball, 404
Japanese Spurge, 383
Japanese Yew, 390
Jasmine, 164
Jasminum, 164
Jekyll, Gertrude, 17
Joe-pye Weed, 153

Joseph's Coat, 28
Judas Tree, 338
Jupiter's Beard, 141
Justicia, 164
Jute, 122
Jute twine, 22

K

Kaempferia, 275
Kaffir Lily, 243, 310
Kale, 34
Kalmia, 369
Kangaroo Paw, 233, 310
Kerria, 370
King's Crown, 164
Kirengeshoma, 371
Knap Hill, 395
Kniphofia, 276
Knotweed, 187
Koelreuteria, 372
Kohleria, 277
Kurume, 395

L

Labiatae, 43, 77, 84, 87, 96, 127, 165–66, 176–77, 182, 184, 193, 195, 397
Laburnum, 372
Lachenalia, 278
Lady's Mantle, 128
Lagerstroemia, 373
Lamb's Ears, 117, 195
Lamium, 165
Larkspur, 44, 110
Lathyrus, 68
Lauraceae, 375
Laurel family, 375
Lavandula, 166
Lavatera, 69
Lavender, 166
Leadwort family, 69
Leaves, 8. *See also specific plants*
Ledebouria, 279
Leguminosae, 42, 51, 68, 137, 170, 338, 348, 350, 353, 367, 372, 407
Lemon Mint, 77, 110
Lenten Rose, 157
Leopard Flower, 32
Leopard Plant, 168

Leucojum, 279
Liatris, 167, 210
Light, 11, 108, 208, 308, 408.
    See also specific plants
Ligularia, 168
Ligustrum, 374
Lilac, 402, 408, 410
Liliaceae, 158, 160, 187, 201, 227,
    235, 240, 242, 244, 246,
    256–57, 259, 262–63, 265,
    271–72, 276, 278–80, 282, 285,
    290, 294, 303–4
Lilium, 221, 280
Lily, 210, 221, 280, 310
Lily family, 158, 160, 187, 201,
    227, 235, 240, 242, 244, 246,
    256–57, 259, 262–63, 265,
    271–72, 276, 278–80, 282, 285,
    290, 294, 303–4
Lily of the Field, 299
Lily of the Nile, 226
Lily of the Valley, 246, 310
Limonium, 69
Linaceae, 70
Lindera, 375
Linum, 70
Liriodendron, 375
Lisianthus, 71
Live-forever, 194
Live Oak, 395
Livingstone Daisy, 52
Lizard's-tail family, 161
Loasaceae, 75
Loasa family, 75
Lobelia, 72, 169
Lobeliaceae, 72, 169
Lobelia family, 72, 169
Lobster Claws, 269
Lobularia, 73
Loganiaceae, 331
Logania family, 331
Lonicera, 169
Loosestrife, 172
Loosestrife family, 373
Loppers, 321
Louisiana Iris, 274
Louisiana Nursery, 11
Love-in-a-mist, 82
Love-lies-bleeding, 28
Lucky Clover, 286
Lungwort, 190

Lupine, 117, 170
Lupinus, 170
Lychnis, 171
Lycoris, 281
Lysimachia, 172
Lythraceae, 373

M

Macleaya, 173
Madagascar Periwinkle, 38
Madder family, 337, 360,
    363, 379
Magnolia, 376
Magnoliaceae, 375–76
Magnolia family, 375–76
Mahonia, 377
Maidenhair Tree, 361
Mallow, 173
Mallow family, 26–27, 69,
    173, 365
Malpighiaceae, 195
Malpighia family, 195
Malus, 378
Malva, 173
Malvaceae, 26–27, 69, 173, 365
Mandevilla, 174
Mandeville, 174
Maple family, 327
Marguerite, 142
Marigold, 100, 210
Marlberry, 328
Matthiola, 74
Meadow Rue, 197
'Medallion' Daisy, 74
Megasea, 138
Melampodium, 74
Melastomaceae, 403
Melastoma family, 403
Mentzelia, 75
Mexican Bamboo, 187
Mexican Hat, 91
Mexican Petunia, 192
Mexican Shellflower, 300
Mexican Sunflower, 102
Mexican Tuberose, 289
Mexican Tulip Poppy, 64
Mezereum family, 349
Michaelmas Daisy, 135
Mignonette, 92, 110
Mignonette family, 92

Milk-and-wine Lily, 248
Milkweed, 134
Milkweed family, 134
Mimulus, 76
Miniature Amaryllis, 252
Mint family, 43, 77, 84, 87, 96,
    127, 165–66, 176–77, 182, 184,
    193, 195, 397
Mirabilis, 76
Miscanthus, 175
Mist Flower, 153
Mitriostigma, 379
Mock Orange, 385
Mollis, 395
Monarda, 77, 176
Monkey Flower, 76
Monkshood, 118, 127
Montauk Daisy, 142
Montbretia, 249, 301
Moonflower, 67
Morning Glory, 67
Morning-glory family, 45, 67, 274
Moss Pink, 183
Mountain Laurel, 369
Mourning Bride, 98
Mullein, 203
Mum, 142
Muscari, 282
Mustard family, 34, 65, 73–74,
    130, 136
Myosotis, 78
Myrsinaceae, 328
Myrsine family, 328
Myrtaceae, 333, 357
Myrtle family, 333, 357

N

Naked Lady, 281
Nandina, 380
Nannyberry, 404
Narcissus, 217, 221, 283, 310
Nasturtium, 104
Nasturtium family, 104, 301
National Arboretum
    (Washington, D.C.), 117
Neem tree sprays, 208, 408
Nemesia, 79
Neomarica, 284
Nepeta, 177
Nephrolepis, 177

Nerine, 285
Nerium, 381
New American garden
    scheme, 117
New England Aster, 135
New York Aster, 135
Nicotiana, 80
Nierembergia, 81
Nigella, 82, 110
Nightshade family, 35, 37, 49,
    80–81, 88, 95, 99
Nolana, 83
Nolanaceae, 83
Nolana family, 83
Nut Orchid, 224
Nyctaginaceae, 76, 139

O

Oak, 395
Obedient Plant, 184
Ocimum, 84
Oehme van Sweden &
    Associates, 117
Oenothera, 178
Oleaceae, 164, 340, 357, 374,
    382, 402
Oleander, 381
Oleaster family, 352
Olive family, 164, 340, 357, 374,
    382, 402
Onagraceae, 41, 155, 178, 360
Opium Poppies, 84
Orange-flowered Sweet Olive, 382
Orchidaceae, 238, 288
Orchid family, 238, 288
Oregon Grape, 377
Oriental Poppy, 121
Ornamental Cabbage, 34
Ornamental Onion, 228
Ornamental Pepper, 37
Ornithogalum, 285
Orpine family, 193–94
Osmanthus, 382
Oswego Tea, 176
Oxalidaceae, 286
Oxalis, 286
Oxalis family, 286
Oxeye, 157
Oxeye Daisy, 142
Oxydendrum, 383

P

Pachysandra, 383
Paeonia, 179
Paeoniaceae, 179
Painted Daisy, 142
Painted Nettle, 43
Painted Tongue, 95
Palmae, 398
Palm family, 398
Pancratium, 287
Pansy, 105, 110
Papaver, 84, 180
Papaveraceae, 54, 64, 84,
    173, 180
Paper Flower, 139
Pardancanda, 32
Parsley, 88
Parsley family, 152
Passiflora, 181
Passifloraceae, 181
Passionflower, 181
Passionflower family, 181
Patience, 66
Paulownia, 384
Peach, 410
Peacock Ginger, 275
Pea family, 42, 51, 68, 137, 170,
    338, 348, 350, 353, 367, 372, 407
Pear, 394, 410
Pea-vine sticks, 118, 122
Pelargonium, 85
Pennants, 242
Penstemon, 86, 180
Peony, 117, 122, 179, 210
Peony family, 179
Perennial garden. See also
    specific plants
  bringing into your home, 210
  buying and planting, 118–21
  caring for, 121
  planning and designing,
      114–18
  propagation, 121
  soil preparation, 118
  tools, 121–22
  troubleshooting guide, 208
  year-round calendar, 122
Perennial Larkspur, 146
Perennial Poppy, 180
Perilla, 87

Pernettya, 384
Perovskia, 182
Persian Violet, 251
Peruvian Lily, 230
Peruvian Squill, 294
Petroselinum, 88
Petunia, 88, 110
Philadelphus, 385
Phlox, 89, 121, 183, 210
Phlox family, 60, 89, 162,
    183, 186
Photinia, 386
Physostegia, 184
Pieris, 387
Pinaceae, 387
Pincushion Flower, 98
Pine, 387
Pineapple Guava, 357
Pineapple Lily, 259
Pine family, 387
Pink, 50, 110, 147
Pink family, 50, 147, 171
Pinus, 387
Pittosporaceae, 388
Pittosporum, 388
Pittosporum family, 388
Plaintain Lily, 160
Planting schedule, 8–11. See also
    specific plants
Platycodon, 185
Pleione, 288
Plum, 392
Plumbaginaceae, 69
Plumbago family, 69
Plume Poppy, 173
Plumeria, 389
Podocarpaceae, 390
Podocarpus, 390
Podocarpus family, 390
Polemoniaceae, 60, 89, 162,
    183, 186
Polemonium, 186
Polianthes, 289
Polygonaceae, 187
Polygonatum, 187
Polygonum, 187
Polypodiaceae, 177
Polypody family, 177
Poncirus, 390
Poor-man's Orchid, 99
Poplar, 391

Poppy, 310
Poppy family, 54, 64, 84,
    173, 180
Populus, 391
Portulaca, 90
Portulacaceae, 90
Potentilla, 188
Pot Marigold, 36
Pot of Gold, 46
Power chain saw, 322
Prairie Coneflower, 91
Primrose, 114, 117, 189
Primrose family, 172, 189, 251
Primula, 189
Primulaceae, 172, 189, 251
Princess Flower, 403
Privet, 374
Propagation, 11. See also
    specific plants
Pruners, 22, 321
Pruning, 11. See also specific
    plants
Pruning saw, 321
Prunus, 392
Pulmonaria, 190
Purple Coneflower, 150, 210
Purple Hyacinth Bean, 51
Purple Osier, 399
Purslane, 90
Purslane family, 90
Puschkinia, 290
Pussy Willow, 410
Pyracantha, 314, 393
Pyrethrum, 142
Pyrus, 394

Q

Quaking Aspen, 391
Quercus, 395
Quince, 347, 410

R

Raceme Redbud, 338
Raffia, 22, 122
Rain Lily, 218, 267, 306
Raised planting beds, 118
Ranunculaceae, 44, 82, 127,
    129–30, 143–44, 146, 157, 197,
    202, 232, 255, 291

Ranunculus, 291, 310
Ratabida, 91
Redbud, 410
Red-hot Poker, 276
Red Star, 291
Reseda, 92
Resedaceae, 92
Rhamnaceae, 336–37
Rhodanthe, 63
Rhododendron, 395–96
Rhodohypoxis, 291
Ricinus, 93
River Lily, 293
Rock Cress, 130
Rock gardens. See under Uses
Rock Spray, 345
Roman Hyacinth, 310
Rosa, 396
Rosaceae, 128, 132, 188, 339,
    345–47, 370, 378, 386, 392–94,
    396, 400
Rose, 210, 310, 314, 396, 410
Rose family, 128, 132, 188, 339,
    345–47, 370, 378, 386, 392–94,
    396, 400
Rosemary, 397
Rose Moss, 90
Rose of Sharon, 365
Rosmarinus, 397
Royal Poinciana, 350
Roystonea, 398
Rubiaceae, 337, 360, 363, 379
Rudbeckia, 94, 191
Rue family, 148, 390
Ruellia, 192
Running Myrtle, 405
Russian Olive, 352
Russian Sage, 182
Rutaceae, 148, 390

S

Sage, 110, 193
Salicaceae, 391, 399
Salix, 399
Salpiglossis, 95, 110
Salt Tree, 403
Salvia, 96, 193
Sambucus, 399
Sanvitalia, 97
Sapindaceae, 372

Sassafras, 410
Satin Flower, 41
Saururaceae, 161
Saxifragaceae, 136, 138, 159, 199, 351, 366, 368, 371, 385
Saxifrage family, 136, 138, 159, 199, 351, 366, 368, 371, 385
Scabiosa, 98, 110
Scadoxus, 292
Scarborough Lily, 304
Scarlet Buckeye, 328
Scarlet Firethorn, 393
Schizanthus, 99
Schizostylis, 293
Scilla, 217–18, 294
Scrophulariaceae, 29, 76, 79, 86, 103, 149, 180, 203–4, 384
Sea Daffodil, 287
Sea Holly, 152
Seaside gardens. *See under Uses*
Season, 8. *See also specific plants*
Sedge, 140
Sedge family, 140
Sedum, 117, 193
Seed packets, 20, 121
Seemannia, 294
Sempervivum, 194
Senecio, 99
Sentry-in-the-box, 227
Sharpshooter, 218
Shasta Daisy, 142
Shears, 322
Shell Ginger, 229
Shirley Poppies, 84
Shiso, 87
Shovel, 321
Showy Bistort, 187
Shrimp Plant, 164
Siberian Iris, 163
Siberian Squill, 294
Silky Camellia, 401
Silver Bell, 362
Silverberry, 352
Silver Farfugium, 168
Silver-king, 131
Silver Lace Vine, 187
Silver Rod, 236
Silver Squill, 279
Singapore Plumeria, 389
Sinningia, 295
Smithiantha, 296

Smoketree, 344
Snapdragon, 29, 110, 210
Snowdrop, 218, 263, 310
Snowdrop Tree, 362
Snowflake, 279
Snow-on-the-mountain, 55
Soapberry family, 372
Society Garlic, 302
Soil, 11. *See also specific plants*
Soil preparation, 18, 118, 217, 317
Solanaceae, 35, 37, 49, 80–81, 88, 95, 99
Solomon's Seal, 187
Sorrel Tree, 383
Sourwood, 383
Southern Yew, 390
Spades, 121, 218, 221
Spanish Bluebell, 271
Spanish Dagger, 207
Sparaxis, 297
Speedwell, 204
Spiceberry, 328
Spicebush, 375
Spider Flower, 42
Spider Lily, 273
Spiderwort, 200
Spiderwort family, 200
Spiraea, 400
Sprekelia, 298
Spring Starflower, 273
Spurge family, 55, 93, 154, 341
Squill, 294
Squirrel Corn, 254
Stachys, 195
Staff-tree family, 354
Standing Cypress, 162
Star Jasmine, 200
Star-of-Bethlehem, 285, 310
Statice, 69, 110
Sternbergia, 299
Stewartia, 401
Stigmaphyllon, 195
Stinking Hellebore, 157
Stinking Iris, 163
Stock, 74, 110, 210
Stonecrop, 193
Storax family, 362
Strawberry Bush, 354
Strawflower, 62–63, 110, 210
Striped Squill, 290
Styracaceae, 362

Sultana, 66
Summer Hyacinth, 263
Summer Lilac, 331
Summer Phlox, 122, 208
Summer Poinsettia, 55
Sun Drops, 178
Sunflower, 110
Swamp Mallow, 365
Swan River Daisy, 33
Sweet Alyssum, 73
Sweet Olive, 382
Sweet Pea, 68, 110
Sweet Potato Vine, 274
Sweetspire, 368
Sweet William, 50
Sword Fern, 177
Sword Lily, 264
Symphytum, 196
Syringa, 402

T

Tacca, 299
Taccaceae, 299
Tacca family, 299
Tagetes, 100
Tamaricaceae, 403
Tamarisk, 403
Tamarisk family, 403
Tamarix, 403
Tampala, 28
Taro, 245
Tarragon, 131
Tassel Flower, 53
Tea family, 335, 359, 401
Tea Olive, 382
Teasel family, 98
Telephone Flower, 283
Temple Bells, 296
Tepees, 118. *See also under Uses*
Texas Bluebell, 71
Texas Bluebonnet, 170
Texas Star, 365
Thalictrum, 197
Theaceae, 335, 359, 401
The Bride, 355
Thunbergia, 101, 198
Thymelaceae, 349
Tiarella, 199
Tibouchina, 403
Tickseed, 145

Tigridia, 217, 300
Tithonia, 102
Tools, 22, 121–22, 221, 321–22
Topiary. *See under Uses*
Torch Lily, 276
Torenia, 103
Trachelospermum, 200
Trachymene, 103
Tradescantia, 200
Trailing Vinca, 405
Transplants, 18–20, 110, 121, 318
Transvaal Daisy, 59
Treasure Flower, 58
Tree Gloxinia, 277
Tree Mallow, 69
Trillium, 201
Tritoma, 276
Tritonia, 301
Trollius, 121, 202
Tropaeolaceae, 104, 301
Tropaeolum, 104, 301
Trout Lily, 257
Trowel, 22, 121, 218, 221
True Gloxinia, 266
Tuber Nasturtiums, 301
Tuberose, 217
Tuberous Begonia, 237
Tulbaghia, 302
Tulip, 210, 217, 221, 303, 310
Tulipa, 303
Tulip Tree, 375
Turkey Corn, 148, 254
Twelve Apostles, 284
Twist-ties, 22, 122

U

Umbelliferae, 46, 88, 103, 152
U.S.D.A. Plant Hardiness Zone Map, 11, 22, 431
Uses, 11
  accents, 93, 132, 173, 229, 245, 248, 256, 327, 341, 353–55, 375, 389–90
  arbor cover, 42, 51, 67–68, 101, 114, 139, 144–45, 164, 169, 181, 187, 195, 198, 200, 407
  arbors, 372, 396
  arrangements, 32, 34, 110, 137–38, 160, 175, 210, 310.

See also everlastings arrangements; ikebana arrangements

background, 42, 61, 151, 175, 229, 340–41, 362, 368, 372, 375, 381, 385, 387, 399, 406

back of borders, 93, 102, 173, 191, 206, 256

banks, 143, 184, 240–41, 248, 383, 399. *See also streamside*

beds, 26–47, 49–50, 52–66, 68–92, 94–96, 98–100, 103–7, 126–27, 129–31, 134–38, 140–43, 145–50, 152, 154–63, 165–67, 169–73, 175–86, 188–97, 199–207, 224–31, 233–55, 257–87, 289–307, 331, 333–35, 337, 339, 341, 343, 349, 351, 363, 365–68, 370–71, 381, 387, 395–96

bee attractors, 33, 176

bog gardens, 172, 176, 202, 240–41, 248

bonsai, 327, 329–30, 332, 335, 338–39, 342–47, 349, 351–52, 354, 356–57, 360–61, 363–64, 366, 372–74, 376, 378, 380, 382, 387, 390, 392–95, 397, 399–403, 406–7, 410–11

border edging, 53, 127. *See also edging*

borders, 26–47, 49–50, 53, 55–57, 59–66, 68–92, 94–96, 98–100, 103–7, 126–27, 129–32, 134–38, 140–43, 145–63, 165–67, 169–73, 175–90, 192–97, 199–205, 207, 224–28, 230–31, 233–42, 244–55, 257–87, 289–307, 326, 328–29, 331–39, 341–44, 348–49, 351–54

bouquets, 17, 27–29, 36–41, 44, 46–47, 49–50, 53, 57, 59–63, 65, 69, 74, 77–78, 82, 91–92, 94–96, 98, 100, 102–7, 110

butterfly gardens, 134, 153, 176, 331, 333, 336, 363, 375

chain-link fence cover, 42

city gardens, 374

climbers, 68

colonizing moist areas, 184

containers, 229, 233, 253, 274, 327–28, 331–34, 336, 339, 341, 343, 345, 349, 352, 357, 360, 363, 365–67, 373, 377, 379–82, 386–87, 389–90, 396–97, 403, 405

cottage gardens, 152–53, 165, 169, 171, 173, 175, 178–79, 182–86, 189–91, 193, 206, 331, 336, 339, 343, 348–49, 355, 362–63, 366–69, 371, 379, 390, 395–97, 400, 402–3

country gardens, 390

cover, 67, 101, 114, 139, 144–45, 164, 169, 174, 181, 195, 198, 200, 301, 396, 407. See also specific covers

creepers, 14

cut flowers, 127, 129–30, 135–36, 140–42, 145–47, 149–51, 153, 157, 161, 167, 169–72, 176, 179–81, 183–85, 189, 191, 202, 205, 207, 225–26, 230, 232–33, 235–36, 240, 242–43, 246, 248–49, 252–53, 256, 258–65, 269–74, 276, 278–83, 285, 287, 289, 291–92, 294, 297–98, 301–5

cutting, 71, 85–86, 110, 126, 131, 152, 166, 228, 231, 326, 338–39, 341–43, 345–46, 348–49, 352, 354, 357, 360, 362, 364–66, 368–70, 375–76, 378, 387, 399, 402, 410

decorative gourds, 48

desert gardens, 398

difficult situations, 76

dry banks/slopes, 52

drying, 38, 60, 62–63, 82, 106, 228. *See also everlastings arrangements*

edging, 14, 33, 46, 50, 54, 56, 58, 60, 66, 72–73, 84, 88, 99–100, 103–5, 107, 128, 130, 133, 136, 138, 143, 179, 183, 397

edible flowers, 105

edible fruit, 347, 357, 378, 390, 392, 399, 404

edible herbs, 46, 84, 87–88, 100, 228

edible seeds, 61

espalier, 333, 337, 339, 346, 349, 352, 354, 357, 360, 363–64, 366, 372, 376, 378, 382, 387, 390, 392–95

everlastings arrangements, 110, 210, 310

fence cover, 48, 51, 67–68, 101, 114, 139, 144, 169, 174, 181, 187, 195, 198, 200, 265, 366, 396, 407

foliage effect, 386

forcing, 272, 274, 282–83, 310, 339

fragrance gardens, 382

greenhouses, 79

ground cover, 14, 17, 30, 58, 89–90, 97, 127–28, 133, 138, 152, 158, 161, 163, 165, 169, 172, 177, 187, 190, 193, 195, 199, 205, 230, 232, 238, 246, 274–75, 294, 307, 326, 328, 342, 345, 351, 354, 364, 373, 383, 387, 399, 405

hanging baskets, 35, 53, 56, 72–73, 81, 83, 88, 97, 101, 103–5, 172, 224, 237, 274, 284, 286, 301

hanging garden, 360

hedgerows, 340, 346, 353, 387, 390, 392–93, 395, 399, 404

hedges, 14, 99–100, 107, 326, 329, 332, 346, 352, 354, 356–57, 363, 366, 370, 374, 377, 380–82, 385–88, 390, 395–96, 399–400, 402–4, 406

hedging, 84, 102, 166

herb gardens, 33, 397

houseplants, 177, 279, 284

hummingbird gardens, 176, 249, 331, 363

ikebana arrangements, 210, 310

interplanting, 64, 78, 117, 232, 271, 359

Japanese gardens, 327, 377, 380, 386, 388

landscape, 386

lattice cover, 42, 101, 114, 265, 407

lawn, 350, 361, 372–73, 375–76, 378, 383–84, 386, 388, 394–95, 398, 401

massed plantings, 369

meadow gardens, 153, 161–62, 169–71, 175, 178, 181, 191

naturalizing, 130, 249

nosegays, 50, 65, 85

orchards, 378

ornamental trees, 346

ornamenting structures, 265

parks, 384, 396, 399, 406

partly shaded summer gardens, 268

between paving stones, 194

pergola cover, 114, 407

perimeter plantings, 240–41

planting under deciduous trees and shrubs, 242

pockets in rock walls, 247

pond banks, 140. *See also banks*

porch cover, 200

potpourri, 110, 210, 310

pots, 26–43, 45–47, 49–50, 52–66, 68–69, 71–74, 76, 78–92, 94–96, 99–100, 102–7, 126–32, 134–36, 139–42, 145, 147–51, 153–63, 165–68, 170–73, 175–77, 181, 184–88, 190, 192–200, 203–7, 210, 224–28, 230–31, 237–39, 241–45, 248–52, 255, 258–61, 264–70, 272–73, 275–82, 284–307, 310

prairie gardens, 344

public gardens, 396, 399

quick cover, 42, 48, 51

quick hedging, 69

quick screeners, 14

roadside, 375

rock gardens, 30, 33, 45, 50, 52–54, 56–58, 70, 72, 83, 89–90, 97, 106, 130, 138, 140, 147–48, 152, 154, 156, 159, 177–78, 181, 183, 185, 188–89, 193–95, 204–5, 246–47, 249, 254–57, 263, 267, 273, 279, 283, 286, 291, 299, 306, 345, 348–49, 384, 397

scented herbs, 110

screening, 139, 187, 363, 365–66, 372–74, 381, 385–88, 390–91, 393, 395–96, 399, 402–4, 406
seaside gardens, 352, 354, 366, 374, 381, 395, 398, 403
seed heads, 32, 110, 175, 210, 310
seedpods for drying, 85
semiwild gardens, 192
shade gardens, 157, 159–60, 165, 177, 187, 196, 199–201, 205, 338, 369, 371, 377, 380, 383, 395–96, 398
shade trees, 328, 347, 350, 356, 361, 372–76, 378, 387
shrubbery border, 169
specimen, 326, 330, 333–35, 337–38, 340–45, 347–52, 357–61, 363–67, 371, 373, 376–78, 380–92, 394–95, 398–99, 401–4, 406
streamside, 132, 140, 169, 176, 342
street, 361, 372, 383, 394–95, 398
tepee cover, 51, 67–68, 101, 144, 164, 174, 181, 195, 198, 200, 301
terrace, 372
terrariums, 295
topiary, 364, 374, 382, 397
trailing over shrubbery or brush, 301
tree-form standard, 360, 366, 381, 390, 395–97, 402–3
trellis cover, 17, 42, 48, 51, 67–68, 144–45, 164, 169, 174, 181, 187, 195, 198, 200, 265, 301, 396, 407
tropical gardens, 398
underplanting, 333
understory trees, 327–28, 338
viners, 14
wall climbers, 364
wall cover, 366
wall gardens, 147–48, 194, 204
wall shrubs, 337
wet sites, 168. *See also banks; bog gardens; streamside*
wild gardens, 75, 77, 130, 137, 143, 148, 152–53, 156–57, 159–62, 165, 167, 169–73, 175–78, 181, 183–84, 186–87, 189–91, 193, 196–97, 199–203, 205–6, 234, 238, 247, 254–55, 257, 263, 267, 271, 273, 279, 283, 286, 306, 338, 344, 368–71, 375, 395–96, 399, 401
wildlife haven, 393
windbreaks, 346, 356, 387, 391, 395, 403
window boxes, 360
woodland gardens, 143, 186–87, 189–90, 196–97, 199, 201, 362, 368–69, 387, 401, 404
Xeriscape, 155, 162, 175, 193, 207

V

Valerian, 141
Valerianaceae, 141
Valerian family, 141
Vallota, 304
Variegated Kerria, 370
Veltheimia, 304
Velvet Flower, 297
Verbain, 104
Verbascum, 121, 203
Verbena, 104, 110
Verbenaceae, 104, 145, 206, 333, 336
Verbena family, 104, 145, 206, 333, 336
Vermiculite, 20
Veronica, 204
Viburnum, 404
Vinca, 405
Vines, 114. *See also specific plants*
Viola, 105, 205
Violaceae, 105, 205
Violet, 117, 205, 210
Violet family, 105, 205
Vitex, 206

W

Wake-robin, 201
Walking Iris, 284
Wandflower, 297
Wax Begonia, 31
Wayside Gardens, 11
Weigela, 406
White Paintbrush, 268
White Snakeroot, 153
White Yulan, 376
Wild gardens. *See under Uses*
Wild Ginger, 133
Wild Honeysuckle, 155
Wild Hyacinth, 240
Wild Petunia, 192
Willow, 399
Willow family, 391, 399
Windflower, 129, 232
Winter Aconite, 221, 255
Winterberry, 366
Wintercreeper, 354
Winter Daffodil, 299
Winter Hazel, 343
Wishbone Flower, 103
Wisteria, 407
Witch Alder, 358
Witch Hazel, 363, 410
Witch-hazel family, 343, 358, 363
Woodland gardens. *See under Uses*
Wood Sorrel, 286
Woody Plant garden
  bringing into your home, 410–11
  buying and planting, 317–21
  caring for, 321
  planning and designing, 314–17
  soil preparation, 317
  tools, 321–22
  troubleshooting guide, 408
  year-round calendar, 322
Woody plant garden. *See also specific plants*
Wormwood, 131

X

Xeranthemum, 106
Xeriscape, 117, 155, 162, 175, 193, 207

Y

Yarrow, 126, 210
Yaupon, 214, 366
Yellow Buckeye, 328
Youth-and-old-age, 107
Yucca, 207
Yucca Do Nursery, 11

Z

Zantedeschia, 305
Zephyranthes, 218, 306
Zingiber, 307
Zingiberaceae, 229, 250, 265, 268, 275, 307
Zinnia, 107, 210

U.S.D.A. Plant Hardiness Zone Map

Average Annual Minimum Temperature

Temperature (°C)	Zone	Temperature (°F)
-45.6 and below	1	below -50
-45.6 and -45.5	2a	-45 to -50
-40.0 to -42.7	2b	-40 to -45
-37.3 to -40.0	3a	-35 to -40
-34.5 to -37.2	3b	-30 to -35
-31.7 to -34.4	4a	-25 to -30
-28.9 to -31.6	4b	-20 to -25
-26.2 to -28.8	5a	-15 to -20
-23.4 to -26.1	5b	-10 to -15
-20.6 to -23.3	6a	-5 to -10
-17.8 to -20.5	6b	0 to -5
-15.0 to -17.7	7a	5 to 0
-12.3 to -15.0	7b	10 to 5
-9.5 to -12.2	8a	15 to 10
-6.7 to -9.4	8b	20 to 15
-3.9 to -6.6	9a	25 to 20
-1.2 to -3.8	9b	30 to 25
1.6 to -1.1	10a	35 to 30
4.4 to 1.7	10b	40 to 45
4.5 and above	11	40 and above

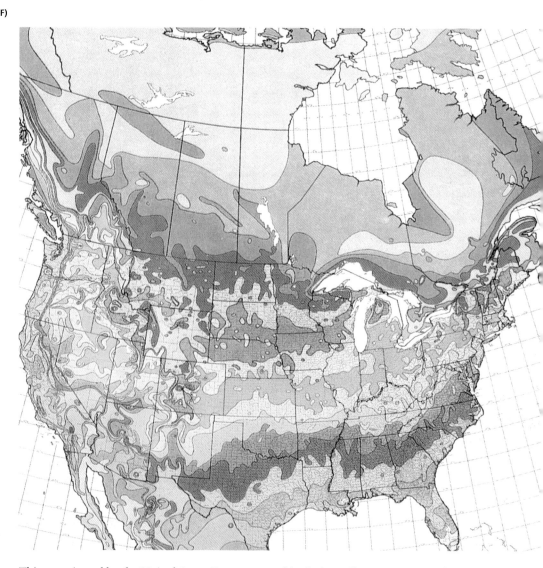

This map, issued by the United States Department of Agriculture, lists average annual minimum temperatures for each zone. It relates directly to the cold-hardiness of plants, but does not address the other extreme, high temperatures. Special considerations with regard to these matters are noted as appropriate throughout the pages of this book.
A new map, in preparation by the U.S.D.A. in cooperation with the American Horticultural Society, will treat equally matters of hot and cold and their effect on plants.

European Plant Hardiness Zone Map

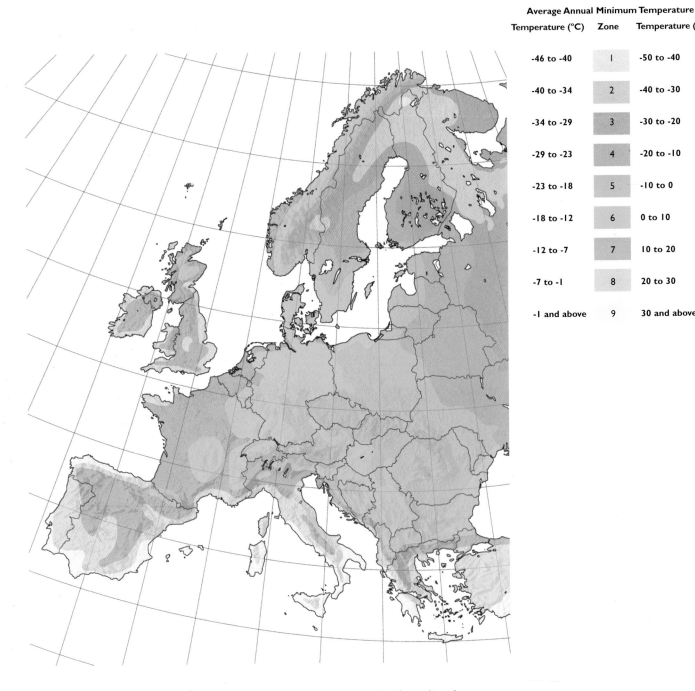

Average Annual Minimum Temperature		
Temperature (°C)	**Zone**	**Temperature (°F)**
-46 to -40	1	-50 to -40
-40 to -34	2	-40 to -30
-34 to -29	3	-30 to -20
-29 to -23	4	-20 to -10
-23 to -18	5	-10 to 0
-18 to -12	6	0 to 10
-12 to -7	7	10 to 20
-7 to -1	8	20 to 30
-1 and above	9	30 and above

This map lists average annual minimum temperatures for each zone. It relates directly to
the cold-hardiness of plants, but does not address the other extreme, high temperatures.
Special considerations with regard to these matters are noted as appropriate throughout
the pages of this book.